1966

EPICURUS AND HIS PHILOSOPHY

✠ ✠ EPICURUS AND

HIS PHILOSOPHY

by Norman Wentworth DeWitt

UNIVERSITY OF MINNESOTA PRESS, MINNEAPOLIS

Library of Congress Catalog Card Number: 54-6368

PUBLISHED IN GREAT BRITAIN, INDIA, AND PAKISTAN BY
GEOFFREY CUMBERLEGE: OXFORD UNIVERSITY PRESS, LONDON, BOMBAY, AND KARACHI

✛ PREFACE

THE aim of this study is threefold: first, to organize the surviving data on the life of Epicurus into a consequential biographical sketch so as to throw some light upon the growth of his personality and the development of his philosophy; second, to present a new interpretation of his doctrines based upon less emended remains of his writings; and third, to win attention for the importance of Epicureanism as a bridge of transition from the classical philosophies of Greece to the Christian religion. This new approach requires a total rearrangement of the pertinent materials, the rectification of grave oversights, and the exposure of time-honored fallacies, even of the fond beliefs that Epicurus declared all sensations to be trustworthy and identified pleasure with the greatest good.

The slanders and fallacies of a long and unfriendly tradition have been enjoying modern sanction ever since Eduard Zeller expounded them with seeming reasonableness and undeniable tidiness a century ago in his *Stoics, Epicureans and Sceptics*. This sanction was confirmed in 1887 by the suave erudition of Hermann Usener in his *Epicurea*. This indispensable work, which ought to have inaugurated a fresh scrutiny of the texts, was unfortunately accepted as authoritative, and after its publication the attention of scholars was diverted to the minor Epicureans, especially Philodemus. In this field an imposing corpus of meritorious studies has long been accumulating, chiefly through the industry of German and Italian researchers, though the hope of making great additions to our knowledge of Epicurus himself has fallen short of expectations.

In England the ignominy to which Epicureanism had been relegated by Puritanism after flourishing briefly under the Restoration, though long enough to administer a smart stimulus to philosophical thought, was terminated at last in 1910 by R. D. Hicks in his *Stoic and Epicurean*, followed in 1925 by his translation of Diogenes Laertius, the chief ancient authority, in the Loeb Library; but in the former he merely enlarged with lucidity upon Zeller's mistakes while in the latter he confirmed tradition by the benedictory *correxit Usener.* A new text and translation was made available in 1925 by Cyril Bailey, soon followed in 1928 by *The Greek Atomists and Epicurus,* the old errors and fallacies being repeated in both books and amplified in the second one with such urbanity that to dissent seems like discourtesy.

It was in Italy that new ground was first broken. This was the good fortune of Ettore Bignone, who in 1936 began to set the account straight in respect of the life of Epicurus and the development of his doctrine in his *L'Aristotele perduto e la formazione filosofica di Epicuro.*

The present study, even if more inclusive than others and based upon less emended sources, is offered with no fond hope of having achieved finality. The feat of rescuing Epicurus from the injustice of centuries will not be accomplished at a blow nor by the efforts of any single researcher. To have made a breach in the wall of false opinion will seem to have been a sufficient advance.

Since the diffusion of knowledge deserves priority over professional scholarship, the level of treatment has been set to meet the needs of students in philosophy and the educated layman. All excerpts from texts have been translated anew to eliminate the traditional slants and elicit the true implications without sacrificing precision. Resemblances to published translations are coincidental. Greek words have been transliterated. Notes have been kept brief and restricted to support for the particular interpretation. Completeness of coverage, in the author's judgment, should be reserved for a critical edition of the texts.

The following acknowledgments are gratefully made: to the American Council of Learned Societies for a grant to defray the cost of an Index to the writings of Epicurus; to the Humanities Research Council of Canada for a grant to defray the cost of typing; to Professors Ben E. Perry and R. P. Oliver and Dr. Edith C. Jones for courtesies in the Library, University of Illinois; to my colleagues Professors R. K. Arnold, P. H. Brieger, and F. V. Winnett for timely assistance; and to Professors R. J. Getty and D. O. Robson, who have read the manuscript and made useful suggestions. It remains to add that the work of printing has been greatly facilitated by the happy liaison maintained by my son Dr. Norman J. DeWitt between myself and the competent University of Minnesota Press.

N. W. D.

✠ TABLE OF CONTENTS

I	A SYNOPTIC VIEW OF EPICUREANISM	3
II	SAMOS AND ATHENS	36
III	COLOPHON: DEVELOPMENT OF DOCTRINE	55
IV	MYTILENE AND LAMPSACUS	70
V	THE NEW SCHOOL IN ATHENS	89
VI	THE NEW EDUCATION	106
VII	THE CANON, REASON AND NATURE	121
VIII	SENSATIONS, ANTICIPATIONS, AND FEELINGS	133
IX	THE NEW PHYSICS	155
X	THE NEW FREEDOM	171
XI	SOUL, SENSATION, AND MIND	197
XII	THE NEW HEDONISM	216
XIII	THE TRUE PIETY	249
XIV	THE NEW VIRTUES	289
XV	EXTENSION, SUBMERGENCE, AND REVIVAL	328
	BIBLIOGRAPHY	361
	ABBREVIATIONS	363
	NOTES	364
	INDEX	378

EPICURUS AND HIS PHILOSOPHY

CHAPTER I ✠ A SYNOPTIC VIEW OF EPICUREANISM

THIS book attempts to present for the first time a fairly complete account of the life and teachings of Epicurus. At the very outset the reader should be prepared to think of him at one and the same time as the most revered and the most reviled of all founders of thought in the Graeco-Roman world.

His was the only creed that attained to the dimensions of a world philosophy. For the space of more than seven centuries, three before Christ and four afterward, it continued to command the devotion of multitudes of men. It flourished among Greeks and barbarians alike, in Greece, Asia Minor, Syria, Judaea, Egypt, Italy, Roman Africa, and Gaul. The man himself was revered as an ethical father, a savior, and a god. Men wore his image on finger-rings; they displayed painted portraits of him in their living rooms; the more affluent honored him with likenesses in marble. His handbooks of doctrine were carried about like breviaries; his sayings were esteemed as if oracles and committed to memory as if Articles of Faith. His published letters were cherished as if epistles of an apostle. Pledges were taken to live obedient to his precepts. On the twentieth day of every month his followers assembled to perform solemn rites in honor of his memory, a sort of sacrament.

Throughout these same seven centuries no man was more ceaselessly reviled. At his first appearance as a public teacher he was threatened with the fate of Socrates. In Athens he never dared to offer instruction in a public place but confined himself to his own house and garden. His character and his doctrines became the special target of abuse for each successive school and sect, first for Platonists, next for Stoics, and finally for Christians. His name became an abomination to orthodox Jews. The Christians, though by no means blind to the merit of his ethics, abhorred him for his denial of divine providence and immortality.

3

EPICURUS AND HIS PHILOSOPHY

Throughout this book certain devices of procedure will be employed which were worked out and practiced by Epicurus himself. One of these has been exemplified in the preceding paragraphs. He laid special stress upon the importance of the diathesis or the attitude to be chosen at the beginning. For instance, in the very first of his forty Authorized Doctrines the disciple is informed that the gods are not to be feared, because "the incorruptible being is immune to feelings of anger or gratitude." If only the disciple could maintain this attitude, it was felt that he would be rightly disposed to receive all subsequent instruction about the nature of the gods. On this same principle the hope is here entertained that, if the reader habituates himself from the outset to think of Epicurus as both the most revered and the most reviled of all ancient philosophers, he will be rightly prepared to judge with impartiality the course of his life and the true structure of his doctrine.

Another device consistently practiced by Epicurus was to begin with the synoptic view. He thought of his writings as maps drawn to larger and smaller scales. The process of learning was regarded as a progression from general maps with few details to regional maps, as it were, with a proportionate increase of detail.

The procedure was regularly from the general to the particular. The truths of Physics were reduced to Twelve Elementary Principles. These corresponded to a general map, affording a panoramic view of the nature of things. Of the Twelve Principles the most important was the third: "The universe consists of atoms and void." Since the void is incapable either of delivering or receiving a stimulus, it followed that the soul, which is capable both of stimulating and being stimulated, must be corporeal by nature, composed of atoms. Hence vision and the other sensations must be explained by the impact of matter upon matter. In this way one detail of truth after another was deduced from the general principle.

From the point of view of logic this progression from the general to the particular constituted a sort of chain argument, a device in which Epicurus had great faith. He looked upon truth in terms of the whole and the part, the integer and the details. The details seemed to him so linked with one another that, if only the beginning was rightly made, one truth after another would infallibly reveal itself until perfection of knowledge should be attained. As Lucretius expressed it: "One point will become clear from understanding another; nor will blind night ever

4

rob you of the path and prevent you from peering into the ultimate realities of nature; so surely will understanding of one thing kindle a gleam to illuminate the next."

The first text to be placed in the hands of the beginner was the Little Epitome, which is extant as the letter addressed to Herodotus. This is contained in a mere twenty pages of print and offers what Epicurus called "the condensed view of the integrated survey of the whole." This too corresponds to a general map. Only the main features of the system are sketched in, the atoms and their qualities, the nature of attributes, such as color, the soul, sensation, the evolution of society and culture, heavenly phenomena. At the same time the objective of study is stressed, which is ataraxy, the quiet of mind that arises from faith in the certainty of knowledge. Incidentally, faith was recognized for the first time as a factor in happiness.

When the student had mastered the Little Epitome, which was, as it were, a First Reader, he would progress to the Big Epitome. This Second Reader, though written earlier, served as an amplification of the Little Epitome and is represented for us by the poem of Lucretius *On the Nature of Things*. The only new topic was the nature of the gods, planned for the seventh book but never written, which leaves the worst gap in our knowledge. The six extant books merely add what seems to us an abundance of detail to the topics already adumbrated in the Little Epitome. This increase of detail, however, is illuminating for the educational procedure involved. The bald outline of doctrine must first be mastered and thereafter the task of the student is "to incorporate all the particulars into it." He might even go on from the Big Epitome to the encyclopedic treatment in the thirty-seven books on Physics but the procedure was always the same, adding details to details until at last perfection of detail should be attained.

In harmony with this method a synoptic view of Epicurus and his philosophy will now be presented in the form of dogmatic general statements. These will be amplified at once by a sparing addition of details in preparation for the yet larger amplification along with footnotes in the chapters that follow. The immediate objectives are two in number. The first has three aspects: to show where Epicurus belongs in the succession of philosophers, how his thought is related to the cultural context in which it arose, and how it survived in the cultural context into which it was finally absorbed. The second objective has two aspects:

so to orientate the reader at the outset as to create the proper attitude for a sympathetic understanding of the man and his work; and not less to warn the reader against the disparagement and prejudice that abound in all the secondary literature.

Unhappily this warning will call for frequent emphasis and repetition. All that we possess of the original texts of Epicurus is comprised in a booklet of sixty-nine pages, though supplemented by the poem of Lucretius. The secondary literature, on the contrary, is abundant and for the greater part hostile. If this were received uncritically we should be thinking of the man as a brawling Thersites in the camp of the philosophers, as an ingrate, an ignoramus, a dullard, a scorner of all culture, a sensualist, and an atheist. The ancient critics who originated these slanders were declared by Diogenes Laertius, whose excellent biography of Epicurus is our chief authority, "to be out of their minds." In spite of this fact our modern scholars prefer to hunt with the pack and with lighthearted disdain for the evidences they denounce Epicurus as a quietist, a friend of anarchy, an incoherent thinker, a moral invalid, and an egoistic hedonist, enlarging the vocabulary of detraction from the armories of modern philosophy.

In the case of these false opinions also it will be convenient to follow a practice employed by Epicurus. It was his way to oppose true opinions to false opinions. For example, it was a true opinion to believe the gods immune to feelings of anger or gratitude, a false opinion to fear them as venal and vindictive. Again, it was a true opinion to believe that happiness was to be found in the simple life and retirement, a false opinion to think it lay in wealth, power, or glory. After this same fashion the false opinions concerning Epicurus and his philosophy will here be paired with judgments based upon the evidences. In some instances, it may be mentioned, the mistakes of scholars are not false opinions but examples of oversight; to particularize, they fail to recognize Epicurus as an acute critic of Platonism. For convenience, however, errors of all kinds will be listed under the heading of false opinions.

TRUE OPINIONS: FALSE OPINIONS

In the succession of philosophers the place of Epicurus is immediately after Plato and Pyrrho the skeptic. Platonism and skepticism were among his chief abominations. The false opinion is to think him opposed to Stoicism. The traditional order of mention, Stoics, Epicureans, and

Skeptics, is the exact reverse of the chronological succession. The philosophy of Epicurus was an immediate reaction to the skepticism of Pyrrho and it was offered to the public as a fully developed system before Zeno the founder of Stoicism even began to teach.

Epicurus was an erudite man and a trained thinker. He made the rounds of the contemporary schools, Platonic, Peripatetic, and Democritean, and he devoted several years to reading and study before offering himself as a teacher. The false opinion is to think him an ignoramus and an enemy of all culture.

Historians persist in judging him only as a philosopher, but to be rightly understood he must be recognized also as a moral reformer. The fallacy consists in damning him as an ingrate and in failing to discern that reformers are rebels and as rebels feel themselves absolved from debts of gratitude.

As a man of science Epicurus returned to the tradition of the Ionian thinkers, which had been interrupted by Socrates and Plato. The chief positive influence on his thinking was Ionian, the chief negative influence Platonic. The error in this instance consists in the failure to recognize Epicurus as an Antiplatonist and a penetrating critic of Platonism.

As a philosopher Epicurus belongs in the class of thinkers who have attempted a synthesis of philosophical thought, and his modern analogues are Herbert Spencer and Auguste Comte. He surveyed the whole field of previous thought and either wrote critiques of his predecessors himself or delegated the task to his colleagues. This aspect of the activity of his school has been completely overlooked.

He was the first to promulgate a dogmatic philosophy, actuated by a passion for certainty and a detestation of skepticism, which he imputed even to Plato. The distinction of being a dogmatist was naturally not denied him, because it was deemed a demerit, the renunciation of inquiry.

He exalted Nature as the norm of truth, revolting against Plato, who regarded Reason as the norm and hypostatized it as a divine existence. The fallacy consists in classifying Epicurus as an empiricist in the modern sense; he never declared sensation to be the source of knowledge; much less did he declare all sensations to be trustworthy.

As an educator Epicurus adopted the procedures of Euclid, parting company with both Plato and the Ionian scientists. The chief mistake in this instance is to foist upon him the method of inductive reasoning; his chief reliance was upon deduction. As for the influence of Euclid, it is regularly overlooked.

Epicureanism was the first missionary philosophy. The mistake is to look upon Epicurus as an effeminate and a moral invalid; by disposition he was combative and by natural gifts a leader, organizer, and campaigner.

Epicureanism was the first world philosophy, being acceptable to both Greek and barbarian. The mistake is to think of Epicurus as an egoistic hedonist, ruled solely by self-interest. He was an altruistic hedonist.

Epicureanism served in the ancient world as a preparation for Christianity, helping to bridge the gap between Greek intellectualism and a religious way of life. It shunted the emphasis from the political to the social virtues and offered what may be called a religion of humanity. The mistake is to overlook the terminology and ideology of Epicureanism in the New Testament and to think of its founder as an enemy of religion.

Epicureanism presented two fronts to the world, the one as repellent as the other was attractive. Its discouragement of the political career was repellent to the ambitious, its denial of divine providence to pious orthodoxy, and its hedonism to timorous respectability. Its candor, charity, courtesy, and friendliness were attractive to multitudes of the honest and unambitious folk.

The influence of Epicureanism, though anonymous, has been persistent in literature, ethics, and politics. In literature and ethics it has survived by amalgamation with Stoicism, chiefly through Seneca and Marcus Aurelius. In politics it fathered the doctrine that the least government is the best government, which was espoused by John Locke and popularized in North America by Thomas Jefferson. All these aspects of influence have been overlooked because of the usual anonymity. It was the fate of Epicurus to be named if condemned, unnamed if approved.

THE CULTURAL CONTEXT

Epicurus was born in 341 B.C. This mute fact will take on significance if it be recalled that barely seven years had passed since the death of Plato and only seven were to elapse before Alexander crossed the Hellespont for the conquest of Persia. The childhood and adolescence of the man were destined to be separated from his adult life by the bold

8

dividing line between the introverted world of Greek city-states and the extroverted world of far-flung Macedonian monarchies. Only a few dividing lines in history are so distinctly drawn.

Boyhood and adolescence were passed in the last years of the so-called great age of Greece, which produced philosophy and eloquence as its final fruitage. Platonism was still dominant in the field of higher education and Athens abounded in gifted orators as at no other time. From Platonism and the political career Epicurus turned away with so passionate a revulsion that this became the chief single factor in shaping his tactics as an educator and his thought as a philosopher. At the same time there were other factors in the cultural context which exercised an active influence. These may be associated with the names of Isocrates, Euclid, Diogenes, Aristotle, and writers such as Aristobulus, Nearchus, and the first Ptolemy, who reported the explorations and campaigns of Alexander. This statement calls for immediate, though brief, amplification.

Isocrates, a great teacher, had inaugurated a shift of emphasis from artistic speech for the benefit of listeners to artistic writing for the benefit of readers and his example was followed up by his admirer Praxiphanes, who became the teacher of Epicurus. The young man seems to have fallen under this spell for a time, and his extant letter to Menoeceus is artfully composed in the Isocratean manner. This fashion, however, was subsequently abandoned in favor of the bald style of Euclid, of which the sole merit was clarity. Along with this unadorned style came the adoption of the textbook form and the deductive procedures. Euclid himself, of course, was merely bringing to perfection a technique of book-making which had gradually taken shape in the circle of geometers. His name is here used to stand for a trend which Epicurus manifestly followed. The school textbook was just beginning to emerge as a distinct type.

In the domain of ethics the influence of the men called Cynics is unmistakable. Diogenes, known as the Dog, was still alive when Epicurus arrived in Athens for his required military training; his pupil Crates was a closer contemporary. These Cynics were staging a riotous rebellion against the conventional smugness and hypocrisy and they affected to make absolute honesty their ideal. Epicurus wholeheartedly endorsed the quest of honesty but repudiated their insolence and vulgarity. He insisted that honesty be joined with courtesy and decorum. His criticism

9

of society was sympathetic and urbane and links the school not only with the better exemplars of the contemporary New Comedy, especially Menander, but also with the best tradition of satire as a literary form. Horace, Juvenal, and Petronius were all communicants of the Epicurean fellowship.

In his approach to the problem of knowledge Epicurus plainly owed an unacknowledged debt to the later Aristotle. One of the latter's innovations was to switch attention from inorganic to organic life; he founded the sciences of botany and zoology. This meant the revelation of a new order of Nature, a terrestrial order as opposed to the celestial order, and in the light of this discovery Epicurus rejected the hypostatized Reason of Plato as the norm of truth and looked instead to Nature as furnishing the norm.

This revolution in the approach to knowledge was fortuitously promoted and confirmed by the simultaneous extension of the geographical horizon by the explorations of Alexander. During the youth of Epicurus Greece was deluged by the new wealth of information concerning the geography, the flora and fauna, and the divergent wisdoms of Persia and India. Even the works of Megasthenes, written under Seleucus, Alexander's successor, were available before Epicurus launched his philosophy. It is consequently not surprising that his new canon of truth was based upon earthly rather than heavenly phenomena nor that his social and political outlook transcended even the Panhellenism of Isocrates and took cognizance of Greeks and barbarians alike, however sundered from the motherland of city-states and parochial politics.

While these positive influences are under survey it should still be remembered that the chief negative influences were Platonism and oratory. The characteristic shared in common by Platonism and oratory was the political obsession. The aim of Demosthenes and his party was to preserve the Greek world of city-states: the political teachings of Plato may justly be appraised as a theoretical extension of the political experience represented by the city-state. It was the assumption of philosopher and orator alike that the happiness of the individual was inseparable from his life as a citizen. The truth of this assumption was destined to be tested in the very presence of the young Epicurus; he was in Athens performing his required military service when the orator Hypereides and others were put to death and Demosthenes escaped a like fate by suicide. The futility of the political career and the folly of continuing to marry ethics with politics could hardly have been more objectively demonstrated.

The result for Epicurus was a violent revulsion from the spirit of the past, though it must not be inferred that this was followed quickly by a reasoned adjustment to the challenge of the new world in the process of becoming. There was an interval of several years consumed in study and in brooding. Even if by disposition the individual be inclined toward rebellion, the obstinate factors of a complicated problem refuse to disengage themselves at once from the pattern of the old to rearrange themselves into the pattern of the new. When this process had at length completed itself, however, it was manifest that Epicurus was determined to divorce ethics from politics and prepared to promulgate a philosophy adapted to the new world of Macedonian monarchs and universal rather than parochial Hellenism.

The promulgation of the new philosophy was bound to mean the declaration of war upon the whole program of Platonic education, not only because it was the system then dominant in the schools but also for the reason that more than others it stood for the tight combination of ethics with politics which disqualified philosophy for universal acceptance.

It was this opposition to Platonism that chiefly determined the shape of Epicureanism; more than half of its forty Authorized Doctrines are flat contradictions of Platonism. It is the mistake of historians to oppose Epicurus to Stoics. This is an anachronism; it comes of throwing back into the lifetime of Epicurus a hostility that arose only after his death. The error is chiefly due to the writings of Cicero, who matches Epicureans and Stoics as if rival schools of gladiators.

Already in 311 B.C. Epicurus was offering a neatly integrated body of doctrine to the youth of Mytilene. At that date the founder of Stoicism, Zeno of Citium in Cyprus, was a new arrival in Athens about twenty-one years of age. In contrast to the precocious Epicurus he was a late beginner and a slow learner. Many years were to elapse before he began to address himself to the people of Athens in the Painted Porch. The assumption of hostility between the two is unsupported even by a scrap of evidence. It was Chrysippus, the second founder of Stoicism, who began the feud and he was a mere lad of nine years living in his native Soli of Cilicia when Epicurus passed away. Stoicism is consequently to be written off absolutely as an influence in the life of Epicurus.

EPICURUS AND HIS PHILOSOPHY

EPICURUS A MAN OF ERUDITION

It should not be necessary to defend Epicurus against the charge of being an ignoramus and an enemy of all culture, but the slanders of ancient and modern writers render refutation obligatory.

As a precocious boy and the son of a schoolmaster it is certain that he received the usual elementary education and that too in advance of his years. Even the scant and fragmented tradition preserves the item that as a mere schoolboy he cornered his teacher over the problem of chaos in Hesiod. In an extant work he denounces the pessimism of Theognis. He is said to have quoted Sophocles in proof of the principle that pain is an evil. He cited Homer as authority for the doctrine that pleasure is the telos or goal of living. He is also reported to have declared the teachings of the poets on the subject of morals to be a hodgepodge, which is true. All of this evidence points to the customary training and some of it to the early manifestation of a bold spirit and an inquisitive mind.

It is inconceivable that he escaped the Platonic training in geometry, dialectic, and rhetoric. He is known to have studied with Pamphilus, a Platonist, in the city of Samos, probably for four years. His extant letter to Menoeceus is composed according to the rules of rhythmical prose and certain excerpts from other writings afford hints of his possessing this skill. There is even reason for believing that he gave instruction in rhetoric for a time.

He declared dialectic a superfluity but was able to criticize Plato with great acumen and he wrote against the Megarians, the contemporary experts in logic. He rejected geometry as having no bearing upon problems of conduct but adopted the procedures of Euclid in the composition of his own textbooks. He refuted the assumption of the mathematicians that matter is infinitely divisible, rightly insisting that the result would be zero. This is not the thinking of an ignoramus.

He also exhibits great familiarity with the writings of Plato and he distributed among members of his school the work of refuting or ridiculing his various dialogues. His own classification of the desires is developed from a Platonic hint and he begins to erect his structure of hedonism from the point where this topic was left by Plato. A paragraph is extant in which he warns his disciples against the Platonic view of the universe as described in the *Timaeus,* and elsewhere he pokes a little satirical fun at that famous opus. More than half of his forty Authorized Doctrines are direct contradictions of Platonic teachings.

A SYNOPTIC VIEW OF EPICUREANISM

The closeness of the relationship between Epicurus and Aristotle may be judged from the fact that two volumes on the subject have been published by the eminent Italian scholar Ettore Bignone. Leaving aside for the moment the undoubted contentions of the two schools, it may be said that common to both founders was the direct analytical approach to problems as opposed to the circuitous analogical approach adopted by Plato. The main difference was that the attitude of Aristotle was analytical while that of Epicurus was analytical and pragmatic at the same time. His injunction "to neglect no opportunity to disseminate the doctrines of the true philosophy" finds no analogue in Aristotle's *Nicomachean Ethics*. On the other hand there is no better preparation for the ethics of Epicurus than a perusal of that treatise and especially of the sections on Friendship, the Magnanimous Man, and Happiness. Many anticipations of his teachings may there be identified: for example, the possibility of man's attainment to a life that in respect of quality may be called immortal or divine.

The debt of Epicurus to Aristotle the biologist is equally manifest for those who are interested in observing it. The mere fact that he rejected Reason from his Canon of truth and set up Nature as the norm is a tacit recognition of Aristotle's discovery of the order in organic life. In its proper place the suggestion will be made that Aristotle's study of the embryo seems to have given rise to the doctrine of innate ideas or Anticipations, as Epicurus styled them, which forecast adult understanding just as the venous system of the embryo prefigures the adult organism. Another subject of interest to both our philosophers was animal behavior, upon which Epicurus based in large part his theory of pleasure and his definition of justice.

The later schooling of Epicurus was also such as to lay the foundations for a broad erudition. After his exciting cadetship there is good evidence for believing that he studied with the acidulous Praxiphanes in Rhodes, a Peripatetic who shared the partiality of his school for literary criticism, while owning "good writing" for a special interest. It is certain that Epicurus spent a longer time in Teos with the Democritean Nausiphanes, who in spite of his indolence was an able, versatile, and original thinker. He gave his ungrateful pupil a fruitful suggestion about a canon of truth.

After tiring of teachers, to none of whom he afterward acknowledged any debt, Epicurus must have devoted himself to an extensive program of reading and study, because a few years later he planned a series of critiques of all previous thinkers, assigning the sophists, dialecticians, and physicians to his trusted Metrodorus, while Empedocles was turned over to the less agile Hermarchus. He chose himself to write against the physicists, among whom he expressed a preference for Anaxagoras and Archelaus, an example of discriminating judgment. He also reserved to himself, as mentioned above, the task of refuting the disputative Megarians, because this school was active and to combat it was an urgent necessity.

When all these facts are added up, the conclusion must follow that Epicurus was not only a man of comprehensive learning but also an ambitious organizer of knowledge. It is doubtful whether any other philosopher made a more earnest attempt to survey the whole field. It should also be borne in mind that those who would have him an enemy of all culture are sometimes driven to emend the texts in order to save their prejudices.

EPICURUS AS MORAL REFORMER

Special abuse has been heaped upon Epicurus because of his alleged ingratitude to teachers. There is some injustice in this charge and a notable lack of discrimination. If he felt no gratitude — and this seems to have been the case — it is unfair to demand the profession of it. The lack of discrimination consists in failing to recognize his double role as philosopher and moral reformer. These two roles may be combined in one person but their respective motivations are quite different and the one role is bound to dominate the other.

Reformers, whether moral or political, feel themselves absolved from debts of gratitude. Epicurus, having become conscious of himself as belonging in this class, denied all obligations to teachers, and this in spite of the fact that he had made the rounds of the schools and acquired the knowledge and skills respectively offered by them. To ascribe this conduct to him as a vice is on a par with vituperating Martin Luther for not proclaiming his gratitude to the Roman Catholic instructors whose skills he had acquired.

The attitude displayed by Epicurus is to a certain degree comparable to that assumed by St. Paul, who declared himself an apostle "not from men neither through man"; he wished the Galatians to know "that the gospel preached by him was not according to man, for he did not receive it from man, neither was he taught it." At this point the similarity ends, and Epicurus and Paul part company as being respectively Greek and Jew. Paul claimed authority by virtue of revelation through Jesus Christ and God the Father, qualifying himself as a prophet, which was a concept familiar to his race. Epicurus declared himself to be "self-taught" and he arrogated to himself the title of Sage or Wise Man, a concept familiar to the Greeks. He could not claim inspiration, because he denied all participation of the gods in human affairs. He was capable, however, of claiming perfection of knowledge, because he had approximated to the life of the gods. Thus to him his wisdom was not a revelation, though it was such to his disciples. Paul's gospel, on the contrary, was a revelation both to himself and to his disciples.

The presumptuous attitude of Epicurus was not only excusable as befitting a rebel and a reformer; it was also virtually imperative for him as the founder and head of a sect. Self-assuredness and even arrogance is rather demanded of a leader by his disciples than resented, however exasperating it becomes to his rivals. The acrimony of rivals really defeats itself, because their very malice and vociferousness operates as an exciter to keep alive and invigorate the loyalty of disciples. In the fourth century A.D., when the Christians fell to attacking one another instead of Epicureanism, this kindly creed began to fade. It had thriven so long as it was under fire.

EPICURUS AS MAN OF SCIENCE

While it was in the role of moral reformer that Epicurus felt himself absolved from the duty of reverence for his predecessors, it was in the role of natural scientist that he became the antagonist of Platonism in particular. It was his choice to revive the tradition of Ionian science, which had been interrupted by Socrates and Plato.

A few details will suffice to amplify this statement. Greek philosophy had made its advances in two separate areas and exhibited two general trends; the earlier was confined to cities of the Aegean Sea, the later to cities of southern Italy. The former trend was observational and speculative, the latter mathematical and contemplative. The Aegean Greeks were familiar with all the industrial techniques of the time, such as spinning, felting, fermentation, ceramics, and metallurgy, and they were acute observers of seasons, climates, winds, waters, and storms. Obsessed by the phenomenon of universal change combined with permanence of the whole, they devoted themselves to the task of discovering the unchanging something that underlay all changing things. After propounding and rejecting or improving one solution after another, they finally arrived at the belief that the ultimate existences were invisible and indivisible bodies, which they called atoms. It was this atomic theory that Epicurus espoused and revived.

The Greeks of Italy, on the contrary, were not greatly interested in physical change or in natural processes. They were addicted to the sitting posture. In art they are represented as comfortably seated with a slender rod or radius in the hand, with which they draw figures on a sanded floor. Counters and writing tablets were also at hand. The advances made by them were in the domains of geometry and arithmetic and these advances were so remarkable as to capture the imagination of the contemporary world and to overshadow for a time the progress which had been made by their Ionian brethren. Geometry in particular, though itself a positivistic study, inspired in the minds of men a new movement that was genuinely romantic.

It was the romantic aspect of the new knowledge that captivated Plato, who was no more than up-to-date as a mathematician himself. In geometry he seemed to see absolute reason contemplating absolute truth, perfect precision of concept joined with finality of demonstration.

He began to transfer the precise concepts of geometry to ethics and politics just as modern thinkers transferred the concepts of biological evolution to history and sociology. Especially enticing was the concept which we know as definition. This was a creation of the geometricians; they created it by defining straight lines, equilateral triangles, and other regular figures. If these can be defined, Plato tacitly reasoned, why not also justice, piety, temperance, and other virtues? This is reasoning by analogy, one of the trickiest of logical procedures. It holds good only between sets of true similars. Virtues and triangles are not true similars. It does not follow, therefore, because equilateral triangles can be precisely defined, that justice can be defined in the same way. Modern jurists warn against defining justice; it is what the court says it is from time to time.

The deceptiveness of analogy, however, does not prevent it from flourishing, and Plato committed himself to the use of it unreservedly. In this he was abetted by a happy coincidence. The method of analysis by question and answer, developed by Socrates recently before, commended itself as the very technique that was needed for the quest of definitions in the domain of ethics. By disposition Socrates was a gifted actor, staging semiprivate theatricals before small groups. As for Plato, in an earlier age he might have become a dramatist. Thus it is not astonishing that the fruit of their joint invention was the dramatization of logic which is called dialectic, best exemplified by the Platonic dialogues.

Yet this was only the beginning. One false step invites another. The quest of a definition, of justice, for example, presumes the existence of the thing to be defined. If equilateral triangles did not exist, they certainly could not be defined. Assume that justice can be defined and at once it is assumed that justice exists just as equilateral triangles exist. Hence arose Plato's theory of ideas. The word *idea* means shape or form and he thought of abstract notions as having an independent existence just as geometrical figures exist, a false analogy.

The theory of ideas was rejected as an absurdity by the young Epicurus, because he was a materialist and denied all existences except atoms and space. The theory once rejected, the instrument became useless; scientists have no use for dramatized logic; they depend chiefly upon their senses.

Plato became guilty of another error upon which the sharp-eyed Epicurus did not fail to place a finger. From Pythagoras was inherited the belief in the repeated rebirth or transmigration of souls. Along with this went the belief that the body was a tomb or prison-house, which blurred the vision of reason and prevented perfection of knowledge. All that the human being perceived was the transient appearance of things as opposed to the eternal ideas. This to Epicurus was virtually skepticism.

This error, moreover, was compounded and also aggravated. Closely allied to geometry was the study of astronomy. The latter, in turn, required the observation of heavenly bodies. Thus Plato was in the position of assuming the validity of sensation in the case of the remoter phenomena and denying it in the case of the nearer terrestrial phenomena. This was a glaring inconsistency.

The aggravation consisted in the belief that circular motion, which was in those days ascribed to heavenly bodies, was the only perfect and eternal motion and identifiable with Reason itself. Reason, in turn, was identified with the divine nature. Therefore the planets were declared to be gods. This seemed both shocking and absurd to Epicurus: shocking because it meant having more gods to fear, absurd because august gods were assumed to become hurtling balls of fire.

These criticisms, plainly explicit or implicit in the writings of Epicurus, were as stinging and penetrating as any to be urged against Platonism in antiquity, and to men of the Academy they seemed nothing short of blasphemy. Violent measures were taken to repress the brash heretic. Learning caution from this painful experience, the chastened Epicurus abandoned as futile the fighting in the streets, withdrew to the security of his own house and garden, and confined himself to the task of disseminating the true philosophy. As a propagandist he soon began to exhibit a marked superiority.

It is remarkable that this man, who exhibited so much acumen in discerning the errors and inconsistencies of Plato, should be denounced today as an incoherent thinker himself. Any thinker, of course, will seem incoherent to a rival of another school; a modern pragmatist seems incoherent to a Thomasite or a logical positivist. Every thinker, however, has a right to be judged within the structure of his own system. If Epicurus be judged within the structure of his Canon, Physics, and Ethics, he will be found to exhibit an admirable coherence of thought.

EPICURUS AS PHILOSOPHER

Of all false opinions concerning Epicurus the most preposterous is that which would dismiss him as a dullard or even as a charlatan. If correctly appraised he will be seen to have attempted a genuine synthesis of philosophy.

He came upon the scene when a great corpus of speculative writings had accumulated, which is precisely the circumstance that invites to a synthesis. A certain progress in this direction had been made by Plato and Aristotle but neither of these was a conscious synthetizer and neither of them was interested in creating an encyclopedic digest of philosophic thought for public use, much less for the amelioration of human life and the increase of happiness. This is precisely what Epicurus attempted. His aim was to survey the whole course of Greek creative thought, to criticize, to cull it, to organize it and make the results available in the form of useful and understandable handbooks.

Insofar as he aspired to become a synthetizer of philosophy his true affinity is with Herbert Spencer or Auguste Comte but more particularly with the latter, and this in spite of their respective contempt and esteem for mathematical studies. The three stages of development recognized by Comte, the theological, metaphysical, and positive, were clearly recognized also by Epicurus, though it was impossible for him so to denominate them. The first stage was represented by the popular religion and mythology, according to which the universe and the destinies of man seemed to be ruled by the gods, by Fate or Necessity, forces external to humanity.

What Comte called the metaphysical stage was for Epicurus represented by Plato and in part by Aristotle. Phenomena were separated from matter and regarded as separate entities. Form was separated from substance and in Plato's theory of ideas was esteemed as the real existence. This meant, as Epicurean ridicule tauntingly insisted, that "horseness" was a real existence but horses were mere apparitions. It seemed less unreasonable, perhaps, to think of justice as existing apart from conduct, public or private. On the physical level the difference between this stage of thought and the next is aptly exemplified in the case of color. Theophrastus believed it to have a separate existence while Epicurus explained it as arising from the arrangement and motions of the atoms comprising the compound, being close to the truth, as so often.

Epicurus was at one with Comte in believing that progress consisted in advancement from the theological and metaphysical stages to the positive. In point of fact he placed these two stages on a par, denominating the first as the age of mythology and the Platonic stage as a new kind of mythology, equally objectionable. Lacking a background of specialized studies such as physics and chemistry, he was unable to formulate a gradation of sciences, but he did subordinate his Ethics to his Physics and in so doing he adumbrated that same direction of logical procedure which prompted Comte to place sociology at the opposite extreme from mathematics and physics. Epicurus was also in accord with Comte in linking human behavior with animal behavior, because he recognized a rudimentary justice of Nature in the organization of certain animal herds.

A third point of agreement between Epicurus and Comte was the recognition that some form of religion was indispensable. In point of fact it is somewhat startling to observe into how many details this agreement extended itself. The new religion of Epicurus, stressing piety and reverence while excluding divine government of the universe, may aptly be described in Comte's terminology as a Religion of Humanity. Both systems exhibited a vigorous distrust of regimentation and political mechanisms; both renounced force in favor of persuasion; and both allowed a generous latitude for the play of human feeling. Finally, they both stressed altruism as opposed to self-love, and neither of them shrank from recognizing at the same time the utilitarian motive or calculus of advantage.

As a last item of similarity it may be mentioned that both men were among the most provoking thinkers who ever lived. In the thought of both there was so much that was exasperating combined with so much that was true and penetrating that no subsequent thinker could ignore them. Total dissent was just as impossible as total agreement. The careers of the two men mark parallel stages in the onward march of philosophic thought, which is an endless progression.

THE FIRST DOGMATIC PHILOSOPHY

Although men contemporary with Epicurus were incapable of recognizing him as a moral reformer, they were quick enough to know him for a dogmatist, which counted for a demerit and a reproach. The modern scholar, however, being long habituated to observe historical processes and laws of development, will easily discern that moral reform and dogmatism are logically related. The moral reformer cannot afford to be a doubter. Epicurus is definitely on record as having said, "The wise man will not be a doubter but will dogmatize," and in this he was implying that the wise man is bound to be more than a speculative thinker. He must make his philosophy useful for the increase of happiness; this, in turn, is impossible without faith, and faith is impossible without certainty. Therefore philosophy must be dogmatic.

If appeal be made to the historical process, it will become clear that skepticism and dogmatism are also related by the logic of cause and effect. The man who denies the possibility of knowledge is challenging others to declare that knowledge is possible. This challenge had never been seriously taken up before the time of Epicurus, because to speculative thinkers skepticism is merely another way of thinking and escapes notice as a menace or a danger. Neither could this aspect of it have presented itself to Epicurus before he became aware of a passion for the increase of human happiness. This passion once awakened, however, he speedily developed a special acumen for discerning even latent skepticism, as in the teachings of his own Democritus, not to omit those of Plato and Aristotle. His later critiques of preceding philosophies stressed this feature.

He was first alerted to this danger by his last teacher, Nausiphanes. This able man had been a pupil of Pyrrho of Elis, who in the company of Anaxarchus, a follower of Democritus, had accompanied Alexander the Great on his eastern campaigns. In the course of these journeys Pyrrho made acquaintance with the wise men of Persia and India, who were not less self-confident than the wise men of Greece. The result for him was the loss of all faith in the certainty of knowledge, reason and sensation seeming alike untrustworthy.

Both Nausiphanes and the young Epicurus admired the placidity of Pyrrho but rebelled against his skepticism. This reaction resulted in the erection of a criterion of truth, which Nausiphanes called his Tripod, obviously so named because capable of standing firmly on its three legs. Subsequently Epicurus quarreled violently with his teacher, seemingly on moral grounds, and feeling himself thereafter absolved from all gratitude he published his own Canon with a threefold basis, Sensations, Anticipations, and Feelings. By the Sensations was meant the evidences furnished by the five senses. The Anticipations were innate ideas, such as that of justice, which exist in advance of experience and so anticipate it. The Feelings are pleasure and pain, Nature's educators, her Go and Stop signals.

Insofar as this system was presented as the true and ultimate philosophy Epicurus laid himself open to the charge of discouraging all further inquiry. It must be allowed that he seemed to favor the confinement of research to the discovery of truth that would contribute to human happiness. It must further be admitted that he made it one of his chief objectives to immunize the minds of his disciples against all teachings other than his own. Some justice may even be allowed to the allegation that his disciples read no writings other than those of their own school.

As a clarification of these criticisms it should be recognized that Epicurus, like Plato, entertained a clear distinction between the talented minority of men and the multitude. He knew also that for the multitude dogmatism, which to Plato was "right opinion" as opposed to rational understanding, was sufficient. Unlike Plato, however, he recognized no need of deception. Since his creed was nonpolitical and his society classless there was no call to institute one training for rulers and another for the ruled. He insisted that his teachings were the same for all men, assuming that each would benefit by them to the limit of his capacities and opportunities.

Individual disciples were conscious of no imposed limitations. Each was free to follow his tastes and his talents. Some even became expert mathematicians. Lucretius was none the less a good Epicurean because of the breadth of his reading. One Asclepiades, an Epicurean physician contemporary with him in Rome, made a notable impact upon the theory and practice of medicine. Epicurus himself knew the true joy of the researcher and gave apt expression to it: "In all other activities the joy comes after laborious completion but in philosophy the pleasure keeps pace with understanding, for enjoyment does not come after learning but learning and enjoyment are simultaneous." His system of thought resembled what is called an open-end plan of investment; it was not a closed but an open-end variety of dogmatism.

THE NEW ORDER OF NATURE

Especially conspicuous in the Canon of Epicurus is the omission of Reason as a criterion of truth. Only the Sensations, Anticipations, and Feelings are recognized as direct contacts between man and his physical and social environment. By virtue of being direct contacts, they acquire a priority over Reason and in effect exalt Nature over Reason as affording a norm of truth.

How this revolution came about may be explained by recalling a few details. The Ionian scientists had studied nature chiefly in her terrestrial aspects, taking reason for granted as a faculty. The Italian Greeks had ignored the terrestrial aspects of nature and exploited the faculty of reason. This procedure led from arithmetic and geometry to astronomy, and by astronomy was revealed the celestial order of nature. This inflexible celestial order captivated the imagination of Plato, who was a romantic, and it was this he was imitating when he proposed in his *Republic* and his *Laws* a rigidly regimented polity, of which a travesty now flourishes in Soviet Russia.

After this Platonic interruption the Ionian tradition was revived by the later Aristotle, but he switched the emphasis from inorganic to organic nature. The sciences of zoology and botany were founded by him. In the course of these studies he arrived at the conclusion "that

22

A SYNOPTIC VIEW OF EPICUREANISM

Nature does nothing at random. Of this discovery he did not realize the importance. It signified that organic nature is governed by laws. In reality it marks the discovery of a new order of nature, the terrestrial order, as contrasted with the celestial order of Plato's grandiose cosmogony.

It was the lead of Aristotle that Epicurus chose to follow. He looked to organic nature as furnishing the norm just as Plato had looked to reason. This divergence resulted in two opposing interpretations of the phrase "living according to Nature." To the Stoics, who hitched their wagon to Plato's star, it signified the imitation of the inflexible celestial order by a rigid and unemotional morality. To Epicurus and Epicureans, "living according to Nature," though they never made a slogan of it, signified living according to the laws of our being. Of this being the emotions were recognized as a normal and integral part, undeserving of suspicion or distrust.

How the new terrestrial order of nature and the older celestial order operate as points of departure for inferential truth may be illustrated simply in the case of justice. For Epicurus the Feelings are the criterion. Injustice hurts and justice promotes happiness. Therefore human beings make a covenant with one another "not to injure or be injured." Justice is this covenant. It is of Nature. No dialectic is necessary to discover the fact; it is a matter of observation. The sense of justice is innate; it is an Anticipation or Prolepsis existing in advance of experience and anticipating experience. Even certain animals possess it; elephants, for example, the bulls excepted, do not injure one another and they marshal the herd to protect one another against injury from outside.

Plato, on the contrary, taking his departure from the analogy between geometry and ethics and politics, requires a definition; dialectic is invoked as the instrument and the ten books of the *Republic* are devoted to the quest. In the background are the mathematical notion of ratio and the musical notion of harmony. Thus at long length the conclusion is reached that justice is a harmony of the three constituents of the soul, reason, passion, and desire. Justice in the state is a harmony of the constituent classes.

Plato was complicating philosophy for the few who find self-gratification in complexity. Epicurus was simplifying philosophy for the many who were willing to live by their philosophy. Platonic justice seemed to him a specious pretense. In Vatican Collection 54 he wrote: "We should

23

not pretend to philosophize but philosophize honestly, because it is not the semblance of health we need but real health."

Epicurus analyzed human nature just as the later Aristotle analyzed ethics and politics, like a student of natural science observing the ways of plants and animals. It was this method he was following when he scrutinized human nature in action and reduced the direct contacts between man and his physical and social environment to Sensations, Anticipations, and Feelings. It was the same method he followed when he classified human desires as "natural and necessary, natural but not necessary and neither natural nor necessary." After the same fashion he scanned the behavior of man in society and concluded "that the injuries inflicted by men are caused by hatred or by envy or by contempt."

The best evidence of a certain validity in the Canon was the ridicule heaped upon it; ridicule is available when arguments are lacking. A tacit tribute to its validity is the fact that the idea of the Prolepsis or Anticipation, the innate idea, was adopted by the Stoics and appears as an accepted commonplace in Cicero's thought. The Sensations were seized upon as the weakest leg of the canonic tripod and in this instance misrepresentation scored a victory. The fallacy that Epicurus declared all sensations to be true and hence trustworthy still flourishes. This would mean that vision informs us no more correctly about a cow at twenty paces than at half a mile.

Equally fallacious was the allegation that the Canon had been set up as a substitute for logic. To make such a claim is on a par with asking a trial lawyer to criticize a chemist, or, as Epicurus might have said, to ask the ears to pass judgment on the nose; the phenomena of which they are competent judges would not fall in the same class. The function of ancient logic was to score points and make opponents wince but no adversaries or witnesses were needed for the use of the Canon; solitude was sufficient. The modern scientist in his laboratory follows a like method. He depends upon the sensations as Epicurus did. The researcher works on the basis of an hypothesis, which he puts to the test of experiment, that is, of the senses, and these, exactly as Epicurus said, "confirm or fail to confirm" the truth of the proposition. Even the theory of Einstein, that rays of light from distant stars are bent in passing the sun, was tested by photographs taken during an eclipse, and photographs are merely extensions of vision.

24

A SYNOPTIC VIEW OF EPICUREANISM

EPICURUS AS AN EDUCATOR

When Epicurus is considered as an educator — and he took himself very seriously in this role — a double paradox presents itself. Plato, while stressing the study of geometry, rejected the bald style of exposition proper to that branch and employed instead a very artistic prose. Epicurus, on the contrary, while rejecting geometry, adopted and recommended the bald style as employed by Euclid, who happens to have been a contemporary. Plato rejected also the textbook form as developed by the geometricians and favored the dramatic dialogue. Epicurus took over the textbook form along with certain subsidiary features that consorted with it.

In adopting the bald style familiar to us from Euclid, Epicurus was looking to Nature as a teacher. He even went so far as to say that it was she who revealed the true meanings of words and the right kind of style. The physicist, he asserted, should be content to take words as he found them, in their literal meanings; the sole requisite of writing was clarity. To express this differently, he was denying that Nature was either a dialectician or a rhetorician. With equal justice he might have denied that Nature was a poet, because he was no less rejecting the didactic poetry of Empedocles and his kind than the artistic language of Plato. Indeed he is on record as saying "that the wise man would not compose poems, though he would be the best judge of poetry."

Along with the adoption of the bald style and the textbook form was taken over the demand for memorization. The practice of committing poetry to memory had long prevailed among the Greeks, but with the vogue of geometry there was a new and different necessity for memorization. The new necessity was one of logic. The theorems could not be mastered unless the student had memorized the axioms and learned "to handle them smartly," as Epicurus said of his Elementary Principles. It was just as necessary for the beginner in Epicureanism to have at the tip of his tongue the Principle "The universe consists of atoms and void," or the Authorized Doctrine "Justice is a sort of covenant not to injure or be injured," as it was for the beginner in geometry to know by heart "Things which are equal to the same thing are equal to one another."

The adoption of the Euclidean textbook as a model involved, of course, the procedure by deductive reasoning. The Twelve Elementary Principles were first stated and then demonstrated like theorems. Each theorem, in turn, once demonstrated, became available as a major premise for the deduction of subsidiary theorems. The truth of this subsidiary theorem is then confirmed by the evidence of the Sensations, which operate as criteria. The mistake of believing Epicurus to be an empiricist must be avoided; it is not his teaching that knowledge has its origin in sensation. The status of the Sensations is that of witnesses in court and is limited to confirming or not confirming the truth of a given proposition.

Another innovation demanded by the adoption of the textbook model was the institution of graded texts. For example, the extant Little Epitome is a mere syllabus of selected truths. Next above it stood the Big Epitome, probably in seven rolls, as seems to be indicated by the six of Lucretius and the promised sequel on the gods. Above this in turn stood the famous thirty-seven books on Physics and other special treatises. Similarly, the Authorized Doctrines are to be appraised as a beginner's book in Ethics. From this the disciple would move on to special treatises on Piety, on the Gods, on the End or Telos, and on Justice and the other Virtues, to mention a few. It may be added that an order of procedure was prescribed. For instance, the lore of the gods was placed last in the list and reserved for advanced students.

It deserves to be known also that Epicureans set up their own schools and developed a pedagogical method based upon their own kindly ethics. A good description of their procedures is extant in a Herculanean papyrus containing the treatise of Philodemus entitled *On Frankness of Speech*. It is better preserved than some others and makes clear the essential rules, among which may be mentioned the requirement that the teacher should conceal his own annoyances and be actuated solely by the good of the instructed.

THE FIRST MISSIONARY PHILOSOPHY

Epicureanism was the first and only real missionary philosophy produced by the Greeks. So foreign was such a concept to the thought of the earlier philosophers and the sophists that they failed even to found schools in the sense that Plato's Academy became a school; much less did they found sects. As Epicurus rightly discerned, human institutions arise from the evolution of the unintended. Just as Nature, according to him, is the sole creatrix in the physical world, so Nature, working through the joint and cumulative experience of mankind, is the sole creatrix in the social and political spheres. Language for example, was an innovation of Nature; men merely improved upon her beginnings. On this principle, it must be deemed incredible that Plato's conscious purpose was to found a school in perpetuity when he chose the Academy as his place of instruction; no model as yet existed. The lack of a model, according to Epicurus, would even have prevented the gods from creating a universe.

One model the Greeks did possess and this was the city-state, itself an exquisite specimen of the evolution of the unintended, and by this model their minds were obsessed. It was a city-state that Pythagoras essayed to found upon philosophical principles. The project failed and a scattering of his followers survived like displaced persons. Their creed was exclusive and incapable of evangelism.

Epicurus was not the first to escape the political obsession. The Cynics had preceded him in this, and Diogenes was dubbed the Dog because he advocated a life of vagrancy, absolved from all social and political decencies and ties. This excess, like others of the blatant school, repelled the decorous Epicurus. He knew that a certain modicum of governmental control was a necessity but he rejected utterly the doctrine of Protagoras, Plato, and Aristotle that the state was in the place of a parent and that the laws were educators.

If any model whatever was in his mind when he took up residence in Athens, this is more likely to have been the school of Aristotle, which from the first exhibited the aspect of a research institution and was less a one-man enterprise than Plato's Academy. It must be remembered that Epicurus brought with him three colleagues who were conceded almost equal rank with himself and that even members who remained behind in Lampsacus continued to cooperate in the business of writing under his aegis.

It is, however, to the Hippocratic medical fraternity that we must look for the undoubted model. As a zealot for the increase of human happiness Epicurus was bound to make a pragmatic interpretation of the analogy between philosophy and medicine, which had long flourished as an idle and unctuous figure of thought. If philosophy was to heal the maladies of the soul, the necessity for its involvement with politics was nonexistent. If all human beings stood in need of health of soul as of health of body, then the healing philosophy must be framed for all mankind and offered to all mankind. It was his resolve "to issue the kind of oracle that would benefit all men, even if not a soul should understand him."

The motive that sparked his missionary zeal was likewise of Hippocratic origin: "Where there is love of mankind there will be love of healing." It is true that the power of love or friendship had long been exploited in Greek institutions. Pythagoras had thought of his ideal state as a unit bound together by friendship along with a mandatory pooling of resources, but this friendship was confined to members of the community. Epaminondas had utilized friendship to build up a spirited military force, but this too was a local and limited phenomenon, love of Thebans for Thebans. It was Epicurus who first extended brotherly love to embrace mankind and exalted it as the impelling motive for revealing to men the way to happiness.

As a missionary enterprise the activity of Epicureanism was not confined to the school premises. Every convert everywhere became a missionary. In the view of Epicurus philosophy should begin at home and be disseminated from the home. It was his injunction to his disciples "to apply it in their own households, to take advantage of all other intimacies and under no circumstances to slacken in proclaiming the sayings of the true philosophy." This feature of the creed possessed the advantage of rendering it independent of schools and tutors; it was able to infiltrate itself into small towns and villages where no schools existed and even into rural areas. It was capable also of winning adherents in social groups untouched by more strictly intellectual systems.

In ancient times Epicurus was denounced as effeminate, and in modern times this reproach has been phrased as moral invalidism. Neither can it be denied that a certain plausibility attaches to the imputation in view of his ill health, the espousal of pleasure as the goal of living, his retired life, and his discouragement of the political career. In reality, however, the accusation is a shallow one. Many a spirited enterprise has been directed from a sickbed. Caesar Augustus, the founder of the Roman Empire, was the least robust of the men of his court and plagued by recurrent illnesses. Ill health is even capable of intensifying the tenacity of the invalid. It was so with Epicurus. In his own circle he was a master mind and alone of all the founders of schools he built up and dominated an organization for the dissemination of his creed. As Seneca said, "In that famous fellowship every word that was spoken was uttered under the guidance and auspices of a single individual." The battle is not always to the strong. Inherent in Epicureanism was a quiet crusading spirit which quickly extended it over the contemporary world and endowed it with a tenacity unequaled by rival creeds; it flourished for almost seven centuries. The vogue of Stoicism as a militant creed lasted a mere two centuries.

THE FIRST WORLD PHILOSOPHY

It is no more inevitable that a missionary philosophy should be a world philosophy than it is that a missionary religion should be a world religion. Christianity was first intended for the Jews alone. In the case of Epicureanism it is possible that a similar limitation was followed by a similar extension. From the first, however, it was nonpolitical. Unlike the philosophy of Plato, it was not restricted to adolescent youth nor to males nor even to citizens. By virtue of the analogy between the healing of the soul and the healing of the body the new creed became applicable to women as well as to men and to human beings of all ages, whether slave or free. The political contract was superseded by the social contract. It is significant that in the writings of Epicurus the word *neighbor* is almost as frequent as in the Gospels.

When Epicurus established himself in Athens it was no part of his plan to offer education to the Athenian youth. To forestall persecution he took the precaution of confining his instruction to the house and garden registered in title deeds in his own name. His chief reason for taking up residence there was the renown of the city as the cultural capital of the contemporary world. He wished to have the prestige of the city as a recommendation for the merit of the new philosophy being offered to the public at large.

The time as well as the location was advantageous. His philosophy was being launched just as the whole Orient was thrown open for Greek exploitation by the conquests of Alexander the Great. The migrations that ensued while new cities were being founded all the way from Egypt and Syria to distant Bactria attained the dimensions of a diaspora. His philosophy rode this tide. It had reached Alexandria even before his arrival in Athens. By the second century it was flourishing in Antioch and Tarsus, had invaded Judaea, and was known in Babylon. Word of it had reached Rome while Epicurus was still living, and in the last century B.C. it swept over Italy. Both Greeks and barbarians were becoming Epicureans.

For this ambitious program of expansion the school was prepared as no Greek school had ever been or ever would be. Not only was every convert obligated to become a missionary; he was also a colporteur who had available a pamphlet for every need. "Are you bloated with love of praise? There are infallible rites," wrote Horace, "which can restore your health if only you will read a pamphlet three times with open mind." "Send him a pamphlet," cried Cicero in the senate-house, taunting the Epicurean Piso about the ambition of his son-in-law Julius Caesar. Could better evidence be cited to prove that Epicureans were pamphleteers?

The system of handbooks was carefully planned and diligently maintained. Not only was Epicurus an industrious writer himself; his three colleagues and other members of the school were encouraged to emulate his example. Nor was this activity confined to the parent school; the new schools in Antioch and Tarsus adapted the writings to meet the needs of the changing times. In Rome the pen of Philodemus was busy interpreting the creed afresh for the age in which he lived. For those whose tongue was Latin a certain Amafinius had made translations, and his services were supplemented by those of Catius, an abler man. The evangelical zeal of Lucretius was characteristic of the sect and exceptional only because of its surpassing fervor. The objective was to awaken men to the blessedness of the Epicurean way of life.

As a design for living Epicureanism is patently suggestive of modern hominism or humanism or pragmatism. It was centered in man and not in the state or in theology. The breadth of its humanity is well expressed by one of its later devotees, who wrote "that the whole earth is just one country, the native land of all, and the whole world is just one household." The most potent single sentiment in the development of modern social theory is Epicurean as well as Menandrian: *Homo sum; humani nihil a me alienum puto*. This sentence has suffered a variety of English translations, but the substance is, "I am a man; I deem nothing that concerns mankind to be a matter of indifference to me."

In the light of this manifesto it is astonishing to find Epicurus coldly classified in modern times as an "egoistic hedonist." This mistaken judgment can be traced to the total honesty of Epicurus. It was because of this honesty that he did not shrink from choosing the suspected name of pleasure as the designation of the goal of life. Because of this same forthright honesty he dared to base friendship upon advantage. He knew that human motives are mixed and he possessed the courage to face the fact. This outspokenness laid him open to the charge of basing conduct upon expediency or self-interest, even though he declared "that, if need be, a friend will die for a friend." Consequently, when in the nineteenth century a distinction was made between egoistic and universalistic hedonism, the pleasure of tagging him as an egoistic hedonist was too tempting to be resisted.

This imputation can be disproved by the doctrines, but recourse to them is superfluous. A point of logic will serve the same purpose. When a philosopher chooses the role of missionary and launches a campaign "to awake the world to the blessedness of the happy life," he may still be a hedonist, but he ceases to be egoistic. If correctly described, he must be seen as an altruistic hedonist. This is not a contradiction in terms, but a higher hedonism.

PREPARATION FOR CHRISTIANITY

By virtue of its spirit, its procedures, and certain of its doctrines Epicureanism served as a preparation for Christianity in the Graeco-Roman world. The similarity between the one and the other has long been evident to friend and foe. To the scornful Nietzsche the teaching of Epicurus seemed to be "a pre-existing Christianity," because in his judgment both creeds had been framed for the weak and timorous. To a sympathetic scholar it seemed "like the twilight between the beliefs that were passing away and that which rose on the world after his time."

The first missionary philosophy was a natural preparation for the first missionary religion. The one had been detached from Greek politics and the other was to be detached from Jewish politics. Both creeds were framed for men of peace, militant only for the increase of human happiness. Both offered healing and comforting beliefs for both sexes and all ages of men. Both based their ethics on love and friendliness. The fellowship cultivated by the Epicureans was comparable to the communion of saints as fostered by the Christians. Both stressed the social virtues, mutual helpfulness, forbearance, and forgiveness.

Epicurus distinguished clearly between the inner life and the external life of circumstance; these corresponded to the spiritual life and the worldly life in Christian thought. Both creeds spoke of ignorance as darkness and knowledge as light. Both essayed to deprive death of its sting. Both spoke of the narrow way and warned of the deceitfulness of wealth, power, and glory.

The two sects were singular in taking their names from their leaders and in pledging loyalty to those leaders; both spoke of following in the steps of those leaders. Both rejected the conventional education and founded their own schools, providing new textbooks. The texts provided by the Epicureans anticipated the texts composed by the Christians. The biographies of the beloved Epicurus, whose life "compared with that of other men would be considered a myth," corresponded to the Gospels; he was revered as nothing short of a god; he was called savior. The affectionate memoirs of his colleagues were comparable to the Acts of the Apostles. The letters of Epicurus to various communities of friends were like the Epistles. Even in their style of writing the two literatures resembled each other, aiming only at clarity.

It should also be carried in mind that the adherents of both sects belonged to the lower and middle classes of society; they practiced in common a voluntary sharing of goods; they were alike in holding their meetings in private houses and in having common meals at regular intervals; in the will of Epicurus provision was made for certain rites to be performed in memory of himself, which reminds us of the Eucharist. It would have been singularly easy for an Epicurean to become a Christian.

As a last word on this topic it may be mentioned that the custom prevailed among Epicureans of carrying about with them small images of their founder; they also had likenesses done in marble or painted on wooden panels to adorn their homes or lodgings. His features are well known to this day from surviving portrait busts and exhibit an expression singularly Christlike. In this connection it is remarkable that the beardless Christ so often seen on Christian sarcophagi down to the fourth century gave way to the bearded form which is now traditional. Since the two sects lived side by side for three centuries, it is by no means impossible that in this particular the practice of the one was a preparation for the practice of the other.

THE TWO FRONTS

Epicureanism presented two fronts to the world, the one repellent, the other attractive. Both the repulsion and the attraction were keenly experienced by St. Augustine, who declared that he would have awarded it the palm had it not been for the denial of immortality and judgment after death. It was chiefly the ethical creed that attracted men, based upon love or friendship and all the kindly social virtues that make for peace and good companionship. It was chiefly the eschatology that offended, arousing in succession the hostility of Platonists, Stoics, and Christians.

Another repellent aspect of the creed was its hedonism. The very name of pleasure is quick to accumulate a semantic load of disapproval. This was well expressed by Cicero when he declared that no one dare proclaim the creed "in the senate, in the forum or in the camp." It is not this name of pleasure, however, that alone divorced the sect from the political life; Epicurus discouraged the political career as a surrender of the happiness of the individual to the whim of mobs and monarchs. For two reasons, therefore, the creed became abhorrent to that minority of mankind which is ruled by worldly ambition and in particular to those breeds who, like Cicero, set their hearts upon high office under democracies or, like Platonists and Stoics, prized court appointments under monarchies or patronage under aristocracies. By the same tokens the unambitious creed made itself attractive to the innumerable majority of men who could never aspire to the seats of the mighty or to move in the public eye.

The effect of these opposing aspects of Epicureanism was to win for it the most numerous, the most ubiquitous, and most enduring of all followings among ancient philosophies and to have adverse to it at all times a rancorous and vociferous minority. The written tradition is hostile for the greater part and sometimes malicious, with which the modern scholar too often concurs. Against this tendency to malign and misrepresent it is well that the unsuspecting layman and the candid inquirer should be warned repeatedly.

SURVIVAL

It is hardly possible for a philosophy to perish utterly so long as the continuity of its cultural context remains unbroken. Each philosophy rises to its peak of popularity, fulfills its appointed role in the historical process, and yields place to its successor. Yet certain strands of it will weave their way into the succeeding pattern of the continuous context. Philosophies are not exempt from the law declared by Lucretius: "One thing will never cease to be born from another and life is given to none

33

in fee simple but only in usufruct." Epicureanism in particular, because of its repellent front, has been especially susceptible to this anonymous absorption. It survives anonymously to this day in literature sacred and profane.

When Christian people assemble for the last tribute of affection to a departed friend and the preacher reads, "The dead shall be raised incorruptible" and "O death, where is thy sting?" and "The sting of death is sin and the strength of sin is the law," only the word *sin* and the idea of the resurrection are here strange to the language and thought of Epicurus. These two new ideas were being presented in a context of Epicurean terminology and ideology so as to make them acceptable to Epicurean listeners. Epicurus had taught that the bodies of the gods were incorruptible. Paul is holding out to the convert the hope of being raised in this very incorruption. Epicurus had essayed to deprive death of its sting by reconciling men to mortality; Paul would deprive death of its sting by holding out the assurance of immortality.

Epicureanism was the prevailing creed among the Greek populations to which Paul addressed himself and, in harmony with his avowed practice of making himself all things to all men that he might save some, he here makes himself an Epicurean to Epicureans. He is shuffling the familiar components of that creed so as to erect a new matrix of meanings. It is just as if the older monument were being demolished in order to yield stones for the wall of the new edifice.

In rabbinical literature the name of Epicurus became a synonym for unbeliever and survives in this meaning. In both ancient and medieval art he was depicted as a type of sensualist, sometimes along with Sardanapalus, a notorious oriental voluptuary. In Dante's Inferno a whole section was set aside for a unique punishment for men of his creed. In the seventeenth century his doctrines experienced a tardy renaissance in France and were carried to England in the period of the Restoration, where they enjoyed a high but fleeting vogue, only to be driven once more into anonymity by puritan condemnation. In the nineteenth century the revival of the study of Greek philosophy in learned circles was too exclusively concerned with Plato and Aristotle to accord him more than grudging consideration, subject to an actual exaggeration of ancient prejudices.

As for political teachings, those of Plato have enjoyed the greatest notoriety and those of Epicurus have been steadily despised or ignored.

Yet the latter have affected the direction of political thought in the Western world for three hundred years. Epicurus rebelled against the highly regimented polity of Plato's *Republic* and the *Laws* and advocated instead a minimum of government. The function of government, he believed, was to guarantee the safety of the individual. This doctrine was anonymously revived by John Locke and espoused by Thomas Jefferson, who was an avowed Epicurean. It is consequently not surprising that Safety and Happiness, catchwords of Epicurus, should be named in the Declaration of Independence as the ends of government. Neither is it surprising that the same document should mention Life, Liberty, and the Pursuit of Happiness; these concepts also are Epicurean, as will be made clear in the chapters on the New Hedonism and the New Freedom.

Since classical scholarship, until recent years, has accorded to Epicurus only condescending and prejudiced notice, it is not astonishing that in other circles the neglect has been almost total. This oversight is but natural; nothing else could be expected in view of the anonymity to which the man's acceptable teachings have been condemned because of his unacceptable doctrines. The hidden tradition has been continuous nevertheless. In the main stream of prose and poetry it often survives under Stoic labels. In the terminology and thought of religion it survives in spite of the obliviousness of New Testament scholars. In politics it has been a dominant, though nameless, influence ever since the succession of modern philosophers was started by Thomas Hobbes and John Locke during the brief vogue of Epicureanism in the Restoration period. In North America the Epicurean doctrine that the least government is the best government was virtually made to order for the circumstances of the Revolution, even if not a single Jeffersonian democrat was ever aware of its origin.

CHAPTER II ✠ SAMOS AND ATHENS

IT IS quite possible from the surviving data to piece together a consequential account of the life of Epicurus and of his development as a man and a philosopher.

The relevant dates are known with a precision that is uncommon in the lives of great men of ancient times. He was born of Athenian parents on the island of Samos in early February of the year 341 B.C. At that date Plato had been six years in the grave, and Aristotle was in his second year at the court of Philip of Macedon as tutor to the youthful Alexander.

In Samos Epicurus passed his childhood and adolescence. At the age of eighteen he was called to perform his two years of military service in Athens. This call would have fallen in the same summer as the death of Alexander, 323 B.C. It was not the lot of Epicurus to return to Samos. In 322 the Athenian settlers were forcibly evicted, and the father Neocles found a new home in the neighboring city of Colophon on the mainland. There Epicurus rejoined the family at the conclusion of his military service.

The ensuing ten years, 321–311 B.C., constitute a period of paramount importance. If, as tradition records, Epicurus studied for a time with the Peripatetic Praxiphanes, a certain time must be allowed for residence in Rhodes. Following this will be a considerable interval of study with the Democritean Nausiphanes of Teos. Most important, however, must be regarded the remaining years of the decade, spent in Colophon itself. It was during this interval that Epicurus first discovered himself as a gifted teacher and worked out to substantial completion the outlines of his philosophy. It was only certain details of organization and procedure that awaited subsequent development.

In the year 311 B.C., at the age of thirty, he had gained sufficient confidence in himself to try out his new philosophy in Mytilene on the island of Lesbos. There he offered himself as a public teacher, subject to the regulations and supervision that were usual in Greek cities. This experiment proved to be both painful and profitable. It was painful because within the space of less than a year the local populace and authorities were so incited against him that safety was found only in flight. It was fruitful because sober reflection convinced him of the necessity of making drastic changes in his procedures.

The more important of these changes were worked out in Lampsacus on the Hellespont, where, like the persecuted Anaxagoras before him, he found a safe retreat. The duration of residence there was slightly more than four years, from the winter of 310 to the summer of 306 B.C. From the very first it had possibly been his plan, after trying out his teachings in the provinces, as it were, to establish himself in Athens, where a new philosophy, if bidding for general recognition, was bound to locate itself. In the year 306 B.C. the occasion seemed to be opportune for this final venture. The procedure he adopted, however, was cautious; he did not choose to expose himself to the supervision of public authorities but confined his teachings to his own house and garden. The remaining thirty-five years of his life, until his death in 271 B.C., were marred by no molestation.

The stormy experience of the year spent in Mytilene serves to divide his life into two periods. The first period was characterized by discontent, impatience, and aggressiveness. In the second he exhibits himself as serene, cautious, forbearing, self-confident, and shrewd. During the first period his worse impulses misled him into costly conflicts with his teacher Nausiphanes and subsequently with the then dominant Platonists. These controversies gained for him the reputation of possessing an unbridled and malicious tongue. In the later period, at length master of himself, he devoted his energies exclusively to the dissemination and perpetuation of his healing doctrines, which he asserted to be "true philosophy." Thus a new reputation was built up, for friendliness, considerateness, and gentleness. Both reputations survive in the records to this day.

The story of his life may now be conveniently diagrammed according to periods and places of residence:

First Period

B.C.

Samos: Childhood and Adolescence 341–323
Athens: Cadetship 323–321

EPICURUS AND HIS PHILOSOPHY

Second Period

Colophon: Development of Doctrine 321–311
Mytilene: The New Philosophy on Trial 311–310

Third Period

Lampsacus: Development of Organization 310–306
Athens: The Garden School 306–271

Our chief authority is the tenth book of the *Lives and Opinions of the Famous Philosophers* by Diogenes Laertius, who wrote in Greek and flourished in the first quarter of the third century A.D. His account of the life and teachings of Epicurus, though pitifully meager and dull by the standards of modern biography, is after all the best we possess of any ancient philosopher. The diligence of the author was not matched by any philosophic insight, but he was abundantly supplied with books and he exhibited better judgment in excerpting the material bearing upon Epicurus than in any other part of his work. It is a special bit of good fortune that he embodied in his book four brief writings of Epicurus, interlarded with biographical and doctrinal information, which would otherwise have perished. Three of these writings are in the form of letters, addressed, as was the custom of Epicurus, to certain of his disciples, in this instance Herodotus, Pythocles, and Menoeceus. The first is known also as the Little Epitome and treats chiefly of the Elementary Principles of Physics; the second, of which alone the authenticity has been doubted, is about celestial phenomena; the third discusses charmingly the Fourfold Remedy or Tetrapharmacon, that is, the correct attitude to assume toward the gods, death, pleasure, and pain; the fourth presents the forty Authorized Doctrines, specially recommended for memorization, the chief topics being the gods, death, pleasure and pain, the tests of truth, and the nature of justice.

This outline will now be expanded in conformity with the practice followed by Epicurus himself.

SAMOS: CHILDHOOD AND ADOLESCENCE

Our biographer Laertius loses no time in setting before his readers the contradictory nature of the tradition with respect to Epicurus. According to detractors, of which the succession has never failed, he was quarrelsome, ungrateful, and vindictive. According to friends, persistently loyal if less vociferous, he was serene, considerate, and full of good will. These reputations correspond respectively to the unregenerate and

the regenerate Epicurus. One key to the contradiction may be found perhaps in the contrast between the harmony of his home life and the irritations of his childhood environment.

All of our information points to a home life that was happy and somewhat unusual. The family consisted of four boys, Neocles, Epicurus, Chaeredemus, and Aristobulus.[1] Neocles was certainly the eldest, having been given his father's name. Epicurus was perhaps the second but this is uncertain. He was beyond doubt the gifted one and the rest were devoted to him. The devotion of Neocles in particular seems to have been fanatical. He is reported to have declared [2] right from the time they were children that "no one was wiser than Epicurus or ever had been and that their mother had had in her body just such atoms as by their combination would produce a sage."

The generosity of Epicurus toward all of them is on record,[3] which may be taken to mean that as soon as he found adequate financial support he summoned them to share the common life in his school. Also on record is his gratitude to his parents,[4] which signifies perhaps that by contributing to their support he made recompense for their self-sacrifices in his own regard. Part of a letter seemingly from his pen is extant in an inscription, in which he implores his mother to quit sending him parcels and goes on to say: [5] "For I do not wish you to lack that I may have an abundance but rather that I myself may lack so that you may not." In the same letter it is revealed that his father was sending money. Thus the evidence points indubitably to a family life that was affectionate, harmonious, intelligent, and ambitious.

The external environment, on the contrary, must have been at one and the same time stimulating and irritating. The locale is important. Samos, the same name denoting island and city, occupied a foremost place among the old Ionian communities. The western part of the island is rugged and the better part lies opposite the mainland, separated by only a mile or more of water. It was close to Miletus, for centuries a commercial and cultural metropolis, and not far from Cos, home of the famous medical brotherhood of Asclepius. The Samians had rarely experienced peace and quiet, involved as they inevitably were in both the external wars and the internal conflicts that convulsed the coastal and island cities. Their experience as a member of the Athenian confederacy had been tumultuous and humiliating; on two occasions they had been forced to make room for plantations of Athenian citizens.

It was through the second of these unpopular colonizations that Neocles, father of Epicurus, had founded a home in the island, one of two thousand Athenians transplanted there in 352 B.C.[6] Such settlers were called cleruchs. Their lives can hardly have been deemed happy. At the outset the applicant for an allotment was subjected to social and political discounts. The mere fact of application was an admission of economic adversity and the acceptance was accompanied by a practical diminution of civic rights. The cleruch could no longer exercise the privilege of attendance and voting in the Athenian assembly.

THE SCHOOLTEACHER'S SON

In addition to these discounts imposed upon all the cleruchs and their children as being islanders and economic expatriates there was a special one in the case of Epicurus. His father at some time in his life, probably in Samos or possibly in both Samos and Colophon, kept an elementary school.[7] Among his countrymen, whose democracy did not extend beyond the political sphere, this was equivalent to declassing the whole family, because schoolteachers were lightly regarded as people who spent their lives, like women and household slaves, in the company of children.[8] It was the pleasure of Stoic calumniators after the death of Epicurus to perpetuate the slur that "he used to assist his father in teaching children their letters for a fee that was painfully small." [9] Timon, a cheap and malicious satirist, coined for him in the manner of the Old Comedy a scornful and lengthy patronymic *Grammadidascalides*, "Elementaryschoolteacherson," and in a single couplet combined this reproach with those of island birth and illiteracy: "At the bottom of the list too and the lowest dog among physicists, hailing from Samos, Elementaryschoolteacherson, most uneducatable of living things." [10]

There is even more to be said about this particular slur than has hitherto been observed. It was very ancient and had been aimed at Epicurus before he became famous. For example, he records of Nausiphanes, with whom he studied while still a young man, that on one occasion "he fell to abusing me and called me a 'schoolteacher'." [11] In later days, however, this epithet must have been thought to convey an additional sting, because from the mature educational system of Epicurus the word was banned. At a very early date the conclusion had been reached that "Human nature is not to be coerced but persuaded." [12] In harmony with this conviction not only the head of the school but all subordinate instructors were called by titles that signified 'leader' or 'guide'. This practice will be more fully explained in the chapter on The New School in Athens.

The discounts that applied to the cleruch himself were augmented in the case of the children. The family of every cleruch was bound to take over the dwelling of a local family and to rupture all the neighborly relationships that previously prevailed. The resentments thus arising might be suppressed by adults but would inevitably find an outlet in the petty persecutions of children by children, whose conduct is always less inhibited.

In the eyes of Greeks of the mainland it was a social demerit to have been born on an island. The Athenians in particular had come to look upon islanders as small fry, whose lot it was to require protection, to pay tribute for it and from time to time to be robbed. It was at their cost that Athenian officials enriched themselves. So bitter was the hostility thus aroused that Demosthenes informs us Athenian citizens were unsafe abroad without the protection of a herald's staff.[13]

Ignobility of birth continued to be thrown up to Epicurus as a reproach, against which Metrodorus, who ranked second in the school, was ready with a reply. He published a book entitled *On Nobility of Birth*, in which he made plain that the master belonged to the deme Gargettus and the ancient family of the Philaïdae.[14] Centuries later the disciple Diogenes of Oenoanda still felt the topic to be a living one and declared: "It is not birth, which, of course, is the same for all, that makes men noble or ignoble but their actions and attitudes." [15] That island birth was a part of this alleged ignobility is also made clear by Plutarch, who exclaims: "O muse, why do the Samians entertain this grudge?" [16] The reference is to the alleged scorn of culture, which "does not become any citizen of Athens," and Epicurus is named. Incidentally, the assumption seemed to be that a social discount on the founder was tantamount to a flaw in doctrine.

It remains to mention another opprobrious report that belongs in the Samian period. It was alleged by eminent Stoic detractors that the mother of Epicurus, Chaerestrate, used to go around the cabins of the poor performing rites of purification and that her son accompanied her to read the charms.[17] If this charge be untrue, the explanation must be found in a transference of calumny, because the same combination of slurs was launched against the orator Aeschines by his illustrious adversary Demosthenes and in very similar language.[18] If, on the contrary, it be regarded as true, there is some support for it in a letter of Epicurus to his mother, in which he assures her that certain ominous dreams of hers must be meaningless.[19] She may have leaned toward superstition. It has even been suggested that her superstitiousness may have been a factor in the hatred borne by Epicurus toward superstition in general.[20]

These reproaches of island birth, of having been a schoolteacher and the offspring of a schoolteacher and a sorceress, were sufficient to impose upon Epicureanism from its very outset and for all time a low social ranking. Cicero was correct, if not charitable, in dubbing the disciples of Epicurus "plebeians" and by naming Plato and the Socratics in the same sentence he left no doubt as to the identity of the aristocratic philosophers.[21] It was snobbish of him to declare in another passage that "he would prefer to agree with Plato and be wrong than to agree with Epicurus and be right," [22] but this attitude was widely prevalent and in certain circles perpetual. The son of an obscure island schoolteacher was not to enjoy parity with Plato, whose lineage was traced to the family of Solon. It is hardly necessary to assume the existence of organized opposition to Epicureanism; [23] the real opposition lay largely in snobbishness, which flourishes in all ages.

SCHOOLING

While Epicurus may have begun his schooling under his father's instruction, there is evidence that he was placed in charge of another teacher before he was of an age for the higher branches. The following anecdote has been preserved for us by Sextus Empiricus: "For while still quite a young lad he demanded to know of his teacher, who was dictating to him the line 'Verily first of all chaos was created,' [24] out of what chaos was created if it really was first created." When the teacher with some irritation denied that it was any of his business to teach such things but rather of the men called philosophers, "Then," said Epicurus, "to the philosophers I must hie if they alone really know the truth about realities." [25]

The interest of the story is threefold: it exhibits Epicurus in the process of receiving the orthodox schooling in Greek poetry. If at the time mentioned he was learning his Hesiod, it is certain he had already acquired a due familiarity with Homer. It will be shown later that several ancient authorities agreed in declaring that he had found in Homer, and especially in the *Odyssey,* the basis for his hedonism.[26] A second item of interest is the evidence of intellectual curiosity and a scant respect for authority at so early an age. There was a seed of rebelliousness in his disposition, which first manifested itself as quarrelsomeness and later as unwillingness to acknowledge debt to teachers. He declared himself "self-taught."

The third item of interest attaches to the mention of chaos. In Democritean physics there was no place for chaos. According to this system, the world had always been a cosmos, because the atoms and void were believed to exist from everlasting unto everlasting. Only in creational systems was there need for an initial state of chaos. Thus the question naturally arises, Was Epicurus already at the time of the incident reading Democritus? An affirmative answer is not absurd. By a scholar named Ariston, whose reputation is good, it was recorded in a *Life of Epicurus* that he began to study philosophy at the age of twelve.[27] He was undoubtedly precocious; this is the point that Ariston was making and he adds "that he headed his own school at thirty-two," which contrasted with forty for Plato and thirty-nine for Aristotle when he began to teach in Mytilene. If to the above item be added a second to the effect that Epicurus, "chancing upon the books of Democritus, took eagerly to philosophy," [28] it becomes quite probable that he already knew something of Democritus when he cornered his teacher on the topic of chaos.

It is certain that Epicurus did betake himself to a philosopher and that this man was the Platonist Pamphilus. Cicero records the fact on the authority of Epicurus himself.[29] Laertius quotes as his authority the same Ariston whose biography was mentioned in the previous paragraph.[30] Both records mention Samos as the place, that is, the city of this name. The association may have lasted for four years: Epicurus himself is reported as saying that "he began to study philosophy at the age of fourteen," [31] and he was eighteen when called up for military service. These specific items of information are consistent with general considerations: the Platonic teachers made a specialty of giving instructions to adolescents and Platonism was at the time the orthodox creed; it may be consequently assumed that the enrolment of Epicurus under Pamphilus was a parental plan. It is the custom of parents to favor the paths of orthodoxy.

EPICURUS AND HIS PHILOSOPHY

THE PAIDEIA FALLACY

No correct understanding either of the schooling of Epicurus or of his later attitude toward education is possible without uncovering and dispelling a fallacy based upon the ambiguity of *paideia,* which means either "education" or "culture." This fallacy is the more regrettable because magnified by modern scholars. There is extant a saying of Epicurus which may be rendered: "To sea with your swift ship, blessed boy, and flee from all education *(paideia)."* [32] To Epicurus this meant the Platonic curriculum of education then in vogue, that is, geometry, rhetoric, and dialectic. Ancient detractors, however, exploiting the ambiguity, insisted that it applied to all culture, including the traditional education in music and literature. Plutarch added history and Quintilian echoed the general accusation.[33]

There is a similar saying of Epicurus, which unemended may be rendered as follows: "Bravo, my lad! I congratulate you upon beginning the study of philosophy free of all indiscretion." [34] Plutarch, although unfriendly, makes it clear that the lad was congratulated "because he had kept himself pure by refraining from the studies." [35] What was meant by "the studies" need occasion no perplexity; they were the geometry and arithmetic required by Platonism as prerequisites. Modern scholars, however, fall into the trap baited by the ancients. They emend by substituting the word *paideia,* found in the previous saying, and translating "pure of all culture." One scholar even emends to read "pure of all defilement." [36]

This willful misrepresentation in ancient times and concurrence in modern times is but one factor of error among several. Epicurus is perhaps the most calumniated of all characters out of ancient history. Although his regimen of living bordered upon asceticism and no one had more to say about the simple life, he was reviled on the comic stage as "the teacher of prodigality" and in general as "the master of lusts." [37] Yet the sheer volume and continuity of this calumny should put serious students upon their guard. An utterly uneducated man and an enemy of all culture would hardly have been worthy of the uninterrupted hostility of the other schools over the space of centuries.

It is absurd to impute to Epicurus a scorn of all culture. His real offense was the attempt to establish a new culture that should compete with the prevailing cultures. In this he was successful; his school outstripped all others in the number of its adherents. He was a learned man himself and his philosophy did not repel intelligent men. It attracted men like Lucretius, Horace, and Virgil. At a later time the Christians Arnobius and Lactantius knew their Epicureanism better than their Bibles. St. Augustine was tempted to award it the palm.[38]

GEOMETRY, RHETORIC, DIALECTIC

Another source of error is the tendency of scholars to throw back into the youth of Epicurus the views of the mature man. It is an incontestable fact that Epicurus later discouraged the study of geometry as having no bearing upon the conduct of life. This does not mean that he was ignorant of it himself. He was enrolled as a student of the Platonist Pamphilus, perhaps for four years, and geometry was a prerequisite in Platonic schools. Tradition has it that over the entrance to Plato's Museum, erected near the Academy, were inscribed the words, "Let no one enter unless grounded in geometry." [39]

It should also be remembered that this study during the youth of Epicurus was enjoying a vogue not incomparable to that of Newtonian physics in the eighteenth century and nuclear physics at the present time. Euclid himself was a contemporary and his influence upon Epicurus is manifest. It should be observed that his work on geometry is really an epitome and is entitled *Elements*. Similarly, Epicurus produced among other epitomes a syllabus of his books on physics, which he called *The Twelve Elementary Principles*. Moreover, as will be shown later, his method of procedure, like that of Euclid, is from first principles to particulars. He states each principle as a theorem and then adduces the proof. Lastly, it was the geometers who quite properly, although surrounded by rhetoricians, developed a style of writing unsurpassed for its baldness. Epicurus, again, though partial to rhetoric in his earlier years and capable of writing artfully, reversed himself and turned to the style of the geometers, abjuring all figures of speech.[40] It was his mature view that clearness was the only requisite and that the study of physics, "physiology" to him, would show men how they should write.[41]

It remains to add that the hostility of the mature Epicurus toward the study of geometry was chiefly actuated by the use that Plato and Eudoxus had made of the subject; it resulted for them in promulgation of belief in the divinity of heavenly bodies. Yet, when Epicurus criticizes this astronomical mathematics, it is by no means as an ignoramus that he speaks. So far, according to him, is increase of knowledge in this field from producing serenity of mind that it may even result in greater fears, since the increase of knowledge is the cause of an increase of amazement without furnishing a solution of the ultimate problems.[42]

As a minor addition it may also be mentioned that Epicurus argued against the possibility of dividing matter into less and less to infinity. It was his contention this would result in zero, the annihilation of matter.[43] This is hardly consistent with ignorance of mathematics.

If all this evidence be summed up, it is not only reasonable but almost necessary to infer that Epicurus received the training in geometry that was customary in the Platonic schools in the time of Euclid.

In respect of rhetoric the evidence is excellent. As a pupil of Pamphilus it is impossible that Epicurus could have escaped an introduction to this study. If he next resorted to Praxiphanes in Rhodes, which is probable, he would have made progress there. That he was finally associated with Nausiphanes of Teos is undeniable and that this teacher, though a Democritean, made a specialty of rhetoric is positively attested.[44] These evidences, of course, establish a high probability but they do not stand alone. That Epicurus actually progressed to the point of writing with genuine polish is proved by the extant letter addressed to Menoeceus. This document, in the judgment of a most competent scholar, falls little short of the standard of Isocrates, the greatest of all Greek teachers of style.[45] It exhibits the periodic structure along with rhythmical cadences and also certain charming little antitheses. Among the latter is one often quoted not alone for the sentiment but also, as may be suspected, for its neatness and balance: "Death is nothing to us, because when we are, death is not present, and when death is present, then we are not." [46] It may be added that the whole paragraph, in spite of the profound pathos that attaches to sincere denials of immortality, deserves a place among the minor treasures of Greek literature because of the grace and limpidity of the composition.

In the fortuitous survival of Greek manuscripts it seems that the writings of Epicurus have met a like fate with those of Aristotle. It is common knowledge that the latter in his earlier compositions emulated the graces of Plato's style while those we still possess exhibit a stenographic terseness more reminiscent of Euclid. Quite similar in character are the few extant writings of Epicurus, the letter to Menoeceus alone excepted. Were it not for the survival of this piece we could not be so sure of his ability to write artfully, but possessing this we are justified in believing that other writings of similar merit existed. This inference finds confirmation in certain of the Authorized Doctrines,[47] which exhibit avoidance of the clash between terminal and initial vowels and are reasonably assumed to have been excerpted from various works. Among these, for instance, was one called "the brilliant letter," [48] and this could hardly have stood quite alone. It is possible also to discern here and there an approximation to poetic diction, of which Vatican Collection 17 affords an example.

It is even conceivable that Epicurus became a teacher of rhetoric for a time, which, it must be borne in mind, was the money-making branch of instruction in the ancient world. At any rate, in the *Rhetorica* of Philodemus [49] may be found an elaborated excuse for one who, "finding himself temporarily among men who lightly esteem all the blessings that philosophy bestows upon us and have admiration for rhetoric as of practical benefit, being short also of the necessities and possessing some degree of skill in rhetorical studies for reasons that apply over the period of youth, may possibly teach selected pupils for a limited period to ease his more pressing needs until he shall find himself once more in surroundings friendly to philosophy, just as he may teach the abc's or athletics." It would be strange if an Epicurean would go to such pains to excuse any but Epicurus himself. If Epicurus did teach rhetoric for a time, this would have been in Colophon, or at least in the Colophon period. In Mytilene he wooed Hermarchus, a student of rhetoric, away from his teacher.

As for the third branch of Platonic studies, dialectic, the evidence for Epicurus' familiarity with it is the express and almost total rejection of it. The grounds of this rejection were both ethical and intellectual. It is on record that he condemned the irony of Socrates.[50] It is not difficult to discern the reasons for this. The pretence of ignorance is a form of dishonesty and inconsistent with that absolute frankness (*parresia*) by which Epicurus set great store, as will be shown under the head of the New Virtues. Yet even assuming that Socrates felt himself to be genuinely ignorant of the nature of piety or justice, he was deliberately concealing his mastery of a devastating skill in debate, which could only result in the humiliation of the hapless interlocutor in the presence of witnesses. This was totally opposed to that disinterested concern (*kedemonia*) for the good of the instructed which was required of the Epicurean teacher.

If Cicero disagreed with Epicurus about the condemnation of irony, this was but natural, because, whether as trial lawyer or political orator, the ability to make his victim writhe under mental punishment was a precious part of his equipment. In the judgment of Epicurus the *Second Philippic* of Cicero and the speech of Demosthenes *On the Crown* would have seemed to represent oratory at its ethical worst, whether because of cruelty of intention on the part of the speakers or the love of havoc on the part of the listeners.

A second evil of dialectic was the tendency to become eristic and argue for victory instead of truth. This was incompatible with the Epicurean considerateness (*epieikeia*) for the feelings of others, which fore-shadowed the Golden Rule of Christianity. It was thus no accident that Epicurus, in the manifest division of labor which prevailed in the mature organization of the Garden School, reserved for himself the task of refuting the Megarians,[51] with whom eristic was a specialty. Only the head of the school seemed capable of dealing with methods so contrary in spirit to the new philosophy.

The intellectual grounds for rejecting dialectic were equally funda-mental. Epicurus denied categorically each of its four assumptions, first, that reason was the criterion, second, that sensations were undependable, third, that phenomena were shifting and deceptive, and fourth, that the only real and eternal existences were the ideas. The reality of the ideas he denied on the ground that nothing exists except atoms and empty space. In place of reason he declared Nature to furnish criteria of truth and he held the Sensations, supplemented by the Feelings and innate notions (Anticipations), to be direct and immediate contacts with external reality, whether physical or social. Thus dialectic became a superfluity.

The rejection of Plato's teachings is almost total. If the Authorized Doctrines be read item by item it may be observed that almost all are contradictions of Plato, and thus it becomes plainly manifest that the writings of Plato occupied the chief place in the youthful studies of Epi-curus. The Platonic dialogues were the textbooks of dialectic and in modern parlance would be "required reading."

This almost total rejection does not, on the contrary, preclude exten-sive borrowing and adaptation on the part of Epicurus. Dialectic by virtue of its dramatic form is committed to a very casual employment of a great variety of analytical tricks and logical devices. If incidentally it furnishes instruction in logic, this is by a method analogous to the case system in the teaching of law. This casual use of logic is precisely what we find in the writings of Epicurus, and it was this practice that gave superficial justification to Cicero in accusing him of "abolishing definitions and offering no instruction in classifications and in partitions of subject matter." [52] Epicurus was not so foolish as to think of abolishing logic; he was merely determined to keep it in a subordinate place. This deliberate choice is additional evidence of extreme familiarity with dialectical writings.

CADETSHIP IN ATHENS, 323–321 B.C.

Those who choose to describe the life of Epicurus as uneventful must be forgetting that while he was growing to manhood in Samos the campaigns of Alexander were setting a new and wider horizon for the contemporary Greek world. It was in this new, expansive world of Alexander that Epicurus was to belong. It was not to be his mission, as it was Plato's, to refurbish a traditional political philosophy for existing Greek states, but to work out a social philosophy for Greek-speaking people everywhere, including the tens of thousands of emigrants who forsook the fatherland to populate the new cities founded by Alexander and his successors in Egypt, Syria, and other lands.

At the age of seven Epicurus was not too young to have regarded with wonderment the sight of Alexander's navy filing through the Samian straits to the siege of Miletus. All the years of his adolescence must have been punctuated by astonishing bulletins of the explorations and victories of that incomparable man. When at length it came the turn of his class to begin their military training, it chanced to be in the year of Alexander's death, 323 B.C., and it was their lot to be eyewitnesses, as it were, of the tragic events in Athens that quickly unfolded themselves in the sequel.

Athens must have been in a turmoil when the class of Epicurus reported for service in the late summer of 323 B.C. By this time the death of Alexander on June 13 would have been common knowledge. This event seemed to be that divine intervention for which the Athenians were praying. No time was wasted in mustering an army. Hostilities were hastily begun against the Macedonian regent Antipater, but good fortune did not attend them and in less than a year came decisive humiliation.

49

While the military catastrophe took place in Thessaly and at a distance, the more painful sequels of it were enacted in Athens itself and can hardly have failed to make a lasting impression upon the youthful Epicurus, who only a few years later was to denounce the political career and the studies that prepared for it. It was such politicians as the orator Hypereides, those whose faces had been familiar on the bema, who were executed. Demosthenes, by this time in his second exile at Calauria near Aegina, forestalled a like fate by suicide. A Macedonian garrison took up a menacing position in the Peiraean fort known as the Munychium.

The general scene was fitted to provoke the exclamation of Ecclesiastes — who, by the way, was familiar with Epicureanism — "Vanity of vanities, all is vanity," or the tenth satire of Juvenal on the miseries of human ambition. Very aptly and by no accident this satire is made to conclude with scorn of Dame Fortune, whom Epicurus taught men to defy, and with commendation of the Epicurean prayer for "a sound mind in a sound body." The paths of glory lead not only to the grave but to envy, hatred, and suffering.

Other possibilities of these two years may well be explored. There was much that could hardly have failed to excite the interest of a sensitive, precocious, and ambitious young man. The two great schools, the Academy and the Lyceum, were still manned by pupils of the illustrious founders, eyewitnesses of the word, as it were, Xenocrates and Theophrastus. That Epicurus at some time heard the former is positively stated by Demetrius of Magnesia, and the possibility is admitted by Cicero.[53] If so, it must have been at this time, because Xenocrates was no longer living when Epicurus took up permanent residence at Athens in 306 B.C. This need not mean that he was formally enrolled as a pupil; it was the custom of the heads of schools to give public lectures and the cadets would have many hours of leave.

It may well have been that Epicurus attended also the popular lectures of Theophrastus, who, after the forced retirement of Aristotle to Chalcis, was then assuming the headship of the Lyceum. His real name is said to have been Tyrtamus and was changed, as the story goes, by Aristotle in admiration of the divine beauty of his enunciation. The word *theophrastus* means "speaking like a god." In keeping with this report is the tradition that as many as two thousand would attend his lectures,[54] an item of information which it is well to keep in mind when reading an acrid comment of Epicurus: "The wise man will establish a school but not in such a manner as to become the leader of a rabble. He will give readings in public but only by request." [55] The antipathy of Epicurus toward Theophrastus is well authenticated. Plutarch speaks of him "rising early in the morning and trudging to the theatre to hear the zithers and flutes" but "clapping his hands over his ears in loathing and disgust at the thought of reading the symposium of Theophrastus on symphonic music." [56]

It is improbable, however, that the antipathy dated from the cadetship of Epicurus. Incompatible with such an assumption is the fact that after his cadetship he seems to have studied in Rhodes with Praxiphanes, who was also of Aristotle's school. It is more probable that the bad feeling had its beginning in Rhodes and blossomed into open warfare in Mytilene some seven years later. Thus when Epicurus returned in 306 B.C. to reside permanently in Athens, he brought with him a hostile feeling toward all Aristotelians, Theophrastus included, who himself hailed from the island of Lesbos, of which Mytilene was the chief city. Since Theophrastus flourished as head of the Lyceum until 286 B.C., twenty years after the opening of the Garden School, it may be inferred that the spiteful reference to him as "leader of a rabble" dates from this interval. For such a criticism there is excuse. When two thousand people attend lectures on philosophy there is something amiss; Aristotle's Lyceum had become temporarily a Chautauqua.

While the great schools are under discussion it deserves to be mentioned that the second year of Epicurus' cadetship, 322 B.C., witnessed the death of Aristotle, who had been living at Chalcis in Euboea. In the previous year the notorious Diogenes had passed away in Corinth. He is usually said to have lived in a tub, but his real retreat was a huge wine-jar turned on its side and used like a kennel. It was such behavior that won for him the name of Cynic, that is, Dog. These deaths must have been lively topics of discussion in every intelligent circle.

In the same year would have fallen a celebration of the greater Panathenaic festival, a gorgeous pageant limited to one year in five. Epicurus, as a cadet, must have marched in the procession. He may have enjoyed more the regular Dionysiac festivals, because his tastes were musical. It may have been that the Eleusinian mysteries impressed him deeply, especially those of the early autumn. At any rate, in the dispositions made long afterward in his will for the perpetuation of his own memory, the date was fixed, not for the anniversary day of his birth, which fell on the seventh, but at the twentieth,[57] the day that marked the final initiations at Eleusis. The twentieth was also sacred to Apollo, which gave it an additional sanctity.[58] Such notoriety eventually attached itself to these monthly memorial gatherings that Epicureans were dubbed "Twentyers" by way of derision.

EPICURUS AND MENANDER

It may have been the privilege of Epicurus also to witness the performance of the first play produced by Menander, greatest of writers in the era of the New Comedy. That the two were of the same age and discharged their military service together is well known.[59] It is known also that the first play of Menander was produced in 321 B.C.[60] The degree of their intimacy is not certified. In the Palatine Anthology is an epigram ascribed to Menander, which turns upon the fact that the fathers of both Themistocles and Epicurus were named Neocles: "Salutations to you two, both of you sons of Neocles, one of whom saved us from servitude, the other from folly." [61] The great scholars, of course, look sourly upon the ascription of this to Menander,[62] but they look sourly upon Epicurus in general. Yet the epigram, whatever the true authorship, attests the popular association of the philosopher with the poet.

Scholars have also denied the existence of a single palpable allusion to doctrines of Epicurus in the four plays of Menander which survive in part.[63] Playwrights, however, like modern novelists, when they exploit their friendships and contemporary writings to enrich the material of their inventions, subject their borrowings to a metabolism deliberately calculated to conceal them. Moreover, it is not to be expected that a comedian should find it expedient to reproduce a doctrine in the exact language of a philosopher.

The negativism of positivistic scholarship may be aptly exemplified by the treatment of a passage in Menander's *Guardians*.[64] The topic is divine providence. The slave Onesimus speaks: "I'll enlighten you clearly. The total number of cities, let us say, is 10,000; the number of inhabitants in each is 30,000. Do the gods handle them one by one and deal out tribulation or prosperity?" The father-in-law is amazed: "How could that be? For what you say means a laborious kind of life for them." The possibility of Epicurean influence here is brushed aside summarily by a famous scholar.[65] He declares that all we need to recall is the blessed gods of Homer who "live at ease." For the contrary side of the argument it should be recalled that the gods of Homer caused plenty of tribulation for men, while Epicurus in the first of his Authorized Doctrines asserted the very opposite. Moreover, it was Epicurus who specifically declared that a laborious life was inconsistent with the perfect bliss of the gods [66] and it was his denial of divine providence that made it a hot topic of controversy. Hence its timeliness in comedy.

While evidences of Epicurean influence are manifest in the plays of Menander, it is well to remember that the doctrines of Epicurus were being exploited for their dramatic possibilities, not necessarily adopted. For instance, one of the teachings of Epicurus was the following: "Human nature is not to be coerced but persuaded." [67] This is the basis of the contrast between the two fathers in the *Adelphi* of Terence, a Menandrian play: the one father is hard, despotic, and unsympathetic; the other endeavors to have the confidence of his adopted son and rule him by good will instead of authority. Again, in the *Self-Tormenter* the harsh father who drove his son from home by his severity is set in contrast to the friend who utters the famous sentiment: *Homo sum: humani nil a me alienum puto*, "I am a human being: I consider nothing human of indifference to me." [68] Yet in neither play does the man who recommends the kindlier treatment fare better at the end than his harsh opponent. It was the ethical contrast that possessed dramatic value, not the ethical teaching.

It should be added that Menander was intimate with Theophrastus and enjoyed the patronage of Demetrius Phalereus, governor of Athens under the Macedonians and a Peripatetic himself. It may also be shown that the plays of Menander reflect the teachings of Theophrastus as well as those of Epicurus. Thus the verdict should be that the comedian exploited the doctrines of both philosophers while his social intimacy was with the opponents of Epicurus, who took up his residence in Athens only after Demetrius was expelled.

LOYALTY

The cadetship of Epicurus was of interest to his detractors and a roll on the subject was published by a renegade disciple Herodotus.[69] That the purpose was to unearth something defamatory cannot be doubted, but only a single item has come down to us and this is ambiguously phrased. The Greek text may mean either that he was not "a genuine Athenian citizen by birth" or was not "a loyal citizen at heart." Perhaps both charges were urged. The ground for the former would have been his birth in Samos and his father's diminished status as a cleruch. Flimsy as this imputation would have seemed, it is possible that Metrodorus replied to it in his work *On Nobility of Birth,* as previously mentioned; at any rate this is quoted as authority for the information that Epicurus was of the deme Gargettus and the family of the Philaïdae.[70]

There is better reason, however, to believe that the real imputation was one of disloyalty and that the conduct of Epicurus upon arrival in Lampsacus afforded specific basis for the charge. This view of the matter is confirmed by the fact that Timocrates, another renegade disciple, was a Lampsacene and supported the accusation.[71] The specific offense seems to have been the "shameful flattery" of the barbarian Mithres, Syrian steward of the ruler Lysimachus, to whom Epicurus was in deep debt, probably for assurance of safety after his forced flight from Mytilene. Further confirmation of the view that the accusation was one of disloyalty is afforded by certain items in the vigorous defense of Epicurus by his biographer. He mentions "his piety toward the gods and the warmth of his disposition toward his native city, beyond words to describe," and the fact that "he lived there to the end, in spite of the distressful times that befell Hellas in this day." [72] Statues of bronze erected by the Athenians are also among the evidences.[73]

In point of date, it may be noted, these attacks upon the loyalty of Epicurus belong to the early years of the Garden School in Athens, after 306 B.C., and were an aftermath of dissension within the circle. Epicurus, who ordered his affairs with dispassionate discernment and did not shrink from preferring strangers over his own brothers if their abilities were superior, assigned the post nearest himself to the capable Metrodorus. This slight was more than Timocrates could stomach; perhaps he was older than his brother Metrodorus. At any rate, he withdrew in anger and returned home to take service under Lysimachus in Lampsacus. There he joined up with the other deserter Herodotus, whose feelings may have been similarly hurt, and began a campaign of pamphleteering with a view of stirring up trouble for Epicurus among the Athenians. More will be said of this dissension under the head of the New School in Athens.

CHAPTER III ✣ COLOPHON: DEVELOPMENT OF DOCTRINE

D URING the ten years between his cadetship in Athens and his adventure as a public teacher in Mytilene Epicurus was domiciled with his parents and brothers in Colophon. This decade, from 321 to 311 B.C., comprises the interval between his twenty-first and thirty-first years, a crucial time of life for a thinker. It may be called the Colophonian period and its importance is paramount.

At the beginning of it he seems to have been still deferring to the wishes of his parents and looking to orthodox instruction for guidance toward the truths of philosophy. At the end of it he emerged as a self-confident and independent thinker with a fully developed and neatly integrated body of doctrine. What he still lacked for the foundation of a successful school was an organization and a procedure adapted for the dissemination of his new design for living. The remedies for these deficiencies were to be discovered later as the fruits of his sojourns in Mytilene and Lampsacus.

If we follow the practice recommended by Epicurus himself and plot the synoptic view before attempting to fill in the details, the outline of this period will be about as follows. The year 322 B.C., the second of his cadetship, was hardly less eventful in Samos than in Athens. All Athenians were evicted under orders from the Macedonian regent Antipater. The father Neocles found a refuge in Colophon on the mainland. There Epicurus arrived the following year and, probably after a family conference, sought the instruction of Praxiphanes in Rhodes. This association failed to prove satisfactory but lasted long enough to find a place in the records. After an interval the still restless Epicurus was permitted to turn aside from the path of contemporary orthodoxy and return to his first love, Democritus. He enrolled in the school of Nausiphanes of Teos, which was close to Colophon. During the course of this instruction, which must have lasted for a considerable time, he seems to have found his feet, to have fought out with his teacher such problems as those of free will and determinism and the function of philosophy, and at the last to have taken his leave with hostile feelings on both sides. Returning to Colophon he there offered himself as a teacher and gathered about him a body of students.

Colophon was situated on the river Hales a few miles north of Ephesus and not far from the coast. The peak of its prosperity was already two centuries in the past. It was one of several cities that claimed to be the birthplace of Homer and it possessed the undisputed honor of having produced the elegiac poet Mimnermus and the philosopher Xenophanes. Even at the end of the fourth century, however, the intellectual life of the Ionian cities had not spent itself, and to take up residence there was by no means a withdrawal among ruins or a sort of exile, as some have gratuitously surmised.

Before proceeding to further details, it is timely also to suggest that Epicurus may have been looking forward to many years of study. If the sophists be excepted, the Greeks may be said to have exhibited a leisurely attitude toward the higher education. The disciples of Socrates followed him about for decades. After the death of Socrates Plato resorted from one school to another and was forty years of age when he began to teach in the Academy. Aristotle remained in the circle of Plato for twenty years and was fifty-two when he began to receive pupils in the Lyceum. Zeno the Stoic is said to have been thirty years of age when he arrived in Athens and sought the instruction of Crates.

PRAXIPHANES

The choice of Praxiphanes as an instructor for Epicurus bespeaks both ambition and discrimination on the part of his family. Praxiphanes ranked among the foremost teachers of his day and was one of five scholars listed by the geographer Strabo as having contributed distinction to the city of Rhodes.[1] It is reported upon dubious authority that he was a pupil of Theophrastus, but superior evidence can be quoted for regarding him as a friend and contemporary, though certainly younger.[2] Both were born on the island of Lesbos, and Praxiphanes in Mytilene itself.[3] While Theophrastus, however, was a pupil of Aristotle in both Mytilene and Athens, it may be inferred that Praxiphanes studied under him only in the Lyceum in Athens.

It is also beyond doubt that he carried on the tradition of the Peripatetics with some originality. He seems to have occupied a middle position between that of the Lyceum and that of Aristarchus, the famous critic of Alexandria. He was the first to be called by the title *grammaticus*,[4] which signified a critical student of literature. He busied himself with Homer and wrote about poets and poetry.[5] His claim to originality is also confirmed by the fact that he separated literary rhetoric from political rhetoric; the objective of grammar as he taught it is said to have been "good writing." [6] This fact also suggests the transition from the scholarship of the original Peripatetics to that of Alexandria, which was little interested in oratory.

Unfortunately these positive merits seem to have been offset by a cold and censorious disposition and by a tendency to picayune criticism. He censured Homer for having the mother of Ulysses reply to his last question first,[7] and as an expert in Homeric diction he denied to the poet Aratus the ability to write correctly or artfully, which provoked a studied reply from the famous Callimachus.[8] It is consequently understandable that he should have failed to make a conquest of the friendly Epicurus, who denied all debt to him by denying that he had been his pupil. About the hostility of the contemporary Epicureans toward him there is no doubt, nor need doubt exist that there was specific reason for it. The promptness with which Epicurus was attacked by the philosophers in Mytilene some years later is readily accounted for if it be surmised that the knowledge of bad feeling between him and the Mytilenean Praxiphanes had preceded him there.

There is, however, better evidence of the hostility than reasonable conjecture. There is extant among the Herculanean papyri an oblique attack upon Praxiphanes by an Epicurean, Carneiscus.[9] From the first years of the sect it was the custom to write eulogistic biographies of deceased members, showing how they had kept the faith. This Carneiscus, in praising his departed friend Philistas, commends especially the propriety of his conduct at the deaths of other friends, declaring that he was neither "hateful nor heartless." [10] From the context it is beyond doubt that by so extolling his friend he was condemning Praxiphanes.

It has been, of course, objected that Praxiphanes, if he was a pupil of Theophrastus, could not have been a teacher of Epicurus, but the evidence by no means precludes the possibility. The sole authority for making him a pupil of Theophrastus is Proclus, the Neoplatonist of the fifth century A.D., who also calls him "an intimate friend" of the same.[11] Thus this evidence is not only to be dated seven centuries after Epicurus but is also indecisive. Against this must be placed the word of Epicurus himself, who in a letter refuting the skeptic Eurylochus denied pupilage to Praxiphanes in his usual way by declaring himself "self-taught." [12] The tradition that he really had been a pupil is confirmed by the word of Apollodorus, a professional historian of literature, who lived close to the time of events.[13] It seems consequently more reasonable to make Praxiphanes a younger contemporary rather than a pupil of Theophrastus and to assume that his teacher was Aristotle himself.

This inference not only dissolves the objection to thinking of Epicurus as a pupil of Praxiphanes but also invites citation of internal and external evidence pointing in the same direction. As already noted, Praxiphanes was interested in "good writing" apart from oratory, and this may account for his sympathy with Isocrates,[14] who was no orator himself and cultivated artifices of style that were specially applicable to literature written only to be read. A specimen of this very kind of writing happens to be extant from the pen of Epicurus, the charming letter to Menoeceus, in which the rules of rhythmical composition along with artful antitheses are deftly observed. It is consequently quite possible that this specific skill of Epicurus was improved under the instruction of Praxiphanes.

So much for the internal evidence. The external evidence for believing that Epicurus once sojourned in Rhodes consists of the remains of two letters preserved in fragments as parts of the long inscription of the devoted Epicurean Diogenes of Oenoanda. In reading these it should be recalled that the letters of Epicurus possessed the rank of holy scriptures among his followers and were widely circulated. The worshipful attitude of disciples toward the founder is aptly described in Vatican Collection 36: "The life of Epicurus in respect of gentleness and self-sufficiency, if compared with those of other men, would be considered a fairy tale." A very special item of the tradition was his devotion to his parents, as mentioned by his biographer,[15] and it was as a testimony to this devotion that one of the two letters now being considered seems to have been inscribed on the stones.

The occasion of writing was the receipt of a letter from his mother, who told of seeing him in dreams. In reply he assured her that these visions foreboded no evil to him and that every day he was making progress toward a happiness like that of the gods. Part of the remaining text may be rendered as follows:

"Think of us, Mother, as living among such blessings as these and rejoicing always and let yourself feel uplifted at what we are doing. Be sparing, however, of the parcels, I implore you, which you persist in sending us, for it is not my wish that you should lack anything in order that I may have an abundance, but rather that I may lack to the end that you may not. As a matter of fact, I am even faring bountifully in all things because of the money being sent regularly by my father and by friends and especially because of the nine minas which Cleon has lately sent. There is consequently no sense in each of you worrying yourself separately on my account but you should rather be sharing one with the other (your common grounds for contentment)." [16]

This letter does not, of course, afford evidence that Epicurus was in Rhodes at the time of writing but it does demonstrate rather conclusively that he was still a student and dependent upon others for the expenses of living away from home. Apart from its intrinsic interest, the reason for quoting from it is to enhance the probability that the second letter is from the pen of the same person, who explicitly refers to his sojourn in Rhodes.

This second letter, apart from its association with the first, exhibits specimens of that effusiveness in the expression of gratitude with which Epicurus was frequently twitted.[17] The reference to a lady with whom the writer lodged must remain cryptic to us, though it is well known that Epicurus had a way of winning the adherence of women to his side. The extant part of the text is brief:

"And I am minded the more to make another visit, having been introduced by you to her, because of your own friendly attitude toward us, dearest Meneas, and the assiduity of the wonderful Carus and our dear Dionysius throughout the whole time that we were sojourning in Rhodes at her house. Again, farewell." [18]

The idea may suggest itself, of course, that this letter has reference to some later visit of Epicurus, but against this assumption may be quoted the express statement that after taking up his residence in Athens he continued to live there, "only two or three times running over to visit friends in Ionia and adjacent parts." [19] To think of Rhodes as adjacent to Ionia is hardly possible.

If the evidences for a sojourn of Epicurus in Rhodes as a pupil of Praxiphanes be now summed up, we have the following items: first, a specific statement that he did study with Praxiphanes and a specific denial of debt to him by Epicurus; second, specific evidence of the location of Praxiphanes at Rhodes; and third, the probability that the first letter, like the second, was written from Rhodes. To these items may be added the fact that Rhodes was in those days becoming increasingly attractive. Its commercial prosperity was increasing as that of Athens diminished and especially after the death of Alexander, which occurred in the student days of Epicurus. It may have been this increase of prosperity that induced Praxiphanes himself to abandon Mytilene, where philosophers were in oversupply. The famous Aristotelian Eudemus had already preceded him in Rhodes.[20]

NAUSIPHANES

Of the three named teachers of Epicurus it should be kept in mind that Pamphilus was a Platonist, Praxiphanes a Peripatetic, and Nausiphanes a Democritean atomist. It would consequently appear that Epicurus, probably with family approval, first explored the paths of orthodoxy and at last returned to his first love, Democritus. That atomism had become heterodoxy is undeniable, because Platonism during the fourth century had established itself widely as the standard creed. Of this Platonism the Aristotelians were allies rather than competitors.

It should also be observed that our knowledge of Pamphilus is mere mention, that rather more is known of Praxiphanes, and relatively much more of Nausiphanes and his relationship with Epicurus. This would indicate that the above order represents the order of time. Epicurus would have been under eighteen as a pupil of Pamphilus, just entering upon his twenties when he enrolled with Praxiphanes, and already approaching maturity when he parted angrily with Nausiphanes. Thus it was to be expected that this last relationship should have left more ample information in the records. This inference accords with a malicious statement of Cicero that in the case of Nausiphanes Epicurus was "on the spot," as it were; he could not deny his debt to him, though he might to Pamphilus.[21]

Nausiphanes taught in the ancient Ionian coastal city of Teos, which was a short voyage north of Samos and not far from Colophon by land. In spite of the Platonism that flourished farther north in Mytilene and at Assos and Scepsis on the mainland,[22] it is not surprising that a cell of the languishing atomism should have there survived, because Teos had furnished citizens for a refounding of Abdera,[23] the home city of Democritus, and family connections between the parent city and the colonists may well have been kept alive. Nausiphanes, however, was no narrow physicist. His reputation for learning was high, and specific testimony to his proficiency in rhetoric has been preserved.[24] Attention to this subject was perhaps a necessity, because it was the money-making branch among contemporary studies.[25]

No specific evidence exists to indicate that he shared an interest in mathematics with the Platonists or in plants and animals with the Peripatetics. His claim to originality arises from his reaction to the contemporary skepticism of Pyrrho, who, after the upsetting experience of viewing the wisdom of Persia and India in the train of Alexander, had returned to deny the possibility of knowledge. Nausiphanes, while yet a young man, became his pupil and was captivated not by his doctrines but by his disposition, which was imperturbable.[26] Epicurus, in turn, becoming the pupil of Nausiphanes, conceived a like admiration of Pyrrho's conduct "and was continually asking for more information about him." [27] Here may consequently be discerned one possible origin for the famous Epicurean doctrine of ataraxy or tranquillity of soul. The practice of Pyrrho was closer to this than to the cheerfulness (*euthumia*) of Democritus, although Epicurus cultivated this also. It is to be remembered too that Pyrrho recommended abstention from public life (*apragmosune*), which should remind us that Epicurus disapproved of all public careers.

THE QUARREL

How long Epicurus sojourned with Nausiphanes it is impossible to say, but the duration of the discipleship was certainly long enough to engender exceptional bitterness of feeling. Cicero records in a malicious moment that being "on the spot," as it were, and unable to deny obligation, Epicurus assailed his teacher with all sorts of insulting epithets.[28] This statement can be documented, thanks to the researches of later Platonistic adversaries, who rummaged the records for damaging items of evidence. From a single list we learn that among the opprobrious epithets were "lung-fish," "dumb animal," "imposter," and "prostitute." [29] These insults call for comment. Of the four words the first two and the second two constitute pairs.

The word here rendered "lung-fish" has been erroneously translated "mollusc" and "jelly-fish." The Greek is *pleumon*, "lung," and Pliny describes the creature as having no more sensation than a block of wood, while Sextus Empiricus explains the word as equivalent to "insensate." [30] The word rendered "dumb animal" above is usually translated "illiterate." To so describe Nausiphanes would be absurd. The Greek is *agrammatos* and when used of animals it signifies "dumb," just as the psalmist speaks of the horse and the mule "which have no understanding." Just what justification Epicurus may have had for so characterizing his teacher can only be surmised. In their opposition to skepticism and acceptance of dogmatism they were agreed. It is conceivable therefore that the bitterness of Epicurus arose from his inability to bring his teacher around to his own views on the topics of free will and determinism and the function of philosophy, which were the chief grounds of his rupture with the teachings of Democritus. At this stage of his career he was litigious and shunned no controversy.

This is not the whole story, however. The imperturbability of Pyrrho was indifference and a sort of resignation to belief in the impossibility of knowledge. With this sort of resignation it is clear that neither Nausiphanes nor Epicurus had any patience. The distinction of becoming the first dogmatists may perhaps be claimed for them. Nausiphanes admired only the disposition of Pyrrho and rejected his skepticism. He erected a canon of knowledge, which means that he asserted the possibility of knowledge. He called his canon the Tripod, though information is lacking us concerning the three legs of this triad. The astute Epicurus did not take over this name, but he did set up three criteria of knowledge, the Sensations, Anticipations, and Feelings. These he chose to call his Canon. That it was in reality filched from Nausiphanes is expressly stated by a reliable writer.[31] If there be truth in this report — and such charges were often made with little justification — the achievement of Epicurus was to bring the idea to universal knowledge; his gifts as a publicist were of a high order.

There remain the epithets "imposter" and "prostitute." For these it is the most plausible explanation that Epicurus discovered his teacher to be living a double life, preaching virtue, as all philosophers did, and at the same time practicing vice. Cicero informs us that most philosophers condoned the practice of homosexuality, and for once he agreed emphatically with Epicurus in condemning it as against Plato.[32] The latter, as is well known, had essayed in his *Symposium* to sublimate this passion into a passion for knowledge. Epicurus also wrote a *Symposium*, in which he retorted: "Intercourse never was the cause of any good and it is fortunate if it does no harm." [33] In the case of Nausiphanes there is another item of evidence from the pen of Epicurus: "As for my own opinion, I presume that the high-steppers (Platonists) will think me really a pupil of the 'lung-fish' and that I listened to his lectures in the company of certain lads who were stupid from the night's carousing. For he was both an immoral man and addicted to such practices as made it impossible for him to arrive at wisdom." [34] The practices here referred to have been interpreted as the study of mathematics,[35] but the mention of adolescent lads, of drinking, and of immorality make the true reference unmistakable to any reader conversant with the shadier side of student life among the Greeks.

As for Epicurus himself, even if strict in his views about chastity, there is no doubt that he was an irritating pupil. It will be recalled how he put his early instructor in a corner over the topic of chaos. The following extract reveals no more the irritable teacher than the irritating pupil; the reference is to Nausiphanes: "Well, good riddance to the braggart, for that rotter, when in a temper, would have a torrent of the sophistic bluster at the tip of his tongue, like many another of the servile creatures." [36] It may be mentioned that Epicurus classified all men as slaves who, like the physicists, believed in Necessity, or, like the poets, in Fate, or, like Theophrastus, in Fortune, or, like the people, in divine interference, or like the Platonists, in astral deities, or those who, by pursuing the conventional education, surrendered their freedom for the pursuit of power, fame, or wealth.

Having made the round of the contemporary schools, Platonic, Peripatetic, and Democritean, Epicurus seems to have retired to Colophon to devote himself to independent study and teaching. It is expressly stated in the records that he remained there for a considerable time.[37] It may even be assumed that not as yet had he developed his aversion to rhetoric and that he offered public instruction in this subject as the one from which the much needed income could most readily be gained. It may be also that he made use of his father's elementary school as a laboratory. It is positively known that his scheme of education reached down to this level, and it is also known that his ultimate aim was to make play hours of study hours, as it were. Specifically the record runs that he wished to turn "education into recreation." [38] It is also related that his disciples were held fast under the spell of his teachings as if by the voices of sirens.[39]

These items of the tradition, if added up, bespeak a fascinating skill in the art of instruction, which must have been brought to excellence somewhere, and the speed with which disciples were won over to him in Mytilene and Lampsacus points to Colophon as the place. These years must also be recognized as an interval of incubation during which the numerous details of the new philosophy were pieced together into a consistent pattern. Even if such basic problems as the question of free will and determinism and the function of philosophy had already presented themselves, no sudden illumination could have been adequate to effect the end-result, which was nothing less than the synthesis of the physics which the Ionians had cultivated to the neglect of ethics with the ethics which Socrates and Plato had cultivated to the neglect of physics. Very properly, this unique synthesis of Ionian and Athenian thought was the achievement of an Athenian born and raised in Ionia.

SELF-TAUGHT

Since the pupilage of Epicurus was terminated by this quarrel with Nausiphanes, the time is opportune to discuss the charge of ingratitude to teachers and the justice of Epicurus' claim to have been self-taught. Ancient critics passed up few opportunities to belittle him on these grounds. Cicero speaks of his "fear that he might ever seem to have learned anything from instruction," [40] and Sextus Empiricus writes: "Although he had been the pupil of Nausiphanes, yet for the sake of appearing to be self-taught and a natural-born philosopher, he used to deny the connection in every way, was eager to wipe out the record of it and became a constant assailant of those studies for which that man was revered." [41]

In order that a verdict on these charges may be just and fair it will be the duty of modern readers to be on their guard, because most of the witnesses are hostile and scornful. On every score it will be found that something may be said in favor of the defendant. It will be a convenient plan to arrange the items in the order adopted by the defendant himself, Canon, Physics, and Ethics.

On the question of the Canon there is certainty and uncertainty. It seems certain that Nausiphanes set up a canon which he called the

Tripod. It is certain also that Epicurus set up a canon with a threefold partition into Sensations, Anticipations, and Feelings. In respect of this item it would be obstinacy to deny the appearance of indebtedness. On the other hand, nothing is known of the Tripod of Nausiphanes beyond the name, and we do know that Epicurus demoted Reason to a subordinate place and exalted Nature as the norm.[42] This substitution, as will be shown later, was in line with the researches of Aristotle and certain of his school in the realm of zoology and animal behavior,[43] in which not one of Epicurus' teachers was engaged, so far as we are informed. It is a reasonable verdict, therefore, that the elevation of Nature above Reason was the fruit of reading and reflection, not instruction.

In the domain of physics the charge of ingratitude is aggravated because the sin is against Democritus. "What is there in the Physics of Epicurus that is not from Democritus?" demands Cicero, and elsewhere he says: "What he changes he seems to spoil." [44] Incidentally, every offense that was charged to Epicurus seemed more heinous than those of others. The defection of Epicurus from the teachings of Democritus, however, is almost wholly in the domain of ethics. To him as a moral reformer two things ranked foremost as abominations, skepticism and physical determinism. To such moral indignation Nausiphanes seems to have been immune; even if he rejected Pyrrhonian skepticism, this need not mean that he became alert to the evil of skepticism in general. To Epicurus he seemed insensate. The pupil was advancing beyond the teacher.

As for Democritus himself, he committed himself to a certain degree of skepticism when he declared "atoms and void to be the only existences and all else to exist by convention." [45] This, however, was only individual skepticism, which did not prevent him from practicing cheerfulness (*euthumia*) any more than Pyrrho was prevented from enjoying indifference. To Epicurus, on the contrary, belief or disbelief had become a matter of morals and the happiness of mankind. He was incapable of taking comfort in a negative attitude, as did Democritus and Pyrrho. Thus he was compelled by the inward urge to become a pragmatist as well as a dogmatist and to insist that knowledge must not only be possible but also have relevance to action and to happiness. In this matter none of his teachers had set him an example.

A second ground of his defection from Democritus was physical determinism. Determinism is not offensive to intellectuals, but to moral reformers it is neither conceivable nor tolerable. Moral reform is synonymous with the experience of conversion, and conversion presumes freedom of the will. To Democritus the prime and only causation in the universe was the motion of the atoms. In this motion there was no deviation, no freedom possible. It constituted an absolute determinism. In order to open an escape from this intolerable physical necessity Epicurus postulated sufficient play in the motion of the atoms to permit of freedom of the will.[46] Thus he introduced into the sum of things a new cause, human volition, which was to him at one and the same time a necessity of thought and a necessity of action. This innovation may not be commendable in physics, but ethical considerations had become paramount and in ethics the desired end had been served by the innovation. For this invention he was in debt to no teacher.

Neither was he in debt to his teachers for his hedonism. None of them was a hedonist. He was in debt to Plato for suggestions concerning the classification of desires and the calculus of advantage in pleasure,[47] but differed from both Plato and Aristippus in his definition of pleasure. To neither of these was continuous pleasure conceivable, because they recognized only peaks of pleasure separated either by intervals void of pleasure or by neutral states. In order to escape from these logical dead ends Epicurus worked his way to a novel division of pleasures into those that were basic and those that were decorative.[48] The pleasure of being sane and in health is basic and can be enjoyed continually. All other pleasures are superfluous and decorative. For this doctrine, once more, he was in debt to no teacher.

In respect of his teleology he was also independent of his teachers. It is true that he may have learned of the teleology of Plato from his first teacher Pamphilus, but this brand of teleology became an abomination to him. In his view the universe was eternal and had always been an orderly cosmos. All creationism was thus ruled out and along with creationism all arguments drawn from evidences of divine design or superintendence. As for Praxiphanes, if he took time off from literary criticism to expound the biological teleology of Aristotle, the mind of Epicurus was closed to it, because it was not the Epicurean view that ears had been created to hear with or eyes to see with.[49] From Nausiphanes, in turn, if he was an orthodox Democritean, no teleology could have been learned at all, because it was inconsistent with a universe of non-·purposive atomic motion.

COLOPHON: DEVELOPMENT OF DOCTRINE

The limited teleology at which Epicurus finally arrived had nothing to do either with creationism or adaptation of organ to function. It had nothing to do with the universe at large, which was ruled by natural laws. It had nothing to do even with animals, although animal behavior afforded evidence that pleasure was the end or telos of living. It was recognized, to be sure, that animals possess volition and that certain kinds of animals are actuated by innate ideas to organize themselves into herds for mutual protection,[50] but only the rational human being was believed capable of intelligent planning for living and for keeping steadily in view the fact that pleasure is the end or telos ordained by Nature. This amounts to saying that a nonpurposive Nature had produced a purposive creature, for whom alone an end or goal of living could have a meaning. This is teleology at a minimum. For such a belief no teacher had set a precedent.

THE FUNCTION OF PHILOSOPHY

Epicurus was in revolt also against the teachings of Democritus, Socrates, Plato, and the rest concerning the function of philosophy. The Phi Beta Kappa idea that "Philosophy is the guide of life" was already commonplace,[51] but no one was interpreting it very practically. To the great atomist Leucippus, Epicurus even denied right to the name of philosopher, because he concerned himself with physics to the exclusion of ethics.[52] The ground upon which this was denied was neatly expressed: "Vain is the word of that philosopher by which no malady of mankind is healed." [53] This position was arrived at by way of the analogy with medicine, itself an inert commonplace in the then current philosophies. He proposed to put life into it: "For just as there is no profit in medicine unless it expels the diseases of the body, so there is none in philosophy either unless it expels the malady of the soul." [54] With Democritus himself Epicurus was impatient because of his implicit skepticism, which to him was a sort of pessimism, paralyzing to action.

Epicurus is thus seen emerging as a natural pragmatist, impatient of all knowledge that lacks relevance to action. Platonic dialectic was to him a superfluity and consisted in "walking around uselessly and harping upon the question, What is the meaning of 'good'?" [55] At times his zeal becomes truly religious, and his language anticipates the terminology of the New Testament. Of this a specimen is his advice to the young

67

Pythocles: "From the outset you must believe that no other end is gained from the knowledge of celestial phenomena, whether viewed in their associations [with the astral deities] or by themselves, than peace of soul and an abiding faith." [56] He did not believe in "following the logos" nor in following "knowledge like a sinking star beyond the utmost bound of human thought." The thing of supreme urgency was not knowledge but the happiness of mankind. He called his teachings "true philosophy," but they approximated to a religion. He claimed for himself the title of "sage," but he was really a prophet.

When once Epicurus had discovered himself as a prophet and a pragmatist, a dynamic significance was injected into the analogy between philosophy and medicine. Unlike the Platonists, he was bound to be concerned not only with adolescent males but also with human beings of all ages, including women and children. This new note is promptly and beautifully struck in the opening words of his exhortation to philosophy, the letter to Menoeceus, which was perhaps intended to compete with the famous *Protrepticus* of Aristotle: "There is no one for whom the hour has not yet come nor for whom the hour has passed for attending to the health of his soul." [57] This new outlook demanded the offering of instruction to junior pupils, and it may have been this proposal that provoked the scorn of Nausiphanes: "Upon hearing this he so lost his temper as to begin abusing me and taunting me with being a schoolteacher." [58] As a matter of fact, the Epicureans did establish elementary schools of their own, an example that was followed by the Christians.

Two observations remain to be made in respect of the Colophon period in the life of Epicurus. First, in view of the bitterness engendered in the clash with Nausiphanes, it will seem plausible to assume that the fundamental problems of doctrine above enumerated were threshed out in face-to-face controversy between teacher and pupil. Second, since the Greeks loved gossip, and communication was frequent between city and city, it may be assumed that reports of the contentious heterodoxy of the young Epicurus preceded his arrival in Mytilene and paved the way for the hostile reception there accorded him.

Furthermore, in view of the furor occasioned by his offering himself there as a public teacher, it seems reasonable to assume that the new body of doctrine was worked out to completion in Colophon. A brief chain argument will make the grounds of this assumption explicit.

COLOPHON: DEVELOPMENT OF DOCTRINE

As will be revealed in due course, the populace of Mytilene was incited to rage against the newcomer and a gymnasiarch was prodded into action. This would mean that an indictment for impiety was either threatened or lodged. From this it can safely be inferred that the denial of all divine participation in human affairs was already part of the offending doctrine. This denial, in turn, was to Epicurus a pragmatic necessity because of his determination to assert the freedom of man. The freedom of man, again, was a pragmatic necessity because of belief in pleasure or happiness as the end established by Nature. To be happy, man must be free to plan his whole life.

Yet again, the free planning of life required, along with the rejection of all shapes of determinism, divine or physical, belief in the possibility of knowledge and the denouncement of skepticism. Moreover, once skepticism had been denounced, it was imperative to set up a canon of truth. Lastly, Epicurus showed himself in Mytilene to be singularly aggressive, and this quality had its origin in his discovery of himself as a prophet and a missionary as well as a sage. It must consequently be inferred that before leaving Colophon he had already worked out to its pragmatic implications the old analogy between philosophy and medicine, that all human beings, regardless of age or sex, stood in need of health of mind and the services of the teacher no less than of health of body and the services of the physician.

CHAPTER IV ✛ MYTILENE AND LAMPSACUS

FTER the sojourn of ten years at Colophon came an interval of five years spent in Mytilene and Lampsacus, 311 to 306 B.C. The stay in Mytilene for the purpose of teaching in public was brief and tempestuous, terminating in forced flight, probably within the year 311–310 B.C. In a mutilated papyrus which once recorded the life of Epicurus is found mention of "the power of mobs or of a monarch or of a gymnasiarch." [1] Plutarch quotes a writing of Epicurus himself as containing mention, among other hazards, of "the passions of mobs, the cruelties of pirates," and the danger of shipwreck in the course of a voyage to Lampsacus.[2] These and similar items can be pieced together into a coherent story.

The sojourn in Lampsacus lasted for four years, from 310 to 306 B.C. It was characterized by the emergence of a regenerate Epicurus, by the winning of financial support, by the assembling of talented disciples, and by the development of an organization suitable for maintaining a new school and disseminating its doctrines.

THE NEW PHILOSOPHY ON TRIAL

It has always been known from the records that Epicurus once offered himself as an instructor in philosophy at Mytilene,[3] but until recent years no serious effort had been made to piece together into a connected story the numerous but scattered evidences of his activities. It happens fortunately, however, that a first effort in this direction produced a very plausible synthesis of the data applicable to this particular year.[4] Since the beginning is half of the whole and certain landmarks have now been recognized, it is not too difficult a task to insert additional details and arrive at a more satisfying narrative of the whole episode.

At the outset it is well to inquire for what reason Epicurus chose

Mytilene for this venture. On this point it may be permitted to adopt the method recommended by Epicurus himself in fields where certainty is impossible and to suggest several possibilities, any one of which may be the true one. In the first place, it must be remembered that Greece was then divided among various Macedonian generals and that absolute freedom of migration is not to be assumed. For example, Athens was at that time governed by Demetrius Phalereus, agent of the ruthless Cassander, while Asia, where Epicurus resided, had fallen to Antigonus Monophthalmus, or the "One-Eyed." Moreover, the island of Lesbos, where Mytilene was situated, belonged to the domain of this same Antigonus.[5] It would consequently have been permissible for Epicurus, who perhaps still lacked influential friends, to make this remove without crossing a frontier.

The city of Mytilene itself may have been an attraction. It was important as an educational center. Aristotle himself had taught there for two years, 346/5–344/3 B.C., immediately before joining the suite of Philip of Macedon as the tutor of his son Alexander. Those were the days when the dream of a Platonic philosopher-king was flourishing and Aristotle was sharing it. He would have ranked as a Platonist, and his later fame as the founder of the Lyceum school may well have enhanced without changing essentially the educational loyalties of the Mytileneans. That several philosophers were teaching there when Epicurus invaded the city and that they were of one color is indicated by his famous attack upon them as a group. This was entitled *Against the Philosophers in Mytilene*.

It is also thinkable that a simultaneous motive on the part of Epicurus was the desire to try out his new doctrines in a more challenging environment than Colophon. Neither is the possibility to be ruled out that he was indulging a long simmering spirit of vendetta. The seed of rebellion was in him from the first. He had submitted to no teacher and had battled openly with Nausiphanes. In this fray he may have believed himself the victor and so become sufficiently indiscreet to invade hostile territory and, like Goliath, to proclaim a general defiance. At any rate, this seems to be what he did.

To say that he "opened a school" in Mytilene may be misleading. The Greek city-states assumed very limited responsibility for furnishing education, but they took somewhat seriously the responsibility for supervising it. This came about from the fact that the custom of the sophists and philosophers was to seek their pupils in the public palaestras and gymnasiums, where boys of high school and college age resorted for their physical exercise and training. These exercise grounds consisted of rectangular spaces, partly shaded by trees, partly open and sanded, and usually surrounded by colonnades along with benches for intervals of relaxation. All these properties were subject to the supervision of officials called gymnasiarchs.

As the custodians of public properties these gymnasiarchs possessed police powers. It is recorded, for instance, that one of them in Thebes gave orders that Crates the philosopher should be flogged.[6] In particular they were charged with the duty of protecting the young men from corrupting influences. Thus we learn from Demosthenes that the lodgment of indictments for impiety fell within their province,[7] and this accords with the statement of Aristotle that their superior was the King Archon.[8] Consequently little doubt can exist that when "the power of a gymnasiarch" is mentioned in the life of Epicurus the inference should be that a charge of impiety was either threatened or actually lodged against him. Such an inference gains added credibility when it is recalled that atheism was imputed to him throughout his life.

THE SORITES SYLLOGISM

If now we begin to piece our evidences together it will be clear that Epicurus began his campaign with a frontal attack and went from one group to another heckling the practicing teachers in his usual irritating way. It will be clear also that he chose to make hedonism the issue. The following passage is first-class evidence; it was translated by Cicero with the text of Epicurus *On the End* before him: "Time and again I demanded to know of those who were called wise what they had to leave in the list of goods if they subtracted those pleasures (of taste, vision and other senses) unless they chose to pour forth a stream of meaningless words. I could get no information from them." [9] That the locale of this questioning was Mytilene can reasonably be inferred. While yet a student in Rhodes the thinking of Epicurus would hardly have progressed to such a point as to impel a public challenge. In smaller towns like Teos and Colophon it is unlikely that many philosophers were available for questioning. After the removal to Athens in 306 B.C. he confined himself to his own house and garden.

It is also clear that his attack was directed against Platonists, with whom Aristotelians would be one so far as he was concerned. It must be remembered that he looked upon Platonists as "high-steppers." Cicero's translation proceeds: "These men, if they will only get rid of their fancy notions of virtue and wisdom, will mean nothing else than the means by which those pleasures which I have listed above are obtained." [10] Here there is little cause for hesitancy. The teaching of Epicurus was realistic; pleasure was the good; justice was practiced for the sake of it. The fancy notions at which he scoffed were the belief in absolute justice, in the theory of eternal ideas in general, and the concept of true knowledge as the apprehension of them.

This is not the limit of our information, however. It is fairly plain that Epicurus chose for his assault upon the Mytilenean philosophers one of the more irritating of all forms of argument, the "sorites syllogism." In the same context in which we learn of Epicurus making his rounds to nettle the practicing philosophers we find this statement: "For my own part I am at a loss to know what meaning I shall attach to the good, subtracting the pleasures of taste, subtracting the pleasures of love, subtracting the pleasures of the ears, subtracting also the pleasure of the eyes in beauty of form and beauty of movement." [11]

The true import of this passage has escaped detection. It is the sorites syllogism in narrative form. The key word is "subtract." For a correct understanding the argument must be restored to dialogue form, where it belongs. It consists of a chain of questions: "Do you deny the name of good to the pleasures of taste?" "Yes." "Do you deny the name of good to the pleasures of love?" "Yes." And so on with the rest. At the end of the chain the interlocutor has denied the name of good to everything that the man in the street calls pleasure and there is left only the pleasures of the mind. That the argument did arrive at this termination is made plain by Cicero, who quotes the passage with more fulness. In his account is added: "Neither can this be said, that the pleasure of the mind alone is to be ranked among goods." It was thus that the imprudent Epicurus chose to exasperate his competitors.

HOMER A HEDONIST

While this application of the sorites syllogism was irritating enough, Epicurus possessed another weapon capable of administering perhaps a meaner sting. He was able to quote a passage from the Phaeacian episode in the *Odyssey* which seemed to be a pronouncement of the hedonistic creed in the very terminology of the Platonic-Peripatetic schools. Not only the scholium on this passage but a bevy of other notices from antiquity inform us that upon this authority Epicurus based his espousal of pleasure as the end or telos.[12] This view, it need hardly be interposed, is only superficially true. The real basis of his hedonism was the sanction of Nature herself, which for him furnished the norm. The persistence of Homer's name in the tradition is merely a tribute to its superior news value and to the smartness of the sting so administered.

The nature of the sting will be better understood if two points be recalled to mind: first, that for the Greek public everywhere the poems of Homer enjoyed the status of a textbook on morals and were revered as a sort of Bible; the second point is the fact that the Peripatetic school made a specialty of the study of Homer, as was noted in the case of Praxiphanes at Rhodes.

The Phaeacian king is addressed and the speaker is Odysseus: "Verily this is a beautiful thing, to be listening to a bard such as this man is, with a voice like the gods. For to my mind, I say, no consummation (*telos*) is nearer perfection than when rejoicing (*euphrosune*) prevails among the whole people and the banqueters seated in order in the halls are listening to a bard, when the tables abound in bread and meats and the wine-bearer draws the sweet drink from the mixing bowl and pours it into the cups." [13]

The sting in this quotation is not single but multiple. To the populace, which was later incited against Epicurus, it was sacrilege, equivalent to quoting the Bible in certain circles in support of evolution. To the rival philosophers it must have been most disconcerting, not only because of the fortuitous sanction of the word *telos* to denote pleasure, but also because of the term *euphrosune,* which to Plato and Aristotle signified a pleasure superior to *hedone* and denoted the enjoyment of pure reason contemplating absolute truth.[14] As an addition to the irritation it may be mentioned that Aristotle himself had quoted the passage to demonstrate the need of music in the best education.[15] If Homer was to be an authority on this question, why not on that of the end or telos?

If this assumption be correct that during this adventurous sojourn in Mytilene Epicurus was deliberately needling his adversaries, a second item also deserves mention under the Homeric heading. The text of the *Iliad,* 24.525–526, reads: "This is the lot the gods have apportioned

74

to miserable mortals, to live in sorrow, but no care have they themselves." To the second of these lines is found a scholium: "From this
Epicurus infers that the incorruptible and blissful being has neither
cares nor worries, nor occasions them to others and for this reason is
susceptible of neither anger nor gratitude." These will be recognized
as the words of the first of the Authorized Doctrines, and little doubt
need exist that the alert and learned Epicurus quoted also the passages
in which Homer speaks of the blessed gods as "living at ease," [16] nor
that he read these to mean that the gods enjoyed freedom from toil or
worry (aponia).

While appealing to Homer as an authority in his teaching concerning
pleasure and the life and nature of the gods, Epicurus was able also to
quote Sophocles in proof of a companion principle, that pain was to be
classed as evil. To this end he cited, and possibly in Mytilene, the following couplet of the Trachiniae, which describes the agonies of Heracles perishing in the fateful shirt of Nessus: "Biting, screaming in pain,
and all around his moans were echoed by Locria's mountainous rocks
and Euboea's beetling headlands." [17] He may also have cited the humor-
ous passage of Homer where the wounded god of war is described as
"bellowing like nine thousand or ten thousand men when they raise
the battle-cry, joining in the strife of battle." If Ares himself, like
Heracles, bellowed with pain when wounded, why should not the wise
man moan and wail aloud when on the rack? Pain was manifestly evil
just as pleasure was manifestly good.

It is difficult to think of tricks of controversy better calculated than
these to exasperate adversaries and to afford them grounds for arousing
the populace.

RHETORIC

To the exasperation engendered by these skirmishing tactics a substantial addition must have been made by the denunciation of rhetoric,
dialectic, and mathematical studies. The Platonistic teachers were
thrown into the same predicament as the silversmiths of Ephesus when
St. Paul's preachings threatened their emolument. This was especially
true of rhetoric, which was recognized as the chief money-maker in the
ancient curriculum. That Epicurus did make converts in the rival
schools is indicated by the fact that he afterwards addressed a letter
To the Friends in Mytilene, and of these we know the name of one, the

very Hermarchus whom he chose to succeed him as head of his school. Of this man's study of rhetoric we are expressly informed,[18] and some teacher must have been incensed by the defection of his pupil. It may well be added that the Platonists of those days did not shrink from violence. Some had become tyrannicides and others had attempted revolutions, in Cyzicus and Lampsacus, for example.[19] It was the age of the "lawless *Laws*" rather than the "noble *Republic*," [20] and the word *academic* had not yet come to mean "having no relevance to action."

Retaliation was prompt and drastic. Mention is made in the papyrus of "the power of a monarch." This would have been Antigonus the One-Eyed, within whose domain the island of Lesbos was included. The Platonists and Aristotelians were sympathetic with monarchy. Epicurus, as an Athenian, was an alien in Mytilene and might well have been reported as a subversive influence. Specific information on the point is lacking. More understandable is the reference in the papyrus to "the power of mobs" and in the words of Epicurus to "the passions of mobs." The incitement of the populace would have been necessary whether to put pressure on the gymnasiarch to lodge an indictment or to ensure condemnation once an accusation had been laid.

That the tension of the situation at large was augmented by the determined hostility of a private group is indicated by a mysterious detail in the record. Along with "the passions of mobs and the cruelties of pirates" the account of Epicurus mentions "the injustices of heirs." [21] It would fit the situation if either Epicurus himself or some newly gained disciple had been denied possession of a legacy legally bequeathed, but this must remain a surmise. Certain it may be regarded that Epicurus chose the part of discretion and made his escape by ship while it was yet winter, being almost "swallowed up by the sea," as he reveals, on a stormy voyage.

It is now possible to corroborate the truth of this version of the Mytilene episode by citing a statement of his biographer, the importance of which has up to now escaped notice: "Down to a certain date he mingled with other philosophers in pursuing his calling; afterward he drew apart by himself, having founded the sect named after him." [22] The "certain date" here mentioned makes plain that our biographer Laertius, who was a redactor, had before him a fuller account in which a definite turning point in the life of Epicurus was identified. This turning point must certainly have been his expulsion from Mytilene. Never again, so far as we know, did he essay to teach in a public place. In Athens the famous garden was his personal property.

LAMPSACUS

Since the flight of Epicurus from Mytilene occurred in the season when regular navigation was suspended, it may be placed conjecturally in the late winter of 310 B.C., slightly less than a year after his arrival there. Since his removal to Athens is known to have occurred in 306, the duration of his stay in Lampsacus would have been slightly more than four years.

It is possible to suggest various reasons for the selection of Lampsacus as a refuge. The influence of the hostile Mytilenean school was not extending itself in this direction and the Platonists must have been losing ground. In Lampsacus itself the abortive attempt of the Platonist Evaeon to make himself tyrant was not likely to have been forgotten.[23] A similar antipathy may have survived in the neighboring Cyzicus because of an attempt at revolution by the Platonist Timolaus.[24] In this city the school of the brilliant mathematician Eudoxus had survived his death but was quite independent of both the Academy and the Lyceum. Equally independent was the school of Heracleides beyond the straits in Pontic Heraclea, and the founder was possibly still living. With both of these our Epicurus was subsequently at odds, but there is no need to think of this hostility as preceding him. In Lampsacus itself the very speed with which he came to the fore is evidence that no outstanding rival was there to oppose his progress. The city may also have preserved repute for toleration, since a century earlier Anaxagoras had found safety there when driven from Athens.

It may also be deemed certain that Epicurus was removing himself from the jurisdiction of the one-eyed Antigonus. This end might have been attained by fleeing to Athens, where, as a citizen, he was free to reside, but unluckily this refuge had been virtually closed to him by his own rashness in Mytilene. The philosophers whom he had there embittered were in the descent from Aristotle, and in Athens his school was then riding its highest under his pupil Theophrastus, supported by the governor Demetrius Phalereus, himself a Peripatetic and a philosopher of high pretenses. Thus the inference is more than plausible that what deterred him from taking flight in that direction was the fear of being followed by angry letters from Mytilene and consequent reprisals.

It must be recalled that four years later, when the Peripatetic governor was expelled, Epicurus immediately did make the remove to Athens. It is also worth recalling that some years later Epicurus himself, when his own disciple Timocrates became a renegade, dispatched letters with the intent to injure him at the court of Lysimachus.[25]

With good reason, therefore, it seemed to Epicurus the preferable choice to avoid an almost certain antagonism and to take his chances in a court where he was unknown. In the division of Alexander's empire the portion that fell to Lysimachus was Thrace, but control of the Hellespont very logically went with it. In Thrace itself there was no city suitable for a capital, as is demonstrated by the fact that a new city called Lysimachia was planned and built on the neck of the Chersonese.[26] This was not yet ready, however, when Epicurus arrived, and the temporary seat of the court seems to have been Lampsacus. Although this fact is not mentioned in the extant narratives of his campaigns, it is impossible to point to another city so conveniently located for the reception, storage, and dispatch of the vast equipment necessary for the serious wars which engaged the attention of Lysimachus from the moment of his accession.

The suppliant Epicurus seems to have arrived in the absence of Lysimachus and to have found in charge a certain Mithres, an able Syrian whose duties were those of a steward. What happened between the two is not recorded, but it seems most likely that Epicurus begged for protection and received assurance of it. At any rate he was ever afterward accused of truckling to a barbarian, and in aggravation of this offense a published letter was willfully misinterpreted. It was the custom of Epicurus, as we are informed by the Christian scholar Origen, to sprinkle his writings liberally with the names of the Greek gods.[27] One of his favorite expressions was *Paian Anax,* an exclamation meaning no more than "Thank Heaven" or "Glory be," or "Hallelujah," but in their original use the words were an apostrophe to Apollo, "Lord and Savior." Taking a petty advantage of this fact, the detractors accused Epicurus of addressing Mithres as a god.[28]

It was the fate of Mithres himself at a later time to become a fugitive, having fallen from favor. He sought refuge in Athens and was there befriended by Epicurus, to the advantage of his detractors.[29] He was also honored by the dedication of a roll entitled *Doctrines about Diseases and Death.*[30] Gratitude was exalted by Epicurus to the rank of a cardinal virtue, and nothing could deter him from displaying it.

So much capital was made of this association with the unfortunate Mithres that Epicurus thought fit to make public a defense, as is evidenced by one of the Authorized Doctrines, No. 6: "As for the assurance of safety from the attacks of men, by virtue of the nature of political dominion and kingly power this is a good thing, no matter by whose aid one is able to procure it." Since these Doctrines are rightly regarded as excerpts from published writings, it is reasonable to infer that these words are of early date, that the men whose attacks were feared were the rival philosophers, Platonists, who incited mobs to violence and prodded gymnasiarchs into action, and that by the last clause Epicurus was justifying himself for receiving aid from a barbarian.

The friendship of Mithres did not make a court philosopher of Epicurus but may have brought him at least to the margin of the courtly circle. Lysimachus was hostile to his one-eyed neighbor Antigonus and the constant friend and ally of the first Ptolemy of Egypt, which meant frequent comings and goings of envoys. Among these on a certain occasion was one Theodorus,[31] an egotistical and insolent hedonist of Cyrene, from whom Epicurus was later accused of filching part of his doctrine.[32] The character of the man may be judged from the anecdote that during a court banquet he was put into a logical corner by Hipparchia, wife of the philosopher-envoy Crates of Thebes, and by way of retaliation made a motion to pull the clothes off her, the point being that she dressed like a man.[33] He was insolent also to Lysimachus himself and insulted the steward Mithres.[34] Whether he was introduced to Epicurus is not in the records but the suspicion is justified that he became his enemy, wrote at least four books against him, and accused him of impropriety in his correspondence with Themista,[35] a brilliant married woman of the Lampsacene circle. It is far from improbable in the light of these items of information that he had encountered the sharp tongue of Epicurus. The recorded facts are also indirect evidence of the prominence of the young Epicurus at this early date.

This is not the whole story, however. Plutarch, twitting the long dead Epicurus with the inconsistency of scorning fame while publishing many books, employs the second person and writes: "Don't try to make recruits of the visitors from Egypt." [36] This item affords ground for inferring that Epicurus shared to some degree the court life under Lysimachus and this inference is supported by the knowledge that the first Ptolemy himself became interested. It was to him that Colotes, a charter member of the Epicurean circle in Lampsacus, dedicated his satirical work on the Greek philosophies, to which Plutarch wrote a counterblast four centuries later.[37] Cicero, moreover, relates how this same Ptolemy gave testimony that nothing ever tasted better to him than some coarse bread obtained in a humble cabin in Egypt when he had fallen into dire want.[38] This experience exemplifies the Epicurean doctrine of the natural limit of pleasure, that the pleasure afforded by the satisfaction of hunger is a maximum and cannot be exceeded by the gratification of any whipped-up appetite.

If all the foregoing items of information be now assembled, it becomes very probable that Epicurus was already practicing his known precept: "Under no circumstance pass up an opportunity to disseminate the doctrines of the true philosophy." [39] It becomes also reasonable to believe that some knowledge of his teachings actually reached Ptolemy himself. How explain otherwise the latter's expressed testimony to a doctrine of Epicurus? Even a further inference is justified: if it be assumed that Ptolemy, who was already a patron of the hedonist Theodorus, became interested in the new hedonism of Epicurus through the reports of his envoys or through writings, we have another very plausible ground of explanation for the bitter hostility of this hot-headed Theodorus after he had fallen from favor in the royal court. That he did fall from favor seems certain.[40]

THE LAMPSACENE CIRCLE

Having once secured the assurance of protection, which for him as an alien was required by law or custom or both, Epicurus was free to disseminate his new philosophy in Lampsacus itself. Among his first converts were Idomeneus and Leonteus along with the latter's talented wife Themista. These two men were named centuries later by Strabo as foremost citizens of Lampsacus and friends of Epicurus.[41] It may well have been that the introduction was due to the Syrian steward Mithres, because Idomeneus occupied an office of importance under Lysimachus.[42] Like all high officials under the Macedonian regimes he was amply rewarded in point of income, and with this he was generous from first to last in his support of Epicurus. This is the more understandable when it is learned that he was a man of education and some ability as a writer. He joined in the campaign of Epicurus against his recent assailants by writing a book *On the Socratics,* almost certainly in answer to another of the same title by the Aristotelian Phanias of the Mytilenean group.[43]

Just as Epicurus had won over Hermarchus to his side from the study of rhetoric in Mytilene, so in Lampsacus he made a convert of the mathematician Polyaenus. It is generally agreed that this man had studied in Cyzicus under the Eudoxans, and this belief is confirmed by the circumstance that his lady friend was of that city. Even among the Greeks such attachments could be exploited for their value as scandal, especially if Epicureans were the target, and after the lapse of centuries Plutarch was capable of so demeaning himself as to write of Epicurus "begetting children along with Polyaenus from the strumpet of Cyzicus." [44]

Polyaenus eventually ranked third in the school of Epicurus and along with Metrodorus and Hermarchus was conceded the title of *kathegemon* or associate leader. He is described as "a sympathetic man with a gift for making friends," [45] and there is extant from his pen a tender letter written to a child, though generally ascribed to Epicurus himself.[46]

The chief recruit was Metrodorus, esteemed as "a second Epicurus" and a prolific writer. His family was one of high standing, as is evidenced by the fact that his sister Batis was taken in marriage by Idomeneus.[47] It is also possible, since Greek names were very persistent, that another Metrodorus who befriended the exiled Anaxagoras in Lampsacus a century earlier was among his ancestors.[48]

The chief sponsor and the principal financial supporter of the school was, of course, Idomeneus. Close to him stood Leonteus, who was deemed worthy of mention by Strabo, and his talented wife Themista. Her standing as an author may be judged from the fact that Cicero named her in a speech before the Roman senate.[49] The theme which established her reputation was the vanity of fame, which may have provoked Cicero to write his *De Gloria,* nor is it improbable that she inspired Ecclesiastes and Juvenal, kindred in spirit though remote in space. Her correspondence with Epicurus was published and afforded material of research for diligent detractors in quest of scandal.[50]

A welcome addition of information concerning the circle is furnished by a papyrus fragment of the life of Epicurus by Philodemus: "As for a certain astronomer-geometer of Cyzicus, [Epicurus] puts him in the same class as Xenophanes and Idomeneus and Leonteus and their circle, who are going too far in their abolition of the possibility of proof and he seems to feel anger at their arguments as positively wicked." [51] The inferences to be drawn from this are several in number. The name of the astronomer is undoubtedly Eudoxus, who is known to have lived in Cyzicus during the last lap of his life. At the date of Epicurus' arrival at Lampsacus in 310 B.C. he had been dead for some forty-five years, but his school continued to flourish. To this school it is clear that Idomeneus, Leonteus, and other young men had resorted while Lampsacus itself lacked a resident philosopher.

These young men are being reproved for holding skeptical views that were there imbibed. This open reproof exemplifies that absolute frankness which was a rule of the Epicurean circle; it was required of every adherent to accept correction without resentment. The skepticism in this instance was concerned with the gods of the Greeks. Xenophanes is mentioned; it was his doctrine that certainty concerning them was impossible; men could only have opinions. As for Eudoxus, it was his settled judgment that it made no difference what men thought about the Greek gods, but it is best to quote what may be his own words: "About Zeus and Hera each man is at liberty to believe what he will but the greatest gods and the most worthy of reverence and the most endowed with volition and surpassing wisdom are those visible to all men in the heavens, that is, the stars." [52]

This is the teaching that seemed "wicked" to Epicurus and aroused his anger. The same man who had recently been accused of impiety in Mytilene is here seen as the defender of Greek religion; he is also, as it were, reclaiming the young men of Lampsacus for orthodoxy.

This indignation is by no means feigned; it is a reflex from genuine convictions. As will be shown in the chapter on the New Piety, Epicurus insisted not only upon belief in the existence of the gods but also demanded true reverence for them. Skepticism, the offense of Xenophanes, was consequently intolerable. The offense of Eudoxus, however, was wicked; he declared it a matter of indifference what opinion was held about Zeus and Hera.

It was, moreover, not merely to true orthodoxy that Epicurus was recalling his circle in Lampsacus. He appealed to their patriotism. He denounced the Cyzicenes as "enemies of Hellas." [53] Editors have emended the word *Cyzicenes* to read "Cynics"; it is not even certain that this word was yet current in those days and the substitution is pointless at best. The followers of Eudoxus, that is, the Cyzicenes, were sponsoring the introduction and worship of foreign gods, because the astral gods hailed from Chaldea. This was worse than wickedness; it was treason, like siding with Persia in racial wars. Epicurus even went so far as to declare that only those who spoke Greek were capable of philosophizing, and Philodemus would have it that the gods themselves spoke some form of the Greek language.

This condemnation of the astral gods because foreign in origin and the unique amalgamation of religion, philosophy, and patriotism are perfectly understood if regarded as a sort of manifesto intended to wean the young men of Lampsacus away from the teachings of the Cyzicene school. Quite possibly it provoked the retort that Epicurus himself had recently presented himself as a suppliant before the barbarian Mithres.

As a stage in the development of Epicurean doctrine it also possesses interest. Just as the new teachings of Jesus were confined to the Jews and only after his death extended to the gentiles, so the new philosophy of Epicurus was confined to Greeks and only after his death disseminated among other races.

Another outstanding recruit in Lampsacus was Colotes. His talent was for satire, a favorite weapon of the school, and his burlesque treatment of Greek philosophers remained throughout antiquity a scandal to the older schools. Extant in papyri are also remnants of attacks upon the *Lysis* and the *Euthydemus* of Plato.[54]

The role of a handsome Alcibiades in the school has been assigned to the youthful Pythocles. He migrated to Athens along with other members of the circle and is named as a companion of the friendly Polyaenus on a return visit to Lampsacus.[55] He seems to have been too generously assisted by Idomeneus, which drew a famous reproof from Epicurus: "If you wish to make Pythocles really rich, do not give him more money but try to lessen his desires." [56] This advice was repeated poetically by Horace, quoted with particulars of origin by Seneca and found its way into proverbial literature.[57]

Two desertions are on record from this early group of adherents, an occurrence notoriously rare in the camp of Epicurus. One was that of Timocrates, the unpredictable brother of the capable Metrodorus, because he could not endure the assignment to an inferior place. After the removal of the school to Athens he broke away, returned to Lampsacus and began a written campaign of vilification, supplying eager detractors with precious items of distorted facts.[58] The other deserter was Herodotus, who made common cause with the spiteful Timocrates and discovered specious grounds for impugning the genuineness of the loyalty of Epicurus to Athens.[59]

The conduct of Timocrates and Herodotus invites mention of a phase of the character of Epicurus which came to prominence during this Lampsacene period. He insisted upon absolute frankness and was opposed to the concealment of any facts concerning himself, even though they might be construed to his disrepute. It is on record, for example, that "he used to praise Idomeneus, Herodotus and Timocrates, who had made known to the public inside information concerning himself and that he encouraged this very thing." [60] It seems as if he felt it was no cause for shame to himself if he had arrived in Lampsacus a destitute refugee and had thrown himself upon the mercy of the barbarian Mithres, steward of Lysimachus. He adhered to the same principle of candor in respect of his correspondence, all of which was published, even if some of it should give excuse for scandal to his detractors.

The high regard in which Epicurus was held by the people of Lampsacus in general is evidenced by the testimony of Strabo, who knew that region at first hand in the time of Augustus. He found him regarded almost as a citizen.[61] At the end of the first century A.D. Plutarch still knew of a roll of Epicurus addressed to the cadets or ephebes of Lampsacus.[62] It is doubtful whether this could have been written or published unless by the request or encouragement of the authorities. Epicurus, on his part had exercised his usual care that the original friendships should not be allowed to lapse; fourteen years after his removal to Athens, in 293/2 B.C., he published a letter *To the Friends in Lampsacus*.[63] Such letters were forerunners of the epistles of the apostles to the various churches.

By this time it is possible to discern an important phase of the character of Epicurus in true focus. It is plain to see that his emotional reflexes had been conditioned to a pattern usual among his countrymen, of loving friends and hating enemies, because it was no foreign ideal described by Xenophon when he recorded of the younger Cyrus that he once prayed to live long enough to outdo both friend and foe in benefit and injury, returning like for like.[64] The wisdom that Epicurus had not yet acquired when he recklessly threw down the gauntlet to the philosophers in Mytilene was that of a kindred spirit, Ecclesiastes, who advised, "To every thing there is a season, and a time to every purpose under the heaven. . . . a time to love and a time to hate." [65] The error of Epicurus had been one of timing, and an error of timing is an error of judgment, an insufficiency of reason.

The item of doctrine not as yet reasoned out by Epicurus when he rashly assailed his enemies was the interpretation of individual human happiness in terms of the happiness of the gods, which by rights should furnish the model. This divine happiness is described in the first of the Authorized Doctrines: "The blessed and incorruptible being neither knows trouble itself nor occasions it to another." After the bitter lesson of Mytilene, and not before, Epicurus was able to produce the corollary to this theorem: "The man at peace with himself is inoffensive to his neighbor also." [66]

No cult of martyrdom arose among the Epicureans. Their partisan Ecclesiastes spoke acceptably for them when he exclaimed, "Better a living dog than a dead lion." [67] It was the mature judgment of Epicurus after his escape to Lampsacus that Peace and Safety were essential conditions not only for the tranquillity of the individual but also for the successful promulgation of a new philosophy. It was from this time that the word Safety, *asphaleia* in Greek, attained the status of a watchword. Eventually it conferred a new vogue upon *securitas* in Latin,[68] as also upon *praesidium*. When the poet Horace in his first ode hails Maecenas as his *praesidium,* he recognizes him as the assurance of his safety from attacks by enemies.

It may be observed in passing that St. Paul quoted the words Peace and Safety as catchwords of the Epicureans, to whom he refused the honor of mention by name.[69] In this collocation Peace signified harmonious relations with neighbors while Safety meant the security of the man as a citizen, the sort of safety that Paul himself enjoyed by virtue of Roman citizenship.

The desirability of being a living dog rather than a dead lion is indicated by no fewer than nine references to safety, either by specific mention or implication, in the Authorized Doctrines.[70] Two of these have reference to the protection afforded by princes. The safety thus to be obtained ranked low in the judgment of Epicurus, which was not warped by the protection of Lysimachus. In his own day, when the several Macedonian rulers were in the first flush of power, the question whether the philosopher should seek or accept their patronage became a pressing one. Epicurus did not share the monarchical sympathies of the competing political philosophers, the Platonists and Aristotelians. His verdict was a grudging one: "The wise man on occasion will pay court to a monarch." [71] In Doctrine 39, listing the expedients for assuring personal safety, he mentions dynastic protection last, as if a final resort. In Doctrine 14, while allowing that dynastic protection, like abundance of means, is effective up to a certain limit, he asserts: ". . . the security that arises from the retired life and withdrawal from the multitude is the most unalloyed." The "withdrawal from the multitude," it may be remarked, signifies the aversion from democratic political life.

This distrustful attitude toward the life of royal courts involved important consequences. It marked Epicureanism as a nonconformist creed, as it were, and tended to confine its membership to the bourgeois stratum of society. The court posts were left to the Platonists and Peripatetics, as also to the Stoics, whose exaltation of virtue qualified them peculiarly for the role of chaplain. As the Epicurean Horace perceived, Stoicism was especially comforting to the "silk cushion" class; [72] a moral front makes the best counterpoise to moral laxity. It was this use of Stoicism as a moral front for the nobility that aroused the scorn of Juvenal, whose best satire, the tenth, is distinctly Epicurean.

A caution is nevertheless in order in respect of this Epicurean attitude. The avoidance of courts is a recommendation, not an imperative, as is also the avoidance of democratic political life. The eminent Epicurean mathematician Philonides was court philosopher to the notorious Antiochus Epiphanes in the second century B.C. It is made clear by his biographer, however, that his independence was not sacrificed and his influence was used for good. It may be noted also in the case of the poet Horace that his determined maintenance of his own self-respect as the client of Maecenas is apparent even to those who know nothing of the Epicurean teaching. He was drawing upon Epicurus for his argument when he asserted his rights as a client. [73]

It is worth while also to have the exact truth concerning the attitude of Epicurus toward the democratic political life. The Platonists, as champions of a political philosophy, misrepresented his teaching, but Plutarch, though usually a scornful critic and often an unfair one, has done posterity the favor of recording a covering statement from the master's pen verbatim: "We must explain how best he will guard the end as established by Nature and how a man will not deliberately from the outset proceed to obtain the offices in the gift of the multitudes." [74] Thus Epicurus did not unconditionally condemn the holding of public office; what he did condemn was making a career of it, which meant studying rhetoric and "deliberately" placing one's happiness "from the outset" at the mercy of others.

It may be regarded as certain that both these items of his creed on its practical side were first thought out to finality in Lampsacus. To his experience with the angry populace in Mytilene may be attributed in part his often expressed antipathy for the multitude, but he knew that some sort of government must prevail and counted upon enjoying its protection. The threat of a monarch's displeasure in Mytilene and the subsequent enjoyment of monarchical favor in Lampsacus through the steward of Lysimachus must also have forced upon his attention the necessity of accommodating himself to existing realities. Thus the attitudes he assumed had been well considered and expressed themselves in recommendations, not imperatives.

The profitable experience of Mytilene also brought home to him the folly and futility of the frontal attack upon the prevailing Platonism. This creed was at the time tied in with the prevailing political life, and to attack the teachers in a public gymnasium was to invoke punitive measures from the civil authorities. He therefore settled upon the plan of attacking Platonism and not Platonists. Colotes, for example, was accused of cowardice because in his burlesque of the philosophers he named the dead but turned to anonymity when he dealt with the living.[75] In reality he was following the new injunction of the leader, who prescribed the procedures. As for Epicurus himself, he referred to Plato as "the Golden" and his followers as "the high-steppers." In the extant remains of the eleventh book of the Physics no proper names are found. False doctrines alone are attacked. It is as if he were discouraging his disciples from reading any writings but his own, and for this they were upbraided.[76]

It is thus in Lampsacus that the birth of a new literary genre is to be recognized, the treatise in epistolary form with propagandist intention and anonymity as regards adversaries. To this class belonged the doctrinal masterpiece entitled *Against the Philosophers in Mytilene,* which is with good reason believed to date from the residence in Lampsacus. This was the first of a long series, which were collected and republished and attained the rank of sacred literature among the disciples. It is doubtful if a previous parallel can be cited. Plato, it is true, had published letters, but these are extant and they abound in proper names; their intention was apologetic and not propagandist. Thus the epistles of Epicurus seem to have been unique and must have furnished the model for New Testament writers. One immediate purpose of the latter was to create for the benefit of converts from Epicureanism a substitute literature which should preserve the form of the texts with which they were familiar. Common to both was the practice of addressing each epistle to an individual or a group, though the intention was that copies should be distributed among circles of adherents everywhere.

This picture of the regenerate Epicurus, rendered discreet and cautious by experience, though not less determined and persistent, may be rounded off by mention of two desires that in his case, to resort to his own vocabulary, were "both natural and necessary": the first was the desire to have many friends and the second was for dominance.

The irritability consequent upon the lack of friends had tempted him to acquiesce in the Greek practice of "loving them that love you and hating them that hate you," which, even if practicable for a war lord, was incompatible with the task of disseminating a new philosophy of happiness. By good fortune this need was satisfied in Lampsacus, where he found a group of intellectual people already willing and prepared to be drawn together into a coterie of friendship for the purpose of sharing in philosophic converse, research, and writing.

This same circle offered satisfaction for the first time to the desire for dominance. There was in the city no resident philosopher and educated men, such as Idomeneus and Leonteus, busy men of affairs themselves, proved willing to underwrite, both morally and financially, the project for launching a new school of thought and to allow to the promoter a free hand. Epicurus, on his part, was amply prepared to draw up the needed prospectus and to assign to each subscribing member a suitable role in an extensive program. For the improvement of this opportunity a not unimportant adjunct was frailty of body, which often confined him to his couch. Invalidism, as observant people know, even those who have never read the life of Mary Baker Eddy, may be made an instrument of dominance, and perhaps no discount is to be imposed upon Epicurus if it be suspected that he thought a noble purpose justified the seizure of an ignoble advantage.

CHAPTER V ✚ THE NEW SCHOOL IN ATHENS

E PICURUS left Lampsacus to take up his residence in Athens in 306 B.C. It may be assumed that the voyage was undertaken between April and October, which was the open season for navigation in the Aegean.

So far as his career was concerned, this remove was a matter of judicious timing. He was by this time thirty-five years of age and a mature man. His doctrines had been worked out to finality and the attitudes he was ever afterward to maintain toward the multitude, monarchs, and competitors had been fixed. It was his settled intention to subject himself no more to the interference of gymnasiarchs but to confine his teachings to his own house and garden. It was not his aim to convert the Athenians but to make use of Athens as a cultural capital for the promulgation of his philosophy to the Greek world. With this aim in view he was bringing with him a staff of capable workers and a definite division of labor. He was not to be dependent upon the patronage of Athenian students, because he was assured from outside of adequate financial support. In the sequel certain methods of instruction alone remained to be developed by practical experience.

There was also an element of judicious timing so far as external circumstances were concerned. The year 307–306 B.C. was a tempestuous one. Lysimachus, who by this time possessed a safer capital across the straits from Lampsacus, was about to assume the title of king and make war on the one-eyed Antigonus to the south. In Athens Demetrius Poliorcetes, or "the Besieger," was ousting the other Demetrius, called Phalereus, who was a philosopher in his own right and a patron of Theophrastus, Aristotle's successor. At this juncture a certain Sophocles secured the passage of a law requiring all philosophers under penalty of death to secure the approval of the senate and the assembly before offering themselves as public teachers.[1] To the credit of the Athenians, although an example of their usual fickleness, it is recorded that this law was repealed within the same year.

Two details connected with the incident, however, are significant. The fact that Theophrastus was compelled to undergo a brief exile is sure evidence of hostile feeling toward his school. Moreover, Demochares, nephew of Demosthenes, in his defense of Sophocles, the sponsor of the law, cited the treachery of the Platonist Timolaus in attempting to overthrow the government of Cyzicus and also the attempt of the Platonist Evaeon to make himself tyrant of Lampsacus.[2] This, in turn, is clear evidence that the arrogance and violence of such men had pulled down Platonism from the high repute to which it had risen in its earlier years.

It must therefore have seemed to Epicurus that at last he was free to establish himself in Athens, because neither of the schools whose hostility he had rashly incurred was any longer in a position to injure him. As for the law of Sophocles, he had nothing to fear from it, even had it not been repealed, because it was not his plan to offer instruction in public places such as the Academy and Lyceum, but only on premises of his own.

The suggestion has been made that Epicurus would have required an assurance of safety in taking up his residence in Athens and that this was possibly secured through the pleadings of his brilliant courtesan friend Leontion with Lamia, the notorious mistress of Demetrius the Besieger.[3] This would afford explanation of the affectionate missive which detractors quoted to disparage Epicurus: "Glory be, darling Leontion, with what jubilation you filled us when we read your precious note."[4] This theory is interesting and fitted to the time, but highly improbable. Epicurus had been an alien in both Mytilene and Lampsacus and in both cities stood in need of sponsors, but in Athens he was a citizen with full rights. Moreover, it is unlikely that Leontion, an Athenian, was already a disciple. Lastly, it is doubtful whether there was sufficient time between the victory of Demetrius the Besieger and the arrival of Epicurus for messengers to fare back and forth between Lampsacus and Athens.

THE SCHOOL PROPERTY

The new school was unique in several respects and may be conveniently described under the headings of Property, Ranks and Titles, Personnel and Students. The organization will be described under the headings of Reverence, Friendship, and Fellowship.)

(The statement has been made that only in the form of a religious brotherhood could a school of philosophy be recognized as a corporate unit under Athenian law.[5] It may well be that a level of abstraction existed within which this principle held true, but for practical purposes such a school may be viewed merely as a specialized example of that highly adaptable institution, the Hellenic household.

The Greeks were not only political animals; they were also extremely social in their habits and seem to have felt little need of that privacy upon which some Western races, as opposed to Orientals, set such high store. Consequently, when wealth permitted it and circumstances required it, no inconvenience seems to have arisen from the presence of numerous slaves and many friends, relatives, and guests within the walls of a home. "What huge throngs of friends," wrote Cicero, "did Epicurus keep in a single house, and that a far from spacious one." [6]

Such a school of philosophy with fixed location and permanent physical assets was slow in making its appearance. The sophists had been vagrants by the nature of their profession. As for the Ionian philosophers, their households were dissolved at their deaths after the fashion of all heritable properties. The first real school was that of Plato. This has been always associated in the minds of laymen and scholars with the walled park known as the Academy, which lay to the northwest of the city about a mile outside the Dipylon Gate. Nevertheless the real school of Plato was located in his own house and not in the Academy. The house and the park were not even contiguous. It is on record that Speusippus, the nephew, heir, and successor of Plato used to be hauled on a small wagon to the Academy, because in his old age he was paralyzed.[7]

Moreover, if the story be encountered that over the entrance to the Academy Plato had caused to be incised the inscription "No one shall enter unless grounded in geometry," this is an error. It was over his Museum, a shrine of the muses, schoolhouse, and library, that this prohibition is recorded to have been placed.[8] This Museum was his private property and located in the suburban district named from the Academy but not in the walled precinct bearing that name.

From the Dipylon Gate it was possible to follow a road around the north margin of the city to the precinct known as the Lyceum.[9] It was from this that the second of the permanent schools took its name when founded by Aristotle. The precinct was sacred to Apollo Lyceus, and in addition to an ample gymnasium possessed a colonnade, or *peripatos,* from which the name Peripatetic was derived. The real school, however, was housed in private property, as may be gleaned from the last will and testament of Theophrastus.[10] There was the usual Museum along with living quarters opening on a garden. As in the case of the Academy, it was by virtue of these private properties, living quarters, library and seminar rooms, as it were, that the permanence of the school was assured.

In neither the Academy nor the Lyceum were heritable rights or privileges existent. The Stoic Chrysippus is on record as lecturing in the Lyceum [11] and the same privilege was open to any philosopher, subject to the oversight of the gymnasiarch.

The school of Epicurus was the third and last. The teachers known as Cynics were dedicated to vagrancy on principle. The Stoics were ethical kinsmen of the Cynics and as a sect did not possess a fixed habitation with library and archives.

The school of Epicurus resembled those of Plato and Aristotle insofar as it was associated with two physical properties, a house for residence and a place for lectures. It differed because both properties, and not the house alone, were registered in title deeds in his own name, as is evidenced by his last will and testament.[12] The two properties were not contiguous and there is evidence for believing that Epicurus, whose health was uncertain, sometimes fared back and forth in a three-wheeled chair.[13] The house was situated within the city walls in a respectable district known as Melite,[14] and the garden was not far distant, outside the old Dipylon Gate on the same road that led to the Academy. This coincidence of location is positively known to us from the testimony of Cicero, who describes with some vividness a visit made by him as a young man along with Atticus and others in 78 B.C.[15] Myriads of other tourists at various times must have combined a peep at the Garden with a visit to the Academy.

It is well, however, to be on guard against the glamor that haunts the Academy, the Lyceum, and the Garden. It was on the premises where the philosophers and their students lived, worked, and slept that the real schools were located. It was there that the confidential instruction was imparted. It was there that the true fellowship prevailed. It was there that the slaves were housed without whose assistance the operation of publishing could not be carried on. As for the house of Epicurus in particular, this was virtually a publishing concern, because the leading members were all engaged in compiling and distributing textbooks for their disciples at home and abroad. It follows that many slaves were employed in the labor of copying manuscripts. We are to think, therefore, of a huge Hellenic household, intolerably crowded from the American point of view, but nevertheless effectively organized and surprisingly efficient.

That the garden was small may be inferred from the price, which was eighty minas, less than the sophist Gorgias charged for a single course of instruction.[16] This inference is confirmed by references to it as the *kepidion* or *hortulus*, "little garden," not without a touch of derision.[17] For the smallness of the house the testimony of Cicero has already been quoted.

RANKS AND TITLES

The principles adopted for the invigoration of the new school of Epicurus were leadership, reverence of superiors, love or friendship, and fellowship. The title chosen for himself as head was *hegemon*,[18] which Cicero rendered by *dux,* "leader" or "guide." [19] Pupils younger than adolescents were admitted, but the word *schoolteacher* was banned. This was not done because Epicurus had been taunted with being a schoolteacher and a schoolteacher's son, but for the reason that the word was associated with what was believed to be a false principle of instruction. The new principle is stated in Vatican Saying 21: "Human nature is not to be coerced but persuaded." Human beings, Epicurus believed, could not be driven to the goal of happiness. Only by leading could this end be attained. Instructors of all grades were consequently designated by titles that mean "leader" or "guide."

Fortunately we have from the pen of Epicurus himself a discerning statement on leadership as he understood it: "There are certain men who have gone out and arrived at truth without the aid of any man; they have carved out their own path." [20] It follows therefore that Lucretius was speaking strictly by the book and not merely inventing a pretty compliment when he wrote that it was Epicurus who "revealed what was the supreme good, toward which all might strive, and, what is more, pointed the way, whereby along an unerring path we might struggle thereto." [21] It follows that Cicero, no less than Lucretius, was speaking by the book

93

when he wrote: "If it is to such goods as these that you recall me, Epicurus, I am ready to obey you, to follow you, even to adopt you as my guide." [22] Every disciple voluntarily took the pledge: "I will be faithful to Epicurus according to whom it has been my choice to live." [23]

Next in rank to the supreme leader stood the three men Metrodorus, Hermarchus, and Polyaenus. The title bestowed upon them was *kathegemones*,[24] which may be rendered "associate leaders," and the understanding was clear that such men were capable of leading only after another had blazed the way. In the words of Epicurus himself: "There are certain men who need the aid of another; they will not go forward unless another goes ahead but they will make good followers." [25] Metrodorus was assigned to this class. It is somewhat surprising to find the abilities of Hermarchus more narrowly circumscribed. He was ranked among those "who could be forced and driven to the right philosophy and needed not so much a leader as an inciter and, so to speak, a driver." [26] The general principle of leadership seems to have been sufficiently flexible to admit of kindly compulsion as a legitimate procedure. Hermarchus succeeded Epicurus as head of the school.

It must have given Epicurus exceptional satisfaction to enroll the mathematician Polyaenus among his associates, especially for the reason that he had been trained in the school of Eudoxus, but the abilities of this man fell below those of his colleagues. He was a kindly man, however, and was eminently qualified in his own way to lead; his success in this mission is praised in fragments of an extant papyrus.[27]

Parallel to the distinction between the head as "leader" and the three next in rank as "associate leaders" was the difference between *sophos,* the *sapiens,* "wise man," and the *philosophos,* "philosopher." [28] The former title was reserved by Epicurus for himself alone, a seeming arrogance which elicited the sneers of his detractors.[29] The three below him were merely "philosophers," which marks the title as being on the same footing as "associate leaders."

For all instructors of still lower rank the title *kathegetes* was chosen.[30] This word is built upon the same root as the others and may be rendered "assistant leaders." It also fell to this word to replace the term *schoolteacher,* which had been banned. To each of these assistant leaders was assigned a group or class of pupils, while leaders of higher rank seem to have been assigned students for individual guidance. At any rate we have on record one such instance in the case of Polyaenus.[31]

THE NEW SCHOOL IN ATHENS

Since the three brothers of Epicurus, Neocles, Chaeredemus, and Aristobulus, are all listed in the school and are not named among the associate leaders, it may be assumed that they ranked among these assistants. The fact that they were brothers would not deter Epicurus from relegating them to an inferior rank; this realistic behavior was part of that absolute honesty by which he set high store.

PERSONNEL AND STUDENTS

Since the school was also a publishing concern, the staff must have included a number of literate slaves to serve as secretaries and copyists. The oversight of these would undoubtedly have fallen to the talented slave whose name was Mys. His position was comparable to that of Tiro in the household of Cicero. He was rewarded by freedom at the master's death, and tradition reports him as a philosopher in his own right.[32]

Among the unique features of life in the school was the presence of women, since only females of leonine courage had been able to break the barriers raised against them elsewhere. Naturally the status of the majority was that of courtesan. The reproach attaching to women of this class was inconsistently made to depend upon the status of the patron. There was no universal outcry if Aspasia was domiciled with the illustrious Pericles, but it remained a perpetual scandal that the beautiful Leontion was a member of the inner circle of Epicurus, even if in that household she lived with Metrodorus as a wife.[33] Cicero, for instance, no doubt thought it quite proper that Plato should have incorporated in one of his esteemed dialogues a speech that purported to be from the pen of Aspasia and he was aware that this speech was read annually in public assembly in Athens, but declared it disgraceful that Leontion, a mere courtesan, should presume to attack Theophrastus in a published book, while candidly admitting that her manner of writing was both clever and good Attic Greek.[34]

This Leontion was perhaps the most distinguished courtesan of her time and the hostility of detractors did not bar her from fame. Portraits of her were painted by two of the most illustrious artists and one of these bore the fascinating title *In meditation*.[35] Her courage — for her name signifies "lioness" — passed to her daughter, called Danaë, who at the court of Antiochus II saved her lover's life at the price of her own.[36]

The same detractors to whom the life of Aspasia gave no offense whipped up their indignation over the names of other courtesans who

95

were domiciled in the house of Epicurus, the hedonist, and to them we owe the list, which is worth repeating for its very prettiness: Mammarion, Hedia, Erotion, Nicidion, and Boïdion.[37]

Since so many women shared the life of the school, it must be assumed that the number of female slaves was proportionate. The oversight of these would have fallen to one Phaedrium, since she was singled out for manumission in the will of the master.[38]

Concerning the student body much may be learned by reasonable inference. In the first place, consistently with the principle that all human beings without respect to age require guidance toward happiness no less than to health, it must be assumed that pupils of various ages were admitted. This, in turn, must have called for the classification of pupils consistent with the division of instructors into associates and assistants. Again, since the new school was not planned for local instruction alone but also for the dissemination of the true philosophy to all parts, provision had to be made for extramural students. Lastly, within the school itself it was necessary to make a division between those who should follow the course of study to the end and those who were compelled to stop short of that goal.

Resident adults were styled "fellow-students in philosophy," as is revealed by the will of Epicurus.[39] These would have attended the lectures in the Garden. It was at such a lecture, possibly in Lampsacus, that Colotes was so overcome by admiration of the siren voice of the master that he threw himself to the ground before him and hailed him as a god.[40] Adults would also have participated in the mystical nocturnal sessions, which took place at regular intervals. Adolescent lads were assigned to one of the associate leaders, as already mentioned.[41]

Suitable corners of the Garden must have been allocated to elementary classes. A principle objective at this stage was to habituate pupils to taking correction kindly.[42] They were in charge of the assistant leaders and called *kataskeuazomenoi*,[43] a passive participle meaning "in course of preparation." It was this word that furnished the model for the Christian term *catechumens, katechoumenoi*, of the same meaning. These classes would be in session from early morning until late in the day, and if it should occur to the modern reader that one class would disturb another, the answer is that the ancients felt as little need of privacy in their education as in their social life. In a public gymnasium, if interference became intolerable, appeal was made to the gymnasiarch.

It is on record that this official sent an attendant to the Academic philosopher Carneades, whose tones were stentorian, asking him to lower his voice.[44]

The Epicurean satirist Colotes in his burlesque of the Greek philosophers had chosen to pour ridicule upon Socrates and upon the Delphic oracle which declared him the wisest of men. This was sacrilege to the Platonists, for whom Plutarch is the known spokesman, and they retaliated by drawing up a list of scornful terms to stigmatize the effusive admirations of the Epicureans: "Vociferations, Hallelujahs, Hullabaloos, Venerations, Adorations." [45] The Platonists, however, could not boast of innocence themselves, because their own Arcesilaus was on record as hailing the founders of the school as "almost gods or relics of the race of gold." [46] Thus Epicurus, when dubbing Plato "the Golden," was possibly mocking his followers and not merely deriding his division of mankind on the basis of iron, silver, and gold.

Much adulation, it is admitted, flourished in the school of Epicurus. For instance, both Leonteus and Metrodorus called their sons after him, and this in spite of the rule that first sons should be named for the grandfather or father.[47]

Distinct from these spontaneous feelings, however, stood the attitude of reverence expressly demanded for Epicurus. This possessed a doctrinal basis and was integrated with the whole Epicurean scheme of life and of learning. It was demanded for him and by him as the discoverer of the true philosophy. To himself alone he arrogated the title of sage or wise man. He thought of himself as standing in the relation of father to his adherents, who upon the same principle were counted his children.

Among passages preserved for us from the writings of the master, which were diligently searched by zealous adversaries for grounds of ridicule, we have the following excerpt from a letter to Colotes: "For because of the reverence you felt for what was then being said by us an unaccountable desire fell upon you to embrace us, to clasp our knees and to exhibit every gesture that is customarily performed in acts of reverence and supplication to certain beings. Therefore you caused us to reciprocate by sanctifying and reverencing your own person in our turn. I bid you go your way as an immortal and to think of us as an immortal." [48] By the term *immortal*, it may be explained, is signified in this metaphorical usage the enjoyment of perfect serenity and happiness such as was characteristic of the Epicurean gods. As with the use of *eternal* in the New Testament, it is the quality of the life, not extension in time, that is signified.

Plutarch, after quoting this passage, adds by way of invidious comment that Colotes was disappointed, because Epicurus, while bestowing the epithet of immortal upon him, took care to withhold the title of wise man, *sapiens*. This taunt may be dismissed with a smile, but the comment serves to call our attention to the fact that another reason for the reverence claimed for Epicurus was his reservation of the title of sage or wise man for his sole use. There is no doubt about the truth of the report. Cicero in one of his meaner moments allowed himself to sneer at Epicurus as one who "had donned merely the mask of a philosopher and caused this title to be inscribed upon himself." [49] If this seems like arrogance on the part of Epicurus, what founder of a sect has not been arrogant? Arrogance in leaders is to disciples an attractive trait. Without it leaders fail to draw the devotion of disciples.

In the highly emotional preface to his fifth book the poet Lucretius exclaimed:

> deus ille fuit, deus, inclyte Memmi,

"that man was nothing short of a god, a god, I say, illustrious Memmius." In this worshipful outburst of enthusiasm the casual reader may well believe that before him is the record of a singular experience of the poet. Sincere the enthusiasm undoubtedly is, but it was not singular. Lucretius, as so often when his feelings seem to be strictly personal, was in reality speaking by the book. Spontaneous this acclamation undoubtedly was; yet at the same time it coincided with a principle of the school. The pronouncement of Epicurus on the topic is extant in Vatican Saying 32: "Reverence for the wise man is a great blessing for the one who feels the reverence." It is even thinkable that the concept of leadership as Epicurus conceived it was influenced by stories of the gymnosophists, the wise men of India, who came to the knowledge of Greece in his day. It is on record that he inquired very diligently from Nausiphanes about Pyrrho, who had been in India with Alexander. Certainly among his followers he commanded and demanded a reverence not unlike that enjoyed by Mahatma Gandhi in recent times.

Over and above the reverence due to Epicurus as the discoverer of the true philosophy and the sole person in the school to bear the title of sage or wise man, there was reverence due to him as bearing the title of father. Thus Lucretius is as usual speaking by the book when in the ardent preface to the third book he hails him by this title: "Thou, Father, art the discoverer of truth; thou dealest precepts to us as a father would." Moreover, the fact that Epicurus had assumed this title along with that of sage is attested by a fragment from a letter which, like so many other excerpts, has been mistranslated. Rightly rendered, the words make clear that the master thought of himself as parent and his disciples as his children: "Send us therefore your first fruits for the sustenance of my sacred person for its own sake and for that of my children, for so it occurs to me to express it." [50] Among later Epicureans this reverence for Epicurus as a father was extended to Metrodorus and Hermarchus, and a passage is extant in a papyrus which reads that "those who contradict the teachings of these men are not far from incurring condemnation as parricides." [51]

This fatherhood, it should be mentioned, has its origin in the assumed analogy between the true philosophy and the art of medicine. In the opening words of the Hippocratic oath we find that the novice swears "to reckon him who teaches me this art equally dear with my parents." Incidentally, it was on this same principle that the disciples were expected to contribute voluntarily to the financial support of the school. To contribute was merely to discharge a debt due for instruction and fatherly oversight. A saying of Epicurus is extant on the topic: "As a precious reward he will have the instruction given him by me." [52]

In the illuminating essay of Philodemus entitled *On Frankness* we find valuable evidence on the organization of the Epicurean school. The disciple who is choosing Epicurus for his guide in life is compared to Diomede choosing Ulysses as his aid on the famous nocturnal foray: "With this man as my companion we should both return safe even out of a flaming fire, because he is exceeding cunning to invent." [53] From the same source we learn that disciples should look to their head as a father-confessor; to him their mistakes and shortcomings should be frankly disclosed in confidence; they were to regard him as their savior. There was also a pledge, as already mentioned: "We will be obedient to Epicurus, according to whom we have made it our choice to live."

Life within the school was looked upon as a progress toward wisdom by stages, as indicated by the treatise of Metrodorus *On the Progress toward Wisdom*. The school was graded. Each member from the youngest upward was trained to respect and obey his superiors, and no superiority was recognized beyond precedence in the progress toward wisdom. On this principle one member could be said to be better than another only so far as he had made more progress. This is the point in a line of the poet Horace, whose writings are strewn with atoms of Epicureanism: "Are you unwilling to learn, to listen and to trust a better man?" [54] Thus we discern a veritable pyramid of reverence, each grade of disciples looking up with due respect to the smaller numbers in the grades above, until the peak is reached, where the inspired leader reigned alone, the sole sage, the unique discoverer of the true philosophy and the ethical father.

From this concept of study as a progress toward wisdom by stages it logically follows that the ultimate goal is a kind of perfection. Like other ideas of the Epicureans, this was a target for ridicule, and Cicero was speaking by the book when he wrote of the Hellenomaniac Titus Albucius "that he was in Athens in his early years and had graduated as a 'perfect Epicurean'." [55] The sting of the irony depends upon the same idea when he suggests that Calpurnius Piso make a convert of his ambitious son-in-law Julius Caesar: "You will speak as a graduate of the school, a man primed for the task of persuasion, elegant, perfected, polished," [56] the epithets carrying an implied comparison with a statue fresh from the sculptor's hands.

IMAGES

The reverence of devout Epicureans for their ethical father impressed itself upon people outside the sect by the affection with which they regarded his likenesses in paint or in carvings. On one occasion Cicero and his friends were indulging freely in sentimental memories while looking upon the thrones in the Academy from which the great masters had taught. Thereupon the Epicurean Atticus began to banter them with his accustomed blend of frankness and suavity: "I live in the present; still, I could not forget Epicurus even if I would, for we followers of his not only have his portrait in paintings but also on drinking cups and finger-rings." [57]

The elder Pliny a century later, lamenting the passing of the good old days when images of the ancestors adorned the atrium, gives expression to his disgust as follows: "They actually put the features of Epicurus on display in their bedchambers and carry them about with them." [58] To the Christian scholar Origen in the second century this Epicurean cult seemed nothing short of idolatry; he seems to have thought that prayers were addressed to the images of Epicurus.[59] From the point of view of the sect itself, however, there can be little doubt that the use of the images was not mere adulation but part of a systematic plan to gain and maintain cohesion and perpetuity for all Epicureans as a body. As for Epicurus, he may have instituted the practice and assuredly did not discourage it. He gave sittings for his own portrait, which he must have known would be copied. Naturally, the custom was not peculiar to Epicureans, because statuettes of Socrates are extant and Origen mentions portable images of Aristotle and Democritus.[60] What was peculiar to the Epicureans was the integration of the custom with their doctrine. The Pauline doctrine of "all members in one body" was anticipated by them.

There is, however, still something to be added. During the first three centuries of Christianity the representations of Christ exhibit a youthful and beardless face, not unlike that of Apollo. The bearded portraits began to appear at a later date and simultaneously with the absorption of the Epicurean sect into the Christian environment. These new pictures of Christ exhibit a similarity to those of Epicurus, then growing obsolete. This similarity is such as to be manifest to the most disinterested observer.

FRIENDSHIP

Just as the analogy between philosophy and the art of healing placed founder and disciple in the relation of parent and child, it evoked also a doctrine of friendship or brotherly love. The love of mankind, *philanthropia*, must actuate the healer of souls no less than the healer of physical maladies. Moreover, this affection could not be reserved to males in the manner of the Platonic love, of which the founder of the Academy wrote so feelingly, nor to aristocrats, as in the creed of Pythagoras. It embraces mankind, as declared in the dictum of Epicurus: "Love goes dancing round and round the inhabited earth, veritably shouting to us all to awake to the blessedness of the happy life." [61] For this kind of love the Greek word is *philia*, and when this is rendered by the Latin *amicitia* there is a regrettable narrowing of meaning. In dealing with Epicurean doctrine, therefore, the Latin tradition is inadequate and the scope of love or friendliness must be extended to include humanity, just as in Christianity.

Nevertheless, in this field also there is a certain division and a certain gradation. The love of mankind is one thing, and the perfection of love among close friends is quite another. Similarly, the biographer draws a distinction between the friends of Epicurus at large and those who were resident in the school. For example, when he writes of "his friends, so many in multitude as not to be counted even by whole cities," [62] he follows this up with mention of "his devotees, held fast by the enchantments of his doctrine." [63] Shortly afterward also, in a passage usually mistranslated, he writes of "the succession of his devotees, though that of almost all other schools had lapsed, perpetually continuing and throwing off numberless fresh beginnings, one from another." [64] In these excerpts two grades of adherents are clearly recognized, first, the friends, *philoi,* associate members of the sect, as it were, and second, the devotees, *gnorimoi,* the members of the inner circle in the lifetime of Epicurus, or of any Epicurean circle anywhere in later times.

In integral relation with this idea of fellowship stands a subsidiary doctrine of the fullness of pleasure. As will be shown in the chapter on the New Hedonism, Nature is represented as having fixed definite limits to the magnitude of pleasures. For example, the natural limit to the pleasure of eating and drinking is the satisfaction of hunger and thirst. Consequently Epicurus wrote: "I am gorged with pleasure in this poor body of mine living on bread and water." [65] For this very reason, because "limits of Nature" exist, and pleasures are not limitless, as Plato taught, the fullness of pleasure is possible.

Next, this fullness of pleasure from the satisfaction of the natural desires is a prerequisite of the fullness of fellowship, that is, the pleasure arising from friendship. It is true, of course, that friends, like food, are a necessity of living, and it is also true that measures must be taken to obtain friends, but it is not true that friendship continues forever to exist on the level of utility. On this point we possess an authoritative pronouncement: "Friendship has its origin in needs. It is true that beginnings must be made in advance, for we also sow the ground, but it crystallizes only in the course of close association among those who have come to enjoy the fullness of pleasure." [66] This phraseology is technical in Epicureanism. It means that true fellowship can be enjoyed only among those who live within "the limits of Nature," for whom alone "the fullness of pleasure" is logically possible.

This subsidiary doctrine of fullness, though an essential and integral part of Epicurean hedonism, has escaped the acumen of scholars. It has a bearing on the question of mourning for the dead, which was a live one between Epicureans and their adversaries. Why, for instance, should the friend feel pity for the friend who in this life, however shortened, had arrived at the enjoyment of the fullness of pleasure? The pronouncement of Epicurus upon this survives in the last of the Authorized Doctrines: "As a class those who have found it possible to assure themselves of complete safety from the dangers of their surroundings have also lived most happily (fullness of pleasure) and, having reaped the utmost fullness of fellowship, do not mourn the untimely decease of the departed as something calling for pity." The Greek language lacked a specific term for fellowship; the word employed in the passage quoted is "intimacy," *oikeiotes,* which etymologically means "membership in the family."

This particular teaching of Epicurus seems to have gained for "fullness" the status of a catchword and to this fact may be attributed such phrases as "the fullness of God" and "the fullness of Christ," [67] because Epicureanism was the prevalent philosophy in New Testament days. The Romans knew only an attenuated version of Epicurean fellowship. They were not mystics. The Latin term that most happily assumed the meaning of "fellowship" was *contubernium,* which signifies "living in the same quarters." [68] Thus the historian Tacitus aptly and understandingly designated the close association of Virgil and his friends as *illud felix contubernium,* "that illustrious and fruitful fellowship." [69] Somewhat earlier the philosopher Seneca employed the same word when he wrote, "It was not instruction but fellowship that made great men out of Metrodorus, Hermarchus, and Polyaenus." [70]

In the circle of Epicurus, however, the institution of fellowship was made to signify more than the sharing of a common life and lodgings. By calculated arrangement he endeavored to invest it with a mystical and religious character, not only during his lifetime but also in perpetuity, and in this he had a measure of success. In spite of his denial of immortality and of divine providence his apprehension of the ethical influences of religious ritual was extremely keen. He scrupulously observed the performance of the customary rites in honor of his father, mother, and brothers and also of members of his circle who predeceased him.[71] In addition to this he instituted the custom of composing and publishing pious memoirs of the deceased associates.[72] In so doing he anticipated the practice of the Christians, who wrote lives of the saints and martyrs. It was as if he was bent upon having his disciples believe

that the fellowship they enjoyed was imperishable, extending backward
into the past and forward into the future.

Yet this is only part of the story. The view has already been mentioned
that only as a religious brotherhood could a school of philosophy gain
recognition as a corporate body under Greek law. There is no evidence
that Epicurus desired or sought such recognition under law. It is possible, however, that the underlying principle actuated him. It may have
seemed that only in the guise of a religious brotherhood could he gain
coherence and perpetuity for his organization. Fairly early in the years
of his residence in Athens, if not from the outset, certain nights were set
apart for a sort of philosophical symposium, where special formalities
were observed. We may assume that it was open to adult members only.
On these occasions the customary austerity of diet was abandoned, and
the wine and viands, if we can trust the testimony of adversaries, were of
the best.[73] This is quite credible, because it was the teaching of the
master that those who feel the least need of luxurious diet or partake of
it after intervals of abstinence have the greatest enjoyment of it.[74]

As for the intellectual fare of these ritualistic banquets, an enlightening clue is furnished by the title inscribed by the renegade Timocrates
upon his satirical account of the same. In derision he dubbed them
Euphranta, "Feasts of Reason," as it were.[75] The point of this title is a
distinction shared in common by the contemporary schools between
pleasures of the body, which were *hedone,* and the higher pleasure of
the mind, *euphrosune,* with which goes the verb *euphraino,* whence the
title *Euphranta,* coined for the occasion. It is undoubtedly to these feasts
of reason that Metrodorus refers when he speaks of "ascending to infinite
space and eternity and looking down upon 'the things that are, the
things that shall be and the things that were before'." [76] It is thus safely
inferred that at these nocturnal sessions the topic of discussion was the
nature of the universe and the ultimate causes of things, the knowledge
of which revealed the only path to the perfection of pleasure.

Especially enlightening is the knowledge that these gatherings were
appointed for the twentieth of each month. If after the death of Epicurus they were to be perpetuated in memory of himself and Metrodorus,
why not on the anniversary of his birth, which fell on the seventh day
of the month Gamelion? The answer is that the twentieth in the Greek
calendar was invested with something of the sanctity of a sabbath. It had
a name of its own, *eikas,* like the Ides in the Roman calendar. It was a

sacred day in a cult of Apollo and it was on the twentieth that the final rites of initiation were performed in the mysteries of Demeter.[77] It follows that once in every year, at the same time that the secrets of the afterlife were being revealed by the hierophant at Eleusis, the disciples in the house in Melite were celebrating what Metrodorus styled "the divine orgies" of Epicurus. Thus the master himself was a hierophant; he actually spoke of his own pronouncements as oracles, and Lucretius ranked them higher than those of the Pythian priestess.[78]

These monthly banquets which provoked the scorn of the renegade Timocrates quickly became a public target of ridicule. One of the first to engage in this literary sport was the Cynic satirist Menippus, who devoted a book to the topic.[79] The theme still seemed a good one for the Peripatetic Sotion in the time of Tiberius.[80] Scattered mention occurs over an extent of five centuries.[81] Because of the custom the Epicureans were dubbed *eikadistae,* "Twentyers," as already mentioned. A Greek epigram from the pen of Philodemus takes the form of an invitation to his patron Calpurnius Piso to be present on one of these occasions.[82]

Seriously considered, the institution may be compared to the *agapai,* or "love-feasts," of the Christians. This is only one among many similarities too numerous to be merely coincidental.

CHAPTER VI ✠ THE NEW EDUCATION

THE new school in Athens began to offer to the Greek world an integrated program of education consisting of the Canon, Physics, and Ethics. This was supported by specially prepared textbooks and eventually by graded texts. It was designed to rival the Platonic program, which was then suffering a recession from the high peak of popularity to which it had risen spectacularly during the lifetime of its founder.

This Platonic program consisted of music and gymnastic, inherited from the Athenian past; of rhetoric, which had been introduced by the sophists; and of dialectic and mathematics, especially geometry, which were the addition of Plato himself.

Toward every component of this prevailing education the attitude of Epicurus was determined by the nature of the objective adopted for his own program. This objective was not the production of a good citizen but a happy and contented man. For practical purposes this happiness was defined as health of mind and health of body. The famous prayer for *mens sana in corpore sano,* "a sound mind in a sound body," recommended by Juvenal, is genuine Epicureanism.

This being the case, there was no reason for rejecting physical training, and approval of it was the easier not only because the laws required it — and Epicurus recommended obedience to the laws — but also for the reason that the amateur athlete and the citizen soldier were being replaced by the professional athlete and the professional soldier. Thus the rigors of the required exercises could be relaxed.

As for music, there need be little doubt that the approval of Epicurus was enthusiastic. His own capacity for appreciating good music seems to have been keen. It is told of him that he would arise early in the morning and trudge to the theater to enjoy the performance.[1] Neither is it to be overlooked that the drama of the Greeks corresponded rather to modern grand and light opera than to the Shakespearean plays and that the worship of the gods consisted largely of vocal and symphonic music. It may also be safely said of Epicurus that he would have shared with conservative critics the disapproval of the libidinous tendencies of the softer Lydian and Ionian modes in music. As a serious moralist, as an advocate of the simple life, and as the avowed enemy of erotic pleasures, no other attitude would have been consistent for him. On the other hand, it would be unreasonable to ascribe to him any partiality for the Dorian mode; it was no part of his plan that the young men should be specially trained for the political career or the military life. From the treatise of Philodemus on music it is known that the Epicureans disparaged the influence of music as an instrument of ethical training.[2]

When these reservations have been made, the conclusion remains to be drawn that the basis of Epicurus' preference was liturgical. He was genuinely pious and insisted upon employing of the gods only such language as was consistent with their perfection of happiness, which was to him a sort of majesty.[3] The proper feeling toward them was reverence. Quite rightly, then, he is reported as saying: "The wise man will experience a higher enjoyment than the rest of men in the public spectacles." [4] The pleasure here described is of the nobler sort; it is *euphrosune*; it is best understood as having reference to the emotional uplift, a sort of communion with the divine.

As for the poetical components of the traditional curriculum, Homer, Hesiod, and Theognis, there can be no doubt that his attitude was hostile. With the genealogies of the gods he could have had no patience. As for the moral teachings of the poets, it was his considered judgment that these were a hodgepodge[5] and he took an unholy pleasure in showing how Homer could be employed to endorse pleasure as the supreme end of living. This hostile judgment, however, does not mean that he condemned all poetry. He assumed that poetry will be read, and in the Epicurean school as described by Philodemus there is mention of a *philologus,* which means a teacher of literature.[6] Of poets themselves he felt a certain disapproval, as the following judgment indicates: "Only the wise man would be able to discourse rightly on music and poetry, but he would not actually compose poems." [7] This attitude was determined in part by his choice of style, from which he banned figures of speech, but at least two of his disciples, Lucretius and Philodemus, ignored his prohibition and became poets; nor did a partiality for his philosophy deter others from becoming poets, for example, Horace and Virgil.

Outstanding among the refutative writings of Epicurus, to be mentioned presently, was his work *On Rhetoric*. This study is denied a place in the new curriculum. As Plutarch sourly expresses it, "These men [Epicurus and his circle] write about oratory to deter us from becoming orators." [8] As usual, the happiness of the individual is the criterion: to be happy a man must be free and no longer is he free if he submits his fortunes to the whims of the multitude; he is consequently to be discouraged from choosing to make politics a career, and by the same argument forensic rhetoric is banned. The tricks of the demagogue lose value, and no quality of style is required except clarity.

In his rejection of dialectic and mathematics Epicurus was motivated partly by his animosity toward Platonism. Dialectic he declared to be superfluous and this judgment followed logically from the dethronement of Reason and the exaltation of Nature as furnishing the norm. Geometry was repudiated as having no bearing upon the happy life. The adoption of this particular attitude was largely determined by the application of geometry to the explanation of heavenly phenomena by the Platonists. It was the observation of Epicurus that increase of knowledge in this field was actually inimical to peace of mind.[9] Such a fear is readily understandable today, because the fission of the atom, even apart from its military involvements, has been an achievement extremely upsetting to the comfort of traditional faiths.

The choice of an unfriendly attitude toward geometry and astronomy, however, was unfortunate. It betrayed Epicurus into his worst blunder; he declared the sun to be no larger or little larger than it appeared to be. His treatment of certain other celestial phenomena is equally ludicrous.

THE HEAVENLY APOCALYPSE

In spite of all these rejections and his hostility toward mathematical astronomy Epicurus was incapable of escaping the trends of contemporary thought. There is no point of departure for any thinker except from things as they are. The causes of each new philosophy are bound to be found in the surrounding cultural context.

Even the Ionian philosophers had concerned themselves with heavenly phenomena and had constructed cosmogonies. These speculations remained highly theoretical until the emergence of geometry and the prodigious increase of skill in arithmetical calculations among the Pythagoreans. Then for the first time in Greek lands the art of measurement began to be applied to heavenly phenomena.

This art of measurement was of course rejected by Epicurus, but along with Plato he took over from the Pythagoreans the fruitful conceit of a flight of the soul through the universe. This was originated by Archytas, pupil of Pythagoras, but is most familiar to us in the version of Plato, the spectacular myth of the *Phaedrus*.[10] In this, it will be recalled, the soul is described as ascending to the heavens in a chariot drawn by two steeds and from a supernal point of vantage looking down upon the nature of things as they truly are.

The history of this fascinating conceit in later times and its appropriation by the thievish Stoics need not concern us here. The item of immediate consequence is the fact that Epicurus tacitly took it over and more or less consciously framed his pedagogical procedure upon it. This fact is readily demonstrated both from his own extant Little Epitome and from the poem of Lucretius. The belief that according to Epicurean doctrine the soul was incapable of existing outside of the body was considered no obstacle. Instead, the thinker was thought of as projecting his mind into space.

This flight of the mind possessed a fascination for Lucretius. Early in the first book we read: "Therefore the vital vigor of his mind pressed victoriously through and far he fared beyond the flaming ramparts of the world and all infinity explored in mind and thought." In another striking passage Lucretius imagines his own self in the role of hierophant: "The terrors of the mind are scattering in flight; the ramparts of the universe are parting asunder; lo, I behold the operations of nature going on throughout the whole void; in plain view is the divinity of the gods and the realms of perfect quiet." [11]

Quite logically, moreover, Lucretius concludes on a prosaic note: "But on the contrary the regions of Acheron are nowhere to be seen." [12] In all the more antique religious lore the mysteries of life were to be learned by a "descent"; for Epicureans it will be an "ascent." This is not mere fancy. It is doctrine and it can be documented. Here are the words of Metrodorus, which at the same time designate the teachings of Epicurus as "orgies," that is, mysteries, and indicate the heavenly trend: "Let us crown fine actions by another — only not sinking downward with feelings common to the mob — and, shaking free of this life upon the earth, rise to the divinely revealed orgies of Epicurus." [13] If this evidence is not convincing, a more specific confirmation is available from the same author, addressed to one Menestratus, Vatican Saying 10: "Remember that, though mortal by nature and allotted a brief span of life, still through our conferences concerning Nature you have ascended to the infinity of space and time and have looked down upon 'the things that are, the things that shall be and the things that were before'." Thus to the Epicurean the descent in quest of truth has become obsolete and the ascent a standard conceit.

Incidentally, the ascent and the descent became rival conceits in philosophy and literature. Cicero resorted to the conceit of the ascent in his *Dream of Scipio,* an exquisite piece of writing, but Virgil, as the Roman Homer, was bound to revert to the descent. Christianity, with the doctrine of hell, threw its weight on the side of the descent and so Dante's great achievement was bound to be an Inferno.

THE TOUR OF THE UNIVERSE

In order to make clear how this conceit of the ascent to the heavens integrates itself with the Epicurean system of knowledge it is necessary to make a brief detour into the terminology of Greek geography and of Aristotle. Epicurus calls his system a *periodeia,*[14] which is the same as the Latin *peregrinatio,* either "journey" for exploration or "tour" for pleasure. Thus the wise man not only ascends but also explores the heavens, and Cicero writes of Democritus that, though blind, "he used to go exploring (*peregrinabatur*) into all infinity without finding any extremity that forced a halt." [15] Similarly, Lucretius, whose language afforded hints to Cicero, said of Epicurus "that he explored (*peragravit*) all the infinite void." [16]

There is something to add, however. The Greek *periodos,* a more common term than *periodeia,* like the Latin *itinerarium,* means not only a tour or journey from place to place but also a map or guidebook. This meaning also is implied in the terminology of Epicurus. In imagination he conducts his pupils on a tour of the universe. He offers a large-scale map, as it were, such as his encyclopedic work on Physics in thirty-seven books; he also offers a small-scale map, which he calls a *puknoma,* "condensation," that is, an epitome. Consistently with this idea and in the same context he writes of discussions "compressed to the form of simple elements and terse statements." [17]

THE NEW EDUCATION

As if to make his meaning more clear by variation of description Epicurus writes also of "the sketch of the whole system reduced to essentials" and the view of the system "at one glance." [18] It is at this point that an item of Aristotle's terminology is of help. In his system the various arts are staggered in respect of importance: the art of making bridles is subordinate to that of horsemanship, and this in turn to that of generalship; generalship in turn, along with the arts of oratory and finance, is subordinate to the political art or government. The latter is then the *kuriotate episteme*, "the supreme science" or "the most com manding science." [19]

Epicurus, in a phraseology analogous to this, writes of "the most com-manding view over the nature of things," [20] the meaning flickering between the conceit of the panoramic heavenly outlook and the synoptic view of truth afforded by an epitome. His addiction to the use of the adjective *kurios* becomes fetishistic. His chief criticism of the Platonic system is its alleged failure to arrive at the *kuriotatai aitiai*, "the ultimate causes." [21] To him these ultimate causes, which had precedence over all others, were the atoms and their motions.

The title chosen for his famous collection of forty doctrines was *Kuriai Doxai*. The precise meaning of this has remained so uncertain that a variety of renderings are in circulation from the pens of the best scholars: Peculiar Propositions, Established Beliefs, Principal Doctrines, Fundamental Tenets, Cardinal Principles, Sovran Maxims, Authentic Doctrines, *Pensées Maitresses*. In this book they are being called Authorized Doctrines, an approximate rendering of Cicero's *maxime ratae sententiae*, "doctrines specially endorsed"; Cicero was near the truth in believing them so named "as being of supreme importance for the happy life." [22] They were authorized for commitment to memory and stood opposed to the "false doctrines" of other philosophers and the multitude. An anonymous scholar has rightly styled them Articles of Faith.[23]

THE USE OF THE EPITOME

For the reason that the epitomes furnished the most panoramic or commanding view of truth, they became the basic textbooks in the educational procedure of Epicurus as finally elaborated. All four of his extant writings are epitomes. These were intended to serve the purpose of breviaries and to be carried about so as to be available whenever an interval of leisure presented itself.[24] They were regarded as a means to self-help and home-study for those too deeply involved in gainful occupations to be free for oral instruction.[25] Lucretius, himself a product of home-study, urges Memmius to follow this procedure: "You will be able by your own unaided efforts to discern one truth after another." [26] Memorization was required and the student was warned against undue haste; he was to proceed leisurely and to commit to memory only so much at one time as would enable him to get the commanding view over the field.[27]

Nevertheless the epitomes are in no true sense to be regarded as primers to be mastered and laid aside. They are rather syllabuses to be kept in hand and used in conjunction with the Big Epitome or the special treatises. For example, let it be supposed that the beginner has learned by heart the third of the Twelve Elementary Principles: "The universe consists of solid bodies and void." The Little Epitome informs him only that the existence of solids is proved by sensation, that from sensory data the nature of subsensory bodies must be inferred and that the existence of void is proved by the obvious facts of motion and rest. If he wishes to have further details, he is recommended by Laertius to consult the Big Epitome or the first of the books on Physics.[28]

The supreme requirement on the part of the student is "to be able to handle smartly the synoptic views" and the supreme objective is "the perfected precision" or perfection of detail.[29] The method of procedure — to adopt the phraseology of Plato and Aristotle — is not "from the particulars to first principles" but "from the first principles to particulars." [30] The reasoning is deductive. For example, let it be assumed that the problem is to decide whether the number of worlds is finite or infinite. The student has learned among others the following principles: (1) "The multitude of atoms is infinite." (2) "The void is infinite in extent." From the first it follows that the supply of atoms of any given kind could not be exhausted by the creation of one world or of any number of worlds. From the second principle it follows that space would not be lacking for any number of worlds. Therefore the number of worlds is infinite, or, to express it differently, if the number of worlds were finite, the universe would not be infinite.[31]

It is customary to classify Epicurus as an empiricist, because of his alleged reliance upon the sensations. To do so is to misunderstand the function of the Canon and to ignore the manifest procedures of his reasoning. One of his epitomes was devoted to the Twelve Elementary Principles of Physics. Since the procedure was to begin with these and to commit them to memory, it follows that the method was deductive throughout. These principles became major premises. Ideas arrived at by deduction from these were called *epinoai*, which by etymology means "inferential" or "accessory" notions. For instance, the third principle declared: "The universe consists of solid bodies and void." From this was deduced, on the principle of the excluded middle, the inferential idea that the soul is corporeal. Again, the fifth and sixth principles declared the infinity of the universe. From this was deduced, on a principle called isonomy, the existence of gods. Unless perfect beings existed somewhere in addition to imperfect beings, the universe would not be infinite; infinity applies to values no less than to space and matter.

The function of the Sensations as part of the Canon is to test the correctness of the inferences drawn from the Twelve Principles. These Principles themselves were not based upon the evidence of the Sensations; the truth of them was demonstrated by a deductive syllogism, as will be shown in the chapter on the New Physics.

THE NEW TEXTBOOKS

In support of this new program of education a complete series of textbooks was composed and published by Epicurus and his colleagues. These writings fall into three classes: Dogmatic, Refutative, and Memorial.

The dogmatic writings comprised a series of textbooks on the Canon, Physics, and Ethics. Most of them were by Epicurus himself. The outstanding example was the thirty-seven on Physics.

The refutative writings comprised a series belittling and refuting the teachings of all rival schools, especially the Platonists. An outstanding example was the letter of Epicurus entitled *Against the Philosophers in Mytilene.*

The memorial writings consisted of sympathetic and eulogistic biographies of deceased members of the school. An example is the memoir of Epicurus on his brother Neocles.

These three classes were logically integrated with the whole body of doctrine. Since Epicurus was convinced that his teachings were "true philosophy," the *vera ratio* of Lucretius, it followed that dogmatic textbooks were the requirement.

113

Again, since the teachings of Epicurus were "the truth," it followed that all others were "false opinions" and "defilements." It followed likewise that the minds of novices must be kept pure from these and that the minds of converts should be purged of false doctrines already imbibed. To accomplish this second purpose was the aim of the refutative writings. These were not strictly controversial. They were not published with the idea that adversaries should reply in kind and be answered again. Satire was a frequent ingredient, such as the ridicule of the irony of Socrates.

The nature of the memorial writings has been completely overlooked but they belong no less logically in the scheme than the two previous classes. One of their aims was to confer a new kind of immortality upon deceased members of the circle. It was the teaching of Epicurus that happiness was attainable; it was possible for mankind within the limits of mortal life to approximate all but completely to the happiness of the gods. This happiness embraced two elements, blissfulness and incorruptibility. Although the soul of man was corruptible, it was still possible for the memory of him to be made imperishable in the records and in the rites of the Epicurean brotherhood. It was with the aim of securing this new kind of immortality for himself and his associates that Epicurus established during his lifetime the regular celebration of the twentieth in each month and provided for its perpetuation in his will. These celebrations were memorial sacraments and the memoirs of deceased members are comparable to the Acts of the Apostles and the Lives of the Saints in the Christian church. A number of specimens are extant in the usual fragmentary condition among the Herculanean papyri.[32]

Thus behind the whole program of writing there existed a coherent logic, and it must be added that behind the logic of it was a compelling personality. A certain Apollodorus, the fifth successor of Epicurus, won for himself the nickname "Tyrant of the Garden," [33] but he can hardly have been more of a tyrant than Epicurus himself, only less artful. In the original garden there was a single will directing all and we have a reliable witness in Seneca: "Among these men whatever Hermarchus said, whatever Metrodorus said is directed to a single objective. Everything that anyone said within that famous fellowship was said under the guidance and direction of a single mind. We cannot, I say, try as we may, select something out of the vast accumulation of coordinated teachings and exalt it above the rest." [34]

THE NEW EDUCATION

While the titles of the dogmatic writings have become scrambled in the course of a fortuitous tradition it is easy to restore them to some degree of order.[35] They fall under the three heads of Canon, Physics, and Ethics. It is a unique tribute to the ability of Metrodorus that he was permitted a share in this field and wrote on the Sensations.[36]

Metrodorus was also permitted to write on Change, which means physical change, but the field of Physics was naturally dominated by the master himself. In addition to the thirty-seven books there were rolls on Atoms and Void, Touch, under which fell all sensations, Idols, that is, the images discharged by solid bodies, Vision and Phantasia; the last was concerned with immediate and dependable perceptions, whether of vision or the mind. A marginal topic was Diseases.

In the field of Ethics the coverage was ample. Here also Metrodorus was permitted a share; he wrote on the Progress toward Wisdom, on Magnanimity, and on Wealth. The fundamental topics were naturally reserved for the master. There was, as fashion had begun to require, a Protreptic or exhortation to the study of philosophy. The chief topic was the End or Telos and along with this went Choice and Avoidance, because the nature of the end determines every decision to do or not to do a given thing. Since Epicurus was the first outstanding champion of the freedom of the will, the work on Fate was of prime importance; it must have discussed determinism. The fashion set by predecessors also called for a work on Lives, which included the political life, the contemplative and other careers. Fashion demanded too a discussion of Occupations, callings below the rank of the Lives, even that of a porter. The discussion of the virtues was by this time enjoying vogue and called for books on Justice and the other virtues and on Just Dealing. The question of the gods was also to the fore and elicited specific treatment, as also Piety. The rise of the Macedonian monarchies and the practice of patronage occasioned discussion of Kingship and Gifts and Gratitude.

In this field the talented Themista of Lampsacus had a share. She wrote on Glory, showing the vanity of it, and to this work Cicero accorded a grudging admiration, because he named her before the Roman senate and seems to quote her.[37]

In the case of the refutative writings the warning deserves to be repeated that the objective was not victory in controversy but rather to discredit all rival teachings, whether earlier or contemporary, and to insulate the minds of disciples against all other doctrines. Lucian the satirist, who knew Epicureanism exceptionally well, describes the attitude for us precisely: "Well, let us be of good cheer, my dear friend, we possess a powerful antidote for such poisonous influences in 'the truth and the philosophy that is invariably right'." [38] This is the infallibility that Epicurus claimed for his doctrines and the reference is unmistakable.

The coverage of the refutative writings is so wide and inclusive as to leave no gaps, and the division of labor is easy to discern. In general it may be said that Epicurus reserved for himself the task of dealing with living rivals and the more essential problems. To his colleagues was accorded the privilege of dealing with the dead and with topics unsuitable for himself or of less immediate urgency. As a rare exception to this principle of dividing the labor may be mentioned the approval given to the brilliant courtesan Leontion in writing against the living Theophrastus, head of Aristotle's school.[39]

Satire was a favorite weapon of the school from the very first. The burlesque treatment by Colotes of the older Greek philosophers and especially Socrates has already been mentioned. The Platonists came in for the chief share of ridicule. The revival of the fashion of law-giving that sprouted from the *Republic* and the *Laws* gave occasion to Metrodorus to become satirical: "The truly free man is justified in having a good laugh at all men and at these would-be Lycurguses and Solons." [40] In a similar vein Epicurus, whose aptitude for hitting upon satirical epithets was not unknown, dubbed Plato "the Golden" in derision of his undemocratic division of citizens into men of gold, silver, and iron. His Platonic adversaries of Mytilene were hit off as "the deep-voiced," a name applied to ambitious second-rate actors, as if "would-be Hamlets." [41] The Platonists as a class he styled "hangers-on of Dionysus." [42] This has nothing to do with Dionysius of Syracuse and Plato's visits there. The meaning stems from Dionysus as the god of the theater. If interpreted in the light of the "deep-voiced" and "would-be Lycurguses and Solons," it may be reasonably taken to describe those who assume a grand air, aspire to do kingly roles, and look down upon others as lowbrows. This was no doubt the attitude of the dominant philosophers toward the schoolteacher's son from Samos and his provincial following from Lampsacus.

The satirical writings were sometimes reinforced by historical research. Idomeneus published a work on the Socratics, in which he essayed to show that the man who offered to assist the condemned Socrates in escaping was not Crito, as Plato reported, but Aeschines, the son of the sausage-maker.[43] This was in line with the general ascription of uppishness to the Platonists.

As for serious refutation of Platonic doctrines, a share in the campaign was conceded to the diligent Hermarchus. He is on record as writing against both Plato and Aristotle; since he also wrote about Studies it is possible that he discussed what branches should be included in the curriculum, discouraging the young from studying rhetoric and mathematics. The outstanding refutation of Platonism was by Epicurus himself, addressed to the Philosophers in Mytilene. This is beyond much doubt the letter called "brilliant" and several excerpts from it are reasonably recognized in the Authorized Doctrines. One curious title, the Corner in the Atom, would remain mysterious were it not known that Plato had accounted for the phenomena of old age by postulating the detrition of the sharp edges of his angular atoms.[44] To Epicurus such an assumption would have been preposterous, his atoms being indestructible.

Other opponents received due attention from the master himself. A single volume against Eurylochus was deemed sufficient to denounce the Pyrrhonian skeptics. Disciples were immunized also against the neighboring Megarians; these comprised a numerous group of eristics, who delighted in arguing for victory instead of instruction. One of them was Stilpo, who espoused a doctrine hateful to Epicurus, that the wise man has no need of friends.[45]

For some of his predecessors in the domain of physics Epicurus was not without respect, because he spoke well of Archelaus, the teacher of Socrates, and of Anaxagoras, who preceded him as a refugee in Lampsacus.[46] He also esteemed Democritus.[47] Against the physicists as a class, however, he wrote several rolls, and the importance he attached to these as textbooks is indicated by his preparation of an epitome of the whole series.[48] Two chief objections urged against them were their neglect of ethics and their teaching of determinism. Upon freedom of the will Epicurus set such supreme value that determinism in any shape became a foremost abomination.

A no uncertain light upon the considerations that determined the division of labor in this field of refutation is afforded by the tasks allotted to the plodder Hermarchus. To deal with Empedocles, who had been dead for more than a century, was his principal chore, and the fruit of it was no fewer than twenty-two books.[49] Obviously his abilities were not such as to qualify him for the performance of the more immediate and urgent assignments.

The more sprightly and vigorous talents of Metrodorus, on the contrary, were such as could be trusted to handle some of the more pressing problems in the field of public relations.[50] In one of his books he placed before the public and the adherents of the school at large the truth about the ill health of Epicurus; in another he wrote on nobility of birth, which must have been a defense of his master against the adversaries who belittled his origin and parentage. He also wrote against Democritus, the physicists, the dialecticians, and the sophists. The thoughtful observer will not fail to discern in this program the completeness of the insulation from all rival influences that Epicurus planned for preserving the integrity of his school.

MEMORIAL WRITINGS

The memorial writings of the Epicureans were unique in their inception, though later the example was copied by the Christians. As for their purpose, the student must be prepared to discern a certain subtlety. A charge of inconsistency was sometimes urged against Epicurus because, on the one hand, he discouraged all public careers and the quest of wealth, power, and fame, while, on the other hand, he wrote and published assiduously and composed sympathetic and eulogistic biographies of all his associates.[51] There was no real inconsistency; just as the purpose of the refutative writings was to insulate his followers from all rival teachings, so part of the purpose in his memorial writings was to bestow an internal coherence upon the body of his followers. When St. Paul spoke of "many members, yet but one body," [52] he was addressing Epicureans and making capital of their own coherence as a sect. Thus it was not world-wide fame that Epicurus was endeavoring to capture for himself and his own but a perpetuity of affectionate recollection within his own circle of disciples.

This judgment is not an inference. Documentation is available. We have the words of the keen-minded Metrodorus, whose special province was public relations: "Epicurus and I have not risen to great prominence but in days to come Epicurus and I shall possess a solid and assured fame among those who shall have chosen to walk in the same footsteps." [53] There is also a pathetic subsidiary purpose in these memorial writings.

Epicurus denied the immortality of the soul. As Metrodorus expressed it in Vatican Saying 30: "The potion mixed for us all at birth is a draught of death." Yet by way of taking the sting out of death, Epicurus offers as a substitute for immortal life an immortality of remembrance within the limited circle of those who have separated themselves from the rest of men by following his precepts. When St. Paul wrote, "O death, where is thy sting?" he was purloining the word "sting" from the Epicureans and also the sentiment.[54] He was offering his Epicurean audience the restoration of an immortality for which they had accepted a substitute.

It follows that we should approach the memorial writings of the Epicureans as we do the Acts of the Apostles and the Lives of the Saints. The earliest title known to us is perhaps a life of one Philistas by an equally obscure disciple Carneiscus; tantalizing fragments of it survive in a papyrus.[55] Most notable were the affectionate memoirs written by Epicurus himself, whom an unkind fate compelled to be present at the last rites of many a beloved disciple. Among these were his three brothers Neocles, Chaeredemus, and Aristobulus, undistinguished men and commemorated in single volumes.[56] A youthful disciple named Hegesianax was similarly honored.[57] Cicero remarks rather shabbily upon the size of the books that were dedicated to the memory of the gifted and loyal Themista; in hinting that they might better have been devoted to someone like Epaminondas, he deliberately chose to misrepresent their purpose.[58] Metrodorus was the beloved disciple; his memory was enshrined in five volumes.[59]

The custom was faithfully pursued after the death of Epicurus and is evidenced in fragments of the papyrus documents from Herculaneum. Outstanding is a memoir of the distinguished Philonides, known also from inscriptions.[60] Only by the papyrus is it revealed, however, that he was an Epicurean and was highly honored at the court of the notorious Antiochus Epiphanes, who furnished the model for the description of Antichrist in a letter of St. Paul.[61] Since this Antiochus was the bitter persecutor of the Jews it would be interesting to make a digression upon the hatred of orthodox Jewry for Epicureanism, but this topic belongs elsewhere. It would be a serious omission, however, were it not mentioned that Philonides kept the faith and did not surrender his precious freedom of action as the price of preferment.[62] This was the test for the faithful Epicurean. It should be recalled how admiring biographers of the poet Horace extol his sturdy independence in his relations with

Maecenas and Augustus Caesar. He was merely showing himself a good Epicurean.[63]

Notable also are the fragments of a papyrus which in true Epicurean fashion offers an epitome of various memorial writings. In these it was the custom to make suitable quotations from collections of letters, which were numerous and reverently regarded. In this particular papyrus is preserved the praise of Polyaenus, who was outstanding for his friendly and sympathetic nature, in illustration of which a tender letter addressed to a child is quoted. In part it runs as follows: "We have arrived at Lampsacus in good health. I hope you are well too and your mamma and that you are always obedient to Daddy and Matro, just as you used to be. For you may be sure, Baby, that I and all the rest of us love you dearly because you are always obedient to them." [64] This letter is ascribed by most scholars to Epicurus himself but only by inference, and that a very flimsy one; the context in which it occurs is totally favorable to the ascription to Polyaenus.[65]

As a sect the Epicureans were assiduous writers of letters and Epicurus had set the example. Of the three hundred odd rolls ascribed to him a large proportion must have been letters. Many of these were serious expositions of doctrine, such as the one addressed to the philosophers in Mytilene and the three extant letters. The files of private letters, however, were diligently kept and widely circulated. In the second century B.C. the scholar Philonides, favorite of Antiochus Epiphanes, was making epitomes of them.[66] Plutarch had copies in his hands in the first century A.D.; [67] Diogenes Laertius was quoting from them in the following century.[68]

The letters, obviously, belonged in all three classes, dogmatic, refutative, and memorial. It was the private letters, however, that were especially adapted to keep alive in the hearts and minds of the disciples the memory of those who had gone before. They constituted a supporting literature that reinforced the effect of the monthly gatherings everywhere celebrated on the twentieth to commemorate the memory of the founders.

It may be added that Epicurus is often described in modern handbooks as "the most prolific of all writers." The truth is that he made a fetish of brevity, as befitted an educator. The total of his output is reported as 300 rolls and the extant specimens are brief. Didymus, a grammarian, is credited with 4,000 and the Christian Origen with 6,000.

CHAPTER VII ✠ THE CANON, REASON AND NATURE

HE Canon was not an afterthought, as the Stoics asserted,[1] but occupied the first place in the triad of Canon, Physics, and Ethics. This arrangement is unalterable, because the Ethics were deduced from the Physics and the truth of both Physics and Ethics was subject to the test of the Canon, which included Sensations, Anticipations, and Feelings.

The task of expounding the Canon would be much simpler were it not for ancient and modern confusions and ambiguities that beset the topic. Epicurus disposed of it in a single roll. The word *canon* denotes a rule or straightedge but metaphorically includes all the instruments employed by a builder. A perspicuous account of it is presented by Lucretius, who mentions also the square and the plumb line.[2] Apart from this passage, however, Lucretius misleads the reader, because he gives exclusive prominence to the Sensations and seems to have lacked a clear understanding of the workings of Anticipations and Feelings as criteria.

These last two criteria, it is manifest, were not discussed in the Big Epitome which Lucretius had before him. In the graded textbooks of Epicurus the topic must have been reserved for advanced students. It is doubtful whether Lucretius was even acquainted with the roll that treated of the Canon. This is unfortunate, because his own one-sided treatment is largely to blame for the classification of Epicurus as an empiricist and for the ascription to him of belief in "the infallibility of sensation."

It is an even worse mistake to have confused the tests of truth with the content of truth, that is, the tools of precision with the stones of the wall. This was the blunder of Pierre Gassendi, who revived the study of Epicurus in the seventeenth century. It was his finding "that there is nothing in the intellect which has not been in the senses." From this position

John Locke, in turn, set out as the founder of modern empiricism. Thus a misunderstanding of Epicurus underlies a main trend of modern philosophy. This astonishing fact begets an even greater concern for a correct interpretation, which may cause Locke to appear slightly naïve.

The institution of the Canon reflects a contemporary striving for an increase of precision in all the arts, sculpture, architecture, music, and mathematics, but the immediate provocation is to be found in the teachings of Pyrrho the skeptic and of Plato. Pyrrho's rejection of both reason and the sensations as criteria rendered acute the need of establishing a canon of truth. In the judgment of Epicurus Plato also ranked as a skeptic, because he belittled the sensations as undependable and phenomena as deceptive, the only real and eternal existences being the ideas. Thus in his system reason became the only contact between man and reality, and human reason was crippled by the imprisonment of the soul in the body.

Epicurus denied the existence of Platonic ideas on the ground that the only existences were atoms and empty space. Thus to his thinking man stood face to face with physical reality and his sensations constituted the sole contact with this reality. Had he stopped at this point he would have been an empiricist, but he did not. He made room also for a kind of intuition, which is incompatible with empiricism. He postulated that man was equipped in advance by Nature for living in his prospective environment, and not in his physical environment alone but also in his social environment. In addition to the five senses this equipment included innate ideas, such as that of justice, and these ideas, because they existed in advance of experience, were called Anticipations. Moreover, as Epicurus postulated, each experience of the individual, the sensations included, is accompanied by a secondary reaction of pleasure or pain. These pleasures and pains are the Feelings, which also rank as criteria, being Nature's Go and Stop signals.

Thus Nature, having equipped man with a triple contact with his environment, becomes a norm, while the Platonic Reason is eliminated along with the Platonic Ideas. It now remains to explain in more detail the dethronement of Reason and the recognition of Nature as the norm.

THE DETHRONEMENT OF REASON

It will have been noted that the Canon makes no mention of reason. This means that reason is denied rank as a criterion of truth. It will be worth while to observe by what procedure this exclusion may be justified and what the consequences will be for the concept of reason itself. The position of Epicurus becomes seemingly paradoxical because there is no instrumentality by which reason can be dethroned except reason itself. Consideration of this paradox may be postponed until it has been shown how the Platonic concept of reason may be rendered absurd. The conclusions will be absolutely logical if the premises are accepted.

As will be set forth in the chapter on Physics, Epicurus adopted and declared Twelve Elementary Principles, one of which reads: "The universe consists of atoms and void." This is a positive statement. If the implied negative be made explicit, it is this, that there is nothing incorporeal except void. This is destructive of certain teachings of Plato. According to him the sensations inform us only of the things that are transient, that have a beginning and an end. The realities are the eternal forms or ideas, which are not joined up with matter and so are incorporeal. Moreover, according to the same teachings the ideas are apprehensible only by pure reason, which, being, like the ideas, discrete from matter, is itself incorporeal and divine. Logically, therefore, if there is nothing incorporeal except void, the eternal ideas and the divine incorporeal reason are alike absurdities.

By this same principle it should be noted that the incorporeal soul is also eliminated. Thus, the soul, being corporeal and incapable of preexistence or survival, is reduced to a parity with the body. This means farewell to all the disabilities imposed upon it through imprisonment in the body and to all mystical ideas associated with successive incarnations. Corporeal reason alone is left, that is, human intelligence.

There is another of the Twelve Principles that has a specific bearing upon the Platonic concept of reason: "The atoms are always in motion." If we seek the implied negative of this positive statement — and Epicurus reasons after this fashion — it will be this, that nothing else in the universe is in motion, because the void is incapable of motion and outside of atoms and void there is nothing. It will follow also that no other cause of motion exists. It will be nonsensical, therefore, to think of divine reason as the cause of motion.

There is yet another of the Twelve Principles that possesses a bearing upon the function of reason in the universe. The second Principle reads: "The universe has always been the same as it now is." [3] This principle is known to us as the law of the indestructibility and uncreatibility of matter. To Epicurus it meant that the idea of primeval chaos was absurd; the universe has always been a cosmos. Specifically, speaking of the various motions of the atoms, he said: "Of these there has been no beginning, the atoms and the void being eternal." [4] To him the universe was a cosmos solely because of the various weights, shapes, and magnitudes of the atoms and their motions, all of which were constant factors. Consequently there was no need of the ordering mind (*nous*) according to Anaxagoras or of the divine demiurge of Plato. Both of these become absurdities. In the extant remains of Epicurus the word *nous* does not occur; it seems to have been deliberately avoided.

While by this line of argument it will be observed that the incorporeal, eternal, and unerring reason of Plato and Aristotle is eliminated, the purely human, mortal reason remains. Even this is subordinated to the sensations: "Not even reason can refute the sensations, for reason depends wholly upon them." [5] This does not mean, as Gassendi imagined, that the whole content of thought is derived from the sensations, which was not the teaching of Epicurus, but rather that the deprivation of sensation is virtually death.[6] The basic idea is the conviction that reason is incapable of making direct contact with reality; reason is active only when the sensations are active. Without the sensations reason possesses no criteria, since they along with the Anticipations and Feelings function as contacts with reality.

Moreover, it is not in sensation but in human intelligence that error arises. Of sensation he wrote: "Sensation is entirely irrational." [7] This is not cited as a demerit but as a merit. It is the justification for regarding sensation as a criterion. It cannot "stimulate itself" and, unlike reason, "when stimulated by something external cannot add anything or take anything away." [8] For example, let us say that the color of white registers itself on the vision. It is not sensation that tells the observer he is seeing a white ox. This is a function of the intelligence and the recognition is "an immediate perception of the intelligence." [9] Even to such a perception as this Epicurus denied the rank of criterion, though his successors did not,[10] and the ground of his rejection is manifest. If the observer says, "It is a white ox," this is a judgment and as such it is secondary to the sensation itself and it can err. Thus it does not qualify as a criterion. The sensation, however, does not err. As Aristotle said,[11] "The sense of sight is not deceived as to color, nor is that of hearing as to sound."

THE CANON, REASON AND NATURE

It remains to mention that Epicurus minimized the value of reason even in dealing with things beyond the range of sensation, whether too minute or too remote for observation. To denote the notions relative to these unseen phenomena he raised a familiar word to the rank of a technical term, *epinoiai,* which by virtue of the prefix means "secondary" or "accessory" ideas. This is the sense in the following pronouncement: "For all accessory ideas (*epinoiai*) are derived from the sensations by virtue of coincidence, analogy, similarity and combination, reason also contributing something." [12] While this grudging concession to reason should be noted, it is observable also that procedures which employ comparison and analogy seem to Epicurus an inferior kind of reason. By analogy, for example, it should seem possible to have a heap of atoms, since we have heaps of dust, but a superior reason intervenes and reminds us that atoms are endowed with motion.[13] Consequently, a heap of atoms is inconceivable. This superior reason employs the method of inference from the Twelve Elementary Principles. The procedure is deductive; Epicurus is not an empiricist.

Three kinds of reason are thus recognized: first, a dependable kind that proceeds by deduction from first principles; second, an inferior kind that proceeds by analogy from the visible to the invisible and is subject to correction by the former; third, ordinary human intelligence (*dianoia*), which is normally automatic and hence fallible and is subject to correction by the volitional intelligence.

Common to all these forms of reason is their restriction to the human mind; all are faculties of that mind. Outside of this human mind there is no reason in the universe, no world-mind which expresses itself in eternal ideas, regularities of motion, harmonic relationships, and spherical perfections and is identifiable with truth itself.

It still remains to glance at the paradox in which Epicurus involves himself by employing reason to dethrone reason as the chief criterion. He places himself in a position similar to that of the skeptic who denies the possibility of certainty in knowledge, thus depriving his own skepticism of certainty.

This paradox, moreover, does not stand alone. It is also paradoxical that Epicurus should have omitted reason from his Canon and at the same time accepted a great body of truth accumulated by the reasonings of predecessors and set these down among his Twelve Elementary Principles of Physics. From this inconsistency he thought to escape by treating each of these principles as if a theorem of geometry. For example, to demonstrate that the universe is infinite in respect of both matter and space, he resorts to a disjunctive syllogism.[14] If matter were infinite and space finite, the latter could not contain the former. Again, if matter were finite and space infinite, then matter would be lost in space and no clashes or combinations of atoms would occur. Since these alternative assumptions lead to absurdities, the conclusion is that the original proposition is true. With such reasoning even a Stoic logician could find no fault.

This treatment of the Elementary Principles as theorems does not save Epicurus from the charge of inconsistency. It gains for his system of knowledge merely the semblance of being logically self-contained. Reason is employed as a criterion to set up criteria by which it should itself be demoted, if not quite superseded. Reason, however, as he conceives it, is purely human, not divine.

The elimination of the divine reason entails a curious logical consequence: the universe is split in two, the terrestrial and the extraterrestrial regions. The former becomes anthropocentric, since the human Sensations, Anticipations, and Feelings are the norm; the latter is left impersonal and nonpurposive, being governed by natural laws. Plato's universe, on the contrary, is undivided, being completely theocentric and ruled by the divine and incorporeal reason. In the terrestrial sphere Epicurus approximates to the position of Protagoras, who said "Man is the measure," while Plato said "God is the measure."

RIDICULE

It is a tribute to the merit of the Canon that the chief weapon employed against it was ridicule. To have set up a criterion of truth in place of reason, if not impious or sacrilegious, was at least heretical and outrageous. Few concepts are so flattering to the vanity of mankind as the hypothesis that the possession of reason exalts it above the brutes and offers it an affinity with the divine. Mystical notions receive a warmer welcome than cold facts and figures, divine creationism than biological evolution. Plato's mysticism exercised a subtle flattery all its own, especially by the separation of form and matter, by the assumption of a pure reason contemplating absolute truth, by the identification of reason with God. Part of its charm consisted in a vague self-pity for the soul imprisoned in the body, pondering wistfully on the theme of previous existence and future incarnations. To declare the soul corporeal and to make it the equal partner of the body seemed repulsive realism, more easily satirized than refuted.

The language of Epicurus sometimes swerves toward poetical diction, and in one of his more enthusiastic moments he seems to have been moved by gratitude to blessed Nature to characterize the Canon as *diopetes*, "fallen from heaven," as if it were a holy palladium. It was this epithet that Cicero was echoing when he dubbed it "the celestial rule" and more literally in another passage styled it as "fallen from the sky." [15] Plutarch, who employed part of his leisure in digging up old slurs out of the archives, wrote scornfully: "It was not because Colotes had read 'the heaven-descended Canons' that bread was perceived by him to be bread and fodder fodder." [16] Even after the time of Plutarch the Canon seemed good to the frivolous Alciphron for a joke between two courtesans, the Epicurean Leontion and Lamia, mistress of Demetrius the Besieger: "How long will one have to put up with this philosopher? Let him keep to his books on Physics, to his Authorized Doctrines and his cock-eyed Canons." [17]

NATURE AS THE NORM

In order that the benefit of the synoptic view may be enjoyed at all times, it is well to bear in mind how the vogue of one philosophy waned and that of another waxed. Ionian science reached a peak with Democritus and then suffered a recession in popular interest. It was outshone for the space of three generations by the revolutionary teaching of Socrates and the brilliant teaching and thinking of Plato. Students came from the remotest parts to study in the Academy. The recession from this enthusiasm may escape recognition at this distance of time, but it was nevertheless real. Even the theory of ideas was abandoned by Plato's immediate successors. Simultaneously the tradition of Ionian science was reviving under the leadership of Aristotle, who was sympathetic with this direction of things by virtue of birth, early training, and cast of mind.

The revived science, however, exhibited a shift of focus. The preceding Ionians had unwittingly confined their studies in the main to inorganic nature. The later Aristotle was a biologist and concerned himself with organic life. It was his particular service to discover a new kind of order in nature, that of the organic structures and processes in living creatures.

This new order, in its turn, became a rival of the order of the heavenly bodies, which had been brilliantly exploited by Plato.

The immediate net effect of this was to create a competition between Nature and Reason for the command of philosophic attention. When Aristotle arrived at the conclusion "that Nature does nothing at random," he was speaking of plant and animal life and was bringing to the fore a new teleology. It is this concept of creative nature that Epicurus took over. He calls the study of nature by the name physiology, the *rerum natura* of Lucretius, which includes nature in all manifestations, but he denied importance to the study of astronomy and eliminated mathematics from the curriculum of study.

By the word *nature* Aristotle the biologist meant the creative force in plant and animate life. This is precisely what Lucretius in one passage meant by *natura creatrix*.[18] In practice, however, the scope of the meaning was narrowed by Epicurus to signify "human nature"; this is the meaning undeniably when he wrote: "Nature is not to be coerced." [19] Only slightly different is the force of the word when he wrote of the beginnings of civilization: "Furthermore it must also be assumed that Nature was taught many and diverse lessons by sheer force of circumstances and compelled to put them into practice." [20] In this instance Nature signifies the composite and accumulative experience of the human race.

A still different color of meaning is to be discerned in the saying: "Gratitude is due to blessed Nature because she has made the necessities of life easy to procure and what is hard to procure unnecessary." [21] The gratitude here signified exhibits an advance over the pagan gratitude to Mother Earth as the giver of bread. The word *nature* has taken on an ethical connotation. Nature is not merely the creatrix. She seems to be also benevolent and provident. The concept of her is close to that of Aristotle when saying "that Nature does nothing at random."

PRIORITY OF NATURE OVER REASON

This ascription of benevolence to Nature and the narrowing of the concept to denote human nature or the composite experience of the race all reflects the pronounced ethical bias of Epicurus. Along with this bias goes a deliberate plan to exalt Nature over reason. In point of time and succession Nature is made to possess precedence.

His most telling argument has been preserved by Cicero.[22] Let it be assumed that a human being has been deprived of all his five senses. This is tantamount to death and the subject has ceased to be a rational creature. In a muddled paragraph our biographer Laertius ascribes to Epicurus the idea "that the Sensations lead the way." [23] In the present context this notion seems to have apposite application: the possession of sensation seems to be construed as antecedent to rational activity.

The priority of Nature was also insisted upon in establishing the identity of the end or telos. Aristotle had furnished a precious hint in this connection; he wrote "that perhaps even in the case of the lower animals there is some natural good superior to their scale of intelligence which aims at the corresponding good." [24] To this principle Epicurus adapted his procedure. By the promptings of Nature alone, apart from reason, every animate thing, the moment it is born, reaches out for pleasure and shrinks from pain. Consistent with this reasoning is the steady practice of referring to pleasure as "the end of Nature," which occurs five times in our scant remains. As analogous phrases may be cited "the good of Nature" and "the pleasure of Nature," all of them implying that reason played no necessary role in establishing the truth. Similar is the implication of parallel phrases such as "the wealth of Nature," signifying that Nature and not reason reveals the true meaning of wealth; and also "the limits of Nature," implying that Nature and not reason teaches the true limits of the desires. [25]

Another aspect of this priority of Nature over reason is manifest in the beginnings of human institutions. Since the sole cause of growth and change in the universe is the ceaseless motion of the atoms and this activity is nonpurposive, it follows that actions invariably precede thought. On this point the judgment of Epicurus is explicit: "Moreover, it must be assumed also that human nature by sheer force of circumstances was taught a multitude of lessons of all sorts and compelled to put them into practice, though reason subsequently contributed refinements and additions to these recommendations of hers, in some fields more rapidly, in others more slowly." [26] Lucretius in his fifth book enlarged liberally upon this theme: human beings wore skins before they manufactured garments; they lived in caves before they built huts; they employed clubs before they made weapons; they lived dispersed before they organized governments and built cities. [27]

The illustrative examples just cited were probably drawn by Lucretius from the Big Epitome of Epicurus. Special interest attaches to the topic of the origin of language, because this was the only example chosen by Epicurus in his extant Little Epitome for the enlightenment of beginners. There was a controversy in his day whether language had its origin in invention and enactment or in natural evolution. The former theory assumed that some god or some gifted individual invented the names of things and prescribed them for the multitude. This notion was scouted by Epicurus. The following quotation, though hardly a verbatim report, expressed his judgment: "These men did not assign names to things intelligently but stimulated by a natural instinct, just as men cough or sneeze, cattle bellow, dogs bark and suffering men moan." [28] Subsequently, the talented few, according to his account, taking their cues from Nature and impelled by expediency, by slow degrees brought human speech to its perfection among various races in various environments.[29]

The specific logical ground upon which Epicurus based this view of the origin of language was the postulate that action is bound to precede thought. The involuntary act is the indispensable stimulus to the voluntary effort through which refinement and improvement are achieved. Let Lucretius speak for Epicurus: "Besides, if other men too had not employed spoken words in their intercourse one with another, from what quarter was this notion of utility implanted in this man's mind and from what source was this capacity in the first instance bestowed upon him, so that he knew and envisaged in his mind what he wished to do?" [30] From this disability not even the gods were believed to be exempt. Unless Nature had first presented a specimen of creative activity, Lucretius demanded to know,[31] how could the gods have known how to plan or create a world?

Since Nature is assumed to be the sole creatrix and man is restricted to improving upon her suggestions, it follows that Nature is the supreme teacher. By the same reasoning Physics is the supreme science, because through the study of this the teachings of Nature come to knowledge. As Cicero correctly informs us, "Through this body of knowledge the force of words, the meaning of style and the distinction between the logically consistent and the logically inconsistent can be discerned." [32]

In this quotation three topics are broached, words, style, and logic. The first two may be discussed together. By implication it seems to be declared that Nature is neither a poet nor a rhetorician nor a dialectician. Words must be taken at their face value, just as Epicurus advises the young Herodotus.[33] This means for one thing that the use of figures of speech is abjured. Although the wise man may become a good critic of poetry, he will not compose poems.[34] Consistent with this is the information that the writing of Epicurus was characterized by propriety,[35] which means the avoidance of figures of speech. The critic Aristophanes is said to have censured it as "highly peculiar." [36] In this attitude toward style Epicurus was certainly influenced by the contemporary vogue of geometry, which instituted a way of writing unprecedented for its baldness, yet undeniably adapted to its needs. His declaration that the sole requisite was clearness,[37] was no more applicable to himself than to geometers.

This exaltation of clearness and the rejection of figurative language is consistent with another dictum of Epicurus: "The wise man will leave writings behind him but he will not compose panegyrics." [38] It was in composing such speeches for festive occasions that the rhetoricians really gave themselves free reign and swung over to the diction of poetry.

The same priority of Nature over reason that predetermined the right kind of writing and rendered rhetoric superfluous eliminated dialectic, but the logic of this judgment can be given more precision. The effect of the doctrine that nothing exists except atoms and void was to deny the reality of Plato's eternal ideas. Thus dialectic, which was the avenue to comprehension of those ideas, became a superfluity. The testimony of Laertius is explicit: "Dialectic they reject as superfluous, for it should suffice physicists to get along with the names of things as they find them." [39] While this advice seems to overlap the recommendation concerning style, the application is different. It means that the quest of definitions is useless. This quest is capable of terminating in fantastic concepts, such as Other, Same, and Essence in Plato's *Timaeus,* possessing no meaning unless on the highest level of abstraction. Since Epicurus rejected the reality of the eternal ideas, such terms could possess no meaning at all. Hence the following dictum: "There are two kinds of inquiry, the one about realities, the other ending up in sound without sense." [40] In the same vein is the advice to the young Herodotus to take words at their face values "so as not by our endless attempts to define have all our ideas in confusion or have mere vocables that mean nothing." [41]

As a parting comment it may be stated that, when once Nature has been established as the norm, it follows logically that man should live according to Nature, but the Epicureans seem never to have followed this inference through. It remained for the Stoics to identify Nature with Reason and to make a fetish of living according to Nature. They believed her supreme teaching was to be found in the divine order of the celestial realm, where Nature and Reason were at one.

CHAPTER VIII ✛ SENSATIONS,
ANTICIPATIONS, AND FEELINGS

THE criteria are three, but the prevailing custom is to reduce them to one by merging the Anticipations and the Feelings with the Sensations. This error arises from classifying Epicurus as an empiricist, ascribing to him belief in the infallibility of sensation, and then employing this false assumption as a major premise.

The three criteria are neither three aspects of a single capacity nor yet three discrete capacities which function separately from one another. To Epicurus body and soul are alike corporeal; they are also coterminous. Consequently all reactions of the individual to his environment are total or psychosomatic. Thus in the case of every reaction Nature is on the alert to register approval or disapproval by the signals of pleasure and pain. This is the function of the Feelings in the meaning of the Canon.

It is true that in the Greek language all three criteria may be called *pathe*, in modern parlance "reactions," but they are not identical. It is true also that all three may be components of a given reaction but still they occur in sequence. Sensation is irrational and merely registers a quality, for example, sweetness. It is the intelligence that says, "This is honey," and it is the Feelings that report, "I like it" or "I don't like it." Again, it is positively known that Epicurus postulated the existence of an innate sense of justice and called this an Anticipation. Now injustice hurts and it is the Feelings that register this fact. If a man is condemned to pay an unjust penalty, the pain is a reaction distinct from the aural sensation of hearing the verdict.

When once the criteria have been recognized as three distinct reactions occurring in close sequence, the next point is to recognize the general approach of Epicurus to the problem of the Canon as being biological or, more precisely, genetic. This attitude reflects the contemporary increase of interest in the study of biology, which included animal behavior. The starting point is the behavior of the newly born, whether brute or human, which reach out for pleasure and shrink from pain.

When once this genetic approach has been recognized it becomes easy to discern that the three criteria correspond to three levels of experience, which may be styled somatic, social, and emotional.

It is proposed to call the first level somatic because at this stage the bodily sensations are of paramount importance. At this level the Feelings denote physical pains and pleasures. The innate ideas, that is, the Anticipations, are still latent or barely emergent, awaiting their due call to activity.

The second level may be called social because the child is becoming an active member of the family, the neighborhood, and society. The Feelings extend their function so as to operate in the sphere of justice and injustice. At the same time the child begins to participate in the religious life. In these two spheres, those of justice and injustice and of religion, we know positively from our texts that the criteria called Anticipations were thought to be operative.

The third level may be called emotional because physical pains and pleasures have been superseded in importance by fears and hopes, suspicions, hatreds, envies, ambitions, and the like. At this level the Feelings reach their peak of importance as criteria. For instance, if the individual is tortured by fear of death and divine vengeance, it is a sure indication of false opinions concerning death and gods. On the contrary, if the individual enjoys peace of mind, it is a sure indication of right opinion.

On this third level the telos attains importance and functions as a criterion. On the level of infancy pleasure was pursued by instinct and without thought. On the third level the intelligence has at length identified pleasure as the goal of living and the telos is purposively pursued. It also becomes an incentive.

SENSATIONS

The Sensations in the meaning of the Canon denote the five senses, vision, hearing, smell, taste, and touch, and nothing else. They qualify as criteria because they are direct physical contacts between the living being and the external physical reality. They also qualify as criteria because they are irrational, are incapable of memory, and pronounce no judgments. Sensation is incapable of memory. It can no more recall a given stimulus than a house can recall the impact of a ball thrown against its wall. The sensation merely registers a stimulus, a melody, for example; it is the memory that says, "I have heard this before"; it is the intelligence that says, "Home Sweet Home."

Unfortunately the discussion of the Sensations has become clouded because of prejudice, negligence, confusions, and ambiguities.

The prejudice consists in classifying Epicurus as an empiricist and the negligence in not putting this assumption to the full test of the evidences and in failing to define the precise meanings of all the terms employed.

The confusions are two in number. The first is between concepts of "truth" and concepts of "value." It is quite possible for a sensation to be true and yet valueless as a criterion. A square tower, for example, appears at a distance to be round; the sensation is true, relative to the distance, but false to the facts. The second confusion is between primary and accessory or derivative notions. This is to say that the ideas represented by the Twelve Elementary Principles of Physics are primary while all other ideas are derivative. The former are *ennoiai*, the latter *epinoiai*.

The chief ambiguities are also two in number. In the dictum of Epicurus that "all sensations are true" both terms are ambiguous. The English word *sensation*, like the Latin *sensus*, is employed to render various words and phrases in Greek, while the word *true*, like its Latin and Greek equivalents, may have any one of three meanings: first, absolutely true, as the statement that two and two make four is true, or second, relatively true, as the distant view of the tower is true, though false in detail, or third, real, in the sense that the sensation corresponds to a real object, such as an ox.

EPICURUS NOT AN EMPIRICIST

In the chapter on the New Physics it will be shown that Epicurus set up Twelve Elementary Principles, which he demonstrated like theorems of geometry, thus classifying himself as a deductive reasoner. The presumption that he was an empiricist has been based in large part upon the zest with which he brandished certain arguments in refutation of the skeptics, who denied the validity of sensation. These arguments are succinctly recorded by Laertius and more amply by Lucretius. The succinct account begins: "Nor does anything exist that can refute the sensations, for neither can a sensation in a given class refute the sensation in the same class, because they are of equal validity, nor can the sensation in a given class refute the sensation in another class, because they are not criteria of the same phenomena." [1] The first limb of this statement has reference to the objection urged by the skeptics that one drinker reports the wine to be sour and another sweet or one bather reports the water to be warm and another cold. The answer of Epicurus was sensible, that the difference was in the observers.[2] Neither does the one judgment cancel the other, because each has validity for the observer, nor does the contradiction prove the fallibility of sensation, because the sensation in each instance performs its function as a criterion.

The second limb of the statement means that the ears cannot contradict the nose if the latter registers the smell of peppermint, which calls for no comment.

A subsequent item in the list of Laertius may seem to support the advocates of empiricism: "nor again can reason refute the sensations, because it depends upon them entirely." However, to interpret this as meaning that the whole content of consciousness is derived from the sensations would be in violation of the Canon, which makes no mention of reason, and would also be contrary to the belief in Anticipations, that is, innate ideas, which is a kind of intuitionism and incompatible with empiricism. The meaning is rather that bereft of the sensations a human being is virtually dead, which, as already mentioned, we know to have been an argument of Epicurus.[3]

There is still another item in the list of Laertius that has been so translated as to lend plausibility to the charge of empiricism. One version runs, "For all thoughts have their origin in sensations," and another, "For all our notions are derived from perceptions." [4] The source of the error is an imprecision. The Greek noun translated above as "thoughts" or "notions" is *epinoiai,* which by virtue of its prefix signifies accessory, derivative or inferential ideas. These secondary ideas are not to be confused with others which to them are primary, *ennoiai* or *ennoemata.* For instance, Epicurus in the Little Epitome outlines seven of his Twelve Elementary Principles and then adds: "Even this brief statement affords an outline of the nature of the real existences sufficient for inferential ideas (*epinoiais*)." [5] To illustrate: the principle that the universe consists of atoms and void is a primary idea; the knowledge that the soul is distributed over the whole organism is secondary; it is inferred from the sensation of touch and other phenomena. [6]

Other plausible reasons for ascribing empiricism and belief in the infallibility of sensation to Epicurus will disappear if the ambiguities be cleared up that inhere in the statement "all sensations are true." If "sensation" and *sensus* be a rendering of *aisthesis,* which means the perception of particulars such as color and shape, then it was idle for Cicero to be arguing against Epicurus, because Aristotle often enough declared the perception of particulars to be always true.[7]

It consequently follows that *sensus* must correspond to "phantasia," an inference confirmed by the evidence of Plutarch and Sextus Empiricus.[8] This term was employed in the same sense by Aristotle and Epicurus; it signifies the composite image of particulars. Both recognized the possibility of error, but Epicurus was more keenly interested in this factor because by his time the vogue of skepticism had made the erection of criteria a vital necessity. He was consequently at pains to locate the source of error, and he found it in the hasty action of the automatic mind. For example, the boat on which the observer is a passenger is standing still but it seems to be moving when a second boat is passing by. In such an instance the eyes are not playing the observer false; it is the hasty judgment of the automatic mind that is in error. However odd it seems in English, Epicurus called this "the addition of opinion." In explanation of this the statement should be recalled, that "sensation is irrational and incapable of adding or subtracting anything." It is the automatic mind that adds motion to the standing ship and subtracts it from the moving ship. Lucretius cites several examples of similar errors.[9]

In order to follow this topic through it is necessary to elucidate a point of terminology and semantic development. In all ages of the Greek language terminology was plastic. Thus Artistotle could employ *phantasia* to denote the imaginative faculty while using *phantasm* of the individual appearance, whether true or false.[10] Epicurus, having a different concern, truth and error, restricted *phantasia* to true and real appearances, using *phantasm* only of the false visions of the insane or of dreamers and also of the phenomena of the heavens, which he declared too remote for clear observation.[11] He even urged his disciple to scorn "those who concede dependable vision (*phantasia*) from distances," where the best scholars emend with misplaced ingenuity.[12]

Yet this is only part of the story. With Aristotle the term *phantasia,* not being restricted to true presentations, readily serves to denote visions of the imagination as a faculty. It is from this use that the English language has been enriched by the derivatives *fancy* and *fantasy,* which denote the absolutely unreal. From this same drift of semantic change we have the word *fantastic.* Epicurus, on the contrary, having chosen *phantasia* to denote a true presentation, employed *fantastic* to describe the objectively true or real. It becomes a synonym of *immediate* and opposed to the remote. For instance, it makes no difference whether he writes "the immediate perceptions" or "the fantastic perceptions." Both alike pertain to the joint activity of the senses and the mind, by which it is recognized that the animal standing over there is an ox or that the man approaching is Plato. These perceptions are "fantastic," strange as the usage seems, because they result in recognitions. The imagination is not involved.

While Epicurus was adamant in his determination to defend the validity of the sensations as being the means of direct contact between man and reality and as possessing precedence over reason, he exhibits no desire to defend the individual sensation. The fallacies of those who impute to him belief in the infallibility of sensation lie partly in their failure to observe the ambiguity of the word *true* and in their confusion of "truth" with "value."

It is not difficult to differentiate the various meanings of *true* and it is essential to right understanding. For example, when Epicurus declared that "the phantasms seen by the insane and in dreams are true," he meant that they were "real" and existed independently of the madman or the dreamer, because "they act as a stimulus and that which does not exist does not deliver a stimulus." [13] These phantasms, however, are not "true" in the sense that a sensation experienced by the waking observer is true. The dreamer may have a vision of a centaur but no centaurs exist in real life. If the waking man sees an ox, then the sensation is true because the stimulus is delivered by a living ox.

A still different meaning of *true* may be discerned when Epicurus denominates his system as "true philosophy." He means it is true in the sense that his Twelve Elementary Principles are true or in the sense that the modern scientist believes the accepted calculation of the speed of light to be true. This may be called absolute truth, if there is such a thing.

It remains to speak of the relatively true. The views of a tower at various distances may be cited as examples. Each is true relative to the distance; its value as evidence of the facts is another matter. This distinction was no novelty to the ancients; Sextus Empiricus sets it forth at some length in a discussion of Epicureanism.[14]

Also worthy of mention is the sensation which is optically true but false to the facts. An example much brandished by the skeptics was the bent image of the oar immersed in the water.[15] Epicurus made logical provision for this difficulty: "Of two sensations the one cannot refute the other,[16] because we give attention to all sensations." This statement alone would acquit him of belief in the infallibility of sensation, because it is distinctly implied that some sensations are employed to correct others.

The example of the tower will serve as a transition from the topic of ambiguity to that of confusion. When modern scholars seize upon the saying "all sensations are true," which appears nowhere in the extant writings of Epicurus, and stretch it to mean that all sensations are reliable or trustworthy or "that the senses cannot be deceived," they are confusing the concept of truth with the concept of value.[17] They overlook the fact that even a truthful witness may fall short of delivering the whole truth or may even give false evidence. The distant view of the square tower is quite true relative to the distance but it fails to reveal the whole truth about the tower.

To assume that Epicurus was unaware of these plain truths, as one must if belief in the infallibility of sensation is imputed to him, is absurd. It is because he was aware that the value of sensations, apart from their truth, varied all the way from totality to zero, that he exhorted beginners "under all circumstances to watch the sensations and especially the immediate perceptions whether of the intellect or any of the criteria whatsoever." [18] Obviously, so far from thinking the sensations infallible, he was keenly aware of the possibility of error and drew sharp attention to the superior values of immediate sensations.

When once these ambiguities and confusions have been discerned and eliminated, it is possible to state the teaching of Epicurus with some of that precision by which he set high store. In the meaning of the Canon, then, a sensation is an *aisthesis*. All such sensations may possess value; otherwise there would be no sense in saying, "We pay attention to all sensations." Their values, however, range all the way from totality to zero. The value is total only when the sensation is immediate. For example, when Aristotle says, "The sense of sight is not deceived as to color," this is true only of the close view, because colors fade in more distant views.

Sensations, however, usually present themselves in combinations of color, shape, size, smell, and so on. An immediate presentation of such a composite unit is a *phantasia*. All such presentations are true, but they do not rank as criteria in the meaning of the Canon, for the reason that the intelligence has come into play. An act of recognition (*epaisthesis*) has taken place in the mind of the observer, which is secondary to the primary reaction that registered color, shape, size, smell, and so forth.

That Epicurus did not regard these composite sensations as criteria is made clear by a statement of his own: "The fidelity of the recognitions guarantees the truth of the sensations." [19] For example, the animal standing yonder is recognized as a dun-colored ox. This is a secondary reaction. Only the primary perceptions of color, shape, size, and so on constitute a direct contact between man and the physical environment. The truth of these perceptions is confirmed by the fidelity of the recognition.

Again, let it be assumed that the quality of sweetness is registered by sensation. It is not, however, sensation that says, "This is honey"; a secondary reaction in the form of a recognition involving intelligence has taken place. This, in the terminology of Epicurus, is "a fantastic perception of the intelligence." These were not given the rank of criteria by Epicurus for the reason already cited. It is on record, how-ever, that later Epicureans did so.[20]

So far is Epicurus from believing all sensations to be true in the mean-ing of the Canon that he guards against error in various ways. In the first place, attention must be paid to all sensations, as already mentioned. Next, the sensations of the individual must be checked by those of others: "Consequently attention must be paid to the immediate feelings and to the sensations, in common with others in matters of common concern and individually in matters of private concern and to all clear presentations of every one of the criteria." [21] This guardedness was imperative, because contemporary skepticism was flourishing.

The problem of skepticism is attacked disjunctively in the Authorized Doctrines: either all sensations are rejected as valid evidence or some are admitted and some rejected. The former procedure is dealt with in Doctrine 23: "If you are going to make war on all the sensations, you will not even have a standard by reference to which you shall judge those of them which you say are deceptive." This makes it plain once more that not all sensations are true but the validity of some must be checked by the evidence of others.

The Doctrine above is directed at the outright skeptics. The second limb of the disjunctive approach deals with the Platonists, who rejected terrestrial phenomena as deceptive while accepting the evidences of celestial phenomena. Epicurus denied "clear vision (*phantasia*) from distances," if only the text be not emended.[22] He wrongly insisted that heavenly phenomena could be explained from the terrestrial. This betrayed him into committing his most notorious blunder; for the reason that the magnitude of a fire does not seem to diminish with distance as does that of concrete objects he declared the sun to be no larger or only a little larger than it appears to be.[23] This ridiculous judgment calls for no comment, but it may be mentioned that Plato's belief in astral gods, however grandiose, is no more acceptable. Epicurus not only censured Plato for accepting the evidence of celestial phenomena while rejecting that of terrestrial phenomena but also condemns him as a mythologer: "Whenever a man admits one phenomenon and rejects another equally compatible with the phenomenon in question, it is manifest that he takes leave of all scientific study of nature and takes refuge in mythology." [24] Hostility to Plato was combined in this case with contempt of mythology.

Nevertheless Doctrine 23 throws light upon the working of the mind in respect of the criteria. Mental activity may be automatic or volitional. It is the automatic mind that errs; it may judge the distant tower to be round; this is the error of "opinion." The discreet observer knows the distant view to be deceptive and suspends judgment until the tower is observed at close hand. A tentative judgment is then confirmed or disproved.[25] In the case of the size of the sun, which is visible but never at close hand, the judgment held good, as Epicurus believed, because not contradicted.

The sensations are consistently regarded as witnesses in court.[26] Their evidence may be false, as in the case of the oar half-immersed in the water, which appears to be bent. False evidence is to be corrected by that of other sensations. The evidence of all witnesses must receive attention. The volitional mind, as opposed to the automatic mind, which errs, functions as judge.

By way of concluding this account of the Sensations as criteria it is well to present a synoptic view of the evidence. Nowhere in our extant Little Epitome or the Authorized Doctrines do we find the statement "that all sensations are true." On the contrary, the Epitome begins by urging the student "to give heed to the sensations under all circumstances and especially the immediate perceptions whether of the intelligence or of any criterion whatsoever," which manifestly allows some value to all sensations and special value to immediate sensations.[27] At the end of the Epitome the student is warned to check his own observations by those of others.[28] These authentic statements are incompatible with belief in the infallibility of sensation. They presume belief in gradations of value among sensations and also the need of perpetual caution against error.

Of three Authorized Doctrines devoted to the topic, 23, 24, and 25, the first urges attention to "all the clear evidence"; the second warns that the rejection of all the sensations leaves the observer without the means of checking sensation by sensation; the third warns of the confusion resulting from rejecting any particular sensation. All of these are of the nature of warnings and completely belie the reckless verdict of an otherwise meticulous scholar "that the Epicureans boldly said that every impression of sense is true and trustworthy." [29]

Lastly, in every instance above mentioned the word for sensation is *aisthesis* and not *phantasia*. That somewhere Epicurus had actually written "all phantasias are true" seems certain; in which of his writings it is unknown, but the evidence is sufficient.[30] This statement, as being assailable, was pounced upon by his detractors and zealously ventilated. If, however, the extant texts of Epicurus be taken as a guide, the phantasia or "fantastic" perception is merely the highest grade of evidence; the *aisthesis*, the perception of particulars, is the criterion.

ANTICIPATIONS

The second criterion of truth is the Prolepsis or Anticipation, such as the innate sense of justice. Between Sensation and Anticipation there is an obvious bridge of connection. The innate capacity to distinguish colors is an anticipation of experience no less than the innate capacity to distinguish between justice and injustice. The difference is that the color-sense is part of the individual's preconditioning for life in his physical environment and emerges in early childhood, while the sense of justice is part of the preconditioning for life in the social environment and emerges later, developing in pace with experience, instruction, and reflection. How the Anticipation functions as a criterion may be seen in the case of the gods: it is impossible to think of them as in need of anything, for example, because according to the idea universal among men their happiness is perfect.

Unfortunately the traditional accounts of the Anticipations have gone far astray. Three excellent reasons can be cited for these aberrations: first, in the graded textbooks of Epicurus the topic was reserved for advanced students and entirely omitted from both the Little and the Big Epitome; consequently Lucretius has no help to offer; second, already in antiquity the concepts of such abstract things as justice had become confused with the general concepts of such concrete things as horses and oxen; third, modern scholars have become victims of the confusion of the ancients and on their own account have committed the error of merging the Anticipations with the Sensations.

It is highly probable that Epicurus allowed even to certain animals, especially elephants, the possession of these embryonic anticipations of social virtues. The tendency of the day was to have recourse to the study of irrational creatures in order to learn the teachings of Nature. It should be recalled too that not only was Epicurus very eager to have information of Pyrrho, who had been in India, but also that the writings of Alexander's associates, Aristobulus, Nearchus, and Onesicritus concerning India were available in his youth, and the same is true of the description of India by Megasthenes of the time of Seleucus. The elder Pliny, who quotes three of the above writers, ascribed to elephants "a sort of divination of justice," [31] an excellent equivalent of the Epicurean Anticipation. Pliny also ascribes to elephants the possession of pride, honesty, prudence, equity, and even religion.[32] All of these fall squarely into the category of abstract notions, where the Anticipations belong.

The term *prolepsis* was correctly rendered by Cicero as *anticipatio* or *praenotio* [33] and less precisely, though intelligently, by the elder Pliny as *divinatio*. It is wrongly rendered as "concept" by those who confuse the general concept of such a thing as an ox with the abstract idea of justice. One scholar prefers "preconception," but perhaps "preconcept" would be preferable. It seems most advantageous, however, to adhere to "Anticipation" because this is the meaning of the Greek word *prolepsis*.

143

Two explicit accounts of the term have fortunately survived from antiquity, the first from Cicero and the second from Diogenes Laertius. Unfortunately there is virtual unanimity among modern scholars that the authority of Cicero is to be rejected and that of Laertius accepted. This would mean that the word of a stodgy compiler weighs more with us than that of the gifted Cicero. It means also that we, who possess about seventy pages of the text of Epicurus, are in a better position to form a judgment than Cicero himself, who knew all the outstanding Epicureans of his time, whether Greek or Roman, and enjoyed access to all the original texts.

THE ACCOUNT OF LAERTIUS

The account of Laertius would not deserve more than brief mention were it not approved by eminent scholars. It is a hodgepodge of Epicurean and Stoic terminology and doctrine. The essential part of the text may be rendered as follows: "By a prolepsis they mean, so to say, an apprehension or right opinion or notion or general idea stored away in the mind, that is, a recollection of something that has often been presented from without." [34] In his exposition he mentions general concepts of a man, a horse, or an ox.

The objections to this are both numerous and cogent. In the first place, the statement is false to the facts. General concepts are formed instantly, as is well known.[35] A little child who has only once seen an elephant will be able to recognize an elephant under any circumstances. In the second place, we know from Epicurus himself that the term *prolepsis* was applied to the concept of the divine nature.[36] Does it not follow, then, if the general concept of a horse is the result of having seen many horses, that the concept of the divine nature must be the result of having seen many gods? This is absurd.

Again, we learn from the text of Epicurus himself that the term *prolepsis* applies to the general concept of justice.[37] If, then, the definition of Laertius be adopted, it follows that the general concepts of such brute things as horses and oxen are to be placed in the same logical category with that of justice.

The following objections may also occur to the mind of the reader: if the formation of the general concept ensues upon acts of sensation, then all elements of anticipation are removed; again, if it is formed as the residuum of acts of sensation, this is a sort of inductive process and no result of a rational process can itself be a primary criterion of truth, which Epicurus declared the prolepsis to be; still again, if the general concept is the sum of a series of sensations, then the prolepsis is merged with sensation, and the second criterion of Epicurus disappears. This, in turn, would mean that Epicurus possessed no criterion of truth on the abstract levels of thought. Such a conclusion is hardly to be tolerated.

THE ELEMENT OF ANTICIPATION

The core of the problem is to be recognized in the element of anticipation. It is positively stated by Cicero that the use of the term *prolepsis* was an innovation on the part of Epicurus.[38] It is agreed that this term *prolepsis* also denotes some sort of concept or idea. No one denies that its proper signification is "anticipation." Therefore, if an idea precedes or anticipates something, this can hardly be anything but experience. The said idea must therefore be innate. Quite correctly, therefore, Cicero wrote with studied precision when reporting on the gods of Epicurus,[39] "implanted or rather inborn conceptions of them." Nevertheless it has been deemed unnecessary to believe that Epicurus held such an opinion and it is even declared that "the notion of 'innate ideas' would be wholly repugnant to Epicureanism." [40] Yet there is compelling evidence for believing the precise opposite, that he thought of all infant behavior as anticipatory of later experience.

Let the faithful Lucretius be called to the witness stand. Among his more striking and better remembered passages is one that emphasizes the proleptic or anticipatory behavior of all living creatures, including animals.[41] Their first gestures anticipate the activities of their adult state. Children point with the finger before they can talk. Calves butt before they have horns. The cubs of lions and panthers fight with tooth and claw almost before they have teeth and claws. Young birds go through the motions of flying before their wings are fit for flight. Obviously all living things are preconditioned for life in their terrestrial environment. Is it, then, inconsistent with this observed fact to assume that human beings are preconditioned for life in their social environment?

Let Epicurus himself be allowed to testify. Basic to his hedonism is the observed fact that all living creatures, brute or human, however young and helpless, reach out for pleasure and shrink from pain. Even before the five senses have begun to perform their parts, long before the dawn of conscious motivation, and long before the development of understanding, pleasure seems to be a good and pain an evil thing.[42] This initial behavior, like the subsequent gestures of play, is at one and the same time prompted by inborn propensities and anticipatory of adult experience. In the growth of the living being and the unfolding of the faculties the attention of Epicurus is manifestly focused upon this principle, the priority of Nature over reason.

Another aspect of this priority is the speed of learning, especially as displayed by gifted children. This topic had received attention before the time of Epicurus. Plato, who believed in the immortality of the soul and in its transmigrations, expressed his judgment of it by the term *anamnesis*, or "recollection." To him the process of learning was one of reviving prenatal memories, while the function of dialectic was to bring this dimly remembered knowledge once more to consciousness.[43] Epicurus, on the contrary, since he denied both the pre-existence and the survival of the soul, found his explanation in the preconditioning of man by Nature for life in the prospective environment. His word for this phenomenon, Prolepsis or Anticipation, is thus the philosophical antonym of Plato's *anamnesis* or recollection, and so far is it from being true that "the notion of 'innate ideas' would be wholly repugnant to Epicureanism" that it is part of the marrow of his doctrine. His materialism, on this point, is idealistic Platonism in reverse.

EVIDENCES FROM SPECIFIC CONTEXT

In the extant texts of Epicurus the term *prolepsis* occurs four times in a specific context. The first has reference to the divine nature and the second and third to justice; the fourth applies to the concept of time. These are sufficient to indicate that the area of semantic reference falls in the domain of the abstract. To deny this would mean that the concepts of justice and the divine nature are on the same level with the general concepts of a horse or an ox.

The discussion of the divine nature is found in the letter to the youthful Menoeceus.[44] It is there declared "that the pronouncements of the multitude concerning the gods are not anticipations (*prolepseis*) but false assumptions." What the correct assumption is may be gleaned beyond doubt from the antecedent context: first, the divine nature is imperishable, which means that the bodies of the gods are "incorruptible"; second, the happiness of the gods is unalloyed, falling in no way

146

short of perfection. This idea of godhead is styled a *noesis koine,* a notion common to mankind, a "universal idea."

This universal idea of god is said by Epicurus "to be sketched in outline," the verb being *hypographo.* This compound word exhibits a prefix known to semanticists as "imperfective," implying that the action stops short of its utmost limit. The lexicon cites the verb as signifying "to trace letters for children to write over" or "to trace in outline, sketch out," as painters sketch figures to be filled in later with colors. Even more illuminating, however, is a usage to be found in Aristotle's *Generation of Animals,*[45] where the network of veins in the embryo is described as prefiguring the adult organism. Here is plainly discernible that element of anticipation or prolepsis which conditions the thinking of Epicurus. These innate ideas, which Cicero categorically ascribed to him, stood in the same relation to later and fuller understanding as the venous structure of the embryo to the developed organism. Incidentally, it should be again recalled that the study of biology gained sudden vogue in the interval between Plato and Epicurus.

The second and third examples of the term *prolepsis* are found in Authorized Doctrines 37 and 38; the topic is justice. Just as in the case of the divine nature, the first requisite is to discern the essential attribute or attributes. It is Nature that furnishes the norm and implants in men the embryonic notion or prolepsis of justice in advance of all experience. Hence it is called "the justice of Nature," as in Doctrine 31: "The justice of Nature is a covenant of advantage to the end that men shall not injure one another nor be injured." Setting aside the idea of the covenant, which is a separate topic, it will be noted that the essential requirement of justice is to protect citizens against injury. Thus "safety" becomes a catchword of Epicureanism. Since the laws are the instruments of justice, it is they that must be tested by this criterion. Like other observers of his time, Epicurus was aware of the diversity of laws from age to age, from city to city and race to race. If a given law serves to protect the individual, it is just; if after a time it ceases to perform this function, it loses the attribute of justice. This is the gist of Doctrines 36, 37, and 38.

The fourth occurrence of *prolepsis,* although negative in its bearing, is particularly illuminating. It deals with the nature of time. The prolepsis, as has been indicated, reveals the attributes of a thing at their minimum definition. Therefore, Epicurus virtually says that a prolepsis of time is a contradiction in terms, since time has no attributes. His finding is that time is "an accident of accidents," and, if his reasoning be closely scrutinized, time seems to be even less than this.[46] The line of reasoning may be sketched as follows: a human being is susceptible of sickness but sickness is not a permanent attribute, only a temporary condition, that is, an accident. Sickness in its turn may be long or short, but this quality of length or brevity is not a permanent attribute but an accident. Therefore it is an accident of an accident. Next, by analogy, since we associate time with states of health or sickness, the time of their duration is said to be long or short. Thus long and short become predicates of time while in reality they apply only to states of health or sickness. This amounts to saying that in the phrases "a long time" or "a short time" the adjectives are transferred epithets.

Incidentally, in the text of Epicurus this paragraph on the topic of time follows immediately upon the discussion of attributes and accidents. This juxtaposition confirms the assumption that the prolepsis is rightly interpreted as an anticipatory notion of the essential attributes of the subject of examination.

LATER EVIDENCES

The word *prolepsis,* once launched by Epicurus as a technical term, was taken over by the Stoics,[47] who cribbed freely from the sect they vilified. It still enjoyed vogue in Cicero's time but the sharp edges of the original idea had suffered detrition through careless handling. The Stoics had developed the study of formal logic and one ingredient of this was the general concept. This denotes the essential attributes of the subject under examination and, if the thinker be not too meticulous about his categories, it is permissible to speak of the general concept of either justice or an ox. Then by a familiar type of semantic shift it became possible to speak of "the prolepsis of an ox," just as people call a lighting fixture a chandelier even if candles have been replaced by gas or electricity. As Epicurus employed the term, however, it was no more possible to have a prolepsis of an ox than of a duck-billed platypus or a caterpillar tractor; the pre-existence of the idea in advance of the experience was essential.

Even within Epicurean circles the term *prolepsis* underwent unjustified extensions. For instance, Epicurus, recognizing Nature as the canon or norm, had asserted that, just as we observe fire to be hot, snow to be cold, and honey to be sweet, so, from the behavior of newborn creatures,

we observe pleasure to be the telos or end. Certain of his followers, however, shaken no doubt by Stoic criticism, took the position that the
doctrine was an innate idea, that is, a prolepsis.[48] In strict logic this
error was a confusion between *quid* and *quale.* The problem was not
to decide what could be predicated of the end or telos but what was
the identity of the end. Was it pleasure or was it something else?

Several examples of the word *prolepsis* occur in the writings of Philodemus, all of them falling in the domain of the abstract.[49] One of these
is worthy of special mention. It is found in the essay entitled *On the
Management of an Estate.* Other writers are there criticized for not
describing the good manager in conformity with a prolepsis; they concern themselves instead with popular ideas on the subject and then
endeavor to hitch the resulting description to the wise man. What they
ought to do is to ask themselves what kind of business and what size of
business and what sort of management are compatible with a philosophic
life and intellectual companionship.[50] This may be a sound procedure
to follow in writing an essay of this kind, but it is very questionable
whether Epicurus ever thought of ascribing to the human being an
innate idea of what a good landlord should be.

As a technique of invention in the practice of writing, this Epicurean
doctrine of the prolepsis came to enjoy a vogue. Cicero employed it
rather charmingly. For example, in his book entitled *On Duties* he was
endeavoring to arrive at a description of the virtuous man, *vir bonus,*
a popular topic of the day.[51] The procedure is to assume that the
interlocutor already possesses a proper preconcept of the object of the
quest, folded up in the mind like the leaves in a bud, or wrapped up
in a sheet, which was an ancient method of carrying luggage. With such
assumptions in mind Cicero wrote: "Unfold your intelligence and
shake it out that you may see the shape and preconcept (prolepsis) of
the virtuous man that is found within." [52] In the same context the reader
finds the following: "But once a man has consented to unroll the preconcept that is folded up in his own mind he can readily teach himself
that the virtuous man is he who will do a good turn to whom he can
and will injure no one unless attacked." [53]

In these passages the comparison of the prolepsis to the leaves folded
in the bud or to an article of value rolled up in a parcel was probably
a refinement of Stoic teachers. It is not known from Epicurean texts and
has the appearance of a pedagogical invention. Another comparison

149

that attached itself to the concept of the prolepsis was Platonic in origin: according to this, for example, every notion of the divine nature should match the prolepsis in the mind as a foot matches its own footprint.[54] Hence Cicero, with his usual genius for adaptation, spoke of a mold or matrix resident in the mind into which the perfect orator or perfect oration should be capable of being fitted.[55]

While these refinements bear witness to the utility of the Epicurean prolepsis as a device of exposition, they are false to the original idea, which adhered to a vocabulary of its own. The practice was to speak of the prolepsis as something that could be looked to or envisaged, as a builder looks to a model. Philodemus, for instance, allows that the Epicureans agree with the multitude in what they believe to be just and honorable "according to the *prolepseis* envisaged by them," but he declares they differ from the multitude as to the actions that "square with the *prolepseis*." [56] In this he is speaking by the card; the same vocabulary, applied to the same topic, justice, is found in Authorized Doctrines 37 and 38. The comparison implicit in the Canon is that between the thinker and the builder. To the informed reader a certain analogy with Aristotle's formal cause may suggest itself; if it is a temple that the architect is building, this fact controls all his work.

Lucretius affords the student no assistance whatever. He makes no attempt to translate the word *prolepsis* either by periphrase or coinage. He might well have preceded Cicero in the use of *praenotio* and *anticipatio*, which, at least in the nominative case, would have fitted into hexameters. His *notities* translates only *ennoia* or *ennoema*. The two passages in which it is alleged to denote prolepsis exemplify an entirely different doctrine, that nonpurposive Nature is the sole creatrix. Human intelligence can only improve upon Nature's beginnings; man could not invent language before Nature had furnished a model in involuntary cries.[57] To this restriction even the gods were subject; they could not have created a universe before Nature had furnished a model.[58] It is unlikely that Lucretius even understood the workings of the Anticipations and Feelings as criteria.

FEELINGS

"The Feelings are two," wrote Laertius, "pleasure and pain, characterizing every living creature, the one being akin, the other alien, through which the decisions are made to choose or avoid." [59]

This means that pleasures and pains are Nature's Go and Stop signals on all levels of existence, that of the lower animals included. They are distinct from the Sensations by two removes: in the meaning of the Canon sensation is restricted to the sensory stimulus; it is the intelligence that registers recognition or nonrecognition; it is the Feelings that register pleasure or pain. These are accompaniments of sensation, as Aristotle observed in advance of Epicurus.[60]

The prevailing belief that Epicurus was an empiricist has led scholars to merge the Feelings with the Sensations. It is true that both may be called by the Greek word *pathe,* but this coincidence of predicate is offset by logical absurdities. Since the Sensations are confined to the five senses, the merging of the Feelings with the Sensations would exclude fears and hopes and all the higher emotions. Again, since Epicurus reduces all sensation to touch, the merging of the Feelings would confine these also to touch. Still again, according to Epicurus the higher emotions, which are included in the Feelings, have a different seat from the Sensations, deep in the breast.[61] How then could they be one with the Sensations? Lastly, unless the Feelings are something distinct from both Sensations and Anticipations, Epicurus would lack a criterion on the level of the higher emotions, where the issue of happiness and unhappiness is ultimately decided.

It would also be obligatory, should the Feelings be merged with the Sensations, to ignore all gradations in pleasures, which Epicurus did not. Like Plato and Aristotle, he recognized the existence of higher and lower pleasures and he employed the same terminology. The pleasures of the flesh are denoted by the noun *hedone* and the verb *hedomai,* the higher pleasures by the noun *euphrosune* and the verg *euphrainomai.* For instance, it is the latter verb he employs when he speaks of the "higher enjoyment" experienced by the wise man in attendance upon public spectacles and also when he speaks of the "serene joy" with which the wise man approaches the end of life.[62] He has still another synonym to employ, *chara,* when he denies that unlimited wealth can bring any "worthwhile happiness," [63] and he uses the same word of that "peak of happiness" that comes of the confident expectation of health of body and peace of mind.[64] These are Feelings but not Sensations in the meaning of the Canon.

It is true, of course, that Epicurus sponsored a doctrine of the unity of all pleasures on the ground that body and soul are coterminous and cosensitive and both corporeal,[65] but this does not mean that the pleasures and pains of the flesh are on a level with the pleasures and pains of the mind. In the meaning of the Canon there are two classes of Feelings, the one class accompanying the activity of the senses, the other accompanying the social and intellectual activities of the individual and specifically located in the breast.[66] Neither class of Feelings is identical with Sensations.

The Feelings operate as criteria on all levels of life, somatic, social, and, if a term may be borrowed from religion to denote the higher emotions, spiritual.

On the somatic level the cub of the wolf no less than the child must learn by trial and error to choose the pleasant and avoid the painful. As the child begins to participate in the life of the family and society the usefulness of lessons learned from burns and bruises shrinks in importance as compared with the edifying approval and disapproval of parents, elders, and teachers.

This sequence of experience was aptly condensed by Epicurus into an oracular statement: "Pleasure is the beginning and the end of the happy life." [67] By this he meant that pleasure was both the starting point and the goal. The approach was genetic. On the level of infancy activity is merely instinctive; there is as yet no intelligence to take cognizance of sensation. On the level of adolescence the young man is apt to exult in his strength and drift at the mercy of chance.[68] On the level of maturity, however, if wisdom is attained, pleasure, that is happiness, becomes a conscious objective and also an incentive. In other words, pleasure or happiness becomes the telos or end and thus on this last level the telos itself becomes a criterion, by which the decision is made to choose or to avoid.

This recognition of the telos as attaining the rank of a criterion on the level of the mature man was deemed by Epicurus of sufficient importance to be included in the Authorized Doctrines, No. 22: "We must take into our reckoning the established telos and all manifest evidence, to which we refer our judgments; otherwise all life will be filled with indecision and unrest." This pronouncement was directed against the Platonists, who, as astronomers, were bound to place dependence upon celestial phenomena and, as accepting the theory of the ideas, were bound to distrust terrestrial phenomena. Hence Epicurus insists upon taking into account "all the manifest evidence," terrestrial as well as celestial. If the latter alone is studied, there will be an increase of wonderment and an end to peace of mind.[69] He also insists that the sole reason for studying the heavenly bodies is "peace of mind and an abiding faith." [70] Thus the telos, happiness, becomes the criterion.

It is chiefly with reference to the gods and death that the Feelings operate as criteria, as may be inferred from the first two of the Authorized Doctrines. If the individual is rendered miserable by the fear of death and of the possible punishment after death, this misery is a Feeling in the meaning of the Canon and a sure evidence of "false opinion." He must habituate himself to the thought "that death is nothing to us," that death is incidental to life, and that "the fulness of pleasure" may be attained within the narrow limits of mortal life.

The case is similar with respect to the gods. If the individual is rendered miserable through fear of the gods, if he feels that he must perform sacrifices to avert their hostility and win their favor, if he feels that at every mischance he must consult a soothsayer to discover which god must be appeased, this is Feeling in the meaning of the Canon.[71] He must learn to believe "that the blessed and incorruptible being is neither susceptible of trouble itself nor occasions it to another."

The Feelings operate as criteria also in the sphere of justice and injustice. The Pauline doctrine "The power of sin is the law" is straight Epicureanism. Among sayings of Epicurus covering the point is the following, Authorized Doctrine 34: "Wrong-doing is not an evil in and by itself; the evil lies in the uneasy feeling, amounting to fear, that he will not escape detection by those appointed for the punishment of such offenses." [72] This fear is a Feeling in the meaning of the Canon; it differs from the child's fear of the fire only by being operative on a higher level of understanding. Adverse criticism of such utilitarian teaching was inevitable.[73] On the side of Epicurus it may be said that, while arguing within the scheme of his premises, he was also discerning the dependence of happiness upon a clear conscience. The concept of conscience, slow to crystallize, is here seen in the nascent state.

The Feelings also serve as a criterion in the choice of a proper attitude or diathesis toward competitive careers. For instance, Diogenes of Oenoanda points out "that the career of the orator allows a man no rest and fills him with anxiety for the success of his plea." [74] The extant sayings of Epicurus himself abound in references to the deceitfulness of the quest for riches, power, or fame.[75] On this level the telos and the Feelings coincide as criteria of choice. The individual must bear in mind that the goal of living is happiness and submit every decision to the test of the Feelings that will ensue upon that decision. As Epicurus himself expressed it: "What will be the result for me if the object of the desire is attained and what if it is not attained?" [76]

As a criterion the Feelings may take precedence over reason. Plato, for example, argued endlessly about the meaning of "good." Epicurus scorned this dialectic and arrived at a simple solution. His line of attack is as follows: the greatest good must be associated with the greatest pleasure. This greatest pleasure is easily identified: "What causes the unsurpassable joy is the bare escape from some terrible calamity." [77] This joy arises from the saving of life, the escape from shipwreck, for instance. Therefore life itself is the greatest good. To think of pleasure as the greatest good is an error; pleasure is the telos and is not to be confused with the greatest good. The testimony of the Feeling functioning as a criterion is decisive. More will be said of this in the chapter on the New Hedonism.

CHAPTER IX ✛ THE NEW PHYSICS

IN THE Epicurean scheme of knowledge the Physics takes precedence over the Ethics because it furnishes the major premises from which the nature of the soul is deduced and the proper conduct of life is formulated. The Sensations, Anticipations, and Feelings, that is, the Canon, are not represented as furnishing the content of knowledge but as being instruments of precision by which the certainty of knowledge is tested at all times.

The topic of physics was given encyclopedic treatment in the famous thirty-seven books entitled *On Nature*, which Lucretius rendered *De Rerum Natura*, "On the Nature of Things." By implication this title signified "the true nature of things," because Epicurus styled his system "genuine physiology," plainly indicating that all other systems were false.[1] Consistently with this assumption Lucretius incessantly employed the phrase *vera ratio*, "true reason." Similarly Lucian speaks of "the truth and the philosophy that is invariably right," [2] referring to Epicureanism, and his friend Celsus published his slashing attack upon Christianity under the caption *alethes logos*, which is usually rendered "true account," but its equivalence to the Epicurean "true philosophy" ought to be manifest. It implies that Christianity is a body of false doctrine.

For the use of younger pupils the contents of these thirty-seven books on physics were subsequently reduced to a single roll. This bore a title which means "the twelve simplifications" or "the twelve principles reduced to elementary form." [3] A single mention of this has survived, but the twelve principles themselves may be readily assembled from the first two books of Lucretius and the extant Little Epitome addressed to Herodotus. These two accounts are in essential agreement in respect of both content and arrangement. The chief difference is that the Little Epitome omits mention of the doctrine of the swerve of the atoms, manifestly for the reason that in the judgment of Epicurus this principle was a topic more suitable for the advanced student.

EPICURUS AND HIS PHILOSOPHY

In this book the title of the epitome of Physics is being rendered the Twelve Elementary Principles. The greater interest attaches to this lost work because its importance has been overlooked down to the present time; the very title of it suggests a more orderly and coherent statement of the principles of physics than is elsewhere known to us from classical antiquity. It calls attention to the talents of Epicurus as a teacher and an organizer of knowledge and ought to be somewhat disconcerting to those who dismiss him as a muddled thinker. It also deserves attention from those who call him an empiricist, because these principles are treated as major premises from which the rest of knowledge is derived by deductive reasoning.

Before listing these Twelve Principles it will be well to recall that Epicurus was averse to the use of technical terminology and declared clearness the sole requisite of style. As a substitute for technical terms he resorted often to the use of synonyms and paraphrases as a means of attaining the desired clearness. To illustrate, in the foreword to the Little Epitome, as a preparation for the tabulation of the Twelve Principles he refers to them in seven different ways: the most comprehensive doctrines; the outline of the whole system; the panoramic view; the most commanding view over the universe of things; the most general outlines; truths condensed to elements and succinct statements; the condensed view of the integrated survey of the whole.

THE TWELVE ELEMENTARY PRINCIPLES

The arrangement of the principles is orderly and easily discerned. The first six tell us what can be predicated of the universe, the next four deal with motion, and the rest with the qualities of matter, whether in the form of atoms or compounds of atoms. It is worthy of notice that space is called void as something self-existent and that time is not mentioned; discussion of the latter is found later as a rider to the third principle. In the ensuing list the items have been simplified in the direction of modern terminology:

1. Matter is uncreatable.
2. Matter is indestructible.
3. The universe consists of solid bodies and void.
4. Solid bodies are either compounds or simple.
5. The multitude of atoms is infinite.
6. The void is infinite in extent.

7. The atoms are always in motion.

8. The speed of atomic motion is uniform.

9. Motion is linear in space, vibratory in compounds.

10. Atoms are capable of swerving slightly at any point in space or time.

11. Atoms are characterized by three qualities, weight, shape and size.

12. The number of the different shapes is not infinite, merely innumerable.

The first two principles deal with the indestructibility and uncreatability of matter. If the question be raised how the truth of these propositions is established, the answer is by deduction. It must be observed that Epicurus makes no show of his logical procedures and, like the layman, employs the enthymeme or elliptical syllogism. Nevertheless, if his omissions be discerned and then supplied, the procedure is as follows. The purpose is to demonstrate the uncreatability of matter. Let it then be assumed for the purpose of the argument that the reverse is true: Matter is creatable. This assumption becomes the major premise and the method becomes deductive. The deductions would be that there would be no need of seeds of plants, no limits of size, no geographical distribution, no part for the seasons to play, and no necessity for fish to be born in the sea nor animals on the land.[4] These inferences are all contrary to observed phenomena. Therefore, the assumption is false and the contrary must be true: Matter is uncreatable.

Again, let us assume that matter is destructible and that material things can be reduced to nothingness. Why, then, should they not vanish before our eyes instead of weakening and declining and decaying as we actually see them do? Again, whence would come the substance of the fruits that the earth produces, the waters that feed the springs and the rivers, or the fuel that feeds the stars? To such questions the only true answer can be that the death of one thing is the birth of another. The turnover of material is perpetual in nature. Otherwise all things in the long lapse of time would have passed into nothingness.[5] It then follows, as in the previous instance, that the assumption of the major premise is false. Therefore the contrary is true: Matter is indestructible. It is not to the point to inquire here whether this logical method is sound in this particular application. The point is that the method should be recognized as deductive, not inductive.

WHAT CONSTITUTES THE UNIVERSE

The problem of what constitutes the universe is dispatched by Epicurus with extreme brevity. The universe consists of solid bodies and void. That the former exist the evidence of sensation alone is sufficient proof; in the case of bodies too small to be perceived by the senses recourse must be had to reasoning by analogy from the visible to the invisible. As for space or void, if it did not exist, then solid bodies would have no place in which to rest nor room in which to move, as they manifestly do move. Epicurus does not think it worth while that beginners should be told of the Eleatic philosophers, who held different views.

If at this point the student chose to consult the Big Epitome as represented by Lucretius, he would find a slight difference of order and more detail. Lucretius employs the method of reasoning from the visible to the invisible by such examples as the wind, odors, heat, cold, moisture, the invisible detrition of finger-rings and statues and the phenomena of growth. This reasoning is meant to prove the existence of atoms. As for void, he points to the porosity of rocks, which is proved by their absorption of water. Again, the difference of weight between equal volumes of wool and lead is to be explained by the presence and absence of void among the respective particles.[6]

Only after presenting these reasons for believing that atoms and void exist does Lucretius turn to the general principle that the universe consists of solid bodies and void. If we assume, he reasons, the existence of a third something, then this will be either tangible or intangible.[7] If it be tangible, however small, it will be an addition to the sum of matter; if, on the other hand, it be intangible and offer no resistance to a moving body, then it will belong to the category of void. The assumption is therefore false and the original statement holds true, that the universe consists of solid bodies and void. Precisely as before, the argument is deliberately thrown into the form of a deductive syllogism, in this instance of the disjunctive type, and the existence of anything other than atoms and void is excluded.

These examples will suffice to show that the Twelve Principles are treated as theorems to be demonstrated and that the logical procedure is not inductive or empirical. The fourth principle, however, that solid bodies are either compounds or simple, deserves mention both for its intrinsic importance and for the light it throws on the use of the epitome. In the Little Epitome it is briefly asserted that, if matter is not going to be annihilated, there must be ultimate bodies which are indivisible, unchangeable, and capable of surviving when compound bodies are broken up; they must be solid, that is, have no void in them. If the student desires further information, he is referred to the Big Epitome or the fourteenth and fifteenth of the books on Physics.[8]

It need hardly be added that the word *atom* means "indivisible" and is neuter or feminine, the nouns *stocheion*, "element," or *physis*, "existence," being supplied as the case requires; Epicurus does not himself use *ousia*, "existence" of the atom.

ATTRIBUTES AND ACCIDENTS

When once this principle has been laid down, that the universe consists of atoms and void, the next logical step is to elicit the negative implications. If the universe consists of solid bodies and void, then nothing else, by inference, can exist. Hence the discussion of qualities called attributes or accidents is properly introduced as a rider or corollary to the above principle.

That this arrangement was followed in the Big Epitome and the thirty-seven books need not be doubted. In the Little Epitome, however, the topic is introduced after the description of the soul. This order too is logical, because Epicurus had there designated the phenomena of volition and sensation as accidents of the human organism.[9] Of this startling doctrine some explanation was immediately necessary for the benefit of young disciples.

This second arrangement has its merits also today, because scholars have been attributing spontaneity not to the organism but to the atoms themselves and have thought of hylozoism as a doctrine of Epicurus, which would identify life with matter.[10] These fancies are plainly inconsistent with the teaching of both Epicurus and Lucretius, as will be shown in the chapter on the Soul, Sensation, and Thought.

The account of attributes and accidents given by Epicurus is perspicuous. He states that a given object receives a predicate of designation by virtue of a combination of particular qualities reported by the senses.[11] Some of these qualities are always present in the case of a given object; these are attributes. Others may or may not be present; these are accidents. In the Little Epitome space is saved by the omission of examples. In the Big Epitome, represented by Lucretius, weight is cited as an attribute of rocks, heat of fire, and fluidity of water.[12] Lucretius also defines an attribute, *coniunctum,* as a quality inseparable from an object without its destruction; an accident, *eventum,* is a quality of which the presence or absence is a matter of indifference.[13]

The confident dogmatism with which Epicurus sets forth his doctrine and the space he allows it in the Little Epitome is sure evidence that his immediate purpose was to immunize the minds of disciples against false doctrines.[14] For example, it is declared that attributes are not incorporeal existences, a statement designed to fortify the student against Platonism and its theory of eternal, incorporeal ideas. Again, attributes are denied to be corporeal existences, even if they are apprehensible by sensation; this was designed to immunize the student against certain teachings of Theophrastus, who thought colors corporeal.[15] Of color the Little Epitome gives no further explanation but Lucretius makes plain that it arises from combinations of atoms, which are themselves colorless.[16] As often, this teaching was close to the truth.

GRADATIONS IN THE ATOMS

Having assumed the existence of subsensible, immutable, and indivisible bodies as the ultimate existences the next step was to elucidate the description of them. At the outset it might be assumed that they were all alike or that differences existed. If they should be assumed to be all alike it would be impossible to account for the great variety of qualities exhibited by compound bodies. Therefore it must be concluded that differences exist. For example, they must differ in size. Again, once differences of size have been assumed, the question arises whether the differences in this regard are infinite or finite. If it should be assumed that the differences are infinite in number, then in the gradation downward from larger to smaller the ultimate limit would be zero,[17] which is equivalent to annihilation. If, on the contrary, in the gradation upward from smaller to larger the differences should be assumed to be infinite, visible magnitudes would be reached, which does not occur, and it is impossible to conceive of it occurring.[18] Therefore the differences must be finite in number, falling well short of zero at the one end of the series and well short of visibility at the other. Even between these extremes it is possible that the differences, if not infinite, should at least be innumerable, and such is the doctrine enunciated.[19]

This conclusion once reached, that the differences of size are merely innumerable, another question arises, whether the number of atoms of a given size is infinite or finite. The answer to this is easy: if the number should be finite, then the supply of atoms of any given shape might readily be exhausted in the formation of compounds, which is inconceivable in an infinite universe.[20] Therefore the number of atoms of each particular size must be infinite.

This same reasoning applies to every kind of atom regardless of the particular quality in which it differs from other kinds, smoothness, roughness, rotundity, angularity, hookedness, or any other quality compatible with weight, shape, and size. Thus the sum of matter in the infinite universe of Epicurus is the sum of innumerable infinite classes of atoms.

With respect to the doctrines here expounded it should be noted that nowhere does Epicurus employ a term corresponding to the word *gradation*. This concept of gradations is one that perhaps never clarified itself in the Greek mind. Yet the idea is subsumed and is of great importance. In his account of the natural creative process Epicurus assumed an ascending series of living things, namely, grasses, plants, shrubs, trees, the lower animals, the higher animals, man, and gods.[21] Corresponding to this gradation is the gradation of the component atoms in the several classes. It may be mentioned here, although the topic belongs in subsequent chapters, that the atoms of the human soul, themselves graded according to the various faculties, are represented as being of finer grades than those of the flesh and bones, while the atoms of which the divine bodies are composed belong to still finer grades than those of the human soul. Thus the recognition of this subsumed principle of gradation in atoms will be of practical assistance in understanding both the psychology and the theology of Epicurus.

MICROMETRY OF THE ATOM

The concluding paragraph on the topic of the atom in the Little Epitome deals with micrometry, if this is not too high a compliment. At the same time it affords us the most unmistakable specimen extant of the method of reasoning by analogy from the seen to the unseen. The drift of it is as follows: [22] In the world of sense we have visible and mensurable magnitudes. Descending one scale lower, we have magnitudes visible but not mensurable, such as grains of dust. Of these we can only say "bigger" of the bigger ones and "smaller" of the smaller ones. Descending another step lower in the scale, we have magnitudes neither visible nor mensurable; these are the atoms. In this last step we are merely extending a long way the meaning of the term *small*.[23] The same reasoning holds, however, and we may still say that some are bigger and some smaller. The visible minima have furnished a standard of measurement for the invisible. Here the analogy ends because, though a heap of dust is possible, "a heap of atoms endowed with motion is an impossibility." [24]

MOTION

Of the Twelve Principles four, Nos. 7 to 10, deal with the topic of motion. Epicurus distinguishes clearly between the motions of atoms through the void and the motions of solid bodies under terrestrial conditions. In the latter he points out the presence of acceleration and retardation while denying the same for atoms or visual images moving through the void.[25] The motions of atoms themselves are of two kinds, being linear in the void and vibratory in compound bodies. He also deals specifically and sensibly with combinations of motions; for example, the atoms in a compound body maintain their vibratory motion at the same time that they share the linear motion of the body in which they are contained.[26] In the Little Epitome are also found warnings, without mention of names, of course, against the view of Aristotle that the universe has a top and a bottom; against his criticism of Democritus on the ground that "up" and "down" could have no meaning in an infinite universe; and against Plato's assertion that "up" and "down" could have no meaning in a spherical universe.[27]

At the same time in common with his countrymen he exhibited no disposition to measure motion by defined standards. In the case of high velocities, such as the speed of atoms, this is readily forgiven, because the ancients knew no constant or absolute standard such as the speed of light. In the case of low velocities this deficiency is less pardonable. The Greeks possessed very serviceable linear measures and they also had water clocks, which were capable of achieving at least a moderate degree of precision, but it never seems to have occurred to them that the speed even of a runner could be timed. Thus they never knew, for example, whether the time of a given Olympian race was faster than that of another. Only the names of the winners from year to year went on record.

Lacking a unit for the denotation of extremely high velocity, Epicurus describes it as follows: "Furthermore, motion through the void, so long as no interference arises from conflicting bodies, accomplishes any conceivable distance in a space of time inconceivably brief." [28] Elsewhere he also writes: "For over whatever distance it [an object] holds to either motion [for every motion he assumes there is a motion in an opposite direction], over that distance it will maintain its speed, quick as thought." [29] What he meant by "quick as thought" may readily be surmised. He must have observed, first of all, the extraordinary speed of reaction in the automatic mind, which guards the safety of the individual during his daily rounds. To the ancients the chief hazards seem to have been carts, dogs, ditches, and precipices. We should think rather of the perils of motorized traffic.

At this point it is timely to clarify a detail of terminology. When discussing the vibratory motion of atoms, Epicurus speaks of "intervals of time discernible only by reason." [30] Unfortunately, the modern reader is prone to read into this word *reason* some implication of rational process. This is an error. The word for reason, *logos,* is among the most ragged and ill-defined of all the Greek symbols of thought, and to Epicurus it sometimes signifies only what we call "imagination."

LINEAR AND VIBRATORY MOTION

The primary and original motion of atoms is declared to be straight downward owing to weight. This motion is consequently rectilinear. While a slight deviation may occur, as will be mentioned presently, this deviation is assumed to be insufficient to require speaking of curvilinear motion. Moreover since Epicurus, like the rest of the ancients, lacked any precise concept of force as apart from motion, he could have no concept of fields of force and thus was bound to find other explanations for the curvilinear motions of the heavenly bodies.[31] It is thus correct to think of the motions of his atoms as rectilinear. Oblique motions in all directions, including perpendicular motion upward, were thought to arise through successive collisions and to take place at the same velocity as the original motion downward owing to weight. Because of the solidity of the atoms the speed of the rebound was declared to be equal to the speed of impact. Thus all atomic motion, like the speed of light in modern physics, was at a uniform velocity, without acceleration or retardation.

As an item of interest, it may be mentioned that in claiming equal velocity for all atoms in the void, irrespective of weight, he did better than Aristotle, who believed the heavier body to fall more quickly than the light.[32] He also reasons intelligently in answering the captious objection that one atom will travel faster than another because atoms share the motion of the object of which they are parts and naturally one projectile will travel faster than another. His reply, in effect, is this: "Quite true, but this is linear motion, and even if the motion is linear during the minimum of time during which it is visible, it does not follow that during intervals of time conceivable only by the imagination atomic motion is linear. Even while the motion of the compound body is under observation the vibratory motion of the atoms continues." [33]

The vibratory motion of the atoms was of greater importance for the philosophy of Epicurus; he chose to take little interest in the motions of the heavenly bodies and to concentrate his attention upon terrestrial matters. In particular he needed a vital force to account for life in the organic world. It was the assumption of vibratory motion that met this need. As usual, his argument is syncopated but it is plain. Weight is a permanent attribute of atoms; it is the cause of motion; since weight cannot be separated from atoms, neither can motion. If linear motion becomes impossible, then vibratory motion must take its place. On this point he approximated to the view of the modern scientist and was in total opposition to Plato and Aristotle, who assumed matter to be inert.

The covering principle for this doctrine is the seventh in the list: "The atoms are always in motion." The assumption of vibratory motion, which this involves, made necessary in its turn the assumption that such varieties of atoms existed as would account for the said motion. Certain atoms must exist, for example, as would engage themselves laterally and form a sort of close chain-mail over the surface of a body. The envelope so formed was thought to function as a container within which other imprisoned atoms would ceaselessly vibrate. In the case of animate beings this theory of the envelope was of supreme importance, because the atoms of the soul were thought to be especially volatile and capable of escaping quickly unless closely confined. Incidentally, it was this conceit that led to the habit of looking upon the body as a vessel, which merged itself with a metaphor native to Hebrew thought and is many times found in the New Testament.

In the case of all bodies, whether animate or inanimate, this hypothesis of the atomic envelope was of importance for vision. While the coarser atoms within a given solid could be thought of even as fibrous (*ramosus*),[34] the surface atoms nowhere engaged themselves deeply. Consequently, on account of the pulsations caused by the internal vibrations, every solid body was thought to be incessantly discharging at inconceivable speed filmy replicas of itself in all directions, which, by impinging upon the eye of the observer caused the sensation of vision. The formation of these idols is one of the processes which Epicurus characterizes as "quick as thought," this speed being possible because the component atoms were not engaged with others at depth and thus the replacements could be synchronized with the discharges, no diminution of volume occurring.[35]

For these atoms which engage themselves only laterally Epicurus has a name, *atomoi plektikai*,[36] and the association of the verb *pleko* with wickerwork throws some light on the meaning. In contrast to these atoms stand those that are capable of engaging themselves with others on all sides, even to the extent of being fibrous (*ramosus*) in the case of very hard or tough bodies. These are said to be "locked by the enmeshment," [37] which explains itself. These also, according to Epicurus, are incessantly pulsating, their hardness ensuring the rebound following the impact, the degree of closeness of the enmeshment limiting the vibration.[38] To a modern physicist with definite concepts of energy this would suggest heat, but according to Epicurus heat itself is atomic by nature, certain shapes of atoms giving rise to the phenomenon of temperature.

SWERVE OF THE ATOMS

In addition to the linear and vibratory motions of the atoms Epicurus postulated yet a third: it was assumed that at any point in time or space they were capable of veering ever so slightly from the straight line. This is known as the swerve, *declinatio,* Greek *pareqklisis*. This was an addition to the teaching of Democritus and necessary for two reasons: first, because atoms would never have collided if the motions of all had been downward in parallel lines and consequently no compound bodies would ever have been formed;[39] second, if the atoms were assumed to be incapable of deviating to the slightest degree from a given course, their motions would all have been unalterably predetermined and all events would be part of an infinite chain of causation.[40] This infinite causation, the Necessity of the physicists, was above all things abhorrent to Epicurus and was a prime reason for his defection from the school of Democritus. More must be said on this topic in the chapter on the New Freedom.

ACCELERATION AND RETARDATION

One of the more obscure passages in the Little Epitome has occasioned much tribulation among editors; it deals with acceleration and retardation and aims to make clear the difference between atomic motion in the void and the motion of projectiles under terrestrial conditions. The key to the difficulty lies in recollection of the Epicurean rule that any proposition inconsistent with the Twelve Principles is "inconceivable." Let us apply this to the particular instance. It is uncertain just what moving body Epicurus had in mind, but it suits the context to assume that it was a meteor. The flight of this is invisible for part of its course and visible for the remainder. "How then," the critical observer may be imagined to ask, "can we be sure that its speed was not equal to that of the atoms for the first part of its flight?" [41] "The suggestion is inconceivable," Epicurus replies in effect, "because the very fact that the flight of the object at a certain point became visible is proof that retardation was taking place. The velocity of the atoms, on the contrary, is uniform at all times." [42]

In this whole passage the reader must make liberal allowance for assumptions, as in much of Greek philosophy. The word translated as "retardation" is in Greek *antikope*, "interference." [43] Acceleration is not mentioned but must be assumed. All projectiles are characterized by acceleration and retardation. The motion of the atoms, by way of contrast, has no beginning and no end; their motion in the void is continuous just as their velocity is uniform. Modern readers will again be reminded of the speed of light, which is regarded as a constant.

Epicurus also makes the smart point that "interference" and "noninterference" must not be confused with "speed" and "slowness." [44] The equation of either with the other is illusory. The velocity of the atom is not diminished by collision even if the direction of motion is changed. Again, the duration of flight from a given point to a second given point may be increased by a zigzag course but the velocity remains a constant. In this instance the modern reader may be reminded of light rays from distant stars, the velocity of which remains constant even if they are bent at a certain point by the repulsion of the sun.

166

The highly syncopated reasoning of Epicurus involves still another assumption that is worthy of mention. The motion of the atoms and the flight of a projectile differ also in this respect, that motion is inherent in the atom itself as a consequence of its weight, one of its three permanent attributes. On the contrary, the flight of a projectile arises from a force external to itself. The truth, however, that the atoms comprised in a projectile have two motions, the one being linear, collective, and usually visible, the other being vibratory and always invisible, is clearly recognized and stated elsewhere.[45]

"UP" AND "DOWN" IN AN INFINITE UNIVERSE

Epicurus in a single paragraph [46] essays to immunize the minds of his disciples against certain views propounded by Plato and by Aristotle in criticism of Democritus. The latter had postulated a primary motion downward to infinity, which signified a perpendicular universe. Plato flouted this theory on the ground that the universe was spherical, which implied that it was finite. This was equivalent to denying meaning to "up" and "down," because all points on the surface of the sphere would bear the same relationship to the center. Moreover, as he pointed out, if a man should be imagined to walk over the surface of the spherical universe, any given point would be "down" to him when standing over it and "up" to him when he arrived at the antipodal point.[47]

Aristotle, in his turn, had advanced the criticism that the downward motion postulated by Democritus would imply the existence of an absolute "up" and an absolute "down," which was meaningless in an infinite universe.[48] In modern parlance he was denying the possibility in an infinite universe of setting up any frame of reference for motion.

The paragraph of Epicurus on the topic is designed as much to immunize the minds of his readers against the views of Plato and Aristotle as to refute the same. As for the view of Aristotle that the world has a top and a bottom, he denies its validity for an infinite universe.[49] The cogency of the rest of his statement depends entirely upon the assumption of belief in an infinite number of worlds, situated above and below any given world. If his reasoning be expanded, it amounts to this: The direction from a world A to a world B above it will be "up" and the contrary direction will be "down"; this fact is not denied but significance is denied to it. Plato is tacitly accused of confusing "direction" with "motion." It is true that the same point may be "down" and "up" according to successive positions of a single observer or to simultaneous positions of two observers, but this is not true of any given motion. The conclusion then is, assuming a multiplicity of worlds: "It is possible to take the supposed motion upward to infinity as a unit and the motion downward as a unit, even if ten thousand times the body moving away from us toward the regions above our heads arrives at the feet of those above us and the motion downward from us arrives at the heads of those below us. For the whole motion in the one direction is none the less understood as being opposed to the whole motion in the other direction to infinity." This amounts to the statement of a principle: motion in an infinite universe cannot be cut into segments; it is independent of observers; for any motion to infinity in any direction there is a contrary motion to infinity in the opposite direction.

A PERPENDICULAR UNIVERSE

The principle of Epicurus that the primary motion of the atoms is straight downward owing to weight involves rather startling inferences so far as concerns the shape of his multitudinous worlds. So far as the atoms and their motions are concerned, the principle is indifferent, because, owing to the constant collisions and the consequent rebounds, the atoms are thought of as moving in every conceivable direction throughout the void. Moreover, there is no such position as upside down or downside up to an atom.

With the human being it is otherwise, for whom "up" and "down" have a constant significance. In other words, he must stand upright and he must have something flat to stand on. His major axis must normally be at right angles to a horizontal plane. It follows from these facts that, so far as man is concerned, the universe of Epicurus is a perpendicular one. By the same reasoning, it follows that of his multitudinous worlds only those with a flat top would be inhabitable by man. Furthermore, since motion is conceived of as downward, and not toward a center, the notion of antipodes would be inconceivable, and the proposal to emend the text to make room for this idea is untenable.[50]

THE PROBLEM OF CAUSE

It would have been strange if a thinker who flourished shortly after Aristotle should have had nothing to say on the problem of cause. Naturally it was a topic unsuitable for beginners and the only mention in the Little Epitome is casual; the Platonists are anonymously criticized as not understanding "what were the real existences and the ultimate causes," the reference being to the atoms and their motions.[51] While the topic must have been discussed in the work on Fate and in the Physics in connection with the doctrine of the swerve, all that we have left is a brief treatment by Lucretius, representing the Big Epitome.[52]

The brevity of this account has not prevented it from being perspicuous, so far as it goes. The first cause is manifestly weight, which causes the downward motion of the atoms. It is equally manifest that the second cause is the blows arising from the clash of atoms, which are the cause of all opposite and oblique motions. The third cause is the swerve of the atoms from the perpendicular in their downward motion. This serves two ends: first, it makes possible the collisions of atoms, which otherwise would fall in parallel lines and never meet to form compound bodies; [53] second, it emancipates man from an infinite chain of physical causation, the pet abomination of Epicurus, and makes possible the freedom of the will.[54]

While this brief account is perspicuous, it is also dogmatic and in keeping with the nature of an epitome. In the Epicurean scheme of education it was intended that the student should first acquire right opinions and only after an interval learn the reasons. The modern reader, lacking the larger works to which the original students had access, must expand the meager data of the Epitome as logically as he can.

The swerve, for instance, being inherent in the atoms, cannot be confined to downward motion; it must be extended also to the oblique. Moreover — and this is more important and more subtle — it must be allowed to extend to the vibratory motions, which alone prevail in compound bodies, including the bodies of animate creatures. What then becomes of the *finita potestas,* "the fixed valence," which determines rigorously what can come into existence and what cannot be? Can variable motion produce invariable results? This question remains unanswered.

That the swerve was thought to prevail in the vibratory motions is proved beyond doubt by the doctrine that it made possible freedom of the will. This free will, in its turn, becomes a cause, a fourth in addition to the three. Motion is initiated in the mind, situated deep in the breast, and is communicated to all the parts of the body. In this case, therefore, the swerve of the atom is no longer a cause, as it was described at the outset, but the result of another cause, namely, volition. Consequently, to make the best of a puzzling situation, the swerve must be viewed as an active cause under most circumstances and as a permissive cause in the phenomenon of free will.

As for Plato's idea that the cause of motion in the universe was the divine mind and that the human being was endowed with a share of this mind, this was inconceivable to Epicurus. In his thinking the human intelligence, including volition, was an accident of organic life. For him it was quite thinkable that a purposive being should be the product of a nonpurposive Nature, the sole creatrix. As Lucretius put it, "We must understand that the sensate can be born of the insensate." Laughing creatures can be born of atoms that do not laugh.[55] So with volition, and apart from it the sole causes in the universe were the blind motions of the atoms, limited by their shapes, weights and sizes, which were fixed factors. Thus to him motion was inherent in matter and no external cause of motion existed, while to Plato matter was inert and the cause of motion was external to it.

The error of Epicurus was a confusion of cause and effect. He thought of weight as a first cause, resulting in motion, while in reality both weight and motion are the result of forces. To him, knowing nothing of forces drawing matter to a center, it was possible to think of triangular as well as spherical worlds. His reasoning, however, was no worse than that of Aristotle, to whom it seemed just as natural that heavy things should come to rest at the bottom of his finite universe as it was that they should fall to the bottom.

CHAPTER X ✛ THE NEW FREEDOM

IN APPROACHING the topic of freedom it is essential to be on guard against the error of anachronism and to keep the discussion within the historical context. No doctrine of a divine and benevolent creator was current in the time of Epicurus, and for this reason there was no thought of human equality or the rights of man. So far was any belief from prevailing that man was born for freedom that the Greeks thought of the greater part of mankind as born for slavery. Neither was the determining context for Epicurus of a political nature but rather social and ethical. He believed it the teaching of Nature that pleasure or happiness was the goal and consummation of living. It did not follow from this that happiness was a natural right of man; happiness was rather a prize which it was the part of wisdom to strive after with foresight and diligence.

To achieve happiness, however, it was necessary to be free and consequently it became necessary first to make an achievement of freedom. To employ the terminology of pragmatism, the individual must plan at all times to retain control of his experience.

Since Epicurus was the first to view the rational pursuit of happiness as a practical problem, it was naturally he who first came to grips with the problem of freedom and determinism. Having once assumed that happiness is the goal of life and that the rational pursuit of it presumes both the freedom of the individual and the possibility of planning the whole life, he was bound to single out all those external compulsions to which antecedent and contemporary thought had yielded belief and one by one to demonstrate them to be nonexistent, escapable, or conquerable. In this he was a natural pragmatist, assuming both the need and feasibility of controlling experience.

To begin, as usual, with the synoptic view, this is adequately set forth in a scholium. It should be noted that the problem of freedom arises as part of the problem of causation and that three causes are here pre-

sumed, necessity, chance, and human volition: "And he says in other
books that some things happen of necessity, some from chance and
others through our own choice." [1] To this statement are added supporting reasons, which apply to the three causes respectively: "because necessity is subject to no correction and chance is a fickle thing but the part
that is left to us is free of control, to which, incidentally, blame and
the opposite naturally attach themselves." Thus in outline the limits of
freedom and of moral responsibility are clearly recognized.

The content of the scholium admits of expansion through particulars
that are available. Various kinds of necessity were recognized. One of
these was observed in the movements of the heavenly bodies; mechanis-
tic causes were assigned to these and no significance for human conduct
was recognized.[2] Another sort of necessity was that of infinite physical
causation, sponsored by Democritus, from which escape was discovered
through postulating the swerve of the atoms, that is, a degree of free play
sufficient to permit of free will in the individual. Still another sort of
necessity was that arising from the interference of the gods in the affairs
of men. This was eliminated by declaring the gods to be exclusively concerned with their own happiness. A fourth kind of necessity was dialectical. This was simply ignored. For example, when the disjunctive
proposition, "Tomorrow Hermarchus will either be alive or dead," was
put up to Epicurus, he declined to give an answer.[3] He was too wary
a dialectician himself to swallow a dialectical bait.

A fifth necessity in the list was that of death, which can neither be
escaped nor be denied. It involved the task of reconciling man to
mortality and was pivotal for both the theoretical and the practical
ethics of Epicurus.

Closely associated in the contemporary mind with the steady pressures
of necessity was the fickle play of chance or Fortune and on this topic
Epicurus was bound to produce a doctrine. He was bound also to deal
with those social and economic pressures that consort with poverty,
war, and servitude.

On the social and political levels of conduct the freedom of the
individual demanded the control of experience and this in turn demanded the choice of attitudes toward the laws of the land, toward
public careers, toward neighbors and the style of living. The coverage
of treatment for all these particular problems was complete, and the disciple was left in no doubt about the principles of choice.

THE NEW FREEDOM

CHOOSING AND AVOIDING

Before proceeding from these generalities to details it is timely to issue a warning. During the nineteenth century the educated public was habituated to accepting the threefold division of the faculties into Intellect, Emotions, and Will. This occasioned in press and pulpit an excessive glorification of "will" and "will power," not unlike the deification of abstractions among the Greeks and Romans. Of this isolation and magnification of the will as distinct from other faculties there is no equivalent in Greek and Roman thought. Neither the Greek language nor the Latin possesses a word that admits of being translated regularly as "will." At no time in antiquity did the roving focus of philosophical attention come to rest upon this unhappy abstraction.

In Greek philosophy it was customary to think of freedom as consisting in the liberty to make a choice between doing and not doing a given thing. This practice was followed by Epicurus, but he developed the notions involved in it to such a degree of detail and precision as to give them a vogue in both popular and professional thought that was parallel and equal to the prominence gained by preachers and publicists for "will" and "will power" during the nineteenth century. Where the modern man says "I will" or "I will not," the Greek said "I choose" or "I avoid." The classic textbook of Epicurus on the topic was entitled *On Choices and Avoidances*.[4] While this terminology sounds stilted in English, it became and remained current coin of language in both Greek and Latin for several centuries.[5] An alternative for "choosing" is "pursuing," which appears as "follow" and "follow after" in the King James version of the Bible.[6]

THE DOUBLE CHOICE

The first and foremost refinement of the topic in the hands of Epicurus was to draw a clear distinction between choosing an attitude, diathesis, toward action in a given sphere and choosing to do or not to do a given thing within that field. For example, a man must first choose what attitude he shall assume toward death and the gods, pleasure and pain, Necessity, Fortune, political life, monarchy, fame, friendship, diet, and several others. To exemplify from this list, the right attitude toward Necessity is to deny it, toward Fortune to defy her, toward political life to avoid it, toward fame to ignore it, and toward friendship to look upon it as the most precious of all the acquisitions of the wise man. The

EPICURUS AND HIS PHILOSOPHY

famous collection known as the Authorized Doctrines is rightly understood as a guide for the choice of attitudes toward the essential things in the art of living happily. The first, for instance, advises the disciple that the gods are not to be feared. This is an attitude, which is first to be chosen and then cultivated.

The choice of attitude, however, by no means abolished the necessity of making individual choices. The proper attitude toward pain, for instance, is to regard it as inherently evil and to be avoided; nevertheless, in the individual case the lesser pain, such as that of the surgeon's knife, is endured for the sake of the greater good. Again, the proper attitude toward food is to prefer a simple diet, but this does not preclude and even approves the occasional indulgence. Neither is political life to be avoided under all circumstances; the evil is not in such a life itself but in surrendering freedom by making a career of it. Thus in spite of the choices of attitude the necessity of making the individual choice is perpetual.

FREEDOM AND NECESSITY

The Greeks esteemed the poems of Homer as textbooks of morality and religion and by these they were habituated to thinking of human lives as being externally determined by a sort of Fate, whether known as Moira, Aisa, or by some other name.[7] Even human virtues were restricted to display within the limitations so imposed and the gods were constantly standing by to suggest such actions as might have been internally motivated by prudence or courage.[8] The poems of Hesiod ranked as supplementary textbooks, and from these the people learned of the three Fates, Clotho, Lachesis, and Atropos, who spun into the thread of life the good and evil of man's lot and snipped it off at will.

The tragedians refined without rejecting the traditional fatalism. Their approach to the problem is truthfully, though rather crudely, expressed in the saying, "Whom the gods would destroy they first drive insane." This is the principle denoted by the concept of Ate, "infatuation"; an internal necessity is substituted for an external cause. Oedipus, for instance, is represented as committing voluntarily the very acts that bring to fulfillment a fate externally decreed.

For all this edifice of fatalism Epicurus had only scorn and he abolished it by removing the gods completely from the terrestrial scene into the intermundial spaces and by denying their participation in human affairs. The details of his teaching will be more precisely treated under the heading Freedom and the Gods and in the chapter on the New Piety.

Concurrently with the labors of the tragedians over the problem of fate and freedom the physicists had been busy erecting an edifice of thought of which the end result was a kind of fatalism even more shocking to the sensibilities of Epicurus. We still possess his pronouncement upon the topic: "It were better to follow the myths concerning the gods than to be a slave to the Necessity of the physicists, for the former presumes some hope of appeasement through worship of the gods while the latter presumes an inexorable Necessity." [9] The crime of the physicists, in his judgment, had been their failure to deal with the problem of freedom, and their offense was at its worst in the case of the atomists, who found the sole cause of motion and change in the universe to be the motion of the atoms. On this point the feelings of Epicurus were so intense that he denied to Leucippus even the name of philosopher.[10]

It may be here interposed that the concept of determinism is not offensive to the intellectualist. It was consequently the duty of Epicurus as a moralist, a reformer, and hence a pragmatist, or in ancient parlance, as a truly wise man, "who will be more powerfully moved by his feelings than other men," to declare the significance of determinism for human conduct. His verdict was that it meant paralysis. His solution was to postulate a sufficient degree of freedom in the motion of the atoms to permit of freedom in the individual. This is the doctrine of the swerve.

For the sake of a closer analysis it is worth while to observe at this point that Epicurus, having put the mythologers and the physicists in a single class as teachers of fatalism, wished his disciples to see the new order of his own system as governed by the laws of Nature, *foedera naturae*, as opposed to the laws of Fate, *foedera fati*. Consequently the new freedom he was offering to mankind "had been wrested from the Fates," *fatis avolsa potestas*.[11] In an infinite universe dominated by these physical laws man is miraculously exempt. He is free to walk forward and to turn left or right of his own untrammeled volition. Neither in respect of time nor in respect of place is his action predetermined down to the moment of its beginning.[12] The laws of Nature are in the main restricted to the world of inorganic things.

EPICURUS AND HIS PHILOSOPHY

In the fourth century Chaldean astrology had arrived in Greece under the high patronage of Eudoxus and Plato, but rather strangely it is not as a form of determinism that we find it attacked in the extant remains of Epicurus. What chiefly outraged his feelings was the idea that august beings should be thought to assume the form of balls of fire and of their own choice go hurtling through circles forever. Only at a later date, apparently, did the practice of casting horoscopes become prevalent, which would have been unconditionally condemned as a new form of determinism. Neither did later Epicureans condone it; Stoic doctrine was more flexible; Panaetius held out against the astrologers but the great Posidonius did not.[13]

NECESSITY AND FORTUNE

By the time of Epicurus the ancient and aristocratic cult of Fate or Necessity was finding a vigorous rival in the popular worship of Fortune, Tyche in Greek, the goddess of chance. Epicurus repudiated her as a divinity, "because nothing is done by a god at haphazard," and with equal decisiveness he denied her the Aristotelian status of a fickle cause.[14] It would have been his contention, no doubt, that the hurricane, even though to the agriculturist it appears to be chance and destroys his crops, still follows a law of its own.

For the sake of clearness there is need, however, of separating the sphere of Fortune from that of Fate or Necessity. For instance, let it be assumed that Fate had decreed the death of a man by shipwreck; it still remained for Fortune or chance to determine the time and place. Again, it is the work of Fortune if a man should be captured by pirates and sold into slavery, but the compulsions under which a slave must live are a form of Necessity. Similarly, so far as individuals are concerned, it is the play of Fortune if their city is attacked by an enemy, but the compulsions to which beleaguered citizens are subject is a form of Necessity.

For all such exigencies, according to Epicurus, the wise man will keep himself prepared through addiction to the simple life and the cultivation of self-sufficiency. During a siege of Athens he kept his associates alive by doling out the beans.[15] One of his apothegms applies to such an emergency: "The wise man, when confronted by lack of the necessities, stands by to share with others rather than to have them share with him; so great a reserve of self-sufficiency he discovers." This same

176

truth is epigrammatically expressed in another maxim, which exemplifies his penchant for playing upon words, at which he was adept:
"Necessity is an evil but there is no necessity of living with Necessity."
This means, as another saying, presently to be quoted, makes plain,
that the compulsions of such things as war and poverty can be forestalled
by rational planning.

As a parting comment it may be added that Epicurus, though affecting
to despise dialectic, knew how to employ it with an epigrammatic sting:
"The man who declares that everything happens of necessity can have
no fault to find with the man who denies that anything happens of
necessity, for he is saying that this very denial is made of necessity." [16]
This is a mere polemical retort, calculated rather to silence the opponent than to refute him. Dialectic was a game even when it was a quest
for truth, and often it was no more than a game.

FREEDOM AND FORTUNE

Among both Greeks and Romans Fortune was a deified abstraction
of great popularity, especially among the middle and lower classes; she
was honored with images, temples, and worship. It lay with her to decide
between war and peace, wealth and poverty, peril of life and escape
from peril. The attitude recommended toward her by Epicurus was
defiance.

The poet Horace describes this attitude aptly in two of his most
compacted lines, when he describes the friend "who stands by to give you
courage and show you how to feel independent and hold up your head
and talk back to imperious Fortune." [17] When Epicurus himself extols
the study of Nature as "making men defiant and self-sufficient and proud
of their inalienable goods instead of the goods of circumstance," [18] the
words *defiant* and *self-sufficient* both alike have reference to Fortune.
It is the fool who trusts to luck and feels puffed up over her favors; the
wise man controls his experience.

Metrodorus, the favored pupil of Epicurus, strikes the true note
when he cries exultingly: "Fortune, I have forestalled thee and bar-
ricaded thine every entrance, and neither to thee nor to any other
surprise of life will we give ourselves in surrender." [19] The master himself has recorded the authorized teaching of the school in Doctrine 16:
"Fortune plays but little part in the life of a wise man and the things
that are of most value and consequence are subject to arrangement by

rational planning, and throughout the whole extent of life are subject and will be subject to it." Thus, while Socrates taught that "the unexamined life is not worth while," Epicurus was teaching that "the unplanned life is not worth while." Planning and the lack of planning make the difference between the wise man and the fool. In another passage he speaks of the young man, glorying in his strength but cherishing false judgments of values, "drifting at the mercy of Fortune." [20]

In none of his ethical teachings and judgments does Epicurus display deeper insight or strike a clearer note than when dealing with this theme of the maintenance of moral independence through all the vicissitudes of life. He was not the first, of course, to discern that extremes of adversity and prosperity are supreme tests of character, but none of his countrymen have expressed themselves more appealingly on the subject. To the youthful Menoeceus he wrote: "For [the wise man] does not imagine that any good or evil bearing on the happy life is given to men by her [Fortune]; he does think, however, that many a starting point for great blessings or evils is furnished by her; he believes that it is better to be unfortunate in reason than to prosper in unreason, for in our actions it is better that the well planned should not succeed than for the badly planned to succeed through her agency." [21]

Best of all, perhaps, is a passage never quoted by his regular detractors. His thesis in this little homily is the doctrine that the wise man, and this always means the man whose will remains free, has "no partnership with Fortune": "[Nature] teaches us to appraise as of minor value the gifts of Fortune and to recognize that when fortunate we are unfortunate, and when faring ill not to set great store by faring well, and to accept without emotion the blessings of Fortune, and to remain on guard against the seeming evils from her hand; for everything that to the multitude seems good or bad is but ephemeral and under no circumstances does wisdom enter into partnership with Fortune." [22] It is, of course, the special temptation of the fortunate man to surrender control of his experience.

On this point of control of experience Epicurus was prepared to insist to the last extremity. In spite of his recommendation to his disciples to pursue Peace and Safety, the question of martyrdom came within his purview. His statement on the topic runs as follows: "Even if put to torture the wise man is happy." [23] Cicero perverted this in shabby fashion and wrote: "In the brazen bull of Phalaris he will say

THE NEW FREEDOM

'How pleasant! how indifferent I am to this pain!' " [24] A quibble could hardly be more foul: Cicero chose to ignore the difference between "pleasant" and "happy." The martyr at the stake may still claim to be a happy man, but he cannot claim to be experiencing pleasure. Seneca became an accomplice after the deed and repeated Cicero's cheap fiction as if a genuine saying of Epicurus. [25] The truth concerning his teaching will be clear to those familiar with stories of Christian martyrs.

FREEDOM AND THE GODS

On the topic of freedom and the gods the student of Epicureanism must be prepared for surprises. In the first place, it will be surprising to discover that Epicurus was at no less pains to assert the freedom of the gods than the freedom of man. In his thinking it was no less necessary for the gods to be free from servitude to man than for man to be free from servitude to the gods. In the second place, the inquiry into this aspect of freedom is mined with a type of trap which to the historian of philosophy is especially deceptive. It is easy for the unwary to put the subsequent before the antecedent and become guilty of the preposterous.

It is easy to ascribe to the Greeks of one generation certain emotional reflexes to which they were not yet conditioned. For instance, when the Greeks of the fifth century read "that the will of Zeus was being fulfilled" it would not occur to them that the will of numberless Greeks was being balked. Neither would it occur to them when Aphrodite set out to avenge herself for the slights put upon her by Hippolytus that his will and that of Phaedra were powerless to oppose the will of the goddess. In both instances the feelings of the readers or the spectators were conditioned to respond only to the pity and the terror of the thing. They knew no word for individual human will, and the idea was never a part of the current coin in their thinking.

Another caution: in view of the fact that Epicurus came to be regarded as the archenemy of divine providence and had "the whole pack of philosophers barking around him," [26] it might be presumed that his writings abounded in tirades against this pious and comforting doctrine. Such an expectation is doomed to disappointment. The word for providence, *pronoia*, is lacking from the extant remains; neither do the numerous testimonies of hostile writers ascribe it to him in quotation. On the contrary, the evidence should be convincing that it was the Stoics of later years who gained for the term the status of a catchword. [27]

179

Paradoxical as it may consequently appear, the conclusion seems mandatory that Epicurus had no need to work out his doctrines concerning the gods to their logical effects upon the doctrine of divine providence, and this for the excellent reason that the doctrine as later understood did not yet exist. His writings are thus on a level with Darwin's *Origin of Species*. Darwin did not specifically attack the accepted beliefs of religion, but soon the whole pack of theologians was barking around him, because the implications of his reasonings were so obvious. It was probably so with Epicurus.

That the implications of his teachings were immediately discerned is demonstrated by the passage of Menander on the topic of providence, already quoted in the chapter on Samos and Athens. When Onesimus estimates the population of the world at 30,000,000 and inquires if the gods deal out good or evil to individuals one by one, Smicrines retorts, "How could that be? For what you say means a laborious kind of life for them."

Three details are noticeable in this context: the word for providence, *pronoia*, does not occur; it was not yet a catchword; the second detail is the mention of "the laborious life." This marks the passage as distinctly echoing the views of Epicurus. His major premise was the perfection of the happiness of the gods, with which a life of toil is incompatible. He was insisting on consistency. The people, he claimed, had a correct idea, a natural prolepsis, of the gods as enjoying perfect blessedness along with incorruptibility, but, as he said, "they do not keep them consistent with what they believe them to be." [28] Their error was in this instance to impose upon the gods a life of unremitting toil while believing their happiness to be complete.

The third point of significance in the Menandrian passage is the assumption that tribulations as well as blessings were dealt out to mankind by the gods. Menander died in the year 291/290 B.C. and thus the inference may be drawn that down to this date at least, the sixteenth year of the Garden in Athens, the ancient belief in the jealousy and spitefulness of the gods, well known from Herodotus,[29] was still in the forefront.

This being true, it would be preposterous in the time of Epicurus to think of the goodness of the divine nature. Even the goodness of Plato's supreme god, the demiurge, by no means consisted in benevolence toward mankind. He is good with a virtue that is complete,[30] just as the happiness of the gods of Epicurus is complete, but this goodness is that of perfect intelligence, incapable of anything irregular or unmathematical. So far from being interested one way or another in mankind, the demiurge is contemptuous of all terrestrial matters and not responsible for evil. He turned over to his subordinates the messy task of mixing the earthly ingredient into the nature of man.[31]

It was difficult for Plato to come to grips with the problem of freedom in a practical way,[32] a difficulty inherent in theocentric structures of thought. His principle "that no man is willingly wicked" commits him to a sort of ethical determinism, eliminating both freedom of choice and responsibility. Epicurus seems to enunciate the same doctrine when he writes in Vatican Saying 16: "No man looks on evil and chooses it but he is baited by it as if being good in comparison with the greater evil and so gets trapped." [33] This, however, means merely that the man fails to manipulate properly the calculus of advantage, which measures the pleasure against the pain. The ignorance is specific; the traveler may take a wrong turn even if he follows the right route. There is no implication that his soul is out of touch with absolute knowledge or absolute goodness.

The first guise in which the doctrine of divine providence came to the fore had reference to the divine ordering of the celestial universe with its manifold regularities of movement. This doctrine of Plato was repudiated by Epicurus on various grounds: it would have imposed upon the gods a life of toil and worry utterly incompatible with blessedness. It did not occur to him, being in this respect a pious and orthodox Greek, that a being might exist for whom such a function would be effortless. The concept of an omnipotent deity was yet to come.

Equally unanticipated in contemporary thought was the idea of a benevolent personal providence and the determinism that was elicited from this by a brief chain argument. Divine providence by etymology means divine foresight, foresight means foreknowledge, and foreknowledge spells the sort of determinism that is known as predestination. It belongs in a context of thought that was fabricated long after the time of Epicurus.

If all these items of evidence be added up, the conclusion will be inevitable that, although the problem of divine providence was incipient in the time of Epicurus, it was in the main posthumous to his career. If subsequently he had "the whole pack of philosophers barking around him," to use the words of Lactantius, this was for the reason that the denial of any kind of divine providence was implicit in his whole treatment of the cosmic order and the gods. If the anachronisms be sifted out, the residue of fact may be comprised in the statement that quite unintentionally he sparked the protracted controversy over divine providence, just as Darwin by expounding the theory of biological evolution unintentionally sparked the modern controversy over divine creationism. It is not going too far to say that by his physical and ethical teachings he so manifestly anticipated the arguments against the doctrine of divine providence that the formulation of the doctrine became a philosophical necessity for his adversaries. He was perhaps the most provoking of all ancient thinkers.

THE NECESSITY OF DEATH

There was one form of Necessity which no logical ingenuity of Epicurus could explain away, the inevitability of death. Metrodorus expressed himself on this theme with a mournful and memorable felicity, Vatican Saying 31: "Against all other hazards it is possible for us to gain security for ourselves but so far as death is concerned all of us human beings inhabit a city without walls." The immediate effect of this is to invest the present with a pressing urgency and to demand the control of experience with respect to the past, the present, and the future. This amounts to the control of our thoughts. A choice of attitude is involved: the past is to be regarded as unalterable, the future as undependable, and the present alone as within our power.

All thoughts are to be under control: the proper feeling to cultivate toward the past is gratitude, toward the future hope, as will be explained more fully in the chapter on the New Virtues.

The urgency that accrues to the present is admirably expressed by the Jewish Epicurean, Ecclesiastes, 9:10: "Whatsoever thy hand findeth to do, do it with thy might; for there is no work, nor device, nor knowledge, nor wisdom, in the grave, whither thou goest." A similar admonition is placed in the mouth of Jupiter by Virgil and with an odd sort of poetic irony, because both he and Hercules, to whom he speaks, are immortals:

> stat sua cuique dies; breve et inreparabile tempus
> omnibus est vitae; sed famam extendere factis,
> hoc virtutis opus.[34]

"For every man the day of death stands fixed; for all men the span of life is brief and irremediable, but by good deeds to prolong fame, this is the task of virtue."

The negative aspect of this teaching happens to be more often documented in our texts than the positive. This is the horror of procrastination and misdirected activity. We have a sad dictum on the topic from Metrodorus, Vatican Saying 30: "Some men devote their lives to accumulating the wherewithal for living, failing to discern that the potion mixed for all of us at birth is a draught of death." If the challenge of this sentence is a telling one, still more so is that of another from the pen of Epicurus himself, Vatican Saying 14: "We are born once and we cannot be born twice but for all time must be no more; and you, thou fool, though not master of the morrow, postpone the hour and each and every one of us goes to death with excuses on his lips."

This sentiment may suggest the chapter of Luke in which occurs the verse, "And they all with one consent began to make excuse," though in the New Testament the urgency of the present is based upon the imminence of the kingdom of God, not upon mortality and the brevity of life. Both alike, however, result in the scorn of procrastination.

The brevity and uncertainty of life were naturally a commonplace of Greek thought. The originality of Epicurus consisted in lifting this commonplace from the rank of a sentiment to that of a motive of action. In so doing he was in alliance with the Hippocratic physicians, from whom we have the saying, "Life is short, art is long, the occasion urgent." He would not, however, have subscribed to the rest of the dictum: "Experience is deceptive and decision difficult." As a moralist he could not afford to indulge in doubt, hesitation, or pessimism. He was bound to be positive, dogmatic, and hopeful. It was possible to achieve happiness but men must act promptly and vigorously, living *sub specie mortalitatis*, "in contemplation of mortality."

FREEDOM, GOVERNMENT, AND LAW

It is the paramount importance of individual freedom that determines the attitude of Epicurus toward law and government. He is no anarchist; he knows that a certain degree of legal control over society is a necessity but at the same time he insists that the maximum of liberty implies a minimum of government. In this respect he is totally opposed to Plato, who recommended a highly regimented state and consequently a maximum of government and a minimum of liberty.

His fundamental teaching is enunciated in Authorized Doctrine 5, immediately after the all-important tetrapharmacon: "It is impossible to live pleasurably without living according to reason, honor and justice." In this group of three determinants reason signifies the practical reason that decides the choice of all general attitudes and particular preferences; honor decides the choice in respect of actions not covered by the written law; justice means voluntary obedience to the written law of the land.

The written law involves no infringement of freedom, provided only that the laws are just. In such circumstances the will of the individual and the will of the law are coincident. Authorized Doctrine 31 has a bearing on this point: "The justice of Nature is a covenant of advantage not to injure one another or be injured." The very word *covenant* implies the democratic process and the free choice of the individual as opposed to the imposition of enactments by the law-giver or the golden few, as in Plato's system.

Safety, the equivalent of the modern Security, was a catchword of Epicureanism. The function of government was the protection of the individual along with his property. Epicurus is reported as having said: "Laws are enacted for the sake of the wise, not that they may do wrong but that they may suffer no wrong." [35] He is quite immune to the political nostalgia which afflicted Plato and, to a far less extent, Aristotle. He reflects the influence of his Ionian upbringing. The cities of the islands and the coast of Asia had never been seduced by the sweets of empire but were content if only they could enjoy autonomy.

It may happen, however, that the laws of the state are not such as the wise man would approve. Yet Epicurus still recommends obedience. He took the attitude, for example, that the religious rites prescribed by law or custom should be observed, even if inconsistent with personal belief: "As for us [Epicureans], let us sacrifice reverently and properly where it is required and let us do everything properly in accordance with the laws, not distressing ourselves over popular opinions in matters regarded as the highest and most solemn." [36] In this perhaps he is displaying the caution learned by experience and from history. He could not have failed to recall his own expulsion from Mytilene nor the persecution of Anaxagoras in Athens, nor the fate of Socrates, nor the flight of

Aristotle. He was not a fanatic. He was willing to surrender an insignificant fraction of his liberty for the sake of carrying on the greater task which he believed to be his true mission.

While the starting point of Epicurus was the freedom of the individual, there was also a philosophical and historical basis for his attitude toward law and government. The Nature that he endeavored to exalt as the norm of truth belonged exclusively to the terrestrial sphere of things and in particular to the domain of organic life. In the domain of the inorganic it was imperfection and not perfection that he discerned; the very name of earth connotes imperfection: *tanta stat praedita culpa*,[37] "so notorious is the imperfection it displays." The lot of man was looked upon as a struggle and the physical environment as hostile. It is Nature in the realm of living things that informs man of happiness being his appointed end or telos. Even so he is not born free but must achieve freedom. Thus freedom is not a law of Nature but an option of man.

According to Plato, on the contrary, the regimentation of society is a law of Nature, and this doctrine is important because of the relish and vehemence with which Epicurus revolted against it. He censured Plato for confining his attention to celestial matters and this stricture was not unjust. In the regularity of the heavens Plato discerned what was most worthy of admiration and even worship and, being such, it was worthy of imitation in human society. To imitate it, moreover, it was essential that the behavior of citizens should be reduced to a corresponding regularity and this meant a highly regimented polity. Thus Epicurus and Plato stood at opposite extremes in advocating respectively a minimum and a maximum of government.

FREEDOM AND PUBLIC CAREERS

The question whether the wise man should or should not engage in the political life emerged to prominence in the generation preceding Epicurus. The progress of thought and the march of historical events conspired fortuitously to make the question a pressing one. On the one hand philosophy discovered the contemplative life and on the other hand the fate of men like Hypereides and Demosthenes put a smart discount on public careers in democratic states. At the same time the campaigns of Alexander brought knowledge of the wise men of Persia and India; one of the latter rebuked Anaxarchus for dancing attendance upon princes.[38] Noteworthy is the fact that Pyrrho the skeptic, the companion of Anaxarchus, set an early example of abstention from public activity and was much admired by Epicurus.[39]

Aristotle discussed "the best life" in his *Politics,* but the title under which the question standardized itself in literature was Lives. Theophrastus published three books on this topic. He favored the contemplative life, but Dicaearchus of the same age and school preferred the active life.[40] Epicurus limited himself to a single roll on the topic but heightened the heat of the controversy by rejecting both the political life and the contemplative life as Plato and Aristotle had extolled it. He would have limited contemplation and research to the study of nature and especially as manifested in terrestrial things, since he scorned mathematics and astronomy. Moreover, the objective of study was limited to peace of mind; knowledge was not, in his view, an end in itself.

The writing of Epicurus on the topic has perished, but to discern his approach is not difficult. The objective of life is happiness and to attain this the individual must at all times retain control of experience. This control means liberty of choice and the choice is double, first the choice of attitude and then the choice in the particular instance. The former is the more important. As the faithful Diogenes of Oenoanda expressed it, "The secret of happiness is in the diathesis, of which we are sole arbiters." [41]

There were two sorts of political career, the one in democracies and the other in royal courts. Both of them fell under a single condemnation, because they were competitive activities and placed the happiness of the contestant at the mercy of others. The way of escape was through the simple life and the knowledge that the necessities of life are few and inexpensive. The topic was deemed worthy of mention among the Authorized Doctrines, No. 21: "The man who has discerned the limited needs of life is aware how easy of procurement is that which removes the pain arising from want and renders the whole life perfect, so that he feels no need of adding things that involve competition." The sacrifice of freedom that is entailed by the political career, whether in democracies or royal courts, is set forth in the Vatican Saying 67: "A life of freedom cannot acquire great wealth because of success in this being difficult apart from servitude to mobs or monarchs." The Roman Seneca had in his hands a letter of Epicurus to his patron Idomeneus, high in the service of the Macedonian Lysimachus, in which "he begs him to do his best to escape and to make haste before some major emergency should arise and deprive him of the liberty of withdrawing." [42]

The condemnation of political careers under democratic governments was especially galling to the Platonists because their program of education, which stressed the study of rhetoric, was branded by Epicurus as a preparation for servitude. One of those apothegms which his disciples committed to memory covers the point, Vatican Saying 58: "We must plan our escape from the prison house of the conventional education and political careers." Even after four centuries Plutarch winces under the sting of this criticism. He grimly records "that these men, even if they do write about the political life, do so to discourage us from engaging in it, and if they write about rhetoric, do so to discourage us from becoming orators." [43]

These items may serve as a reminder of the exceptional capacity of Epicurean teachings to disturb the equanimity of conventional minds. Cicero, for instance, who bowed to convention insofar as he chose the political role, was on the verge of losing his patience when he wrote to Atticus in 44 B.C. after the murder of Julius Caesar: "You mention Epicurus and dare to warn me 'to keep out of the political game'." [44] The advice stung because Atticus was in the right; by following the policy he was recommending he had himself maintained the greatest possible freedom of choice under the existing circumstances.

The avoidance of political careers for the sake of preserving personal liberty served to separate the Epicureans from the other schools. The court posts, for instance, were left to the Platonists and especially the Stoics, whose pious pretensions qualified them uniquely for the role of chaplains. The miseries and restrictions of this occupation have been ably described by Lucian in his essay entitled *On Salaried Posts in Great Houses*. The Epicureans were satirists from the beginning, and Lucian was conscious of a close affinity with them.

CONTROL OF ENVIRONMENT

That the quest of freedom demanded for Epicurus the calculated control of environment might have been taken for granted, but fortunately the documentation is ample. The following statement not only demonstrates how carefully the problem had been analyzed but also lays down the general procedure: "The injuries inflicted upon man by man have their origin in hatred or envy or contempt, over which the wise man achieves control by calculation." [45] By calculation is meant a course of conduct rationally planned. It may be added that hatred arises in the competitive life; Aeschines and Demosthenes hated each other. The poor envy the rich or powerful; such men as Miltiades, Themistocles, and Ephialtes paid a bitter penalty for popularity.[46] As for contempt, this was felt for men who defied public opinion by miserliness or other vices, such as Timon the misanthrope.

By what manner of life these dangers should be avoided is made clear by the famous advice of Epicurus *lathe biosas*, "Live unknown." This saying is not found in the extant writings and is reported by Plutarch invidiously, as if Epicurus had courted fame by his writings while advising his disciples to shun it.[47] Epicurus was not averse to fame provided it came unsought; he really desired a fame that was earned and deserved.[48] His warning was against the notoriety that is earned in the public assembly and on the streets. When it is said of him that he remained virtually unknown to the Athenians,[49] this does not mean that his name was unknown but rather his face. If ever he had desired to be in the public eye, this ambition was cured for once and all by the persecution in Mytilene.

Of the three motives for injury, hatred, envy, and contempt, the last may be considered first. On this topic the general prescription is extant: "As for reputation, the wise man will exercise just enough foresight to avoid contempt." [50] In this instance the advice "to live unknown" means rather "to live unnoticed." The rule applies particularly to housing, dress, and servants. A miserly way of life — and misers seem to have been numerous in ancient societies — provokes the contempt of neighbors and invites derision. The judgment of Epicurus is as follows, Vatican Saying 43: "To hoard dishonest gains is impious, to hoard honest gains shameful, for it is a disgrace to live sordidly and penuriously even with justice on one's side." The logic behind this condemnation is obvious. The miser invites the petty persecutions of his neighbors and also deserves them. A man cannot live happily unless he observes the decencies of social life. To do so is not only a duty but an advantage as well; not to do so is folly, for the miser surrenders control of his own experience.

The opposite of contempt is envy and this is provoked by ostentation and parade of luxury. The theme is a favorite of the poet Horace, who reproduces both the teaching and the terminology of Epicurus with fidelity:

> Auream quisquis mediocritatem
> diligit, tutus caret obsoleti
> sordibus tecti, caret invidenda
> sobrius aula.[51]

A paraphrase will serve better than a translation to elucidate the meaning: "Whoever cultivates the golden mean is safe from persecution; he escapes the contempt occasioned by the squalor of a shabby house; he exercises sober judgment; he avoids the envy occasioned by the invidious palace." In this passage "safe," "sordid," "sober," and "envy" are all catchwords of Epicureanism.

St. Paul in I Thessalonians 5 identified the Epicureans by their catchwords Peace and Safety. In this collocation Peace has reference to amicable relations with neighbors, while Safety refers to the security of person and property for the citizen. The best means of obtaining the latter, according to Epicurus, was to withdraw from the multitude and live a retired life, but he thought it equally important to put forward what he called the "false opinions" on the topic, as in Authorized Doctrine 7: "Some men have chosen to become celebrities and to be in the public eye, thinking thus to achieve security from the attacks of men." He does not explicitly label this a false opinion but leaves the inference to be drawn: "Consequently, if the lives of such men are safe, they have reaped the end of Nature, but if their lives are not safe, they lack that for the sake of which at the outset they reached out by the instinct of Nature." They are not free nor in control of their environment; they have placed their happiness at the mercy of a fickle populace.

Another false opinion that did not escape attention was what the New Testament calls "the deceitfulness of riches." In Authorized Doctrine 14 it is paired with the patronage of princes: "Although safety from the attacks of men has been secured to a certain degree by dynastic protection and abundance of means, that which comes of the retired life and withdrawal from the multitude is the most unalloyed." It may be mentioned that riches were condemned as deceitful in another way. Just as they failed as an assurance of safety, so they begot no worth-while happiness [52] but merely administered to superfluous pleasures which removed no pain arising from want.

Only after these false opinions had been exposed did Epicurus arrive at his positive teachings on the topic of security. It was not enough to be on guard against the deceitfulness of notoriety and riches, to retire from the crowd and to avoid envy and derision in one's own neighborhood; it was also necessary to plan for security by diligently and systematically cultivating friendships. In the next to the last of his Authorized Doctrines we find this positive teaching: "That man has best managed the feeling of insecurity from the environment who has made relationships friendly wherever possible; where this was impossible, at least not unfriendly; where not even this was possible, has avoided contacts, and wherever it was profitable to do so, has sought dynastic protection."

It will be observed in this enumeration that recourse to the support of the dynast is listed as a last resort. Epicurus himself had been forced to this expedient after his expulsion from Mytilene, when he fled to the court of Lysimachus, and he persisted in justifying his action; but it is manifest that in his mature judgment every effort must be made to forestall such a necessity.

It is also manifest that he looked chiefly to friendly diplomacy to keep the environment in control. Good will is a catchword of his creed no less than Peace and Safety. It is a precondition of Peace and Safety. He wrote, for instance: "A life of freedom cannot amass great wealth because of success in this being difficult apart from servitude to mobs or monarchs but it does enjoy all things in uninterrupted abundance; if, however, now and then great wealth does fall to its lot, it would gladly disburse this to win the good will of the neighbor." [53]

In the attitude toward friendship as Epicurus shaped it there was both a traditional and an original element: the Greeks were accustomed to look to friends not only for such forms of protection as the modern man obtains by paid insurance, that is, the hazards of sickness, accident, and fire, but also for others, ransom from pirates, for example; even Plato's freedom was once so redeemed. The innovation of Epicurus was to advise making a systematic business of friendship; it was not in his opinion sufficient to leave the winning and keeping of good will to chance and opportunity; to win and keep it was to become an integral part of the control of environment for the sake of happiness and security, which meant freedom. The wording of his pronouncement deserves diligent notice. Authorized Doctrine 27: "Of all the preparations that wisdom makes for the blessedness of the perfect life by far the most precious is the acquisition of friendship." This must be interpreted in the light of the specific prescription quoted above. The environment is deliberately zoned: friends are made where possible, hostility neutralized where possible, and contacts avoided where neutrality or friendship are balked.

It is no accident that the dictum on the wisdom of making friends is immediately followed by another pronouncement on the topic, which even Cicero admired: "The same judgment that renders us confident of no punishment being either everlasting or even long enduring also discerns the security furnished by friendship to be the most complete in the brief span of life itself." [54] The meaning is that the man who has no fear of eternal punishment in the afterlife will experience no fear of brief punishment in the present life. Life at its longest is brief; the sacrifice is the less for this reason. The man who believes "that death is the last line of things," to use the Horatian phrase,[55] will defy the tyrant rather than betray his friend. For the wise man this is the supreme assertion of freedom.

FREEDOM AND THE SIMPLE LIFE

So consistently does Epicurus urge throughout his teaching the maintenance of freedom and the control of experience, which is freedom at its best, that he even brings it into relationship with diet and the general design of living. No one, as Cicero testifies, had more to say about the simple life,[56] and it may be added that no Roman writer had more to say about it than the Epicurean Horace.[57] To Epicurus the simple life meant contentment with little and this was called self-sufficiency, which in turn meant freedom: "Of self-sufficiency the most precious fruit is freedom." [58] That the reference of these words was to food and not to friendship is made clear by the following: "The wise man, when confronted by lack of the necessities, stands by rather to share with others than to have them share with him; so great a reserve of self-sufficiency he discovers." [59] That in respect of friendship the wise man was not sufficient to himself the following indicates: "Before you look for something to eat and drink you should look around for companions with whom to eat and drink, for life without a friend is just the gulping of a lion and a wolf." [60]

In this, as in all spheres of conduct, the rule of the two choices holds good. The proper attitude toward the desires, according to Authorized Doctrine 29, is to regard some as "natural and necessary," others as "natural but not necessary," and the rest as "neither natural nor necessary." The first class has reference to food, drink, clothing, and housing, the second to sexual desires; under the third fall the appetite for luxurious viands and the hankering in public life for crowns and statues, the equivalent in modern life of honorary degrees.

The correct basis of choice with reference to the particular desire is furnished by Vatican Saying 71: "To all desires must be applied this question: What will be the result for me if the object of this desire is attained and what if it is not?" This, of course, is the calculus of advantage in operation, and the correct procedure is defined in Vatican Saying 21: "Human nature is not to be coerced but persuaded, and we shall persuade her by satisfying the necessary desires, and the natural desires if they are not injurious, but relentlessly denying the harmful."

Even these details fall short of representing the whole creed of Epicurus touching the simple life. He says that it "creates a better attitude toward expensive foods when they become available after intervals of scarcity" and that "those who feel the least need of luxury have the keenest enjoyment of it." [61] If credence may be allowed to the slurs of his detractors, as well it may, this principle was practiced and the plain diet of the school was replaced on the twentieth of each month by more bountiful repasts.[62] These celebrations marked the high points of the fellowship for which the sect was notorious.

While these pronouncements are perspicuous enough, it is possible to define still more closely the operation of the calculus. Epicurus discerned no merit in the creed of such a man as Diogenes the Cynic, who eschewed the comforts of life while scorning civilized society; neither did he see merit in the ascetic, who eschewed the comforts without scorning society. His estimate of the proper attitude was based upon a keener analysis: the sole merit lay in the control of experience, which signified freedom. His considered judgment is as follows: "We judge self-sufficiency to be a great good, not meaning that we should live on little under all circumstances but that we may be content with little when we do not have plenty." [63] He does not fail to mention that the simple diet conduces to health but the greater gain is discerned in the feeling of security: it renders the individual "unshrinking before the inevitable vicissitudes of life" and "fearless in the face of Fortune." [64] The sincerity of Epicurus was put to the test when Athens was besieged by Demetrius; according to Plutarch he kept the members of the school alive by counting out the beans.

The same principle was practiced by the poet Horace, who planned his life on Epicurean principles. The covering doctrine is aptly expressed in the line:

Dulce est desipere in loco.[65]

This is poetical understatement, litotes; the meaning is not merely "It is a pleasure to forget one's philosophy on occasion," but "It is a special pleasure." It is abstinence that gives salt to the rare indulgence. It is the moderation of the rest of the year that gives relish to the Christmas dinner. In the language of Epicurus, the pleasure is "condensed."

CONTROL OF DESIRES

In his approach to the problem of the desires Epicurus stands closer to Aristotle than to Plato. In harmony with his usual practice he eschews figures of speech. Courage is not associated with the lion in the soul nor is desire a many-headed beast. He sees evil not in desires but only in the consequences that follow their gratification. Intelligence and the desires stand on a level: they are alike in being accidental capacities of an atomic organism.

He avoids the terminology of both Plato and Aristotle. He has nothing to say about harmony between the parts of the soul nor anything about the mean in virtues. The new context which he sets up for the component ideas has already been mentioned in other connections. Happiness is the natural consummation of life; to be happy man must possess freedom. Freedom, however, is not a right but an achievement; it consists in maintaining and retaining control of experience under all circumstances.

The remaining components of the new logical context are the practical reason or "sober calculation," the diathesis, choice and avoidance, the calculus of advantage, and false opinion. On the last item of this list Vatican Saying 59 is a clear commentary: "People say 'The stomach is insatiable' but it is not the stomach that is insatiable; they have a false opinion about the limitless quantity required to fill the stomach." To emancipate one's self from this servitude to false opinion and to make every act an act of choice is made possible through the practical reason.

The first step in this process is to choose the diathesis, which consists in believing that of the desires "some are natural and necessary, some are natural but not necessary and others are neither natural nor necessary." The second step is to make the choice in respect of the particular desire, Vatican Saying 71: "What will be the result for me if the object of this desire is fulfilled and what if it is not fulfilled?" This is the calculus of advantage in operation. It is plain pragmatism, the control of experience for the sake of happiness.

Into this same context of doctrines it is easy to fit the passion of anger. It is the right diathesis to consider "an outburst of temper a brief madness," as Horace states it; [66] Epicurus himself is on record as saying, "Unbridled anger begets insanity." [67] The false opinion would consist in believing that any worth-while satisfaction comes from revenge.

It is easy also to find place in this context for the calculus of advantage. Anger is a turmoil in the soul and as such is destructive of serenity or ataraxy. There is more to be said, however: angry reprisals invite reprisals and would be destructive of that peace and safety which Epicureans raised to the rank of a practical objective. As a sect, Cicero informs us, "they were to the least degree malicious." [68] They were not revengeful; even while attacking them Plutarch ascribes to them the saying "Let this too meet with forgiveness." [69] With the Greeks and Romans the topic of anger was associated with the treatment of slaves, whose revenges could be dreadful. Hence it is not surprising that Laertius speaks of "his gentleness toward household slaves" when praising Epicurus.[70] Lucian in his encomium makes mention of "the mildness of his disposition, his considerateness, the unruffled calm of his life and his tactfulness toward those who lived with him." [71]

It may be said by the way that the perfect Epicurean approximates closely to our prolepsis or natural preconception of the true gentleman and that those who committed themselves even partially to the practice of his philosophy have proved to be especially likable. The names of Horace and Virgil and even Petronius will suggest themselves. The Stoics whose writings are best known do not elicit affection. Seneca is felt to be insincere, Epictetus a bit priggish, and Marcus Aurelius rather morbid. All three absorbed some Epicureanism but not enough to make themselves lovable.

While the topic of the desires has its context of ethical doctrine, it also fits into a context of physical doctrine. This was no proper subject for beginners, is not mentioned in the Little Epitome, and it may be that Lucretius went beyond the Big Epitome for the information that he furnishes. In ascending order of mobility the ingredients of the soul consist of atoms resembling those of air, wind, and fire; the fourth ingredient surpasses in mobility the atoms of any known existence. Each of these in turn is associated with some quality of character: air with placidness, wind with cowardice, fire with anger. Moreover, it is to be assumed that within each of these classes, including the unnamed fourth, there are subgradations of mobility, far too numerous to have names. Out of combinations of these arise the boundless variety of human character.

In this association of fire with anger and the assumption of varying proportions of component elements in things there is nothing unknown to previous thinkers. The rest of the explanation is peculiar to Epicureanism. It is assumed that for some men education can result in perfection; there is such a thing as a *perfectus* or *politus Epicureus*.[72] This perfection is attained by actually dislodging from the soul the excess of those atoms which are the causes of faults of character. The text of Lucretius is explicit: "In these matters I do seem able to make this assertion, that so infinitesimal are the residual traces of natural faults which reason cannot eradicate from the educated that nothing hinders them from passing a life worthy of the gods." [73]

It is further assumed that such men as attain this perfection through education will resemble one another. Nevertheless, the dislodgment of the evil atoms is not total; traces of the original disposition are left and under suitable circumstances the hot-tempered man will once more give way to anger. Analogous statements may be made of the cowardly, the lustful, and the rest. Thus those whom the perfection of education has raised to a kind of uniformity may still find themselves on occasion differing from one another.

About the identity of the reason, *ratio*, that dislodges the excesses of atoms there should be no doubt. It is the practical reason, *phronesis*, "the sober calculation, which investigates the reasons of every choice and avoidance and expels the false opinions, the chief cause of the turmoil that takes possession of the souls of men." Just how the atoms are dislodged is not explained in detail but the idea is not incongruous with the rest of Epicurean doctrine. The principle is often stressed that the atoms of each specific sort are in boundless supply and prompt to dart forward for the performance of their appropriate function. It may then be inferred that the surges of anger in the bosom of the hot-tempered man are actually caused by an inrush of the atoms resembling those of fire. Contrarily, it may be inferred that the practical reason, measuring the advantage and the disadvantage, actually forestalls the inrush of mischievous atoms. Thus the individual gains control of experience, which is the prerequisite of happiness.

CHAPTER XI ✠ SOUL, SENSATION, AND MIND

HAVING set forth his Twelve Elementary Principles, as shown in Chapter IX, Epicurus proceeds to treat these as major premises and to arrive at all other ideas by a procedure manifestly deductive. In the Little Epitome he expressly denotes these ideas as inferential or accessory, *epinoiai*.

The logical framework of the whole system has been faithfully reproduced by Lucretius. All the major premises of thought, that is, the Twelve Elementary Principles, are contained in the first two books. All the ideas expounded in the following books are to be regarded as inferential or accessory: III, the Soul; IV, Sensation; V, Human Institutions; VI, Celestial Phenomena; VII, the Gods. The last book was promised but never written. In the Little Epitome Epicurus makes a break after the seventh principle for pedagogical reasons but reverts later to the above arrangement.

It is assumed throughout the treatment of all these topics that Nature furnishes the norm and that the Sensations, Anticipations, and Feelings function as the criteria of truth. Concurrently the validity of a sort of faculty psychology is assumed, as was usual among the Greeks. To Epicurus the faculties are sensation, memory, and intellect or reason. Imagination is not, as with Aristotle, associated with vision, but is subsumed under reason.

One principle from which the nature of the soul is deduced is the third: "The universe consists of solid bodies and void." It follows from this by the procedure known in logic as the excluded middle that the soul, like the body itself, is corporeal, consisting of atoms. The contrary doctrine, that the soul is incorporeal, is disposed of by deductive reasoning. Let it be assumed that the soul is incorporeal. There is nothing in nature incorporeal except the void. This, however, is incapable, on the one hand, of initiating motion or of delivering a stimulus and, on the other hand, of receiving a stimulus from a moving body, but these capacities are the characteristic attributes of the soul. Therefore the assumption is false and the contrary proposition holds true: the soul is corporeal.[1]

The next of the Elementary Principles from which information concerning the nature of the soul may be drawn is the last, which declares the varieties of atoms to be innumerable. The problem, therefore, is to determine which varieties of atoms compose the soul. As might be expected, it is the Feelings and Sensations that serve as criteria. Under the Feelings may be cited sudden fright, which instantly convulses the whole being. As for the Sensations, their characteristic is quickness of response to stimulus, *eukinesia*, and with them are to be paired the reactions of thought, *dianoeseis*, as of perception and memory.[2] All of these bear witness to the extreme mobility of the soul.

From the evidence of these witnesses, Epicurus concludes that the soul must be composed of smooth, spherical, and fine atoms, because the coarse, rough, angular, and larger would be incapable of the mobility required for the instantaneousness of thought and feeling. Since the gradations of the atoms in respect of every quality are innumerable, it follows that to have names for them would be impossible. For this reason the best that Epicurus can do is compare the atoms of the soul to those of things remarkable for mobility. His choice fell upon wind and heat.[3] He does not mention air, because this element was associated with serenity and repose,[4] and it is his immediate purpose to dwell upon the quality of mobility. It is because his attention was concentrated upon this quality that he mentions another ingredient of the soul, "possessing a great superiority over wind and heat in point of fineness and thereby being all the more cosensitive with the rest of the organism." [5] The reference is to sudden joys and fears that convulse the whole being.

Incidentally, it should be noted that Epicurus does not declare this last ingredient to be nameless, for the excellent reason that to him the gradations of atoms were necessarily nameless, because innumerable. On this point and on the whole problem of the composition of the soul the modern scholar can be misled by Lucretius, who was not always precise. In stating that the soul was composed of heat, wind, air, and a nameless something, he was inexact; Epicurus in the Little Epitome is careful to say "atoms resembling those of wind and heat." [6] Next, by naming four ingredients Lucretius has encouraged the notion that the number four was canonical with Epicurus as with Empedocles and Aristotle, which is incorrect. Even the name of the famous fourfold remedy, the tetrapharmacon, was not of Epicurean origin; Epicurus would never have compared his doctrines to a household concoction of wax, tallow, pitch, and resin.

Lucretius also gives comfort to those who believe that Epicurus was copying Aristotle, who postulated a fifth and nameless ingredient of the soul. This is unfortunate, because Lucretius himself knew well the number of unnamed atoms to be past counting, and hence nameless. [7]

THE BODY A VESSEL

It is because of this extraordinary mobility and volatility of the soul that a subsidiary doctrine was promulgated, the body as a containing vessel for the soul. Lucretius propounds the idea with explicitness and perspicuity. [8] The atoms of the soul are more mobile than those of mist or smoke, for they are set in motion even by the phantoms of the smoke of incense, such as impinge upon the minds of dreamers. For this reason the soul disperses like water when the containing vessel is shattered or as mist and smoke that dissolve into the air: "Naturally, for how can you believe that this soul can in any way be held together by the air — which, being of a subtle nature, tends to restrain it less — when the body itself, which has been made, as it were, a vessel for the soul, if once shattered by some cause and laid open as the blood is withdrawn from the veins, is incapable of holding it together?" [9] Incidentally, Ecclesiastes, who seems to play hide-and-seek with Epicurean thought, has immortalized the shattering of the vessel as a euphemism for death in the beautiful words "the pitcher broken at the fountain." [10] Moreover, through varied employment in the New Testament the metaphor of the body as a vessel has become a commonplace in the language of religion. [11] In its original Epicurean contexts, however, it was no mere ornament of language but a logical necessity of thought.

Epicurus himself in the Little Epitome does not expressly denote the body as a vessel, but he conveys the idea by circumlocution and repetition, as was his custom. The soul, he says, alone and by itself does not possess the capacity of sensation; it has in itself only "the chief cause of sensation": "for it would not possess this, were it not, so to say, enveloped by the rest of the organism."[12] And by way of driving this truth home he repeats himself: "for it is impossible to think of it as experiencing sensation when not in this combination and as being capable of these reactions when the parts that envelope and contain it, within which it now is and is characterized by these reactions, are no longer such as they are now."[13]

This doctrine of the vessel inevitably provoked the scorn of adversaries, especially the Platonists, whose taunts were revived by Plutarch. For instance, the reference is to this when he speaks of the Epicureans "as pouring pleasure back and forth from the body into the soul and then from the soul into the body, since it spills and escapes them through fault of the container."[14] Moreover, since the metaphor of the vessel readily suggests the detail of the lid, little doubt can exist that Dante was exploiting this ancient gibe when, in the sixth circle of his Inferno, he chose to imagine a cemetery of lidless coffins in which the bodies of the infidel Epicureans upon the occasion of the resurrection were to be sealed along with their own souls. Such was to be the penalty for denying that the soul could exist without the body, an exquisite irony of punishment.

COSENSITIVITY OF SOUL AND BODY

Inseparably associated with the relationship of soul and body as the contained and the container is the phenomenon of cosensitivity. So volatile is the soul by nature that only within the envelope of the body is it capable of existing and playing its part. This fact bestows upon the body a certain priority of causation over the soul, paradoxical as this may seem. It is the more paradoxical because, according to Epicurus, the soul and the body come into existence simultaneously. He insists, however, upon so having it, that the body in the first instance bestows sensitivity upon the soul, whereupon it acquires a share in sensitivity for itself.[15] Nevertheless, it never acquires all the capacities of the soul; its active capacities are limited to touch, taste, smell, hearing, and vision, while the soul possesses also memory, intelligence, and reason. In addition to its active capacities the body also shares passively in the feelings of the soul, as is indicated by the phenomena of blushing, blanching, perspiring, chilling, and trembling.[16] The psychology of Epicurus is thus psychosomatic.

In promulgating this doctrine of cosensitivity Epicurus invoked a new and specialized meaning for the word *sympatheia*, just as Lucretius did for *consensus*. If pressed to its full extension the idea involves three elements: first, participation in sensation by body and soul, second, simultaneousness of participation, and third, mutual causation in the experience. These phenomena have their origin in the fact that body and soul are coterminous and coextensive, being contained within the same limits, as a fluid in a vessel, and intimately connected throughout the whole area at depth. So intimate is this interconnection presumed to be that it afforded ground for denial that the soul entered the body at birth. Its origin must have been simultaneous with conception and, as Lucretius aptly expresses it, while still reposing in the mother's womb "they learn the mutual contacts of the vital impulse." [17] Epicurus himself begins his description of the soul by declaring it "to be dispersed over the whole organism" and later treats the cosensitivity of body and soul as synonymous with "being contained within the same limits." [18]

There is one characteristic of the soul which Epicurus honors only by a hint in his little treatise for beginning students. This is the paucity of the atoms composing it. Once the soul has taken its leave, he tells us, the rest of the organism, whether surviving whole or in part, does not possess sensation, "irrespective of the number of atoms that contribute to bestowing upon the soul its peculiar nature." [19] In this particular, as we learn from Lucretius, he differed from Democritus, who had taught that atoms of soul alternated in the living being with atoms of the body.[20]

In order to ascertain the reasons for this innovation recourse must be had to the Big Epitome, which is richer in detail. The evidence, as usual, is furnished by the Sensations. First, the soul, though corporeal, does not add appreciably to the weight of the body; the living and the dead weigh alike. Secondly, there is a spatial limit to the sense of touch: such things as dust, feathers, and cobwebs are capable of coming to rest upon the body without registering their fall, nor does the sense of touch possess the delicacy necessary for perceiving the individual footsteps of insects that crawl upon the skin.[21] From such phenomena it can only be concluded that atoms of the soul are not so numerous as atoms of flesh and are consequently characterized by larger intervals of separation.

RATIONAL AND IRRATIONAL SOUL

A second characteristic of the soul at which Epicurus merely hints in the Little Epitome is its division into rational and irrational parts. To speak of "parts" is, of course, somewhat incorrect, although an excellent scholium in the extant text ascribes to Epicurus this particular teaching: "The one part of it is irrational, which is dispersed over the rest of the organism while the rational part is located in the breast." [22] Thus Lucretius is strictly correct when in broaching the topic he stresses the unity of the soul and, as if invoking the American principle *e pluribus unum*, insists that no one component is separable from the rest but, "so to say, all exhibit themselves as many capacities of a single unit." They are one, just as a certain odor, color, and taste are joined together in a single article of food.[23]

The unity of the soul, of course, is assured by the extreme mobility of all its component atoms. Yet even here the principle of the gradation of atoms holds good. There is mobility and also supermobility. On the periphery of the body are to be found only those atoms which deliver fleshly sensations such as touch, taste, smell, hearing, and vision. These sensations, as already stated, are irrational, and they represent the soul in its irrational functions. At the other extreme are atoms "far surpassing in perfection of smoothness and rotundity those of fire," [24] which are congregated far from the periphery of the body, in the breast, "so that nothing in our bodies is seated deeper." [25] This last conceit was spotted by Virgil as having poetical value:

Tum latebras animae, pectus mucrone recludit,[26]

"Then with the point of his sharp sword he lays open his breast, the hidden lair of the soul." In this he exhibited better taste than Lucretius, who represents as returning to its "lair" the intelligence of the drunkard, the epileptic, or the victim of a philter after being routed out by hard liquor, disease, or poison.[27]

Between these two extremes, then, the innermost part of the being and the body's periphery, it is the correct view to think of atoms graded minutely in respect of fineness and mobility, all the way from the superlative mobility of those at the center to the comparative mobility of those at the surface.

These atoms of the soul are at the same time homogeneous, because surpassing in mobility, and heterogeneous, because differing in mobility. They constitute a unit because arranged in order of mobility. The rational part cannot be separated from the irrational part. It cannot perform its function without the irrational part, because no stimulus reaches it unless communicated by the irrational part. As Lucretius warns his readers, every argument for the mortality of the soul is an argument for the mortality of the mind.[28] It is inconceivable to think of an incorporeal rational soul, as Plato and Aristotle did, because the faculty of reason is only a contingent capacity of an ordered body of atoms contained within the limits of the living corporeal vessel.

Since body and soul occupy the same space and are so ubiquitously interconnected, they are cosensitive and every reaction is psychosomatic. When the whole organism is in a state of health, the atoms of the soul are characterized by serenity, and they function as an automatic mechanism, the impulses darting back and forth in orderly fashion in both directions between center and circumference. By either disease of the body or terror of the mind the whole body can be convulsed and the atoms thrown into turmoil. The mind can even be routed from the breast, which is its proper seat, just as the ears are the seat of hearing and the eyes of vision.

Impulses originating on the periphery of the organism and transmitted to the center are called Sensations. These are accompanied by pleasure and pain, which are the Feelings. The data furnished by the Sensations and Feelings are processed by the mind or intelligence, *dianoia, animus, mens.* The mind is spoken of as "the rational part" but it is no more rational than emotional and volitional, all three being capacities contingent upon the life of the organism. Volitional and emotional impulses originate in the mind and are transmitted from the center to the whole organism.

The topics next calling for exposition are consequently the Workings of Sensation and Mental Processes. Brief mention will be made also of Motor Impulses because the topic of volition in the chapter on the New Freedom was discussed only from the point of view of ethics.

THE WORKINGS OF SENSATION

In the Little Epitome Epicurus first lists seven of his Twelve Elementary Principles and then turns to the exposition of accessory or inferential ideas, *epinoiai.* His first example is the multiplicity of worlds, easily deduced from the infinity of the universe. His second example is vision. There is consequently no doubt about the classification of this phenomenon in his scheme of thought: it is to be explained inferentially. The reasoning, as usual, is syncopated but the omitted steps are easily supplied. The universe consists of atoms and void. The void by definition is intangible and cannot deliver or receive a stimulus. Every stimulus, therefore, has its origin in the corporeal, which means the atoms; they are always in motion and no motion exists apart from them.

This subsidiary principle, that only the corporeal can deliver a stimulus and only the corporeal can receive one, results in reducing all sensation to the level of touch. This was beyond much doubt the gist of the contents of a treatise of Epicurus entitled *On Touch*.[29] It is also quite possible that from this roll the extant saying has been extracted that "seeing and hearing are just as real as feeling pain." [30] Even this, we may well believe, was not original with him, because Aristotle ascribes to certain physiologists the statement that seeing and hearing actually do cause pain though the human being becomes immune to the feeling.[31] What Epicurus meant, however, by the words quoted above will be this, that seeing and hearing result from corporeal bodies from external sources impinging upon the physical eye and ear and thus causing the sensations bearing corresponding names. These sensations, he might have said, are just as real as if the hand had touched some concrete object.

When once all sensations have been reduced to touch, it follows that taste, at least in part, has been accounted for. Thus only seeing, hearing, and smell need explanation and, as a matter of fact, these alone are mentioned in the Little Epitome. Seeing and hearing are naturally treated at greater length because discussion of the latter involves the mechanism of sound and that of the former the mechanism of vision.

VISION

In his explanation of vision Epicurus sets himself in opposition to both Democritus and Plato. The latter had thought of the eyes as discharging little beams of light, which, being homogeneous with the light of day, were capable of revealing the shapes and colors of external objects and of conveying the impressions of them back to the consciousness of the observer. The essential part of this theory is the homogeneity of the beam extending between eye and object, which ensures that red will be reported red and square square. In darkness homogeneity is lacking and hence vision also. Although stimuli, *kineseis*, are spoken of, it is not made clear how the stimulus is delivered.[32]

According to Democritus the intervening air served the purpose of a medium in vision, being shaped into images by the pulsation of the atoms in an object, and these images caused the sensation by falling upon the soft and moist surface of the pupil, as upon a mirror.[33] If the adoption of the air as a medium was occasioned by a fear that atoms of solid bodies might wound the delicate surface of the eye, we may well understand why Epicurus, in rejecting his master's teaching, dwells so positively upon the extreme filminess of the idols which he represents all bodies as discharging. At the same time that he overcomes this difficulty he gives the opinion that the stream of idols thrown off by the object itself accounts more satisfactorily for the precision of the image impressed upon the eyes, as if by an engraved seal.[34]

The theory of the idols being assumed as true, already described in the chapter on the New Physics, the rest of the exposition may be pieced together with all the perspicuity desired. The stream of idols discharged at high velocity by the external object impinges upon the eye, causing a pressure, *epeireismos*.[35] This, in turn, acts as a stimulus, *kinesis*.[36] The stimulus is recognized by the intelligence, *dianoia*, which is itself, of course, of a material nature, consisting of the most mobile and sensitive of all atoms. The intelligence, in turn, jogs the memory and, if the stimulus corresponds with something on record there, the verdict is a recognition, *epaisthesis* or *epaisthema*;[37] in such a word the prefix *ep-*, for *epi*, has the perfective force, denoting that the action reaches an appointed goal. For instance, the observer may say, "It is a horse." Thus the act of apperception, according to Epicurus, is essentially an act of recognition.[38]

The account of the working of vision deserves comment as a characteristic specimen of his textbook style, avoiding technicalities and achieving the desired clearness by paraphrastic repetition.[39] It is assumed that the presentation is a phantasia, clear and close. The idols streaming from the external object are "of one color and like shape" to those of the original; the magnitude is "proportionate," because reduction in size must be assumed; the number of idols is innumerable but they deliver the phantasia "of the single and undisintegrated object"; they preserve the *sympatheia*, "the likeness of effect," because the pressure exerted by the stream of idols upon the eyes is "symmetrical," that is, not distorted.[40] The student may be reminded of Plato's use of *homoiopathes*, "of like effect," in his account of vision.[41]

The account concludes as follows: "and whatever phantasia, whether of shape or of attributes, we receive by impact through the mind or the organs of sense, this is the (true) shape of the solid body." [42] To this, as if the preceding explanation had been insufficient, it is added that the presentation is true "by virtue of the orderly condensation or residue of the image." This means that the image of a house, let us say, is symmetrically reduced in size in the workings of vision and the image registered in the eyes is a residue of the original idols.

HEARING

The explanation of hearing involves the nature of speech and sound and this in turn the origin of language. According to Epicurus the latter began with the involuntary cries of humankind. Moreover, just as different animals make different vocal responses to a given stimulus, so the different races of men "emitted the air differently, freighted in each instance with sound as evoked by this or that emotion or spectacle." [43] This implies that the sounds are corporeal and that the streams of breath are variously charged with them. The theory that the air itself takes on the shape of words, as Democritus supposed, is rejected.

Both accounts are materialistic and save the principle that only the corporeal is capable of delivering a stimulus to the corporeal. Lucretius, though leaving it uncertain whether or not air is the medium, is emphatic enough on the point that words themselves are corporeal. This is proved by the friction of speech on the throat, causing hoarseness after long conversation, and by the superior penetrating quality of high notes in music over low.[44] He also mentions with scorn the notion that the grating notes of the saw can consist of atoms so smooth as those of the pipe organ's melodies.[45]

The most precise and concise statement on the topic is from the pen of Epicurus himself: "The instant we utter voice, the impulse delivered within us causes a discharge of certain minute conformations capable of forming a stream resembling breath and this discharge is such as to produce the sensation of hearing." [46] These minute conformations, in turn, subdivide into still more minute conformations, otherwise identical with the originals, and scatter into all directions so that all the people in the assembly, for example, hear the voice of a single crier. As a general thing, it is added by Epicurus — and this is an essential part of his theory — recognition takes place. Otherwise, the listener merely becomes aware of the presence of something external. Lucretius makes the same point.[47] This should remind us that to Epicurus a complete sensation terminates in a recognition.

The brevity with which the topic of smell is dismissed in the Little Epitome serves to indicate a diminution of interest and importance.[48] The problem was not controversial; under no system of thought could it be denied that odoriferous substances discharge something corporeal and capable of stimulating the sense of smell. This discharge very naturally invites comparison with the idols that account for vision and the conformations that account for hearing. The idols of vision require a straight and unobstructed runway, since the pattern of the picture is readily disrupted by obstacles. The conformations that cause hearing, on the contrary, are capable of penetrating walls and for this reason must be smaller in dimensions. The conformations that cause the sensation of smell, since they do not penetrate walls, must be coarser. Lastly, since odors wander leisurely about, it must be inferred that they are not discharged with vigor as are the idols and spoken words.

The previous details are furnished by Lucretius from the ampler store of the Big Epitome and he also cites the special capacities of certain creatures to detect certain odors, such as bees, hounds, and geese.[49] The account rendered by Epicurus himself in the Little Epitome is brief enough to quote in full: "Moreover we must believe that smell, precisely as hearing, would never result in sensation unless there were floating off from the substance certain minute conformations of a nature suitable for stimulating this organ of sense, those of one sort being disturbing and offensive, those of another sort being reassuring and inviting." [50] The last item refers to a commonplace of animal lore that wild creatures are diverted by odors from what is poisonous and drawn by the same to their appropriate food, of which Lucretius also makes mention.[51]

MIND AS A SUPERSENSE

It is part of the psychology of Epicurus that the mind under certain conditions is capable of functioning as an organ of sense; thus the procedure of Lucretius is quite regular in discussing the topic immediately after sensation. The exposition presumes certain subsidiary ideas, such as the gradations of atoms, the irrational nature of sensation, the faculty psychology, and a phenomenon of double reactions.

The gradation of atoms is basic to the account of sensation. The conformations that cause vision, for instance, while finer and more mobile than those of odors, are not sinuous enough to penetrate walls, as sounds do. Vision, moreover, is subject to another limitation: unless the idols be discharged from an object in plain view and so constitute a steady stream, no sufficient pressure on the eyes results and no sensation registers itself. Of the random and vagrant idols only the mind can take cognizance because of the extreme mobility of its component atoms and the resulting supersensitivity.

In order to discern the circumstances under which this takes place the principle must be invoked that sensation is irrational. It merely delivers a stimulus and this may fail of registering itself. It is possible to hear without listening and to see without observing.

Down to this point there is nothing peculiar in the thought of Epicurus. The rest of the teaching is his own. He thinks of the mind as a mechanism for processing sensations. Its activity may be automatic or volitional. The automatic mind, though normally dependable, is capable of erring; it may report the square tower to be round. To guard against such errors and to correct them when once made is the function of the volitional mind, directed by reason. Unlike the automatic mind, it pays attention to all sensations and corrects the false by calling the true to witness.

In dreamful sleep, according to Epicurus, the erring, automatic mind alone is active. Bodily sensation, memory and volition are all quiescent. Under these circumstances the stage is cleared for the entrance of all the random, floating idols that survive from the swift, coherent streams that under waking conditions press upon the organs of sense and register themselves as sensations. Of these errant, subsensory idols the passive mind, partly because of its relief from interference and control, and partly because of the supermobility and supersensitivity of its component atoms, alone is capable of taking cognizance. Thus it functions as a supersense.

To complete this exposition a subsidiary doctrine of the two reactions must be invoked. Let it be assumed that the image of a centaur presents itself to the dreamer; it may even be a galloping centaur. This acts as a stimulus to the mind and causes a reaction, *kinesis*. This is not the end, however, because a second reaction follows and the automatic mind registers a recognition: "It is a centaur." The dream carries the conviction of reality because the memory and the volitional mind, which is rational, are quiescent. Thus the deceitfulness of dreams is an error of the same kind as that of the automatic mind that judges the square tower to be round. The waking mind, in command of the total experience, knows that no such things as centaurs exist.

Even this is not the whole story. The mind is capable of functioning as a supersense even in the hours of waking. It loses this capacity if the being is in a turmoil through fears and anxieties. Thus Lucretius warns Memmius that, unless free from such fears "you will never be able to capture with unruffled peace of mind the idols that from the blessed bodies of the gods float into the minds of men." [52] These idols belong in that isolated, vagrant class of images, which, not being part of a pressing stream, are imperceptible to fleshly sensation and register themselves only upon the mind and only under restricted conditions.

The caution must be observed, however, that visions of the mind do not enjoy the status of criteria of truth. They do possess value but only at the level of circumstantial evidence; they afford reason for believing, by way of example, that the bodies of the gods are anthropomorphic.

EMOTIONAL IMPULSES

While Lucretius tells us that sensory impulses originate in the periphery of the bodily vessel and communicate themselves to the mind, which is at the center, he adds that emotional impulses originate in the mind and communicate themselves in the contrary direction to all parts of the body. In no other context is the principle of the gradations of atoms more distinctly assumed. Let us presume that the emotion is the most powerful imaginable, which to Epicurus was the fear of losing one's life or the joy of escaping destruction. The commotion begins deep in the breast, where the finest and most mobile atoms are congregated. It communicates itself in turn to the atoms of heat, wind, and air; next the blood feels the turmoil, the flesh is convulsed, and last of all the distress is registered in the bones and marrow.[53]

This description would be strictly according to the book if only Lucretius had been more precise in his language and instead of atoms of heat and the rest had spoken of "atoms resembling those of heat and the rest." The sweep of poetry, however, must not be impeded by technicalities; to Epicurus himself the medium of poetry had become outmoded for purposes of exposition.

Lucretius was correct in declaring that the majority of emotional impulses terminate at the surface of the body, resulting in blushing, blanching, perspiration, chills, and tremors. The most violent of all emotions, however, might dislodge the mind, "the soul of the soul," from its seat deep in the breast, expel it through the channels of the flesh, and terminate in death.[54]

MOTOR IMPULSES

It was likewise necessary that Epicurus should furnish an account of bodily movement in harmony with his materialistic principles. For information we are again dependent upon Lucretius, because this topic was omitted from the Little Epitome as being unessential for beginning students. It has already been mentioned that all the phenomena of consciousness, or as Epicurus puts it, the capacities "without which we die," were appraised to be accidents, that is, contingent upon the cosensitivity of soul and body. It might then have been thought that volition, being one of these contingent capacities, should have ranked as an adequate cause for the inception of all bodily movements.

Such was not the case. Even for an act of volition an external cause must be found. Before the human being makes the decision to walk, his mind must receive a stimulus from the impact of images of himself in the act of walking. *Inde voluntas fit,* "from this stimulus results the will to walk," if the translation may be expanded to bring out its implication.[55] Incidentally, readers will recognize in this theory a precise anticipation of gestalt psychology.

This explanation, if there were no more to it, might win for itself a certain admiration as a smart invention. To accept the rest of it is very difficult. It is not unacceptable to be told that the impulse which has been started in the mind, though not by the mind, communicates itself to the rest of the soul, dispersed over the whole body, but when we read that movement comes about through the dilation of all the minute channels of the body, allowing the circulation of surges of air to all parts, this is too fantastic to seem reasonable. Neither does the comparison with the winds driving ships or derricks lifting huge stones result in a verdict of plausibility. The theory may well confirm, however, the truth of the tradition that Epicurus believed the earth to be buoyed up by air.[56] By way of excuse for him it may be recalled that he had lived for four years in Lampsacus on the Hellespont, perhaps the windiest spot that was known to his countrymen, and winds do perform miracles.

MIND

It is now possible to summarize the psychology of Epicurus and to describe with more precision and detail his teaching concerning the mind and its activities.

The human being consists of body and soul, both alike corporeal by nature. The two are born at the same time and grow and decline in pace with one another. They are coterminous and cosensitive. They function as a unit and reactions are psychosomatic.

The soul consists of atoms surpassing others in fineness, smoothness, and sphericity and consequently in mobility. All the component atoms are in contact throughout the body, unless in the condition of sleep, when the contiguity is broken, part of the soul escaping from the containing body, part retreating deep within. In daydreaming a less extensive but similar condition arises. Among the component atoms gradations of mobility exist, the less mobile being at the periphery and associated with the operations of sense, which are all varieties of touch. The most mobile of the component atoms constitute the rational part of the soul and are situated deep within the breast. This location is no less fixed than that of the ears or eyes, because the mind is an organ of the being no less than they.

Although it is usual to speak of this part of the soul as rational, the adjective is inadequate. The so-called rational part could with equal justice be called the emotional part, because fears and joys, according to Epicurus, have their seat in the same place.[57] In this instance the Latin language is for once superior to Greek in respect of terminology. The word *mens* is capable of denoting both mental and emotional aspects of the mind's activity, while *animus* can be equated with Greek *dianoia*, "intellect," and *anima* may be used as equivalent to *psyche*, "soul," including all capacities, rational, emotional, and sensory.

The activity of the rational part, *dianoia, animus,* is either voluntary or involuntary, that is, either automatic or volitional. The character of the automatic mind that most impressed Epicurus was its speed. Its function is to receive and process sensations and under normal conditions this is done instantaneously: to cite trite examples, the individual is unerringly warned of ditches and precipices and other dangers in his path. It is this automatic mind that takes care of man in his daily rounds on the physical or somatic level of life.

The Sensations are irrational and merely register a stimulus, *kinesis*. It is the quick and automatic mind that with the aid of memory registers a recognition and says, "This is honey." It is likewise the mind that makes the generalization "Honey is sweet." These are "fantastic perceptions of the intelligence." They do not possess the rank of criteria because they are not a direct contact between mind and matter but are rather the result of a process or operation. "Fantastic" means "immediate." [58]

Under the abnormal conditions of either genuine dreaming or daydreaming the supersensitive mind is capable of operating as a sense, registering the incidence of those vagrant idols which, being detached from visual streams, are incapable of exerting pressure and stimulating the senses of the flesh. These visions, however, do not rank as criteria, being subject to no correction by the conscious, rational mind.

Even under normal conditions, however, the automatic mind is liable to err. This error often consists in adding to and subtracting from the data of sense. For instance, to the observer the moon may seem to be moving and the drifting clouds to be standing still; or the shore may seem to be moving and the passing ship to be stationary; or the anchored ship may seem to the passenger to be moving and the passing ship to be motionless. In all of these examples the error is not in sensation but in the automatic mind, which adds motion to standing objects and subtracts it from moving objects. Epicurus calls this error "the addition of opinion," but the fact that it also includes subtraction is recognized by the statement that sensation "is neither stimulated by itself nor, when stimulated by an external object, is it capable of adding or subtracting anything." [59] In such instances Epicurus is at pains to point out that the reaction caused by sensation is followed by a second reaction within the observer "which is connected with 'the fantastic perception' but distinct from it." [60] This second, involuntary reaction is the source of error.

It is another shortcoming of the automatic mind that its operations confine themselves to the sensations of the moment. It must consequently be subjected to correction by the volitional mind, which is truly rational. The latter is aware of the danger of error; it remembers that the value of sensations depends upon distances; it recollects past sensations; it takes cognizance of all sensations and it appeals to the observations of others.[61]

Unlike the automatic mind that warns the observer of ditches and precipices, the volitional mind takes cognizance of the Anticipations, that is, the innate ideas of justice, of the divine nature, and other such abstractions, and it puts to the test every law of the land to determine whether it harmonizes with the innate idea of justice. The volitional mind also takes cognizance of the Feelings, that is, those fears and anxieties which warn the individual of the false opinions concerning things of supreme importance, the causes of the worst turmoil in the soul.

The status of the volitional mind, which alone is truly rational, is that of a judge presiding in court. The litigants are truth and error. The role of the Sensations, Anticipations, and Feelings is that of witnesses. The judge, as becomes his office, rejects no evidence that is pertinent; he distinguishes between mere opinion and knowledge, between the idea that awaits confirmation by additional evidence and that which is already certain, between the immediate, dependable sensation and the deceptive, distant view, between false pleasures and wholesome pleasures and between true and false concepts of abstract truth. If the mind falls short of performing these judicial functions, the conflict in the soul will be prolonged and no satisfying decision between truth and error will be attainable. This is the gist of Authorized Doctrine 24.

The point that bears the stress in the above exposition is the danger of indecision, which is even more destructive of happiness than false opinion. For example, it is worse to suspect the truth of the tales about Acheron than to believe in them.[62] Again, the sole reason for acquiring knowledge of celestial phenomena is "serenity of mind and an unshakable faith." [63] The lack of faith, *apistia*, is of the same effect as indecision, *akrisia*. Both spell turmoil.

This equivalence of indecision with lack of faith is made clear in two sayings. The first is Doctrine 22: "We must take into our reckoning the established telos [pleasure] and all the manifest evidence, to which we refer the opinions we form. If we fail to do so, our whole life will be filled with indecision and turmoil." The second dictum is Vatican Saying 57: "His whole life will be thrown into confusion through lack of faith and will be wrecked." Epicurus was in the process of discovering the part played by faith in the happy life. In so doing he was preparing popular thought for the acceptance of the New Testament, where faith at last attained to full stature as a virtue. The difference between faith as it first emerged and the perfected faith resides in the fact that the former was faith in the truth of doctrine while the latter was faith in Jesus Christ as a redeemer.

With the idea of mind as a judicial faculty Epicurus anticipated the practical reason of modern philosophy; in the Platonic vocabulary it was *phronesis*. Describing it by paraphrase in his usual way, he called it "sober calculation" and assigned to it the function "of investigating the reasons for every choice and avoidance and of expelling false opinions, the chief cause of the turbulence that takes possession of the souls of men." It was to him the starting point for all the virtues and for this reason more precious than philosophy, by which he meant what is now called pure reason, and when he says "it teaches the impossibility of living happily without living according to reason, honor and justice," [64] he means that geometry was incapable of imparting this lesson. It is true that geometry is not mentioned, but by implication the Platonic program of education, based upon mathematics, is being repudiated.

As an essential precaution it deserves to be emphasized that this concept of the rational mind as a judge, soberly weighing the evidence contributed by the Sensations, Anticipations, and Feelings, which perform the office of witnesses, constitutes a frame of reference without which the teachings of Epicurus are bound to be misapprehended. This frame, moreover, is incomplete without the Twelve Elementary Principles, which are, as it were, a sort of legal code, in harmony with which the judging mind must reach its decisions.

That these Twelve Principles were the starting point for the Epicurean program of education is unmistakable whether from the Little Epitome or Lucretius. The truth of them was not demonstrated inductively from sensation but established deductively and only confirmed by sensation. If this involves a logical fallacy or a philosophical defect, it must be borne in mind that Epicurus was not constructing a theory of knowledge but a philosophy that would serve as a road to happiness. This called for a set of principles, a judging mind, and dependable witnesses, all of which his system furnished.

It was his view that only notions accessory or inferential to the Twelve Principles, such as the nature of the soul, had their origin in sensations. If this is a fallacy or a defect, it should be borne in mind that he was not working out a psychology but merely showing how his system based upon principles, the practical reason, and evidence was intended to operate. The notion of consciousness, as employed in modern psychology, lay outside of his problem and so he had no need to deal with the content of consciousness.

It should nevertheless be remembered that a misunderstanding of his teaching gave rise to Gassendi's doctrine "that there is nothing in the intellect which has not been in the senses" and that this in turn was a starting point for John Locke and modern empiricism. Epicurus was not himself an empiricist but rather an intuitionist: the mind of the infant was to his thinking not a blank tablet but already laced with the faint outlines of ideas that should gradually acquire definition in pace with experience, instruction, and reflection.

CHAPTER XII ✛ THE NEW HEDONISM

I N HIS structure of doctrine Epicurus took up the various aspects
of the problem of pleasure where they had been left by Aristippus, Eudoxus, Plato, and Aristotle and handled them with such
superior precision that this line of inquiry, so far as antiquity was concerned, became exhausted. After his time the various schools merely
bickered over the tenability of his findings. Thus the justification is
excellent for entitling this chapter "The New Hedonism."

Epicurus was following the lead of his predecessors when he found
in the behavior of animate creatures the evidence for identifying
pleasure as the end or telos, but he improved upon their procedure
by narrowing his observations to the behavior of newborn creatures,
which as yet possess neither volition nor intelligence. This procedure
was in effect a sort of genetic approach, which made pleasure "the
root of all good" and "the beginning and the end of the happy life."
It also afforded ground for asserting the essential unity of pleasure,
which in turn made available a telling device, the sorites syllogism,
against the Platonists, who declared some pleasures to be good and
some bad and placed the pleasure of the mind in a class by itself.

Epicurus also displayed intellectual enterprise and ingenuity in discerning and exploiting the logical implications of the belief in the
mortality of the soul. This belief, deduced from the corporeal nature
of the soul, resulted in placing body and soul upon a parity, and from
this parity it followed that the good or telos, which as a unit was
pleasure, must also be dualistic, a sound mind in a sound body. This
same parity, since it minimized the difference between body and soul,
both being corporeal, caused Epicurus to adopt a new antithesis and
oppose the flesh to the soul, a usage which has become commonplace
through its perpetuation in the New Testament.

Moreover, since the denial of immortality and the surrender of its rewards demanded the discovery of an ethical counterpoise, Epicurus developed compensating teachings both negative and positive. The negative teaching took the form of a denial that pleasure could be increased by immortality; the positive teaching consisted in the doctrine of the fullness of pleasure in this mortal life. This subsidiary doctrine affected the thinking of St. Paul and survives under various aspects in the New Testament, such as "the fullness of Christ" and "the fullness of Godhead."

Once again, by insisting upon maintaining a fixed relation between true pleasure and natural and necessary desires, Epicurus was justified in establishing a ceiling for true pleasure. By this step he made possible the continuity of pleasure, which had been considered impossible by Aristippus, who recognized only kinetic pleasures or pleasures of excitement, and also by Plato, who had recognized "mixed states" and "neutral states." As for kinetic pleasures, while recognizing them, Epicurus found a way to discern equal or greater values in static pleasures. For example, if the joy of escaping a violent death is kinetic, why should there not be a static pleasure in possessing life? This required a new way of thinking and was possible only "for those who were capable of figuring the problem out." This marked him as a pragmatist, insisting upon the control of experience, including the control of thought.

He also had something new to say on the true relation of pleasure to pain. Some had believed them true opposites on the ground of universal pursuit and universal avoidance. Others had firmly denied this on the ground that some pleasures were good and some bad, while some denied that any pleasures were good. Neither were either laymen or philosophers agreed upon the nature of pain; Antisthenes and the Spartans classified it as good. Epicurus discovered a logical position for himself by positing an indissoluble connection between pleasure and health and between pain and disease. No one could then with reason deny that pleasure was a true opposite to pain since it would mean denying that health was a true opposite to disease. Neither could men deny that health was a good and disease an evil. By the same token pleasure was bound to be a good and pain an evil.

Finally, Epicurus scored a logical point over his predecessors in drawing a distinction between the greatest good, which he declared to be life itself, and the end or telos. His predecessors, when they defined the good or telos as that to which all other goods were referred while the good itself was referred to nothing, were illogical. Every supreme good, even the eudaemonistic good of Aristotle, is meaningless to the dead; every supreme good presumes life. It was very natural that Epicurus should have been the one to place the finger upon this confusion of thought; since he denied immortality, he discerned that all values must be concentrated in the space between birth and death. Life itself became the greatest good. Modern editors, however, still labor under the old misapprehension that pleasure is the Epicurean *summum bonum* and emend the text in order to save the fallacy.

THE "SUMMUM BONUM" FALLACY

The first step toward understanding rightly the new hedonism of Epicurus is to discern and eliminate this *summum bonum* fallacy. Since the Latin language lacks the definite article, the Romans were unable to say "the good," which is in Greek an alternative way of denoting the end or telos of an art or activity. Neither could the word *finis* be equated with *telos,* because it means *end* in the sense of limit or termination and not in the sense of fulfillment or consummation. Consequently the Romans were forced to adopt a makeshift, which happened to be *summum bonum.* Only by convention was this employed to denote the telos, but so inveterate did the convention become that the ambiguity of *summum bonum* was overlooked. Literally it means the highest or greatest good but this was not necessarily the telos. To Epicurus pleasure was the telos and life itself was the greatest good. Thus the hedonism of Epicurus must be explained from the beginning.

The belief that life itself is the greatest good conditions the whole ethical doctrine of Epicurus. He sees life as narrowly confined between the limits of birth and death. Soul and body are born together and perish together. Metrodorus gave telling expression in figurative language to this melancholy belief, Vatican Saying 30: "The potion mixed at birth for all of us is a draught of death." There was for Epicureans no pre-existence, as Plato believed, and no afterlife, as the majority of mankind believed. Epicurus himself expressed the thought with stark directness, Vatican Saying 14: "We are born once and we cannot be born twice but to all eternity must be no more." Thus the supreme values must be sought between the limits of birth and death.

The specific teaching that life itself is the greatest good is to be drawn from Vatican Saying 42: "The same span of time includes both beginning and termination of the greatest good." If this seems to be a dark saying, the obscurity is dispelled by viewing it as merely a denial of belief in either pre-existence or the afterlife. As Horace wrote, concluding *Epistle* i.16 with stinging abruptness, "Death is the tape-line that ends the race of life." Editors, however, misled by the *summum bonum* fallacy, equate "the greatest good" with pleasure and so are forced to emend. The change of a single letter does the trick but fundamental teaching is obliterated.[1]

While this quoted statement is first-hand evidence of the Epicurean attitude, the syllogistic approach is also known from an extant text, of which the significance has been overlooked. The major premise is the assumption that the greatest good must be associated with the most powerful emotions, that is, the worst of all fears and the greatest of all joys. Now the worst of all fears is that of a violent death and the greatest of all joys is escape from the same. The supporting text runs as follows: "That which occasions unsurpassable joy is the bare escape from some dreadful calamity; and this is the nature of 'good,' if one apprehend it rightly and then stand by his finding, and not go on walking round and round and harping uselessly on the meaning of 'good'." [2] This passage marks the summary cutting of a Gordian knot, the meaning of "good," upon which Plato had harped so tediously. Epicurus finds a quick solution by appealing to the Feelings, that is to Nature, as the criterion; it is their verdict that the supreme good is life itself, because the strongest emotions are occasioned by the threat of losing it or the prospect of saving it.

PLEASURE IDENTIFIED AS THE TELOS

When once the *summum bonum* fallacy has been detected and the difference clearly discerned between the greatest good, which is life itself, and the end or telos, the next step is to apprehend clearly by what procedure the end or telos is identified as pleasure. The nature of this procedure and of the attitude which determined it was one thing in the time of Cicero and quite another in the time of Epicurus himself. In the space of the two centuries between these two men the study of formal logic had been forced into a dominating position in the curriculum through the aggressive genius of the Stoic Chrysippus, and after his time the incessant needling of Stoic adversaries had shaken the confidence of many Epicureans in the word of their founder.[3] The faith of Epicurus himself had pinned itself upon Nature as the norm, not upon Reason. The faith of the Stoic, on the contrary, and of those Epicureans who wavered in their faith, while ostensibly pinned upon Reason, may more correctly be said to have been pinned upon argumentation and disputation.

When Epicurus himself identified pleasure as "the end of Nature" he was setting Reason aside and recognizing Nature as the norm or as furnishing the norm. In this he was merely following a trend of his time. The brilliant Eudoxus, for example, who had preceded him by no great interval, also declared pleasure to be the good and he took his start from the observation that all creatures, whether rational or irrational, pursued it.[4] Confirmation for the truth of this observation was found in the behavior of all creatures toward pain. If we may accept as authentic the tradition as reported by Aristotle, it would seem that Eudoxus thought of the pursuit of pleasure as comparable to the instinct of wild creatures to seek their proper food and to avoid the opposite. This demonstrates clearly the incipient tendency to recognize Nature as furnishing the norm.[5]

Thus the originality of Epicurus did not consist in recognizing Nature as furnishing the norm but in working out this principle to its utmost limit, which he did by setting up his Canon, each item of which, Sensations, Anticipations, and Feelings, was a separate appeal to the authority of Nature.

In identifying pleasure as the end or telos it is both possible and probable that Epicurus was taking up a suggestion of Aristotle, who dropped the hint in this instance that the evidence drawn from the behavior of irrational creatures is superior in value to the evidence drawn from the behavior of rational creatures.[6] At any rate the declaration of Epicurus, as reported by Cicero, runs as follows: "Every living creature, the moment it is born, reaches out for pleasure and rejoices in it as the highest good, shrinks from pain as the greatest evil, and, so far as it is able, averts it from itself."[7]

In the evaluation of this text the important words are "the moment it is born." By narrowing the field of observation to the newborn creature Epicurus was eliminating all differences between rational and irrational creatures. In infancy even the creatures that by courtesy we call rational are as yet irrational. By narrowing the field to the newborn Epicurus was also reducing animate life to its minimum value, because at the moment of birth even some of the senses have not yet begun to function. Consequently, as Cicero says in the same context, "since nothing is left of a human being when the senses are eliminated, the question, what is according to Nature or contrary to Nature, is of necessity being judged by Nature herself."

It is doubtful whether any other item of Epicurean invention is the equal of this in logical acumen. Even if weight be allowed to the later objection of the Stoics that the behavior of the infant has its cause in what we now call the instinct of self-preservation, this interpretation would lead to the recognition of life as the greatest good, which was the doctrine of Epicurus, and it would still be left for pleasure and pain to function as the criteria.

Incidentally, this appeal to the evidence afforded by the newly born exercised its effect upon the terminology of Epicurus. The infant, being still in a state of nature, is "not yet perverted." These words afford a hint of the perversion ascribed to the study of rhetoric, dialectic, and mathematics, which a lad was judged lucky to have escaped. As for Nature herself, she speaks through the newly born "undefiled and uncontaminated." Her word is "true philosophy," the *vera ratio* so often invoked by Lucretius.

Out of this teaching arises a perplexing question. Was Epicurus, in making of Nature a judge, and incidentally a teacher, involuntarily ascribing to her a certain purposiveness and by so doing admitting himself as a believer in teleology? On the face of it this would be going contrary to his fundamental teachings. In his cosmos a single primary cause was recognized, the downward motion of the atoms. In the over-all picture it was true that the good prevailed over the bad, but this was a deduction from the infinity of the universe and the infinity of time; in the individual worlds the forces of destruction eventually prevailed over the forces of creation but never in the universe at large. This ascendancy of the good over the bad, however, does not signify purposiveness or some far-off divine event toward which the whole creation moves. For such teleology there was no room in the cosmos of Epicurus.

How could he, then, with consistency arrive at the conclusion that in the case of human beings there was a telos, which he identified as pleasure? To this question there is an answer. In the reasonings of the preceding atomists there had been a flaw: in effect they had reached the conclusion that a nonpurposive Nature had at last produced a creature endowed with volition and intelligence as contingent capacities; but they had overlooked the fact that this human volition would be incapable of exercise if the universe were ruled by inexorable physical law, a form of Necessity. Epicurus corrected this oversight by postulating that a sufficient degree of free play prevailed in the motion of the atoms to permit man to exercise his volition. This was the famous doctrine of the swerve.

So much for the flaw in the reasoning of predecessors. The question still remains, however, whether the reasoning of Epicurus is faulty when he makes a judge and a teacher of Nature, who seems to deliver the verdict that pleasure is the telos and to inform man of the fact.

This error is not really committed, even if Lucretius personifies Nature and places a poetical and ethical diatribe in her mouth at the end of the third book. The meaning of the word *nature* is to be closely scanned. When Epicurus says, "Nature is not to be coerced," he means human nature. Similarly, when he wrote, "It must be assumed that Nature was taught a multitude of lessons of all sorts by sheer experience," he means human nature, looking upon the experience of the race as a joint phenomenon and as cumulative.

Even this cumulative experience need not be deemed purposive, even if intelligent. When such phrases are employed as "the justice of Nature" or "the limits of Nature," this means only that the intelligent agent looks to the phenomena of Nature in order to observe there the signs by which he shall know the true nature of justice and the true limits of pleasures. In the same way he looks to the behavior of the newly born for the signs that shall inform him of the identity of the telos of living.

In passages where the word *nature* does not mean human nature, it signifies the blind activity of the universe, the sum of all matter and motion, which is nonpurposive and almost equally destructive as creative. Both Epicurus and Lucretius personify Nature, but Epicurus also personifies Prudence or the practical reason, making a teacher of her.[8] This is mere figurative language. There is no fallacy in the thought. Even though Epicurus affected the bald style of Euclid and abjured figures of speech, there was a poetical vein in his own nature to which he yielded at times.

Thus, so far as touches teleology, the net situation may be described as follows: there is no purposiveness in Nature, but in the processes of nonpurposive creation she has brought into being a purposive creature, man. For him, being capable of reason, a telos is conceivable.

THE TRUE NATURE OF PLEASURE

While the identity of the end or telos is declared to have been established by Nature, recourse must be had to observation and reflection to determine what can be truthfully predicated of it. Tied in with this problem is the question of the true relation of pleasure to pain.

On both these points the findings of Epicurus, though clear and explicit, are regularly misrepresented. Pleasure, he declares, is cognate and connate with us, and by this he means not only that the interconnection between life and pleasure manifests itself simultaneously with birth and by actions that precede the capacity to choose and understand; he means also that pleasure is of one nature with normal life, an ingredient or component of it, and not an appendage that may be attached and detached; it is a normal accompaniment of life in the same sense that pain and disease are abnormal.

It follows from this that pleasure is not to be opposed to pain on the ground alone that all creatures pursue the one and avoid the other; the two are true opposites because they stand in the same relation as health which preserves and disease which destroys. It is for this reason that the one is good and the other is evil, Vatican Saying 37: "Human nature is vulnerable to evil, not to the good, because it is preserved by pleasures, destroyed by pains." This may be taken to mean that pleasure, as it were, is nutriment to the human being, as food is, and that human nature reaches out for it just as each living thing by some natural impulse seeks its appropriate food. It is no accident that the following statement of Aristotle is to be found in his discussion of pleasure: "And it may well be that in the lower animals there is some natural good, superior to their scale of existence, which reaches out for the kindred good." [9] With this surmise Epicurus would have concurred: all creatures seek pleasure as if food; they avoid pain as if poison.

THE DUALISTIC GOOD

When once the association of pleasure with health and pain with disease has been established, the next step is to recognize the good as dualistic, being concerned with soul and body alike.

This teaching is ultimately derived from the denial of immortality. The belief in immortality confers upon the soul an adventitious superiority of importance and upon the body an adventitious inferiority. For Epicurus, on the contrary, the belief in the mortal nature of both soul and body, their simultaneous birth, their continuous interdependence, their cosensitivity and coterminous existence conferred upon the two a parity of importance. The body was appraised as a containing vessel but not as a prison or a tomb; there was no incentive to mortify the one for the sake of the other. The physician must be also a psychiatrist, and the point of view is psychosomatic.

From such materialistic reasoning arose the famous Epicurean doctrine of the dualistic good, health of body and health of mind. Even if no longer citable in so many words from the extant remains, it is abundantly assumed; it was absorbed anonymously into the stream of Western culture and survives in thought and literature down to our day. In Rome, where Epicurean teaching under Augustus was forced into anonymity, this ideal was publicized by the poet Horace, though verbally concealed with such painstaking felicity in a mosaic of diction that recognition escapes the commentators:

> frui paratis et valido mihi,
> Latoë, dones, at precor integra
> cum mente.[10]

An expanded rendering is best: "I have made preparations for my old age. Grant me, child of Leto, health to enjoy them, and I beseech you, also with soundness of mind." The same dualism presents itself again in the famous satire of the incomparable Petronius: *bonam mentem bonamque valetudinem sibi optarunt,*[11] "they wished one another health of mind and health of body." It also furnished a memorable finale for the famous satire of Juvenal: *mens sana in corpore sano.*

In each of these three instances it should be observed that the dualistic good is something prayed for. Epicurus was not for abolishing prayer but he limited its scope severely, Vatican Saying 65: "It is idle to seek from the gods what a man is capable of providing for himself." It may be that we have here a curious detail of doctrine. Epicurus is on record as having written: "Each individual is physically constituted from the very beginning of his being for a definite span of life, so that, while he cannot live a longer term, he may live a shorter." [12] By this it is possible that some light is thrown upon the Epicurean attitude toward prayer. The individual is free to choose the kind of life he will lead, but the duration of life is beyond his control. The latter, then, is a fit subject for prayer. If this be true then Horace was a consistent Epicurean when he wrote: "It is enough to petition Jupiter for what he gives and takes away. May he grant length of life, grant the means of living. As for the quiet mind, I'll provide that for myself." [13]

Just as the parity of soul and body based upon their corporeal nature and their common mortality called into being the dualistic good, so it also demanded a refinement of terminology. Soul and body being both *soma*, the Greek for material things, the contrast between them vanished. To preserve a contrast, which is real and useful, recourse was had to the use of the word *flesh*. Thus health of body was described as "the stable condition of well-being in the flesh." [14]

This innovation of terminology pervades the language of Epicurus. Authorized Doctrine 20 begins: "It is the flesh that finds the limits of pleasure boundless and infinite time would have been required to furnish it, but the intelligence, taking into the calculation the end and limit of the flesh and dispelling the fears about eternity, renders the whole life perfect." Here and there the phraseology of Epicurus resembles in its simplicity the language of the New Testament. We read in Vatican Saying 33: "The cry of the flesh is not to hunger, not to thirst, not to shiver with cold." Epicurus also recognized the association of the lusts with the flesh. The opening words of his advice to a certain young man run as follows, Vatican Saying 51: "You inform me that the stimulus of the flesh disposes you inordinately toward indulgence in sexual intercourse."

To return now to the dualistic good, this has been seen to consist, on the one hand, of "the stable condition of well-being in the flesh." The part that is opposed to the flesh is the intelligence. So far as this is concerned, the perfect condition is ataraxy, which is defined by the New English Dictionary as "Stoical indifference." This signifies a confusion with "apathy." The Epicurean sage did not cultivate indifference. It is even said of him: "He will be more susceptible of feeling than other men nor would this be an obstacle to wisdom." [15] If an example be in point, mention may be made of gratitude, of which the sect made a specialty. The general objective was not to attain immunity to feeling but to keep the emotions within natural bounds, Vatican Saying 21: "Human nature is not to be coerced but persuaded and we shall persuade her by satisfying the necessary desires if they are not going to be injurious but, if they are going to injure, by relentlessly banning them."

The word *ataraxy* implies a metaphor derived from the sea and the weather. One of the original synonyms is "calm," *galenismos*,[16] of which the proper application is to the sea, *tranquillitas* in Latin. The turmoils of the soul are specifically compared by Epicurus to storms and squalls at sea.[17] The chief causes of the soul's turmoils are unreasonable fears concerning the gods and death and ignorance of the natural limits of pleasure and pain. If a man has attained to true knowledge of these things and keeps his emotions within their natural limits, the reward is comparable to the peace "which passeth all understanding." For this statement there is a specific Epicurean text, if only the editors did not emend it, Vatican Saying 78: "The truly noble man busies himself chiefly with wisdom and friendship, of which the one is an understandable good but the other is immortal." Paradoxical as it must seem, Epicurus knows no higher praise than to call a thing immortal; being opposed in this text to understandable, it must mean "passing understanding."

THE NATURAL CEILINGS OF PLEASURE

Having established body and soul upon a parity, equal partners in life, Epicurus next proceeded to propound a number of paradoxes: first, that limits of pleasure were set by Nature, beyond which no increase was possible; second, that pleasure was one and not many; and third, that continuous pleasure was possible. These new doctrines were the offspring of controversy, because the contrary doctrines had been sponsored by Plato and his followers, who in this instance agreed for the most part with the multitude.

The first paradox is part of Authorized Doctrine 3, and by this position its prime importance is revealed: "The removal of all pain is the limit of the magnitude of pleasures." The meaning is plain if the pleasure of eating be taken as an example. Nature is the teacher, as usual, and sets the norm. Hunger is a desire of the first category according to Epicurus: it is both natural and necessary. Where this natural and necessary desire for food exists, the pleasure of satisfying it cannot be exceeded. Cicero cites the example of the first Ptolemy of Egypt, who, it was reported, had never been genuinely hungry until on a certain occasion he was parted from his escort and received the gift of coarse bread in a cabin; it seemed to him that nothing had ever been more delicious than that bread.[18] This testimony is the more telling for two reasons: first, because Cicero quotes it in an explicitly Epicurean context; second, because it was this Ptolemy to whom Colotes of Lampsacus, a charter member of the sect, dedicated his satire on earlier philosophers.[19]

Thirst, of course, belongs in the same category with hunger, and Cicero in the same paragraph cites the example of that Dareius who fled before Alexander the Great: in his extremity he drank filthy water polluted with corpses and declared he had never drunk with greater pleasure. This example is contemporary with Epicurus and little doubt can exist that Cicero drew from it the same text as the story of Ptolemy, possibly the book *On the End*, which was in his hands at the time.[20]

It is justifiable to go further: the original source of both stories may have been the book which the talented Ptolemy himself wrote on the campaigns of Alexander. It has been shown already that he was interested in hedonism [21] and it becomes probable that he reported certain incidents with an Epicurean color.

The core of the principle here exemplified is the necessity of keeping true pleasure in a necessary connection with natural and necessary desires, such as hunger and thirst. It is impossible to whip up a thirst or an appetite superior to that created by natural hunger and thirst. To the youthful Menoeceus Epicurus writes: "Plain-tasting foods bring a pleasure equal to that of luxurious diet when once the pain arising from need has been removed, and bread and water afford the very keenest pleasure when one in need of them brings them to his lips." [22] This is the fixed ceiling for pleasure, which he endeavors to establish in opposition to Plato, who compared the appetitive part of the soul to "a many-headed beast" and held to the opinion that desires increase endlessly and that pleasure defied the fixing of a limit.[23]

The natural and necessary desires that still await mention are those for clothing and shelter. The authorized teaching concerning these will be made plain by the first half of Authorized Doctrine 18: "The pleasure in the flesh is incapable of increase when once the pain arising

227

from need has been removed but is merely embellished." The Greek word here rendered "embellished" has also been translated by "varied" and by "variegated," but these renderings fall short of revealing the meaning. Seneca does better when interpreting the word as "to season, as it were, and divert." [24] This is correct; to luxurious men it is a fact that eating is a way of passing the time. Epicurus himself applies the word *poikilmata*, "embellishments," to food, Vatican Saying 69: "It is the ingratitude of the soul that makes the creature endlessly lickerish of embellishments in diet."

Cicero, however, happens to be our best guide, because the meaning of his version is made clear by Lucretius. He says "the pleasure can be *variari distinguique* but not increased." [25] The first of the verbs italicized applies properly to color and the second to needlework, as may be gleaned in the lexicon. Lucretius confirms this: "It hurts us not a whit to lack the garment bright with purple and gold and embroidered with striking designs, provided there still be a plain cloak to fend off the cold." [26]

When once the meaning of *poikillo* has been fixed as "embellish" and applicable alike to diet, clothing, and housing, the doctrine can be extended with precision. The function of walls is to afford protection from the weather; the enjoyment of this is a basic pleasure, and, being basic, cannot be increased. If the walls are decorated, the enjoyment of them is merely a decorative pleasure. Similarly, the function of a garment is to avert the pain arising from cold and the resulting pleasure is basic and, being such, cannot be increased but is merely embellished if the cloth is gaily colored or brocaded.

The case is not different in respect of diet. The satisfaction of natural hunger is the basic pleasure, which is not increased but merely embellished by richness of diet. Epicurus is recorded by a late doxographer as saying: "I am gorged with pleasure in this poor body of mine living on bread and water." [27] Porphyry records him as saying: "It is better for you to lie down upon a cheap cot and be free of fear than to have a gilded bedstead and a luxurious table and be full of trouble." [28]

In the same Authorized Doctrine, 18, in which the ceiling of pleasure for the flesh is defined, the ceiling of pleasure for the mind is set forth: "As for the mind, its limit of pleasure is begotten by reasoning out these very problems and those akin to these, all that once created the worst fears for the mind." These words need not seem enigmatical: the worst fears are created for the mind through false opinions concerning death and the gods, the topic of Authorized Doctrines 1 and 2. These fears rank in point of importance with false opinions concerning pleasure and pain, the topic of Doctrines 2 and 4. The cure for all these false opinions and the fears they entail was dubbed by detractors the tetrapharmacon, or fourfold remedy. It is charmingly elaborated by Epicurus in the letter to Menoeceus, which alone of his extant writings possesses literary grace.

In this letter the doctrine of the basic pleasures and the consequent fullness of pleasure is elaborated: "It is for this that we do everything, to be free from pain and fear, and when we succeed in this, all the tempest of the soul is stilled, the creature feeling no need to go farther as to something lacking and to seek something else by which the good of soul and body shall be made perfect." [29] In speaking of "going farther" and "seeking something more" he refers to the superfluous or merely embellishing pleasures.

PLEASURE NOT INCREASED BY IMMORTALITY

At the same time that the denial of immortality resulted in placing body and soul upon a parity and required the formulation of a dualistic good, it demanded a doctrinal counterpoise for the surrender of belief in immortality. That this surrender was recognized in the reasoning of Epicurus as a further delimitation of the scope of pleasure is indicated by the position of the Authorized Doctrine in which the remedial doctrine is stated; it is No. 19 and follows that on the ceilings of pleasure: "Infinite time and finite time are characterized by equal pleasure, if one measures the limits of pleasure by reason." This is both paradoxical and subtle. It is shocking to Christian feeling and was hardly less so to the pagan of antiquity. To the multitude, as Lucretius observed, it was a gloomy and repulsive thought.[30] To Platonists, with their stately, elaborate, and mystical eschatology, it must have seemed like nihilism.

Its subtlety is equally manifest. As will presently be shown, Epicurus maintained that pleasure is not altered in kind by the fact of duration or extension; here he declares that it is not increased in quantity. All pleasures have fixed ceilings and fixed magnitudes. When in the words of the Doctrine he speaks of "measuring the limits of pleasure by reason," he means recognition of the fact that for the body health and the expectation of its continuance is the limit of pleasure, and that for the mind the limit is the emancipation from all fear of the gods or death. The attainment to this state, he now declares, is a condition of one dimension. He seems to think of it as an Alpinist would regard the ascent of an arduous mountain peak. The pleasure would not be increased by remaining on the peak.

THE FULLNESS OF PLEASURE

It is possible, however, to arrive at a higher degree of precision, always a chief objective in the reasoning of Epicurus. This higher precision depends upon discerning the subsidiary doctrine of the fullness of pleasure. For this there is a double logical basis: the first basis is the infinity of time, from which it is deduced that there can be nothing new. As the Epicurean Ecclesiastes expresses it, 1:9: "The thing that hath been, it is that which shall be; and that which is done is that which shall be done: and there is no new thing under the sun." Lucretius reminds us in similar vein "that all things are always the same" and "no new pleasure can be devised." [31] From this it follows that the exhaustion of pleasures is feasible and the fullness of pleasure is attainable.

The second basis of this subsidiary doctrine is the existence of natural ceilings of pleasure, which, being thus limited, could be enjoyed to the full. Out of this was begotten the familiar metaphor of the aged sage as taking leave of life like a satisfied banqueter. This theme was chosen by Lucretius for the ringing finale of his third book; he personifies Nature and represents her as rebuking the complainer because he cannot depart "as a guest who has had his fill of life" or "as one who is full and has had his fill of experience." [32] The wise man, on the contrary, can say *bene vixi*, "I have lived the good life." This is the cry of triumph uttered by old Diogenes of Oenoanda; to quote his own words: "Facing the sunset of life because of my age and on the verge of taking my leave of life with a paean of victory because of the enjoyment of the fullness of all pleasures." [33]

If still further precision on this topic be sought, it may be observed that this doctrine of the fullness of pleasure is supplementary to the doctrine that death is anesthesia. The latter may help to reconcile men to the state of being dead but it fails to compensate for the surrender of immortality. Only the possibility of having enjoyed all pleasures to the full in this life can counterbalance the relinquishment of the hope of enjoying eternal pleasures in the afterlife. This is the "true understanding" of which Epicurus speaks: "Hence the true understanding of the fact that death is nothing to us renders enjoyable the mortality of existence, not by adding infinite time but by taking away the yearning for immortality." [34] What cancels the yearning for immortality is the conviction that the fullness of pleasure is possible in this mortal life. The ingenuity of this argument is undeniable; it means the victory over death and we have proof of its wide acceptance in the vigor with which St. Paul in his ardent plea to the Corinthians champions the resurrection of the dead as a new means of victory over death.

Incidentally, without close scrutiny it is difficult to discern by what sort of logic this doctrine could be reconciled with the perfect blissfulness of the gods. If pleasure is not increased by the length of its duration, how could the lot of the gods seem more desirable than that of the mortal sage? With this problem Epicurus did not fail to deal. The topic must await detailed treatment in the ensuing chapter on the True Piety. Here it will suffice to say that the superiority of the happiness of the gods is represented as consisting in the perfect assurance of its continuance. Involved with this judgment is a startling paradox: what renders the happiness of the gods eternal is this perfect assurance of its continuance; its eternity is a result, not a factor of causation. It is a quality of life.

The paradox that ranks major to this, that happiness is not increased in magnitude by immortality, has found its way into Western thought through the literature of consolation. Obviously, if happiness is not increased by immortality, neither can it be increased by length of mortal life. The philosopher Seneca expatiates upon this inferred aspect of the doctrine, though without mentioning its source, and comforts his correspondent by dwelling feelingly upon the wisdom of measuring a human life by its achievement rather than its length.[35] In the course of this homily he compares the long and merely vegetative life to that of a tree and this detail survives for us in the poem of Ben Jonson which begins,

> It is not growing like a tree, in bulk,
> Doth make man better be.

But the last lines of the poem hark back definitely to Epicurus:

In small proportions we just beauty see
And in small measure life may perfect be.

The sentiment recurs in Christian hymnology:

He liveth long who liveth well.

Such is often the fate of Epicurus, to be quoted anonymously if approved, by name if condemned.

THE UNITY OF PLEASURE

If at this point the attention be recalled to the synoptic view, it may be observed that the telos has been presented under three aspects: first, as a unitary good it is pleasure; second, as a dualistic good it is health of mind and health of body; third, in a seemingly negative aspect it is freedom from fear in the mind and pain in the body. This seeming negativism was spotted by the antagonists of Epicurus as a chink in his armor, and the arrows of their dialectic were concentrated upon it. The weakness alleged was that of calling two disparate things by the one name of pleasure.

It is plain to see how Epicurus was led to switch emphasis to this aspect of pleasure. As usual, he was working his way to greater precision in his analysis of the subject and, as will presently be shown in more detail, he discerned that according to Aristippus and Plato no such thing as continuous pleasure was possible; they recognized only peaks of pleasure separated by intervals either devoid of pleasure or neutral or mixed. From this it followed with inevitable logic that the wise man could not be happy at all times. This conclusion was repugnant to Epicurus as a thoroughgoing hedonist and was repudiated. This repudiation could be made good only by vindicating for freedom from fear and pain the status of a positive pleasure. This in turn resulted in a doctrine of the unity of all pleasure.

Though we certainly fall short of possessing the whole argument of Epicurus, there is ample evidence upon which to construct the skeleton of a case. The Feelings, as usual, are the criterion. It may be recalled how he proved life itself to be the greatest good by pointing out that the greatest joy is associated with the escape from some dreadful destruction. By a similar argument, even if not extant, it could be shown that the recovery of health is a positive pleasure when the individual has recently survived a perilous illness. It would be a positive pleasure also to be freshly relieved from the fear of death and the gods through the discovery of the true philosophy.

To substantiate this drift of reasoning it is not impossible to quote a text: "The stable condition of well-being in the flesh and the confident hope of its continuance means the most exquisite and infallible of joys for those who are capable of figuring the problem out." [36]

This passage marks a distinct increase of precision in the analysis of pleasure. Its import will become clear if the line of reasoning already adumbrated be properly extended: let it be granted that the escape from a violent death is the greatest of joys and the inference must follow that the possession of life at other times cannot rank greatly lower. Similarly, if the recovery from a dangerous illness be a cause for joy, manifestly the possession of health ought to be a joy at other times. Nevertheless the two pleasures differ from one another and it was in recognition of the difference that Epicurus instituted the distinction between kinetic and static pleasures. The difference is one of intensity or, as Epicurus would have said, of condensation. At one time the pleasure is condensed, at another, extended. In other words the same pleasure may be either kinetic or static. If condensed, it is kinetic; if extended, it is static.

There is a catch to this reasoning, however; it holds good only "for those who are capable of figuring the problem out." This marks Epicurus as a pragmatist, insisting upon the control of experience, including thought. His reasoning about kinetic and static pleasures is sound, but human beings do not automatically reason after this fashion; they fail to reason about the matter at all. Although they would spontaneously admit the keenest joy at recovery from wounds or disease, they forget about the blessing of health at other times. Hence it is that Epicurus insists upon the necessity of being able to reason in this way. Moreover, this reasoning must be confirmed by habituation. The same rule applies here as in the case of "Death is nothing to us." It is not enough to master the reasons for so believing; it is also necessary to habituate one's self to so believe.[37] This is pragmatism.

There is also another catch to this line of reasoning. The conclusion clashes with the teaching of Aristippus and Plato and it also violates the accepted usage of language. It was not usual to call the possession of health a pleasure and still less usual to call freedom from pain a pleasure. It was this objection that Cicero had in mind when he wrote: "You Epicureans round up people from all the crossroads, decent men, I allow, but certainly of no great education. Do such as they, then, comprehend what Epicurus means, while I, Cicero, do not?" [38] The common people of the ancient world, however, for whom Platonism had nothing attractive, seem to have accepted Epicurean pragmatism with gladness. Cicero, being partial to the aristocratic philosophy and having no zeal to promote the happiness of the multitude, chose to sneer.

The irritation which Cicero simulates in the above passage was beyond doubt genuine with those from whom the argument was inherited. They had been nettled by the phraseology of Epicurus, who was mocking Plato. The words "those who are capable of figuring the problem out" are a parody of Plato's *Timaeus* 40d, where the text reads "those who are incapable of making the calculations" and the reference is to mathematical calculations of the movements of the celestial bodies, which "bring fears and portents of future events" to the ignorant. Baiting the adversary was a favorite sport of Epicurus.

Epicureans at a later time were in their turn subjected to incessant baiting by Stoic opponents, and it may have been these who tried the reduction to the absurd by means of a ridiculous example. If those who are not in a state of pain are in a state of pleasure, "then the host who, though not being thirsty himself, mixes a cocktail for a guest is in the same state of pleasure as the guest who is thirsty and drinks the said cocktail." [39]

Cicero, however, had his tongue in his cheek and knew that this was mere dialectical sparring, intended rather to disconcert the opponent than to refute him. He was partial to the New Academy and to Stoicism, both of which tended to turn argumentation into a game and thus make it an end in itself. They could not fail to be intolerant of the procedures of pragmatism, of which action is the primary object and not logomachy.

This extension of the name of pleasure to freedom from fear and pain was not the sole achievement of the new analysis. In popular thought, the correctness of which Plato assumed, pleasures were classified according to the parts of the body affected, eating, drinking, sexual indulgence, philosophical thinking. In respect also of this conventional classification Epicurus exhibited finer discrimination. He not only discerned that the pleasure associated with one organ is brief and intense while that associated with other parts is moderate and extended but also observed that certain pleasures, like that of escaping a violent death, affect the whole organism.

The next step in this new analysis was to declare that this fact of extension or intension was of no fundamental importance. The high value assigned to this principle is indicated by its promulgation as Authorized Doctrine 9: "If every pleasure were alike condensed in duration and associated with the whole organism or the dominant parts of it, pleasures would never differ from one another." Positively stated, the meaning would be that pleasure is always pleasure; it is of no consequence that some pleasures are associated with the mind, others with the stomach, and others with other parts, or that some affect the whole organism and others only a part, or that some are brief and intense, others moderate and extended. In other words, it makes no difference that some pleasures are static and others kinetic. Pleasure is a unit. This unity could be expressed in ancient terminology by saying that all pleasure was a kind of motion, *kinesis* or *motio*, the ancient equivalent of reaction.

To put the colophon upon this topic it should be added that three Authorized Doctrines, Nos. 8, 9, and 10, deal with pleasure and all three imply the quality of unity. The eighth stresses the fact that the evil attaches solely to the consequences; all pleasures are alike in being good: "No pleasure is evil in itself but the practices productive of certain pleasures bring troubles in their train that by many times outweigh the pleasures themselves."

The ninth Doctrine has been quoted above. In it the item about "condensed pleasure" was pounced upon by Damoxenus of the New Comedy as a good cue for merrymaking; quite aptly he allowed a cook to dilate upon it.[40] Some five centuries afterward the frivolous Alciphron testified to the longevity of the theme by assuming it to be still good for a laugh.[41]

The tenth Doctrine, last of the three, serves to shift all ethical condemnation from pleasures themselves to the consequences: "If the practices productive of the pleasures of profligates dispelled the fears of the mind about celestial things and death and pains and also taught the limit of the desires, we should never have fault to find with profligates, enjoying pleasures to the full from all quarters, and suffering neither pain nor distress from any quarter, wherein the evil lies." Such declarations afforded to enemies of Epicurus a means of besmirching his name, but he was absolutely honest; he did not evade the logical implications of his principles; he flaunted them. By disposition he was a teaser; he drew enjoyment from the squirming of the piously orthodox.

A variation of the same teaching appears in an isolated saying. "I enjoy the fullness of pleasure living on bread and water and I spit upon the pleasures of a luxurious diet, not on account of any evil in these pleasures themselves but because of the discomforts that follow upon them." [42] The net effect of these pronouncements is to put all pleasures in a single class, all being good, irrespective of extension or condensation or of the organ affected or of approval or disapproval, which attach only to consequences. This is an instance where Epicurus exhibited deeper insight than Plato in the latter's own field, discerning the one in the many.

THE ROOT OF ALL GOOD

Epicurus had formulated the doctrine of the unity of pleasure at a very early date and it was a chief cause of his conflict with the Platonists of Mytilene.[43] The particular belief with which it clashed was that which postulated an ascending series of pleasures, depending upon the organ affected and culminating in the supreme enjoyment of intellectual contemplation. Aristotle, who had founded the Platonic school in Mytilene, was very explicit on the point.[44] "The sense of sight is superior in purity to the sense of touch, and the senses of hearing and smelling to the sense of taste; in a quite similar way the respective pleasures also differ, both the pleasures of the intellect from those of the senses, and the pleasures in each of these two classes from one another."

Obviously, if the truth of this be denied and the assertion be substituted that goodness can be predicated of the pleasure of the stomach on the same basis that this is predicated of the pleasure of pure reason, it requires no unusual acumen to realize that a doctrine esteemed as sacrosanct was being derided, and one can better understand the fury of the Platonists of Mytilene, who proclaimed a state of riot and dispatched messengers in hot haste for the gymnasiarch.

It fell to the lot of the Platonists to enjoy a double revenge, the one immediate and brief, the other deferred but prolonged. They quickly compelled Epicurus to flee the city, preferring a charge of impiety, but it was less the alleged offense against the gods of the city than the derision of their proud doctrines over which they waxed so indignant, and it was no more the fear of a trial that intimidated Epicurus than the rage of the populace which had been kindled against him. A school that had recently graduated half a dozen tyrannicides [45] was not likely to be finicky about the means employed to bring a hedonistic young scoffer to his uppance.

The deferred revenge was achieved by the trick of rendering evidence incriminating by quoting it out of context, which corresponds to hitting below the belt in a more manly sport. Metrodorus, a more impetuous individual than the master, afforded exceptional opportunities to the adversary. In some publication he had written: "The pleasure of the stomach is the beginning and root of all good, and the things of wisdom and the refinements of life have their standard of reference in this." [46] In detachment these words exhibit a shocking rawness and were employed as evidence for condemning Epicureans as out-and-out sensualists. Part of their import is the unity of pleasure. Pleasure is pleasure, wherever found, and the nature of it does not depend upon the organ affected. The mind is an organ of the body no less than the eyes or the ears; nor does the pleasure of the mathematician in the last analysis differ from that of babes and sucklings. Strict logic is capable of arriving at such startling conclusions.

The offensiveness of the new teaching, however, is mitigated by recognition of the genetic approach. The innovation of Epicurus was to have recourse to the newborn infant for the first of his evidences. He was not taken in by the flattering assumption that man is the rational creature. It was for him to discern and keep in mind that man does not begin life as a rational creature and only by definite stages arrives at that proud eminence, if ever. The phenomena of life must consequently be viewed in series, infancy, childhood, adolescence, maturity, and old age. Thus the planned life becomes a journey or a progress toward wisdom.

Once Nature has been recognized as furnishing the norm, it is imperative that the study of life begin at its minimum values, which are recognized in the newborn infant, as yet lacking volition and intelligence and the greater part of sensation. At this level, while the creature is as yet unperverted and Nature reveals herself candidly, it is discerned that pleasure and life are already indissolubly joined. For this reason Epicurus wrote: "We recognize pleasure as the first good and connate with us." [47] By "the first good" he means that it manifests itself at the beginning as being good, being first in order of time and succession.

Metrodorus meant no more than this; he was only more specific when he called the pleasure of the stomach "the beginning and root of all good," the pleasure of the stomach being virtually the only one known to the infant. As for the words that follow, "the things of wisdom and the refinements of life have their standard of reference in this," the meaning is plain if the principle be recalled that the nature of pleasure does not depend upon the organ participating. Life unfolds itself by stages and the creature at each advance in maturity engages in new activities with their attendant pleasures, but the affinity between the soul and pleasure is continuous and it can be said of the wise man as of the infant that he shuns pain and seeks pleasure. There is no stage of life or culture at which this principle does not hold good.

On this topic there is more to be said. Just as Epicurus and Metrodorus discerned the pleasure of life as manifested at its minimum in the pleasure of the infant, so its maximum was discerned in the fullness of pleasure that came with the attainment of wisdom. There can be little doubt that Metrodorus enlarged upon this in his book entitled *On the Progress toward Wisdom*; to him was sometimes assigned the task of treating in detail what the master had sketched in outline. Epicurus himself possessed a distinct turn for the epigrammatic saying, and one of his best is applicable here: "Pleasure is the beginning and the end of the happy life." [48] This calls for elucidation because of certain double meanings, all of which hold true.

When he says that pleasure is the beginning, *arche*, he means for one thing that it dates first in order of time and succession; it is "the first good" and "connate with us" and "the root of all good." In a second sense it is the beginning of every action because "starting from this we begin every choice and avoidance," that is, every decision to do or not to do. As for the word *end*, *telos*, a triple meaning should be discerned. Viewed from the standpoint of the creature, it is the fulfillment of being; the infant seeks this by the instinct of Nature. From the standpoint of the intelligent being the telos is an objective; this stage is only potential in the case of the infant; with the growth of reason it becomes actual. Lastly, the telos, having been identified as pleasure, becomes the criterion of intelligent choice, because "to this we have recourse as to a canon, judging every good by the Feeling."

A saying capable of being so variously understood is truly oracular, and with good justification Epicurus so classified his own pronouncements.[49] The fact that veneration was accorded them by his disciples on this ground is evidenced by Lucretius, who graded them above the utterances of the Delphian Apollo.[50] As for this particular dictum, it must have been on the lips of multitudes of Epicureans in the days of the New Testament writers, and a counterblast to it may be recognized in the Book of Revelation, 22:13: "I am Alpha and Omega, the first and the last, the beginning and the end." In this expanded version the liturgical appeal has been heightened and the flickering of meaning has also been preserved. By interrogating educated men of various religions it may readily be discovered how divergent are the plausible interpretations. Whatever the true meaning may be it is old wine in a new vessel. The wine is Epicurean, the vessel Christian.

PLEASURE CAN BE CONTINUOUS

The apex of the new structure of ethics erected by Epicurus consists in the teaching that pleasure can be continuous. The discovery of a logical basis for this proposition was essential for the promulgation of hedonism as a practical code of conduct for mankind. No philosophy that offered merely intermittent intervals of pleasure would have possessed any broad or cogent appeal for those in quest of the happy life.

The predecessors of Epicurus had spent considerable thought upon the analysis of pleasure, but their attitude was in the main merely analytical and academic, lacking relevance to action. Their zeal was not for promoting the happiness of mankind. They were rather in the position of men who give themselves to the study of anatomy without contemplating the practice of medicine. The attitude of Epicurus, on the contrary, was pragmatic from the beginning. The declaration that "Vain is the word of that philosopher by which no malady of mankind is healed" has already been quoted.[51]

The desired logical basis for the continuity of pleasure was afforded by the discovery of natural ceilings of pleasures. From this is derived the division into basic and ornamental or superfluous pleasures, corresponding respectively to natural and necessary desires and those that are neither natural nor necessary. Hunger and thirst exemplify the former class while the desire for rich viands and rare wines belongs to the second class. Correspondingly, the satisfaction of normal hunger and thirst is a basic pleasure while the gratification of abnormal desires for rich foods and drinks is ornamental and superfluous.

This recognition of basic pleasures, in its turn, signified the recognition of a normal state of being, consisting of health of mind and of body and freedom from fears and all unnecessary desires, which was called ataraxy or serenity. This condition was denominated static, but allowance must be made for a certain variation. Hunger and thirst recur and call for satisfaction, which is a moderately kinetic pleasure, whereupon the individual returns to the normal state of absence of pain. Epicurus describes it in one of those reciprocal statements for which he had a preference: "Only then have we need of pleasure when from the absence of pleasure we feel pain, and when we do not feel pain we no longer feel need of pleasure." [52] While these words have reference to the natural desires of the body, the description of the normal state must be understood to include freedom from pain in the body and distress in the mind.

The extension of the name of pleasure to this normal state of being was the major innovation of the new hedonism. It was in the negative form, freedom from pain of body and distress of mind, that it drew the most persistent and vigorous condemnation from adversaries. The contention was that the application of the name of pleasure to this state was unjustified on the ground that two different things were thereby being denominated by one name. Cicero made a great to-do over this argument,[53] but it is really superficial and captious. The fact that the name of pleasure was not customarily applied to the normal or static state did not alter the fact that the name ought to be applied to it; nor that reason justified the application; nor that human beings would be the happier for so reasoning and believing.

Even at the present day the same objection is raised. For instance, a modern Platonist, ill informed on the true intent of Epicurus, has this to say: "What, in a word, is to be said of a philosophy that begins by regarding pleasure as the only positive good and ends by emptying pleasure of all positive content?" [54] This ignores the fact that this was but one of the definitions of pleasure offered by Epicurus, that he recognized kinetic as well as static pleasures. It ignores also the fact that Epicurus took personal pleasure in public festivals and encouraged his disciples to attend them and that regular banquets were a part of the ritual of the sect. Neither does it take account of the fact that in the judgment of Epicurus those who feel the least need of luxury enjoy it most and that intervals of abstinence enhance the enjoyment of luxury.[55] Thus the Platonic objector puts upon himself the necessity of denying that the moderation of the rest of the year furnishes additional zest to the enjoyment of the Christmas dinner; he has failed to become aware of the Epicurean zeal for "condensing pleasure."

On a level with this criticism is the allegation of a more recent writer that Epicurus put himself in a corner by defining pleasure as freedom from pain.[56] It was not Epicurus who put himself in a corner but rather Aristippus and Plato, who by recognizing only peaks of pleasure separated by intervals either void of pleasure or neutral or mixed, rendered all continuity of pleasure impossible and consequently all continuity of happiness. The error of the modern critic is to allow ancient controversy to vitiate the independence of modern judgments. The ancient enemies of Epicureanism were not concerned to present a total estimate of its teachings; they pounced upon those doctrines which, when considered singly, seemed susceptible of refutation or ridicule. They kept harping upon the negative description of pleasure as freedom from pain and ignored the positive aspect as health of mind and health of body. The latter, being difficult to attack, is lacking from the hostile testimonies and survives only anonymously in the friendly tradition.

It would have been strange if this doctrine of continuous happiness were absent from the Authorized Doctrines. Its presence is easily overlooked, because the context of the controversy has become blurred with the lapse of time, but the emphasis derived from prominence of position must have been at one time arresting. It forms part of the famous tetrapharmacon, Doctrine 3. The first part, already quoted, identifies the basic pleasure as freedom from pain, the only kind that could be continuous: "The removal of all pain is the limit of magnitude for pleasures." This rules out the "neutral state" as postulated by Plato; it identifies the neutral state as one of static pleasure. The second part of the Doctrine disposes of Plato's "mixed states": "And wherever the experience of pleasure is present, so long as it prevails, there is no pain or distress or a combination of them." This amounts to denying that pain and pleasure are capable of mixing and of resulting in a state that is different from either. Epicurus implies instead and elsewhere teaches that pain is subtractable from pleasure, leaving a balance of the latter.[57] This principle applies either to physical pain or mental distress or to both together. It is essential to the thesis that continuous pleasure is possible.

Those who denied that pleasure was the telos were naturally not concerned with the question of the continuity of pleasure, but there was an analogous question of equal consequence, whether the wise man could be happy under all circumstances. The importance of this revealed itself shortly after Plato's demise and showed no abatement for three centuries. In two passages Cicero lists the names of those who gave an affirmative answer — from which the name of Plato is conspicuously absent — and elsewhere he pretends to cite the opinion of Epicurus, misrepresenting him shamelessly and using his name as an excuse for parading a tedious collection of his own translations from Greek tragedy on the topic of pain.[58] What Epicurus is on record as saying is this: "Even if under torture the wise man is happy." [59] Cicero chose to imagine him in the brazen bull of the tyrant Phalaris, in which the victims were roasted alive, and as saying "How pleasant; how little this torture means to me!" This is a shabby invention and shameless ·quibbling. It ignores the difference between *suavis*, "pleasant" and *beatus*, "happy."

Even Epicurus could not have used pleasure as an invariable synonym for happiness. He died a happy man but in physical agony. His last words, known even beyond his own sect, exhibit the triumph of happiness over pain: "On this blissful day of my life, which is likewise my last, I write these words to you all. The pains of my strangury and dysentery do not abate the excess of their characteristic severity and continue to keep me company, but over against all these I set the joy in my soul at the recollection of the disquisitions composed by you and the rest." [60] He is here exemplifying the subtraction of pain from pleasure, leaving a balance of pleasure, which is happiness. The letter is addressed to Idomeneus but is intended for the whole Lampsacene circle, which made many contributions to the literature of the school. It is the grateful recognition of this service, together with all that it implies, that in this instance is declared to outweigh the physical pains.

It was the discovery of static pleasure, without which continuity of pleasure was impossible, that resulted in the division of pleasures into static and kinetic. There was no call for such a division until the name of pleasure had been extended to denote the possession of health. On this point, however, as on many others, greater precision is possible. The modern use of the word *static* as opposed to *kinetic* is Aristotelian in origin. The Epicurean word is *katastematikos*, from *katastema*, explained in the lexicon as "stable condition." It connotes, moreover, change of state, from action to rest. To Epicurus it denotes a normal state of pleasure to which the individual returns after kinetic pleasure, which is activity. For example, it is the comfortable feeling that follows after the satisfaction of hunger and thirst, the relaxed condition that follows after attending the theater, a public festival or a banquet. Exceptionally, it describes the return to normal after the joy of escape from peril of life.

Since this innovation was, as it were, the keystone of the new hedonism, it is not surprising to learn that it was expounded in the letter addressed to the philosophers in Mytilene, which is rightly regarded as having been written in Lampsacus, nor that it was emphasized in other major writings and kept in the forefront by successors. That it was an innovation is made clear by a sound paragraph of Laertius.[61] Discussing the divergence from Cyrenaic doctrine he quotes a phrase of Metrodorus: "Pleasure being thought of both as associated with motion and as static." Epicurus is quoted at slightly greater length: "Serenity of mind and freedom from bodily pain are static pleasures, but joy and delight are seen to be associated with motion, that is, activity." In both these passages modern usage calls for the adjective *static*; the Greek would demand *catastematic*. *Static* and *kinetic* would apply to the state of a stone, now lying on the ground, now sent hurtling through the air. *Catastematic* and *kinetic* would apply to the pleasure of a healthy Epicurean, now enjoying a quiet evening at home, now having a rollicking time at one of the monthly banquets.

The fact that this extension of the name of pleasure was so long and malevolently contested is merely proof of the jealousy of rival schools and of the real validity in the arguments. The validity of the main contention, that continuity of happiness must be conceded to be feasible, was not contested. The leading philosophers after Plato seem to have made this concession, and much that Plato had said about pleasure became obsolete. Theophrastus was an exception, who, attaching great value to external goods and evils, declared "that Fortune, not wisdom, rules the lives of men" and "that the happy life cannot mount the scaffold to the wheel." [62]

CONTINUOUS PAIN IMPOSSIBLE

Having laid down the two principles that pleasure and pain are true opposites and that continuous pleasure is a possibility, Epicurus was forced by a necessity of thought into positing that continuous pain is impossible. Authorized Doctrine 4: "Pain does not prevail continuously in the flesh but the peak of it is present for the briefest interval, and the pain that barely exceeds the pleasure in the flesh is not with us many days, while protracted illnesses have an excess of pleasure over pain in the flesh." This is among the more unfortunate doctrines of Epicurus and rightly incurred the sharpest ridicule. It reveals more faith in doctrine and more determination to live by it and to maintain control of experience than is consistent with medical knowledge. He seems to have been reasoning from his own malady, stone in the kidney, which is accompanied by spasms of extreme agony separated by long intervals of immunity.

He had taken this stand, however, and continued to maintain it. There is another saying extant which is supplementary to the former: "Acute pains quickly result in death; protracted pains are not marked by acuteness." [63] In protracted suffering the principle of the subtraction of pain from pleasure holds good. Upon this notion depends the so-called Calculus of Pleasure. This title is neither ancient nor precise; it is no more a calculus of pleasure than of pain and it might more rightly be called a calculus of advantage. The supporting text runs as follows: "The right way to judge all these pleasures and pains is by measuring them against each other and by scrutiny of the advantages and disadvantages." [64] Since it is postulated that continuous happiness is possible, it follows that the process is always subtraction. The pain is subtracted from the pleasure.

As for "continuous pleasures," these words acquired the status of a slogan through the teaching of Epicurus. An exhortation of his begins: "It is to continuous pleasures that I summon you." [65] The debate over the feasibility of achieving continuity was part of the protracted controversy over the rival claims of virtue and pleasure, which raged for two centuries and is rehearsed for us in the last book of Cicero's *Tusculan Disputations*.[66] As so often in the courts of law, the old advocate

244

was slated to make the final address, and he won a resounding verdict for virtue, and, at the same time, hypocrisy. The Empire, being founded upon political hypocrisy, required specious labels, which Stoicism was prepared to furnish. Reason, virtue, and duty were unimpeachable catchwords, acceptable to hypocrites even more than to saints.

THE RELATION OF PLEASURE TO VIRTUE

While the question whether pleasure could be continuous or not was of supreme importance for the structure of the new hedonism, there was a second topic that ranked extremely high and even gained an access of importance after the death of Epicurus. This topic was the true relation of pleasure to virtue. The reason for the subsequent increase of importance was the growth of Stoicism, which espoused the cause of virtue as against pleasure and concentrated an inordinate amount of attention upon this not too profitable controversy.

The importance accorded to the problem in the time of Epicurus is demonstrated by its prominent position among the Authorized Doctrines after the famous four. The fifth Doctrine declares in effect that pleasure and virtue are inseparable. They are thought of as being linked to each other like health and pleasure, disease and pain. The reason for this pronouncement becomes manifest if it be recalled that Plato and Aristotle upheld a contrary doctrine. Becoming the victims of a common semantic fallacy, they assumed that pleasure, possessing a name of its own, must be an independent entity, attachable and detachable, which might or might not be combined with a given activity. Aristotle, for example, recognized a pleasure that was proper to the study of geometry, but this pleasure did not always accompany it, as cold experience must have taught him.[67]

This principle, moreover, was assumed to hold good also for the virtues. For example, it was believed that if pleasure should be added to justice or temperance, the value of these goods would be enhanced by the addition, and the same would hold true if any good be added to another; any good would be more desirable when combined with another than when isolated. Aristotle also quotes Plato as denying on this ground that pleasure could be the good "because the good is not made more desirable by the addition of something to it." [68]

In this line of reasoning Epicurus, always on the alert to be exact, would have detected two fallacies. In the first place, he would have denied it correct to put temperance and geometry in the same class and to apply the same reasoning to both. It would not follow from the fact that the study of geometry might or might not be accompanied by pleasure that the practice of temperance might or might not be accompanied by pleasure. The logical procedure here called into question is reasoning by analogy, a tricky kind and valid only among true similars. Geometry and temperance are not true similars. The error will be more unmistakable if modern examples be employed and the study of trigonometry, geology, and chemistry be placed in the same class as the practice of diligence, veracity, and sobriety. While it is not on record that such a criticism was made, it is of a kind in which Epicurus was extraordinarily sharp.

The second fallacy in the reasoning of Plato and Aristotle was expressly urged. The error, according to Epicurus, lay in the assumption that pleasure was an independent entity and capable of being combined with the practice of virtue or detached from it. His reasoning on the point was similar to his reasoning about pleasure and living; life was the greatest good; it was a pleasure to be alive, even if maimed or in pain. Pleasure is virtually an attribute of life and the principle enunciated by Lucretius holds good, that an essential attribute of a thing is incapable of being removed without destroying the thing itself.[69] Heat cannot be separated from fire, sweetness from honey, nor whiteness from snow. Pleasure and virtue are similarly inseparable.

In order to apprehend this fifth Doctrine with complete precision the factor of reciprocation must be clearly recognized: A is impossible without B and B is impossible without A: "It is impossible to live pleasurably without living according to reason, honor, and justice, nor to live according to reason, honor, and justice without living pleasurably." Incidentally, it may be recalled that by reason is meant the practical reason, which guides the individual in every choice between doing and not doing a given thing; by honor is meant the unwritten law that determines the conduct of a gentleman; and by justice is meant obedience to the written laws of the country.

At first glance this reciprocation of pleasure and the virtues may seem to result in placing pleasure and virtue upon a parity of importance, but this inference is readily shown to be illusory. Virtue, unlike pleasure, is not "the first good" nor "the beginning and the end of the happy life." Even if Nature approves of virtue, she first bestows approval upon pleasure, because she links it with life from the moment of birth in advance of volition and intelligence. Pleasure possesses a long precedence over virtue in the growth of the human being; the newborn infant can feel pleasure but cannot practice virtue. By benefit of this priority pleasure becomes a criterion and, when at length the choice to act virtuously or otherwise must be made, this choice must be decided by the criterion that has the priority. Thus virtue is chosen for the sake of pleasure and not the contrary. This reasoning holds good if the genetic approach is admitted to be correct.

In the heat of controversy Epicurus did not shrink from employing strong language: "I spit upon the beautiful and those who unreasonably adore it when it gives no pleasure." [70] When he says "unreasonably" this is more than mere derision; it is fundamental doctrine. Since the only real existences are atoms and void, it follows that no abstractions exist; "justice is nothing by itself"; form cannot exist apart from substance, quality apart from thing, virtue apart from action. This results in a sort of nominalism; virtue becomes an empty name, corresponding to no reality. "You think virtue a mere locution and a stately grove just sticks," wrote Horace; [71] this was alleged to be Epicurean doctrine. The same allegation applied to the saying that passed as the last words of Marcus Brutus: "O unhappy Virtue, so you were just a word after all and I was practicing you as something real." [72]

There is another saying of Epicurus extant which exhibits an exceptional concentration of anti-Platonic teachings: "As for me, it is to continuous pleasures that I invite you and not to virtues that are empty and vain and offer but harassing hopes of reward." [73] In speaking of "continuous pleasures" he is tacitly censuring the intermittent pleasures presumed in Plato's neutral and mixed states; the word "empty" implies repudiation of the theory of ideas, which assumed the existence of such things as absolute justice; the word "vain" implies rejection of Plato's opinion that pleasure was separable from virtue; the "harassing hopes of reward" refers to the Platonic belief in immortality and the hope of happiness in the afterlife, which Epicurus rejected.

These judgments of Epicurus were well deliberated and logically based upon his premises. His denial of immortality resulted in the restriction of pleasure to the brief span of mortal life. The reward of virtue could not be postponed but was bound to be immediate and concurrent. This view is explicit in Vatican Saying 27: "In the case of other activities completion is toilsome and the reward comes after it, but in the study of philosophy the pleasure keeps pace with the process of learning and the enjoyment does not follow after learning but is simultaneous with it." There is no hint of despair or self-abandonment; he does not lightly advise "to take the cash and let the credit go" nor "to eat, drink and be merry, for tomorrow we die"; his attitude is restrained, logical, realistic, and utilitarian. His studied aim is to discover exactly where immediate pleasure is to be found and to seize it.

The success of Epicurus in his sponsorship of pleasure had the effect of embittering the battle of the schools and of advancing it to a new phase. His versatile contemporary Theophrastus devoted some study to the classification of goods, wealth, health, and the like, and after the death of both men the Peripatetics and Stoics pursued this line of inquiry into great detail. Out of this fetishistic comparison of goods arose the question concerning the identity of the superlative good or *summum bonum*, which it was falsely presumed must be the telos.

Another effect of the sponsoring of pleasure was to keep the Stoics at an opposite extreme, maintaining the austerity that was native to the creed. Inevitably they espoused the cause of virtue as the *summum bonum*; and so engrossing was this conflict that both sides forgot that for Epicurus the greatest good was life itself. This fallacy pervades the writings of Cicero, who summarized the controversy when it was dying out. After his time the process of mitigating the harshness of Stoicism with the amenities of Epicureanism set in, and it is this amalgam that survives in English literature chiefly through the influence of Seneca and Marcus Aurelius. The kindlier creed survived under Stoic labels.

CHAPTER XIII ✠ THE TRUE PIETY

EPICURUS approached the topic of piety as a reformer, a materialist, and a dogmatist.

As a reformer he believed that the natural piety of mankind had suffered perversion and that his mission was to recall men to true piety.

As a materialist he rejected belief in all incorporeal existences. This resulted after his death in the discovery of a new category, "spiritual beings."

As a materialist he felt bound also to reject all divine causation, including divine movers and divine creators. He was an evolutionist, postulating the continuous birth of the unintended.

As a dogmatist, declaring the possibility of certitude in knowledge, he felt bound to furnish a rationalized account of the gods, their numbers, attributes, form, abode, and manner of life.

The new theology that resulted is astonishing. Some of the findings are as follows:

The gods are not by nature deathless. They were never called immortal by Epicurus himself, though they were by his followers.

The gods are animate creatures, resembling human beings, that is, atomic in composition and structure. As such they are theoretically not immune to the contingency of dissolution but in practice this event is avertible. Thus they may be styled incorruptible in the sense that they are subject to a contingency that need never occur.

All gods, however, are not of the same kind: some are composed of the same atoms at all times, like human beings; others are composed of like atoms by virtue of the perpetual afflux and efflux of atoms self-arranged in identical formations.

The gods can ensure incorruptibility for themselves by their own vigilance. Just as this vigilance ensures incorruptibility, so the assurance of incorruptibility ensures blissfulness. The happiness of the gods is perfect because the assurance of its perpetuity is perfect.

EPICURUS AND HIS PHILOSOPHY

Between men and gods there is a physical, a psychological, and an ethical nexus. Both are animate creatures in an ascending scale of existence. This is the physical nexus. The idea of god is prenatal in man, a built-in notion, implanted by Nature in man as a Prolepsis or Anticipation of experience. This is the psychological nexus. Just as the happiness of men must be self-achieved, so the happiness of gods must be self-preserved. This is the ethical nexus.

Freedom to preserve happiness is no less necessary for gods than freedom to achieve happiness is necessary for men. The gods must be free from onerous responsibilities. Consequently there is no divine government for the universe, no divine providence for man, and no prophecy.

Strange as these doctrines may seem, they were combined with definite previews of Christianity. The idea of love between man and God would not have seemed a novelty to Epicureans. They were taught "that the gods were friends of the wise and the wise were friends of the gods." Friendship and love were one for the Greeks, though denoted by different words in Latin and English.

Neither would "Blessed are the pure in heart, for they shall see God" have seemed to be an innovation. Epicureans were taught that the images of the gods float down into the receptive minds of the truly pious.

Even "Be ye therefore perfect, even as your Father in heaven is perfect" would not have seemed altogether new. The happiness of the gods was held up to the Epicureans as a model and an inspiration; it was declared possible of attainment. The Christians said, "We shall be like Him"; the Epicureans might have said, "We can become like them here and now."

KNOWLEDGE OF THE GODS

An inveterate tendency to classify Epicurus as an empiricist has resulted in the conclusion that according to his thinking knowledge of the gods comes by vision. The absurdity of this view will become clear as abundant items of evidence are assembled against it.

According to these evidences the sources of knowledge are multiple. The Prolepsis apprises men of the blissfulness and incorruptibility of the gods. The Feelings, that is, fears and worries, serve to inform the individual of the true nature of the divine through the distress that follows upon "false opinions." Reason, by deductive inferences from the Twelve Elementary Principles, informs men of the existence of gods, of their corporeal nature, their number, their gradation in kind and their abode. By the method of analogy, that is, progression from similars to similars, reason also produces confirmatory evidence concerning their form, by a chain argument concerning their nature, and by a disjunctive syllogism concerning the kind of life they lead.

In the expansion of this synoptic view the details will be presented under the following heads: The Proper Attitude or Diathesis, Existence of the Gods, The Form of the Gods, Gradation in Godhead, Incorruptibility and Virtue, Isonomy and the Gods, The Life of the Gods, Communion and Fellowship, Prophecy and Prayer.

In the meanwhile attention should be drawn to the fact that the greater part of the teachings concerning the gods was assigned to the last volumes in the graded texts and reserved for advanced courses of study. The surviving texts of Epicurus, including the Authorized Doctrines, were planned as outlines for beginning students and the immediate objective was indoctrination, not exegesis. So far as they treat of the gods, they concern themselves almost exclusively with the proper attitude to be assumed toward them. The subsidiary principle of isonomy, for example, which requires that in an infinite universe the number of imperfect beings should not exceed the number of perfect beings, is nowhere mentioned; neither does this appear in the extant books of Lucretius and was undoubtedly being reserved for the unwritten seventh book, a position that marks the topic for the last place in the Epicurean curriculum. Were it not for Cicero's mention we should not even know of the word *isonomy* in this connection.

It is equally unmistakable, on the contrary, that the essay of Epicurus entitled *On Piety* was prescribed reading for students of limited advancement. This is exactly what we should expect. The prime necessity for peace of mind and freedom from fear was not a knowledge of the gods, of their number, form and abode, but the proper attitude or diathesis toward the gods. Hence we find that in the very first of the Authorized Doctrines the disciple is assured that the gods are incapable of wrath and hence need not be feared. The prime importance of the attitude is also stressed in the letter to Menoeceus, which warns the disciple against attributing anything to the gods that is alien to their incorruptibility or incompatible with their happiness.[1] In the

Little Epitome it is the necessity of reverence which is stressed and this is the positive aspect of the proper attitude toward the divine.[2] In the letter to Pythocles the young disciple is warned against ascribing demeaning functions to the gods, such as watching over the omens derived from the behavior of birds.[3] This too is an aspect of attitude.

Thus the emphasis upon the proper attitude toward the gods in the previous stages of instruction and the relegation of the details of doctrine to the period of advanced study corresponds respectively to the textbook of Epicurus entitled *On Piety* and that entitled *On the Gods.* It corresponds also to the two sources of knowledge, the inborn idea or Anticipation, which is shared even by children, and the inferential ideas, *epinoiai*, which are attainable only by reason and consequently only by adults. This partition of the study is so broad and so distinct that it decisively determines the order of treatment.

THE PROPER ATTITUDE OR DIATHESIS

"Happiness is mainly a matter of attitude, of which we are the arbiters," wrote the faithful Diogenes of Oenoanda.[4] Of all the attitudes the most vital in importance were those toward the gods and death, pleasure and pain — the famous four — and these were honored with the first place in the list of Authorized Doctrines. Among these four, in turn, the first place was given to the proper attitude toward the gods, the most frequently cited of Epicurean doctrines for the space of seven centuries. It runs as follows: "The blissful and incorruptible being neither knows trouble itself nor occasions trouble to another, and is consequently immune to either anger or gratitude, for all such emotions reside in a weak creature." In spite of its prime importance, however, this first Doctrine is only a particular instance of a more comprehensive principle, which is stated negatively and positively as follows: "First of all, believing the divine being to be a creature incorruptible and blessed, just as the universal idea of the divine being is outlined, associate no idea with it that is alien to incorruptibility or incompatible with blessedness and cultivate every thought concerning it that can have the effect of preserving its blessedness along with incorruptibility."[5] In this translation the word *incorruptible* has been retained for two reasons: first, Epicurus did not believe the gods to be inherently immortal and never called them immortal, though Lucretius and others did; second, the Greek word is the same that is rendered "incorruptible" in the New Testament, 1 Corinthians 15.

To return to the first Doctrine, the disciple is warned against associating anger or gratitude with the gods as being inconsistent with the perfection of their happiness and the assurance of their incorruptibility. In this a syllogism is implicit; briefly stated, the major premise is the assumption that a being whose happiness is perfect and assured cannot stand in need of anything; the minor premise is the perfect and assured happiness of the gods. The conclusion is that men cannot bestow a gift upon the gods and so win their favor nor withhold a gift and so incur their anger. The gods are immune to anger and gratitude because of their immunity to need. To be in need would be a symptom of weakness, which cannot be ascribed to a god.

In this argument a greater degree of precision is attainable. It should first be observed that anger and gratitude are reciprocal emotions; they are a pair, as Lactantius discerned. It should next be observed that corresponding to this pair is another, weakness and need. The feeling of gratitude implies the fulfillment of a need, which cannot be ascribed to a god. The feeling of anger is a turmoil in the soul arising from the threat of wrong or injury, and this would imply a weakness in a god, which is incompatible with perfect and assured happiness.

This question of divine anger became a chief topic of contention only when the Christians took over the battle. At the end of the second century A.D. one of the most stinging criticisms leveled by Celsus against the Christians was the fact that they worshiped a god of wrath,[6] for which the Old Testament afforded ample justification. By way of reply his respondent Origen could think up no better argument than to say that Jehovah was not really given to anger but only feigned it.[7] Proof that the criticism continued to sting is evident from the fact that more than a century later the Christian Lactantius wrote a book entitled *On the Wrath of God.*

In his rebuttal the latter displayed better invention than Origen. He refused to take anger and gratitude merely as reciprocal emotions and resorted to a kind of chain argument.[8] The emotions, he insisted, cannot be separated. If a god feels neither anger nor gratitude, then he will not feel fear or joy or grief or mercy, and if this reasoning be pressed, he will feel no emotion at all, which means that he will not exist. That the defenses of Epicurus were really breached by this reasoning there is no denying. His account of the life and nature of the gods, however logical from his premises, is far from being plausible as a whole.

It must still be admitted that he never forgets his premises. Having logically established the all important doctrine that the gods are not to be feared, which, by the way, is strongly reflected in the New Testament under his influence, the next problem was to identify the proper positive feeling of the happy disciple toward the gods. Consistently with the principle upon which he founded his school and worked out the organization of leadership, this feeling was declared to be reverence. Just as each disciple was indoctrinated with the teaching that he should look up with respectful regard to those who were further advanced than himself on the path to wisdom and should revere Epicurus himself as the supreme example, so he must reverence the gods themselves because of the perfection of their bliss and the assurance of its continuance. Quite correctly Cicero represents his Epicurean speaker as declaring: "Piously and reverently we worship an excelling and surpassing being." [9] The gods are not transcendent creatures; they merely stand at the head of a series in which human beings themselves are members.

In respect of this teaching Epicurus was not making an innovation. The feeling he was enjoining toward the gods was the same that his countrymen entertained in their better moments. The Greek word for it was *eusebeia*, "reverence," and the quality in the gods which evoked it was *semnoma*, "sanctity." The latter is sometimes translated "majesty," which is misleading to modern readers. There is no suggestion of omnipotence, omniscience, or omnipresence, which were not current Greek conceptions but the result of a progression of religious thought that took place beyond the original area of Greek religious ideas. Within this area, however, the feeling of awe and reverence had abundantly flourished, for example, in the dramas of Aeschylus. The innovation of Epicurus consisted in selecting this feeling for deliberate cultivation as something possessing a singular guiding value. He was innovating also in furnishing a more precise conception of the divine nature as possessing a sort of happiness which men should not only admire and reverence but also aspire to and imitate.

Reverence was believed to exercise a guiding power. By habitually associating noble and lofty ideas with the gods the human being would build up a correct concept of the divine nature. An anonymous papyrus throws some light upon this teaching; not even the forms of the gods are to be demeaned but thought of as "tending to the sublime," like their dispositions, because of which "they scorn everything that is low." [10] It was this feeling in part that caused Epicurus to be shocked by the teaching of Plato according to which certain gods assumed the guise of balls of fire; it shocked him especially that they were thought to do so of their own free will.[11] On the same principle he would have scorned the idea that Zeus should have hurled Hephaestus from the sky or assumed the form of a swan or an eagle or a shower of gold in order to consummate an amour. Above all else the augustness of the gods must be cultivated in men's thoughts.

EXISTENCE OF THE GODS

Those who are bound to make an empiricist of Epicurus have been compelled to represent him as finding the evidence for the existence of gods in vision. This is an error and a curious one; it was Eudoxus and Plato who appealed to vision as evidence of the existence of gods.[12] The former declared that it mattered little what a man thought of the gods of Greek mythology but it mattered much what he thought about the visible gods, that is, the planets. It was on account of his revulsion from this teaching that Epicurus damned the Eudoxans as "enemies of Hellas." [13]

So far as vision is concerned, Epicurus denied that the gods were visible to the physical eye, though he did think them visible to the mind when operating as a supersensory organ of vision. The value attached to this evidence, however, was strictly limited. It served two purposes: first, to furnish a hint concerning the form of the gods, and second, to awaken in the minds of men the innate notion of the divine being there residing. This innate notion, Prolepsis or Anticipation, was the prime and primal evidence of the existence of gods. According to this notion the gods enjoyed perfect happiness and were immune to corruption. Add to this the information that they were anthropomorphic, gleaned from visions whether of day or night, and this is the sum total of knowledge attainable without recourse to reason and deduction.

The first approach, as in the letter to the lad Menoeceus, is dogmatic: "For there are gods, because the knowledge of them is manifest." [14] This is the appeal to the authority of Nature. The recognition of the existence of gods is apparent among all races. Cicero makes the meaning clear: "For what race is there or what breed of men that does not possess what we may call an Anticipation of gods, which Epicurus calls a Prolepsis?" [15] This is what Epicurus calls by way of description "the universal idea" of the divine being. Its validity, however, depends only in part upon its universality; its main validity derives from the fact that the human being is believed to be preconditioned by Nature for the reception of the idea in advance of experience. For this reason the idea is called an Anticipation or Prolepsis. This priority to experience is part of its qualification as a criterion.

By Cicero's time, however, the syncretism of Stoic and Epicurean ideas had long been in progress, and he erred in saying that Nature had "stamped" this idea of the divine upon the minds of men as if with a seal upon wax.[16] Such a comparison, it is true, was known to Epicurus but he employed it to illustrate the precision of the impression made upon vision by the pressure of the streams of images or idols which account for the sense of sight. Cicero went even farther astray when he wrote of the notion of godhead as "incised" or "engraved" upon the mind.[17] The word he employed, *insculpsit*, could by no interpretation connote faintness or dimness of outline, which was an essential implication of the theory of Epicurus.

The semantic area in which the terminology of Epicurus belongs is that of biology. He thinks of the beginning and growth of the Prolepsis as a genetic process. The newborn infant lacks the use of certain senses, not to say reason; he is only potentially a rational creature. Still, just as the use of the senses exists potentially in the infant and so precedes and anticipates experience, so the capability of apprehending abstract ideas exists potentially from the first and only by degrees becomes actual in pace with experience, instruction, and reflection. As already mentioned, the idea of god is thought of as emerging in the mind just as the network of veins emerges in the embryo, prefiguring and anticipating the development of the whole organism. The mistake of Cicero was to intrude the Stoic idea of the mind as a tablet, capable of receiving impressions. This was not Epicurean.

Once this "universal idea" of the divine being, congenitally existing in the minds of men, has been assumed to precede and anticipate experience, the question that next presents itself is by what agency

256

this potential experience is made actual. Bearing upon this question is the belief of Epicurus that the stimulus to thought and action of necessity comes from without; even the act of walking is believed by him to be preceded by images of the person in the act of walking, a preview of modern gestalt psychology.[18] It is consistent with this belief in the external stimulus that Sextus Empiricus, who is a rather careful citator, informs us that according to Epicurus man derived his idea of godhead from the visions of sleep, the assumption being that these correspond to external realities.[19] This evidence is confirmed by the testimony of Lucretius.[20]

In scanning the latter's testimony, however, the reader must be on guard to observe that true religion and false religion took their start from the same experiences, and the poet is chiefly concerned for the moment with false religion. Nevertheless, he is in accord with the evidences above quoted when he heads his list with visions of the gods witnessed by day or more often by night. It was from these that men first learned of the form of the gods, their stature and beauty. The rest of the passage belongs to the story of superstition.

In respect of the evidence afforded by dreams it is timely to issue a general and a specific warning: the general warning is against the assumption that the doctrines of Epicurus are easy to understand; the specific warning is against assigning more than a minimum value to the evidence of dreams. The vision of gods seen in a dream is no more evidence for the existence of gods than a vision of centaurs is evidence for the existence of centaurs. Only two functions are assigned to dreams in the extant authorities: one function, as gleaned from Sextus Empiricus, is to act as a stimulus to the innate Prolepsis of godhead, which up to a point is merely potential, and thus render it actual;[21] the other function is to furnish a hint, and no more, of the form of the gods, as Cicero informs us.[22] More will be said of this under the heading that next follows.

Confirmatory evidence for the existence of gods was found in logical deduction; this will be discussed in the section on Isonomy and the Gods.

THE FORM OF THE GODS

It was the teaching of Epicurus that the gods were corporeal beings of human form, as stated in the scholium to the first Authorized Doctrine. This part of his teaching was dogmatic and deemed sufficient for the rank and file of his disciples, as is indicated by the paucity of details in the extant synoptic writings and Lucretius. Only from external sources is it possible to gather the drift of more advanced teachings.

All knowledge of the gods falls under the head of things beyond the range of sensation. Consequently all knowledge of them, apart from hints concerning their form, belongs in the category of inferential truths, *epinoiai,* to be arrived at by analogy or by deduction from certain of the Twelve Elementary Principles.

The fact that knowledge of the gods lay beyond the range of sensation might well have been taken for granted, but it happens to be one of the points upon which, in the judgment of Lucretius, the rank and file of disciples should be explicitly informed: [23] "Subtle is the nature of the gods, far removed from the perception of our senses, and only with difficulty is it seen by the part of the soul that is called mind." This is consistent with the scholium to the first Authorized Doctrine, which mentions the gods as "discernible by reason," and the same truth is expressly repeated by Cicero, who wrote of them as perceived "not by sensation but by the mind." [24]

The mind, however, functions in two ways, first as a supersensory organ of vision, and second, as the organ of reason. As a supersensory organ it is capable of perceiving the subtle images of the gods, whether in sleep or in waking hours, which are too fine to be caught by the physical eyes. The information so acquired possesses authority because it emanates from Nature and is a universal experience. "For what other shape," Cicero's interlocutor asks, "ever presents itself to anyone, either sleeping or awake?" [25] Nevertheless, this information falls short of finality; it is a hint only. Lucretius is writing with precision when he speaks of the images of the gods which float into the minds of the pious as "harbingers of the form divine." [26] He means that they afford only a hint of the form of the gods.

Along with the question of form goes that of the size of the gods. As on the question of polytheism, the teaching of Epicurus was in harmony with tradition, because even the statues of the gods were made larger than human. Ancient authority, an anonymous papyrus, employs the words "even their forms tending to the sublime." [27] Sextus Empiricus lays emphasis upon the size of the images that visit men in sleep, and St. Augustine not only declares that, according to Epicurus, the stimulus that causes men to think of the gods is the images that float down into their minds but also that the explanation for their seeing the gods is the "huge images, so to say, that come from the outer world." [28] This detail of teaching, that the gods were larger than human beings, evoked no controversy, because it was traditional.

Distinctly controversial, on the contrary, both in the time of Epicurus and centuries later, was the question whether the bodies of the gods were corporeal or incorporeal. For the benefit of youthful disciples the teaching was dogmatic. In his syllabus addressed to the young Menoeceus Epicurus loses no time in defining the divine being as "a living creature," incorruptible and blissful, and the term employed is *zoön*, "animal," applicable to beasts as well as to human beings.[29] This is important: the gods are viewed as part of the natural order of living corporeal things, the *scala naturae*. Their place is at the top of the scale but not outside of it.

While deeper inquiry into the nature of the gods was reserved for advanced students and for the very last place in the curriculum of study, the nature of the soul was explained for the young Herodotus, and similar reasoning applies to the nature of the gods.[30] The major premise is the third of the Twelve Elementary Principles, which states that the universe is composed of solid bodies — that is, atoms — and void. From this it is deduced, on the principle of the excluded middle, that there is nothing incorporeal except void, which can neither receive nor deliver a stimulus. If either the soul or the god is incorporeal, they must be equated with void, but both are capable of delivering a stimulus; the gods, for example, stimulate the sensory capacity of the mind in visions. Therefore the bodies of the gods must be corporeal.

So wide an acceptance did Epicureanism gain for belief in the corporeal nature of the soul that the word *psychical* in the New Testament actually signifies corporeal, and "psychical body" is rendered "natural body" as opposed to "spiritual body." [31] This marks a new stage of doctrine: the antithesis of corporeal to incorporeal is replaced by that of natural to spiritual. In this the Epicureans played a part. As atomists, anticipating the chemists, they had a most plausible conception of what is now called chemical change, and the brilliant physician Erasistratus, at least an atomist, if not an Epicurean, proposed that the air breathed in by the lungs was changed by the heart into *pneuma*, "vital breath" or *spiritus*.[32] The elder Pliny knew it as *halitus vitalis*.[33] Thus without

Epicurus it is doubtful whether we should be speaking of the "spiritual body" or "spiritual beings."

It is now time to speak of the ascending scale of living things, plants, animals, human beings, and gods, which was not an invention of Epicurus but an accepted assumption of contemporary thought. Its importance at the moment lies in the bearing it has upon knowledge of the gods, their nature and form. Epicurus took over this assumption and insisted upon certain implications of it. He combined it with the fifth and sixth of his Twelve Elementary Principles, which asserted the infinity of the universe in respect of matter and space. Two inferences follow: first, if an ascending scale of existence be assumed, at the top of it there must be some superlative beings, which can be no other than the gods; second, if the universe be infinite, this infinity must apply to values as well as to space and matter. If no perfect beings existed, the universe would not be altogether infinite. Thus, by a necessity of thought there must exist some beings surpassing all others in perfection, that is, in respect of happiness and incorruptibility. These, again, can be no other than the gods.

While this general conclusion is a logical deduction, certain details must be reasoned out by the subsidiary methods of chain argument and analogy. That the gods must enjoy perfect happiness was part of the universal idea or Anticipation. By a brief chain argument two details can be elicited. Since virtue is a prerequisite of happiness, it follows that the gods, as enjoying happiness, must possess virtue. Moreover, since an irrational creature cannot possess virtue, it follows that the gods must possess reason, and that too in the highest degree.[34]

The gods having been once recognized as possessing reason, the next recourse is to observed facts and analogy. It was a favorite observation of Epicurus that everything in nature had its appointed place, fish in the sea, birds in the air, and animals by land.[35] The faculty of reason is not exempt from this law. It is not to be located in the foot, for example, nor in any part of the body except the chest.[36] Neither is it to be found in air or water or fire or in a clod of earth.[37] It is found only in the human form. Consequently the gods by a necessity of thought must be characterized by the possession of the human form, though somewhat larger, being by virtue of this more beautiful.[38]

This line of argument was employed to refute the Platonists, who associated deity with sphericity, and Epicurus chose to wax witty over it,[39] to Cicero's annoyance. From times very remote the circle had been a symbol of perfection, and with the growth of geometry the sphere had captured the popular and learned imagination alike. Circular motion shared this superstitious regard, and Plato was moved to exalt certain heavenly bodies, falsely believed to move in circular orbits, to the rank of gods. Geometry, however, had also brought to knowledge regular cubes, cylinders, cones, and pyramids. These too were beautiful, and Epicurus rightly demanded to know if the gods might not also assume these forms.[40] Moreover, what kind of a life could one ascribe to a spherical god? Hurtling through space would be a strange conception of happiness. Thus the cardinal question was with what shape the faculty of reason could be consistently associated.

On the same principle of analogy the beauty of the divine form was also inferred. Of all living creatures within knowledge the human being is the most beautiful. "What structure of limbs," it was asked by Cicero's speaker, "what configuration of lines, what shape, what aspect can be more beautiful than that of man?"[41] Even more beautiful, therefore, must be the bodies of the gods, because by assumption they must surpass in all regards.

It is not on record whether Epicurus adduced logical grounds for denying flesh and blood to the bodies of the gods. We are informed that he wrote of them as having "a sort of blood and a sort of body, lacking solidity such as characterizes ordinary bodies."[42] It is quite possible that he was rationalizing a tradition, represented by Homer, who also denied blood to the bodies of the gods. Instead of blood there was in their veins a liquid called *ichor*,[43] which in later Greek signified the straw-colored residue of blood called serum. As for the unsubstantial nature of the divine body, this was only what the general belief of the Greeks assumed to be true. As already mentioned, Epicurus preferred to follow tradition where permissible and was not bent upon introducing new gods, which was an indictable offense, but aimed rather to rationalize existing beliefs and recall his countrymen to true piety.

GRADATION IN GODHEAD

It is one of the more debated problems whether Epicurus recognized the existence of more than one class of gods. Both the specific evidences and general considerations would strongly favor the recognition of two classes, but scholars have been reluctant to make such a concession and they resort, as usual, to the device of emending the text.[44] In view of this situation a synoptic glance over the arguments is in order.

At the outset, as a factor of error, it should be diligently kept in mind that in the main the criticism of Epicurus has been hostile and the general desire has been to represent him as a heretic. In his own view, on the contrary, he was rather a traditionalist. He sponsored the usual polytheism of his countrymen and rationalized it. It has been noted already that his description of the bodies of the gods would not be unacceptable to the Greek who took Homer for a guide.

Although Epicurus had no choice but to call himself a sage or philosopher, he was in reality a reformer and a prophet, concepts for which his language had as yet no names. He believed he had discovered "true philosophy," originating in the teaching of Nature herself, as opposed to the corrupt beliefs of the poets, the multitude, and philosophers. As the upholder of the sanctity and dignity of the gods he rejected all the indecencies ascribed to them by the poets and the venalities and spites ascribed to them by the multitude. He was specially hostile to philosophers such as Eudoxus and Plato, who debased the gods by thinking of them as visible balls of fire coursing in circles around the sky.

On the question of the existence of heroes and daemons the reasoning is easy to supply and there is some evidence. Since the former were represented as the fruit of the amours of the gods with mortal beings, belief in them would have been irreconcilable with the sanctity and dignity of the gods. If Epicurus thought it debasing even for a lesser deity to cooperate with birds for the fulfillment of omens, what would he have thought of Jupiter taking the form of swan? This objection would have been decisive even if all miracles had not been rejected. As for daemons, which in current belief occupied a place intermediate between gods and men, we have the statement of Plutarch that Epicureans exhibited impatience if anyone asserted their existence.[45] In the language employed it is implied that this rejection would be on the grounds of both physics and logic. Here also the reasoning can be readily supplied. Under terrestrial conditions, in which these daemons were believed to live, it would have been inconceivable according to the teachings of Epicurus for a divine being to survive; only in the intermundia, where the forces of preservation remained superior to the forces of destruction, would this have been possible. As for the logical grounds of rejection, if once the doctrine of the sanctity and dignity of the gods be accepted, it would be inconceivable that divine beings would lower themselves to such a vulgar function as trailing after human beings to control their fortunes. The daemon of Socrates himself must have been a subject of ridicule to Epicureans.

Even with heroes and daemons eliminated, however, there still remain reasons for entertaining the belief that Epicurus favored some degree of gradation in godhead. The first of these reasons is the current assumption of an ascending gradation in the order of living creatures. Belief in this was old, and it received a powerful impetus in the growth of biological knowledge that took place in the youth of Epicurus under Aristotle's leadership. According to Epicurus, it must always be borne in mind, the gods are *zoa*, "animals," or, if this word seems offensive to us, at least "animate creatures." They are thus not placed outside the ascending series of living beings but at the top of it. Between man and god a physical nexus remains; they are both corporeal. Moreover, there is a psychological and ethical nexus: the idea of god exists congenitally in the minds of men, a model of happiness to which they may aspire.

When once the gods have been admitted into this ascending order of Nature, their position at the top of it leaves a somewhat chasmic gap between man and god. It would seem strange if there were no intermediate grade. The assumption of such is consistent with the gradations in the atoms themselves. According to the last of the Twelve Elementary Principles, the variety in the shapes of the atoms is beyond numbering, though not infinite. This means that with respect to each of their qualities, weight, size, and shape there is an ascending series. Between these several series and the ascending order of animate things there must be a correspondence. The component atoms of human bodies, and especially those of the human soul, must be finer than the component atoms of beasts. The component atoms of gods, in turn, must be infinitely finer than the atoms of man. Consequently, unless a gap is assumed to exist in the gradations of atoms, it is reasonable to assume at least a moderate degree of gradation in the bodies of the incorruptible gods.

In support of this assumption may be cited a statement of Aëtius the doxographer, which informs us "that Epicurus represented the gods as anthropomorphic and all of them discernible only by reason." [46] Why, unless he understood them to differ in kind, should he have written "all of them"? There is also a passage of Philodemus in which he allows that more reverence is due to certain gods than to others.[47]

Fortunately these general considerations are reinforced by the specific evidence of the scholium to the first of the Authorized Doctrines, if only it be translated and interpreted without emendation: "In other writings he says the gods are anthropomorphic, discernible only by reason, some of them existing under limitation, others [not under limitation] by virtue of identity of form arising from the perpetual afflux of similar images wrought to the same shape." The first two items, about the form of the gods and the avenues of knowledge, have already been discussed.

The rest of the sentence may be expounded in a preliminary way as signifying that the bodies of the one class of gods are limited to the same component elements at all times while the bodies of the others are being continually replaced by the afflux and efflux of identical images.

Increased precision of exposition may be attained by a modern comparison. Let it be assumed that the spectator is looking at a portrait of Abraham Lincoln. The component lines and colors of this portrait are continually the same. Let the portrait be projected upon the screen of the cinema and the resultant picture is composed of identical images continually replaced by others, so many frames per second. These are of two dimensions, of course, but the bodies of the second class of gods must be imagined to be replaced in a similar way in three dimensions.

The fidelity of this comparison may be tested by applying to it the language of Cicero when speaking of this class of Epicurean gods. He writes, if only the manuscripts and not the emended texts be followed: "An interminable shape made up of identical images arises from the inexhaustible supply of atoms and flows to the gods."[48] This is the afflux already mentioned, the corresponding efflux, as usual, being taken for granted.

In another passage, though a scornful one, Cicero paraphrases his own description after the fashion of Epicurus himself: "A transmission of images in close succession takes place so that what is composed of many seems to be a unit."[49] This terminology is native to the Garden. The following statement is made by Philodemus with the intimation that the view expressed was that of Epicurus: "Units can be constituted no less from the same elements than from similar elements."[50] By a unit or unity is meant an organic unity, such as a god, and the implication is clear that the existence of two kinds of gods is assumed, the one characterized by permanence of substance and the other by ever changing substance. This inference would be less certain were not Philodemus writing of reverence and Epicurus of piety.

By the time of Epicurus the strange notion of flux combined with permanence, which now seems bizarre, had been fondled by the Greeks for a century, since the days of Heraclitus. It was especially familiar in the saying that no one can bathe twice in the same river. It underwent refinement; clever thinkers pointed out that it was impossible to bathe even once in the same river; it would be a different river from which the bather emerged. Were the conceit so fondled today, the tourist would be warned that the Niagara Falls viewed by him was not the same as viewed by previous tourists. By way of refinement he would be warned of the impossibility of getting two glimpses of the same Falls; the substance had changed while he glanced.

The theory naturally bred a terminology. The Greek equivalents of afflux and efflux became current coin of language, like neutrons and ions today. A changing unity such a river was said to exist *kat' eidos, ad speciem*, "by virtue of form." [51] This turned out to be lacking in preciseness, and a refinement became necessary. Hence we find in the scholium under discussion that the second class of gods exist *kata omoeideian*, "by virtue of similarity or identity of form." This was what Cicero meant when he wrote *infinita species*, "interminable form," while Lucretius said "the form persisted." [52]

This notion of flux and permanence was no more congenial to the atomists than to the Greeks in general. The latter experienced no uplift from contemplating the "everlasting hills" but discerned divinity and eternity rather in the unfailing springs and rushing rivers. Things of unchanging substance were said to exist *kat' arithmon*, "subject to count or measure" but idiomatically "subject to limitation." This was a versatile phrase, taking its meaning from the context, and might apply to time. For example, Philodemus points out that even a chronically bad-tempered man may be subject to special spells of anger of limited duration, that is, *kat' arithmon*.[53] In our scholium, however, the reference is to substance; the first mentioned class of gods exists "subject to limitation." In this respect they resemble human beings, whose substance does not change, and they occupy the intermediate position between these and the second class of gods, who exist by virtue of perpetual afflux and efflux.

It is now possible to recapitulate. No chasmic gap is left by Epicurus in the upper registers of the ascending scale of existence. Between mankind and all gods there is a physical nexus, because all are animate creatures of atomic structure. Between mankind and the first class of gods the nexus is closer, both being subject to limitation of substance. Between the two classes of gods there was a special nexus, both being capable of incorruption, as will presently be made clear. Their bodies were composed of the finest atoms and described as translucent. It is this quality that Cicero has in mind when he describes the gods as not characterized "by what we may call solidity," [54] though when he adds *nec ad numerum*, "nor subject to limitation," this applies only to the second class of gods, the other class being ignored as less open to ridicule.

For the acceptance of the theory of afflux and efflux the minds of pupils had already been prepared by Epicurus through his explanation of vision in his syllabus for beginners. It was there pointed out that even a solid body was vibrant with internal motion, which caused a perpetual discharge of subtle images preserving the surface appearance of the object. This continuous discharge was possible because the image was not formed at depth and so could be replaced at the speed of discharge. Moreover, an infinite supply of the proper atoms was always pressing close, eager, as it were, to dart into the required conformation.

In the case of the gods, on the contrary, there was no obstacle to the images being formed at depth, because their bodies were constituted throughout of atoms of extreme fineness. For this reason the atomic activity must be all the greater and the stream of images discharged would be composed of perfect replicas of the bodies, formed at depth and of three dimensions. Therefore, by invoking the Elementary Principle that the number of atoms of each particular shape is infinite, it may be said in the words of Cicero "that out of the infinite supply of atoms an interminable form [*species* = *eidos*], consisting of identical images, arises and flows to the gods." [55] This is the afflux already mentioned. It involves the principle *e pluribus unum*, "one made of many," like the image seen on the screen of the cinema, which, though consisting of many, appears to be one.

Mention of Cicero affords excuse for the reminder that he does

266

not confuse the two classes of gods, as some have alleged, but speaks with precision within the limits of his purpose. This purpose was not to present a complete or true account of Epicurean doctrine but to select material apt for disparagement. For this reason he selected the gods of ever changing substance and ignored the other kind. His treatment is brutally brief, and no space was available for details that were recondite or uninteresting to the public. His approach was like that of certain comic poets, for whom only those items that were well known and hence good for a laugh, such as "condensing pleasure," were utilizable. It may be recalled how Cicero causes his spokesman to observe that the gods must be fearful lest sometime the stream of constituent images should fail.[56] He was engaged in a campaign for the belittlement of Epicureanism. Always a trial lawyer, even when philosophizing, he felt under no obligation to present all the evidence but only to make such a selection as would be effective with the jurymen.

INCORRUPTIBILITY AND VIRTUE

If the adoption and adaptation of the Heraclitean theory of flux to explain the nature of the gods, that is, by an afflux and efflux of images, seems astonishing to the modern reader, not less astonishing is the doctrine that the maintenance of their own incorruptibility should be ascribed to the gods as a virtue. This is certainly advanced doctrine, and rather difficult to understand and more difficult to accept. Yet the evidence for it is sufficient and explicit.

At the outset it must be observed and kept diligently in mind that nowhere in his extant writings does Epicurus call the gods immortal. This might be thought an accident of the tradition were it not for the fact that other considerations rule out this possibility. If Lucretius does call them immortal repeatedly, this may be set down as an indication that he never really mastered the Epicurean lore of the gods and did not live to make an intensive study of it in preparation for writing about it.

The reasoning behind this doctrine of incorruptibility is readily discerned. From the doctrine that nothing exists except atoms and void it follows that the bodies of the gods must be corporeal. Gods are *zoa*, "animate beings." They are thus units in the ascending order of Nature, as is man. Being in this order and corporeal, they cannot be deathless. If deathlessness were inherent in their nature, they would be in another class by themselves. Since they do belong in the same class as man, it is a logical necessity to think of their incorruptibility as by some means preserved. Since in the cosmos of Epicurus, unlike that of Plato, this incorruptibility lacked a superior being to guarantee its continuance, the sole possibility was that the gods preserved it for themselves by their own vigilance. Thus it must be discerned that just as the happiness of man is self-achieved, so the happiness of the gods is self-preserved.

However astonishing this doctrine may seem, it is well authenticated. Plutarch, for example, who, though hostile, wrote with texts of Epicurus before him, has this to say: "Freedom from pain along with incorruptibility should have been inherent in the nature of the blissful being, standing in no need of active concern." [57] This manifestly implies that the Epicurean gods were unable to take their immunity from corruption for granted but must concern themselves for its perpetuation.

The incongruity between this selfish concern for their own bodily security and their indifference to the good of mankind was certain to elicit condemnation from believers in divine providence, and this has not escaped record. Thus the Christian Eusebius quotes his Atticus as saying: "According to Epicurus it's good-bye to providence, in spite of the fact that according to him the gods bring to bear all diligent care for the preservation of their own peculiar blessings." [58]

When once it has been discerned that the gods are under the necessity of preserving their own blessings, the next step is to learn that this activity is ascribed to them as a virtue. The recognition of this fact will serve to explain a rather cryptic statement from the pen of Epicurus himself. Writing of the "false suppositions" of the multitude, who thought of the gods, now as punishing the wicked, now as having venal relationships with them, he concluded as follows: "for [the gods], being exclusively devoted to their own peculiar virtues, are partial to those like themselves, deeming all that is not such as alien." [59] The first half of this statement has been variously interpreted, but the recognition of our puzzling doctrine will make the meaning intelligible. Just as it is the virtue of men to achieve their own happiness, so it is the virtue of the gods to preserve their own blissfulness. This task so completely engages their attention that no participation in human affairs is possible.

This notion was so well known as to have been familiar to the dull Horatian commentator Porphyry, who lived early in the third century A.D. Horace had quoted freely from Lucretius: "I have learned the lesson that the gods live a life free from concern." [60] The comment runs: "This derives from the doctrine of the Epicureans, who assert that the gods cannot be immortal unless enjoying leisure and immune from all responsibility."

This doctrine has two facets. The gods are characterized by two attributes, blissfulness and incorruptibility. Neither is inherent in their nature. They are incorruptible only because the contingency of destruction is avertible by their vigilance. If this seems subtle, the notion that keeps company with it is more so and also paradoxical. Let it be allowed that incorruptibility is tantamount to eternal life. Then, according to Epicurus, this eternal life is not to be thought a cause of happiness but rather the perpetuity of happiness is a cause of eternal life. The gods win eternal life by maintaining their own pleasures perpetually. This conceit appealed to Menander, who exploited it in his *Eunuchus*. It survives through transfer to the *Andria* of Terence, where the happy lover is made to exclaim: "I think the life of the gods to be everlasting for the reason that their pleasures are perpetual, because immortality is assured to me if no grief shall intervene to mar this joy." [61] This is labeled as "Epicurean dogma" by the Donatus commentary.

This curious conceit consists in a curious semantic shift. Since the life of the gods becomes immortal only through perpetuity of happiness, it follows that the word *immortal* comes to denote a quality of life, something superb or exquisite. This is the only sense in which it is employed in the extant remains of Epicurus. For example, the good Epicurean "lives among immortal blessings" and friendship is styled an "immortal good." [62]

The notion that this activity should be ascribed to the gods as a virtue seemed as weird to Plutarch as it does today: "This is not what we mean when we speak of virtue as strong and vice as weak; we do not apply the words to the perpetuation and dissolution of body; wherefore [the Epicureans] are at fault when they represent eternal life as accruing to the divine being through guarding against and dispelling the forces that would destroy." [63] Manifestly the gods are not assured of their safety merely by dwelling in the spaces between the worlds. They must also be forever on the watch. This is the view satirically presented by Seneca: "[The divine being] in the space between this heaven and another . . . dodges the debris of the worlds crashing to ruin above it and around it." [64]

Very differently are described the divine abodes in the opening lines of the third book of Lucretius; all is at rest, no wind, no rain, no frost, no snow, and no clouds, but always serenity of sky; Nature unasked supplies all needs and nothing occurs at any time to mar the perfection of peace.[65]

This contrast between Lucretius and Seneca marks a chimerical union in the thought of Epicurus between a relentless logic and a sort of romanticism. The logic can be made clear by a chain argument. It has its source in a tenacious materialism, which demands that the bodies of the gods be corporeal; by the same logic the corporeal cannot be immune from the hazard of destruction; the gods are consequently not deathless, only incorruptible; this incorruptibility, not being inherent, demands some sort of conservation, which can only be ascribed to the foresight and effort of the gods themselves. This, then, is their virtue, to preserve their own happiness and incorruptibility.

The weakness of logic, of course, is its lack of dynamic. Men do not feel called to devote their lives to the propagation of syllogisms. The merit of romanticism, on the contrary, is the dynamic that goes with it. It is powered by emotion. Lucretius often handles the logic of Epicurus with clarity and skill, but the force of propulsion behind the logic is emotion, pity for the superstitious misery of man and eagerness to emancipate him. In respect of this enthusiasm Lucretius seems to surpass his master, and yet Epicurus is on record as saying: "[The wise man] will be more susceptible of emotion than other men and this will be no obstacle to his wisdom." [66] Here we have the recognition of the chimerical blend of logic and romanticism. It is the latter, the emotion, the eagerness to emancipate men from fear and to show them the road to happiness, that leads Epicurus to extol the blissfulness of the gods as a perfection to contemplate and imitate. It is the logic of materialism that compels him to deny it to them as a birthright, so to say, and to impose upon them the necessity of preserving it.

Strange as this contingent immortality may seem, a similar notion was entertained by Plato. According to him the eternity of the cosmos depends upon the will of the supreme demiurge; since he was the creator, he could also destroy. It is impossible, however, to think of him choosing to do so.[67] Thus the cosmos is eternal because it is subject to a contingency that will never occur. Even the immortality of the Christian falls in the same class: being the gift of God it could also be withdrawn by the same power, but perfect faith exists that this contingency will never occur.

ISONOMY AND THE GODS

In spite of a supercilious opinion to the contrary, Epicurus was not a muddled thinker but a very systematic one. He enunciated his Twelve Elementary Principles and adhered to them closely. Two of these, the fifth and sixth, asserted the infinity of the universe in respect of matter and space. To this idea of infinity he ascribed fundamental importance. He exhorted the young Pythocles to study it as one of those master principles which would render easy the recognition of causation in details.[68] Cicero must have been recalling some similar exhortation when he wrote: "But of the very greatest importance is the significance of infinity and in the highest degree deserving of intense and diligent contemplation." [69] He was quoting Epicurus.

It was from this principle that Epicurus deduced his chief theoretical confirmation of belief in the existence of gods. It was from this that he arrived at knowledge of their number and by secondary deduction at knowledge of their abode. He so interpreted the significance of infinity as to extend it from matter and space to the sphere of values, that is, to perfection and imperfection. In brief, if the universe were thought to be imperfect throughout its infinite extent, it could no longer be called infinite. This necessity of thought impelled him to promulgate a subsidiary principle, which he called *isonomia*, a sort of cosmic justice, according to which the imperfection in particular parts of the universe is offset by the perfection of the whole. Cicero rendered it *aequabilis tributio*, "equitable apportionment." [70] The mistake of rendering it as "equilibrium" must be avoided.

The term *isonomia* itself, which may be anglicized as isonomy, deserves a note. That it is lacking in extant Epicurean texts, all of them elementary, and is transmitted only by Cicero is evidence of its belonging to higher doctrine and advanced studies. Epicurus switched its meaning slightly, as he did that of the word *prolepsis*. To the Greeks it signified equality of all before the law, a boast of Athenians in particular. It was a mate to *eunomia,* government by law, as opposed to barbaric despotism, a boast of Greeks in general. That Epicurus thought to make capital of this happy connotation may be considered certain. He was vindicating for Nature a sort of justice, the bad being overbalanced by the good. It is also possible that he was remotely influenced by the teachings of Zoroaster, well known in his day through the conquests of Alexander, according to whom good and evil, as represented by Ormazd and Ahriman, battled for the upper hand in mundane affairs.

Whatever may be the facts concerning this influence, Epicurus discovered a reasonable way of allowing for the triumph of good in the universe, which seemed impossible under atomic materialism. Thus in his system of thought isonomy plays a part comparable to that of teleology with Plato and Aristotle. Teleology was inferred from the evidences of design, and design presumes agencies of benevolence, whether natural or divine. Epicurus was bound to reject design because the world seemed filled with imperfections, which he listed, but by extending the doctrine of infinity to apply to values he was able, however curiously, to discover room for perfection along with imperfection.

That he employed isonomy as theoretical proof of the existence of gods is well documented. For example, Lactantius, who may have been an Epicurean before his conversion to Christianity, quotes Epicurus as arguing "that the divine exists because there is bound to be something surpassing, superlative and blessed." [71] The necessity here appealed to is a necessity of thought, which becomes a necessity of existence. The existence of the imperfect in an infinite universe demands belief in the existence of the perfect. Cicero employs very similar language: "It is his doctrine that there are gods, because there is bound to be some surpassing being than which nothing is better." [72] Like the statement of Lactantius, this recognizes a necessity of existence arising from a necessity of thought; the order of Nature cannot be imperfect throughout its whole extent; it is bound to culminate in something superior, that is, in gods.

It is possible to attain more precision in the exposition. Cicero, though brutally brief, exhibits some precision of statement. The infinity of the universe, as usual, serves as a major premise. This being assumed, Cicero declares: "The nature of the universe must be such that all similars correspond to all similars." [73] One class of similars is obviously taken to be human beings, all belonging to the same grade of existence in the order of Nature. As Philodemus expresses it in a book about logic, entitled *On Evidences*, "It is impossible to think of Epicurus as man and Metrodorus as non-man." [74] Another class of similars is the gods. This being understood, the truth of Cicero's next statement follows logically: "If it be granted that the number of mortals is such and such, the number of immortals is not less." [75] This reasoning calls for no exegesis, but two points are worthy of mention: first, Cicero is not precise in calling the gods immortals; according to strict doctrine they are not deathless, only incorruptible of body; the second point is that Epicurus is more polytheistic in belief than his own countrymen.

The next item, however, calls for close scrutiny. Just as human beings constitute one set of similars and the gods another, so the forces that preserve constitute one set and the forces that destroy constitute another.

At this point a sign of warning is to be raised. There is also another pair of forces that are opposed to each other, those that create and those that destroy. [76] The difference is that the latter operate in each of the innumerable worlds, while the former hold sway in the universe at large. For example, in a world such as our own, which is one of many, the forces of creation have the upper hand during its youthful vigor. At long last, however, the forces of destruction gradually gain the superiority and eventually the world is dissolved into its elements. [77]

In the universe at large, on the contrary, the situation is different and the forces opposed to each other are not those that destroy and those that create but those that destroy and those that preserve. Moreover, a new aspect of infinity is invoked, the infinity of time. The universe is eternal and unchanging. Matter can neither be created nor destroyed. The sum of things is always the same, as Lucretius says. This truth is contained in the first two of the Twelve Elementary Principles. In combination they are made to read: "The universe has always been the same as it now is and always will be the same." [78] This can be true only on the principle that the forces that preserve are at all times superior to the forces that destroy.

It follows that Cicero was writing strictly by the book when he made his spokesman draw the following conclusion from the doctrine of isonomy: "And if the forces that destroy are innumerable, the forces that preserve must by the same token be infinite." [79] This doctrine, it is essential to repeat, holds only for the universe at large. It is not applicable to the individual world and it does not mean that the prevalence of elephants in India is balanced by the prevalence of wolves in Russia. Isonomy does not mean "equal distribution" but "equitable apportionment." It does not denote balance or equilibrium. No two sets of similar forces are in balance; in the individual world the forces of destruction always prevail at last, and in the universe at large the forces of preservation prevail at all times.

By this time three aspects of the principles of isonomy have been brought forward: first, that in an infinite universe perfection is bound to exist as well as imperfection; that is, "that there must be some surpassing being, than which nothing is better"; second, that the number of these beings, the gods, cannot be less than the number of mortals; and third, that in the universe at large the forces of preservation always prevail over the forces of destruction.

All three of these are direct inferences from the infinity and eternity of the universe. There remains to be drawn an indirect inference of primary importance. Since in the individual worlds the forces of destruction always prevail in the end, it follows that the incorruptible gods can have their dwelling place only outside of the individual worlds, that is, in the free spaces between the worlds, the so-called *intermundia*, where the forces of preservation are always superior. There is more to be said on this topic in the section that follows.

THE LIFE OF THE GODS

For the life of the gods there is a moderate supply of evidence. The first avenue of approach was by way of traditional belief, with which Epicurus was glad to be in harmony where logic permitted. More important are the details arrived at by deductive reasoning because the whole topic lay beyond the sphere of sensory knowledge. The Prolepsis of the divine nature, being certified as a criterion, serves as a major premise. Among logical procedures a brief chain argument and a smart disjunctive syllogism will stand out.

Basic for the traditional account was the doctrine of Homer that the gods live at ease for ever.[80] This served as common ground between Epicurus and the belief of the Greeks in general. Traditional also was the assumption of an ascending order of living things of which the gods were the top and crown. It was also accepted that the happiness of the gods was superlative. That Epicurus gave precision to this belief is evidenced by the following quotation: "Happiness is thought of in two ways, the first being superlative, admitting of no intensification, such as belongs to the divine nature, the second admitting of the addition and subtraction of pleasures." [81] It need not be added that the second kind falls to human beings. Their pleasures are subject to increase and decrease, that is, they are sometimes static, sometimes kinetic. To be alive and in health is a static pleasure; to escape from a violent death or recover from sickness is a kinetic pleasure.

The traditional beliefs had been violated by Plato when he discovered onerous functions for divine beings: for his supreme god, the demiurge, the task of creating and superintending the moving universe, and for the astral gods the duty of wheeling through circular orbits for ever. This teaching aroused such indignation on the part of Epicurus that he declared it unpatriotic and denounced the Cyzicene philosophers, who also sponsored it, as "Enemies of Hellas." [82] He found logical grounds for denouncing it in the common belief that the happiness of the gods is perfect. Specifically, the logical basis was the idea connate with man, the Prolepsis of the divine nature as blissful. On this basis a brief chain argument was resorted to: onerous tasks involve feelings of responsibility and worries; these, in turn, are incompatible with perfect happiness; therefore onerous tasks cannot be imposed upon the gods.[83]

In taking this stand Epicurus would to a certain extent have had Aristotle on his side. The great-souled man could not have been described as living otherwise than at ease, except that from time to time he might serve as head of the state or of an army. Much less could divine beings be described as weighed down to all eternity with onerous responsibilities and consequent worries. The result is the anti-Platonic declaration that the gods "have nothing to do, are involved in no occupations," and above all "plan no onerous undertakings." As Cicero expresses it with ponderous alliteration in another passage, the divine nature enjoys *immunitas magni muneris*, "exemption from burdensome responsibility." [84] The universe, being eternal, was never created; it is self-operating and stands in no need of superintendence.

From the proleptic belief in the perfection of divine happiness Epicurus also drew the inference that the gods were immune to all disturbing emotions, such as anger, and were consequently indifferent to human wickedness. This was elementary teaching for young disciples and is on record in the first Authorized Doctrine. There was also the teaching that the virtue of the gods was to preserve their own happiness, in which they were exclusively engaged, which was dogmatically intimated in the letter to Menoeceus.[85] For the benefit of advanced pupils there was a disjunctive syllogism, which covered the topic of worldly evil in a more sweeping way.

This disjunctive syllogism is reported by the Christian Lactantius as follows: "The divine being either would abolish evil and cannot, or he can and will not, or he is neither willing nor able, or he is both willing and able. If he would and cannot, he is weak, which cannot befall a god. If he can and will not, he grudges to do it, which is equally alien to the divine. If he is neither willing nor able, he is both grudging and weak, consequently not a god. If he is both willing and able, which alone befits a god, whence then arise the evils? Or why does he not abolish them?" [86] That rival philosophers were badly upset by this argumentation, as Lactantius admits, may readily be credited, because an apter specimen of disjunctive reasoning is difficult to find. The refutation offered by Lactantius, that without evil there could be neither wisdom nor virtue, is logically pertinent but does not altogether cure the sting of the syllogism. The doctrine of divine providence has always been a difficult one.

Still, the argument offered in refutation by Lactantius was capable of putting Epicurus in a corner. According to his own doctrine, since evil was unknown among the gods, there could be no wisdom and no virtue, because wisdom displays itself in choosing between good and evil. Virtue, of course, could not logically be denied to the gods, because happiness is inseparable from virtue, as stated in the fifth of the Authorized Doctrines. It follows that the virtue of the gods is so circumscribed that it must consist in the preservation of their own blissfulness and incorruptibility. Being corporeal by nature, that is, composed of atoms, they cannot be deathless like the Homeric gods, only incorruptible, and this by virtue of their own vigilance in an environment where the forces of preservation are superior to the forces of destruction.

The same circumscription of the divine activity renders very unsatisfactory the description of the life of the gods. Epicurus was perhaps too much influenced by hostility to the working gods of Plato. The happiness of the Epicurean gods consists in large part of the very immunity from responsibilities. In this respect they resemble gentlemen of leisure, for whom all worldly occupations were sordid. To Seneca the life of the Epicurean gods seemed lonely, "no living thing, no human being, no property." [87] In so speaking there was possibly at the back of his mind his own conception of happiness, the life of a wealthy gentleman living on a rural estate abounding in farm animals, servants, and the physical comforts of life. Lucretius, however, more vague and romantic than logical at the moment, speaks of "Nature unasked supplying every need."

Philodemus, who lived long among wealthy Romans, was of like mind with Seneca. In his essay *On the Management of an Estate* he stresses the importance, when selecting a country property, of ensuring that the purchaser should have neighbors with whom he might enjoy good companionship,[88] which means that they might meet often together and engage in philosophical discussion. This is the very pleasure that in his books *On the Gods* he represents as being enjoyed by the divine beings.

The subsumed logic of this view is the method called analogy and transition or progression from similars to similars, already described. The two sets of similars are men and the gods and the transition is from the life of the one to the life of the other. The language of Philodemus is slightly extravagant: "Philosophical converse with those of their own kind floods good men with ineffable pleasure." [89] It is in the light of this judgment that we must interpret the statement that the pleasure of the gods is "to enjoy their own wisdom and virtue." Like the earthly Epicureans, they were sociable creatures and found the maximum enjoyment in the company of one another.

The rest of the passage of Philodemus presents a brace of interesting details. As usual, the subsumed method is that of analogy and transition. The gods, like human beings, must be endowed with speech, "for we shall not think of them as more happy and indissoluble if not speaking nor conversing with one another, but like dumb people." [90] The second point is the conclusion that they speak Greek. "Yes, and I swear by Zeus," he adds, "we must believe that they possess the Greek language, or something not far different; in no other way do we understand gods existing unless they use the Greek tongue." [91]

If this judgment provokes a smile, its interest need not stop with

277

amusement. It had its influence upon Latin literature through a chain reaction. The Greeks in general arrogated philosophy to themselves, and Epicurus was for confining it to those who spoke the Greek tongue.[92] Lucretius seemed to concur when he dwelt upon the poverty of the Latin language. This lamentation stung the patriotism of Cicero and prompted him to claim not mere equality but even superiority for Latin.[93] This resentment, in turn, was a contributing factor to the burst of anti-Epicurean writing in his last years. He was responding to a challenge and making good a boast. He never assumed a hostile attitude toward Epicureanism until the poem of Lucretius made it a threat to Latin literature; he was determined that this literature should not have an Epicurean color.

To return to the gods, Epicurus was not the only one to employ the disjunctive syllogism. Sextus Empiricus turned it against his teachings: "Either the gods possess speech or they don't. Now to deny speech to the divine being is absolutely absurd and contrary to the universal ideas. But, if he possesses speech, he uses his voice and has organs of speech, that is, lungs, windpipe, tongue, and mouth, and it is this that is absurd and in line with the rest of Epicurean mythology. The conclusion, then, is that there is no god. For, granted that he does use voice, he talks with others. And if he does so, he certainly employs some sort of language. If so, why Greek rather than the barbaric tongue? And if Greek, why rather the Ionian or the Aeolic or one of the other dialects, or for that matter, why not all of them? Therefore he uses none. For, if he uses Greek, how will he use the barbarian tongue, unless someone has taught him? Unless he has interpreters like those who among us mortals are able to interpret. So it must be denied that the divine being has the use of speech." [94]

The logic of this is not quite compelling; if gods be dumb, they should also be deaf. The really logical inference is that all inquiries into the life of the gods terminate in absurdities.

An outstanding paradox of Epicureanism is the combination of traditionalism with innovation, conformity with nonconformity, fervent piety with doctrinal heresy, and devout reverence with the denial of divine providence. The attitudes of Lucretius are typical. In point of fervor his invocation to Venus is not inferior to the hymn of Cleanthes

278

to Zeus. If he falls short of the grandiosity of the Stoic, his ardor is on a par. Yet he inveighs vehemently against the evils of religion.

A kind of communion between the human and the divine was characteristic of both Epicureans and Stoics. The Stoics discovered a basis for this in that spark of the divine fire which resides in every man. The Epicureans found a basis in the images of the divine beings that float down into the minds of the truly pious. "Blessed are the pure in heart; for they shall see God," was a dictum quite in accord with their belief. Writers so diverse as Sextus Empiricus and St. Augustine bear witness to the truth of this view, that the thought of the divine nature has its beginnings in these visitations. These witnesses do not stand alone, however. Lucretius warns the impious man "that he will not draw near the shrines of the gods with a heart untroubled nor will he be able to capture the images that from the sacred persons of the gods float into the minds of men, harbingers of the form divine." It is through these that man first becomes aware of the divine nature.

Enemies of Epicurus and his creed were accustomed recklessly to accuse the sect of atheism and of nullifying the significance of all religious festivals. The attitude assumed by Epicurus himself was dictated by various considerations. No desire to become a martyr or to make a cult of martyrdom occurred to him. He recommended conformity in practice. When he denied that a man could live happily without living according to reason, honor, and justice, he meant by justice obedience to the written law of the land. The state festivals were part of this law and covering their observance his recommendation is explicit: "Let us Epicureans, at any rate, sacrifice piously and properly where it is required and let us do every thing else according to the laws, not troubling ourselves about popular opinions in respect of the things that are highest and holiest." [95]

That Epicurus was not guilty of advising one course and following another is evidenced by one of his own letters, in which Philodemus quotes him as writing "that he had participated in all the festivals," and he specified the Feast of Pitchers and the Mysteries, though the adjective that would define the latter is unluckily mutilated.[96]

The covering principle in such matters is the beneficent effect of reverence upon the worshiper. A dictum of Epicurus on the point has been quoted previously, Vatican Saying 32: "Reverence for the wise man is a great blessing for the one that feels the reverence." The working of this principle, though limited in this context, may be extended in application to the gods. To reverence is ascribed in particular a guiding power of supreme importance. This guidance is toward a correct concept of the divine. Philodemus quotes the master as saying: "The following truth is also of great moment and in respect of its guiding power, so to speak, is of surpassing importance: for every wise man has chaste and pure notions of the divine and takes it for granted that this divine nature is exalted and august." [97]

This guiding feeling, of course, requires diligent cultivation and the first practical rule recommended for this purpose by Epicurus is worthy of a Holy Name Society. He thinks of reverence as in part a product of the language habitually employed. For instance, while speaking of the gods he urges upon the young Herodotus the necessity of "maintaining all reverence of feeling in the use of all epithets applied to such concepts if nothing inferable from them is going to seem incompatible with augustness." [98] The test to be applied to these epithets, in which Greek liturgies abounded, would manifestly be the suggestion of debasing or shabby conduct, spitefulness or vindictiveness.

This recommendation of Epicurus to censor the terminology of religion was bound to provoke condemnation, and Plutarch did not fail to put it on record.[99] He accuses Colotes of quibbling and declares that "the heinous thing is to refuse to say that god is god and not to believe in him. This is what you Epicureans do, refusing to recognize Zeus as Genethlios, 'Protector of the Family,' Demeter as Thesmophorus, 'Bearer of Law,' and Poseidon as Phutalios, 'God of the Orchard'." These cult-names were chosen as having happy connotations. He omitted Apollo Smintheus, "Mouse-Killer," hardly an exalted function, Zeus Alastor, "Avenger," which suggested vindictiveness, and Dionysus Omestes, "Delighting in Raw Flesh," which was revolting. Neither did he cite Zeus Bronton or Hyetios, "Thunderer" or "Rainmaker," phenomena for which Epicurus had physical explanations. Aphrodite Kallipugos, "of the Beautiful Buttocks," might have offended his sense of decorum.

Epicurus was resolute in ascribing high values to the liturgies. Of the three divisions of worship now commonly recognized, adoration, confession, and petition, it was adoration upon which he placed almost exclusive value. Not only did he recommend to his disciples "to sacrifice piously and properly" but it is reported of him that he said: "[The wise man] will take keener delight than the rest of men in public festivals." [100] Even Plutarch informs us of his rising early in the morning to attend these performances. [101] Philodemus also quotes him as saying: "In the festivals in particular [every man who is wise], making progress toward understanding of it [the divine nature], through steadily having the name upon his lips, with stronger emotion becomes seized of the incorruptibility of the gods." [102]

That Epicurus took particular pleasure in music is inferable from the records, and Philodemus in his essay on the subject has this to say: "Let this much be said also now, that the divine being stands in no need of worship but it is natural for us to worship him above all with pious thoughts and next in importance by the rites handed down by our fathers for each of the gods respectively." [103] Of the same tenor is a passage from the work of Philodemus *On the Life of the Gods*: "[The wise man] regards with wonder the nature of the gods and their disposition [tranquillity], and endeavors to draw near to it and yearns, as it were, to touch it and to be in its company, and he also calls wise men the friends of the gods and the gods the friends of the wise." [104]

Such were the teachings of the man who was accused of nullifying all sacrifices, mysteries, religious pageants, and festivals, who was denounced for centuries as an atheist, and whose name survived as a synonym for unbeliever. There was sufficient truth in his conception of the new piety to carry a lasting sting.

By attending the festivals himself and urging the disciples to do so while at the same time denying all participation of the gods in human affairs, Epicurus laid himself open to the charge of hypocrisy. It was alleged that he was merely appeasing the multitude out of fear of reprisals. [105] Another ground for this charge was his habit of interspersing his writings with oaths, as was customary among his countrymen. Dionysius the Great, Bishop of Alexandria, for example, is quoted by Eusebius as writing of Epicurus: "In his own writings he puts oaths in his own mouth and those of others, swearing continually this way and that by Zeus, making all and sundry swear, including those with whom he is conversing, in the name of the gods, having no fear of perjury himself, I presume, nor ascribing any fear to the others, and adding to his words this empty, false, idle, and meaningless appendage of superstition." [106] As a token of the opposition of the Christians to this practice the words of Jesus may be recalled, "Swear not at all."

In the second century the learned Origen, refuting Celsus the Epicurean, had gone even farther afield to lodge a charge of hypocrisy against the Epicureans, who carried about with them small images of the master. These are his words: "It is not only silly to pray to idols but also to pretend to pray to them while circulating among the multitude, as do those who philosophize after the way of the Peripatos and those who cherish the teachings of Epicurus and Democritus." [107] The point of this seems to be that the custom of carrying amulets, including images of gods, was prevalent then as is now the habit of carrying images of saints. The potency of these images is, of course, mainly potential; to render it active and efficacious the image must be caressed by the hand. This gesture, in effect, is a prayer and thus the Epicureans laid themselves open to the charge of hypocrisy, more particularly for the reason that they laid great stress on the virtues of true piety and absolute honesty. Hence Origen concludes: "Because absolutely no insincerity should attach itself to the soul that is truly pious toward the divine."

As a parting word on the subject of fellowship it should be recalled how consistently and ardently communion on the human side was cultivated. The sect has often been compared to the Society of Friends, better known as Quakers. The older members of the school were "fellow-philosophers"; the members in good standing were "associates," Greek *synetheis*, Latin *familiares*. Their staple enjoyment was found in "good companionship." "Philosophical converse with those of their own kind floods good men with ineffable pleasure," wrote the genial Philodemus. This good companionship may be viewed as the antecedent of the "communion of saints," because Epicureanism was flourishing in every community in advance of Christianity. Similarly, the regular monthly gatherings of Epicureans would have furnished a model for the love-feasts of the Christians.

While the sect had no doctrine of the Holy Spirit there was something analogous to it in the reverence with which the memory of Epicurus was regarded. To Lucretius he was a god, and when once the savior sentiment had established itself, the epithet of savior was also applied to him. Both Metrodorus and Lucretius speak of following "in his footsteps" and for all Epicureans there was a pledge: "We will be obedient to Epicurus, according to whom we have made it our choice to live." Every loyal disciple was to conduct himself as if Epicurus were looking on.[108] This makes of the dead Epicurus a living criterion of conduct, and it may well be that it was Epicureanism which gave vogue to a novel concept of immortality which was current in antiquity, an immortality of good influence as the prolongation of a good life. As Virgil put it, "To perpetuate our names by our deeds, this is the task of virtue." [109]

Quite in line with this worshipful attitude toward Epicurus is the Epicurean attitude toward the gods. They are incapable of anger and so need not be feared, but they are not incapable of loving; "they are partial toward those like themselves"; they are "friends of the wise." There is a psychological nexus between men and them, because the concept of the blissful and incorruptible being is implanted in the mind by Nature herself. Moreover, the images of the gods come down to visit the minds of the pious and are recognized by them. To desire to aspire to a perfect happiness such as theirs is natural for men and this goal is attainable. Lucretius is very positive upon the latter point: "This I seem able in these matters to affirm, that so very paltry are the traces of their evil natures which reason cannot expel for the wise that nothing prevents them from passing a life worthy of the gods." [110] Epicurus himself wrote to the lad Menoeceus: "Meditate, therefore, upon these truths and upon others like them by day and by night, both by yourself and with someone like yourself and never will you be troubled whether waking or sleeping but will live like a god among men, for in no respect does a man who lives among immortal blessings resemble a mortal creature." [111] The Christian said, "We shall be like Him." The Epicurean would have said, "We can be like them here and now."

PROPHECY AND PRAYER

Any scholar who would lay the charge of "moral invalidism" at the door of Epicurus has a weak case to present when the topic of prophecy or divination is slated for investigation. A man who possessed the moral courage to deny the existence of prophecy and to defy the immemorial beliefs of his own countrymen and to condemn the public practices of all the Greek states can hardly be set down for a moral invalid. In his own day, although the political influence of oracles had passed its prime, the business of catering to the hopes and fears of individuals was in an upsurge. The various Sibyls were enjoying a revival of popularity, of which one was in Samos, where Epicurus grew up. Near

283

Colophon, where he was domiciled for ten years, Apollo Clarius was beginning to acquire celebrity. It was consequently a growing evil to which he set himself in opposition.

Neither can the man whose pronouncements on religion continued to harass the conditioned reflexes of Greeks, Jews, and Romans be cavalierly dismissed as an "incoherent thinker." The issue he put up to all these races and asserted to be a basic principle, the sanctity and dignity of the gods, was clear-cut and definite. The reason for his criticisms being so biting was an incontestable validity in them.

It is possible to set forth his logical position in detail. Since according to certain of the Twelve Elementary Principles the universe was declared to be infinite, there could be no divine being outside of it to govern its operations and maneuver human events by remote control. Moreover, since predetermination was thus lacking, neither could there be prediction from that source. Again, since all incorporeal existences other than void are ruled out according to the same Elementary Principles, it follows that only the corporeal gods of the intermundial spaces remain, and these were incapable of living under terrestrial conditions even if they had had the will to come down and inspire human beings with prophetic insight, which they had not. One possibility that remained was the potency of magic rites to call up the souls of the dead from Acheron, which was in turn ruled out by the denial of immortality. As for divination through dreams, for this the pertinent text is extant: "The visions of sleep possess no divine nature nor prophetic power but are accounted for by the invasion of images." [112] This is a purely physical explanation. The image of a nonexistent centaur is just as capable of stimulating the mind of the dreamer as is the image of a god.

Neither was there lack of courage in making these opinions known. His pronouncement was forthright and uncompromising and published in several writings. "The art of prophecy is nonexistent and, even if it did exist, external events are to be thought of as meaning nothing to the life within us." [113] The second limb of this sentence is sometimes mistranslated or emended. The meaning becomes clear if the distinction is borne in mind between the inner life of man, which is free, and the external life, which is affected by circumstances. Fortune and Necessity cannot be eliminated, but they can be reduced to virtual impotence.

It is for this reason that prophecy, even if it did exist, would not alter the attitude of the wise man. He is not saying, as some translate, that events are "nothing to us." This would not be true. He means that the wise man remains master of his life under the most trying of circumstances. This fact would not be altered by foreknowledge or prophecy.

One of the weapons employed against prophecy was ridicule. Cicero is authority for the statement "that there is nothing Epicurus ridicules so much as the prediction of future events." [114] Lucian depicts his opposition as "adamantine," and he tells how the false prophet Alexander "waged against him a truceless and undeclared war" and used to apply to him an epithet which in current slang is equivalent to "hard-boiled," because all prophesyings were denominated by him as "something to be laughed at and as childishness." [115]

From the pen of Epicurus himself we possess a mild specimen of this scorn. Writing of the departure of birds, probably the storks, as a sign of winter coming to an end, he has this to say: "For the birds can bring to bear no sort of compulsion to bring winter to an end, nor does some divine being seat itself to watch for the departure of these creatures and then bring these signs to fulfillment, because such silliness would not befit even an ordinary being, even if only a little superior, much less one possessed of perfect happiness." [116] The guiding feeling is reverence. The diligent practice of it, Epicurus believed, would lead the disciple infallibly to a true concept of the divine nature as exalted and august, incapable of any conduct vulgar or degrading.

The followers of Epicurus after his death, though diligent cultivators of peace and safety, continued to display the same belligerency as their founder. According to Lucian it was chiefly the Epicureans who summoned up courage to defy Alexander the False Prophet, and the only man to accuse him to his face on a specific charge was an Epicurean, who almost paid for his daring by his life.[117] Upward of a century before the date of this alleged occurrence it was the Epicureans in Thessalonica who by their derision aroused the indignation of St. Paul, then prophesying the second coming of Christ. In his retort he denied them the honor of mention by name but identified them adequately by those catchwords of their creed, "Peace and Safety." [118] It may be added that the Epicureans, as usual, were in the right; the prophecy was not fulfilled.

That the badgering tactics of the Epicureans were directed also against the Jews is revealed by Josephus. With him, as with his race in general, the question of prophecy was tightly tied in with the belief in the divine government of the world. Since the prophet Daniel, for instance, was believed to have been inspired by God, it was to be expected that his prophecies would be fulfilled by God. Prophecy was subsidiary to divine providence. In conformity with this view Josephus gives a somewhat extended account of the prophecies of Daniel and their precise fulfillments, thus demonstrating for his readers the falsity of the Epicurean doctrines, which he rehearses at suitable length.[119]

The Greek concept of the divine being was more restricted and, perhaps it may be said, less developed. Apollo, for example, unlike Jehovah, was not to be held responsible for the fulfillment of his own prophecies. His prophecies were self-fulfilling. Croesus, for instance, by his own actions fulfilled the prophecy of his own downfall. The gift of foretelling and the power to fulfill were not necessarily joined in the same deity. Again, the quality of ubiquity or omnipresence was not claimed for a deity. It was consequently necessary for Apollo to be ceaselessly commuting between Delphi, Delos, Branchidae, and Claros, not to mention numerous other shrines variously located. His life was therefore a very laborious one, completely incompatible with perfect bliss, even allowing that incorruptibility was maintainable under stormy flying conditions. It is for this reason understandable why Epicurus insisted that the gods should have no occupations, not even that of a prophet. They must have leisure to enjoy their bliss.

Divination must have been abominable to Epicurus also because it was inseparable in his world from the sordidness of magic and sorcery. Alexander the False Prophet, Lucian does not fail to relate, served his apprenticeship to a wizard, who promised to the credulous help in love, revenge on enemies, discovery of buried treasure, and inheritance of wealth. From sorcery Alexander progressed to prophecy, as a means of getting rich quickly, preying upon the hopes and fears of men, for which he perceived "that prophecy was an utmost necessity and the most desirable of things." [120] This was just as true in the time of Epicurus as when Lucian wrote under Marcus Aurelius. Close to Colophon, where Epicurus had his home for ten years, was a mineral spring, sacred to Apollo Clarius. The waters of it had a deranging effect upon the mind, and under their influence the ministrant was thought to reveal the future. Familiarity with this traffic may have been a prime factor in fixing the attitude of Epicurus. It would have outraged his sense of reverence to think that a god should lower himself to participate in such hocus pocus.

Even apart from the degradation of the divine and the deception of men through their hopes and fears, Epicurus had an ethical objection to urge against the business of prophecy. A scholium to Aeschylus runs as follows: "There is a doctrine of Epicurus denying the art of prophecy, 'because,' says he, 'if fate is the master of all, when foretelling calamity you have caused pain before the due time and when foretelling something good you spoil the pleasure.' " [121] This judgment, as usual, is part of a logical context. It is the fool who thinks of the future. The wise man makes a rational choice of attitude toward past, present, and future. He lives in the present. While this rule is essential for avoiding fear, a chief enemy of serenity, the immediate provocation for its espousal may well have been furnished in part by the contemporary prevalence of petty prophecy preying upon men's fears and hopes concerning the future.

The proper attitude toward the future was well defined, "to hope for the best, contemplate the worst, and endure whatever shall be." [122]

That the sordidness of Greek religion on its lower levels was much in the mind of Epicurus is evidenced by an extant saying: "If the divine being complied with the prayers of mankind, all men would speedily be perishing, because they are continually praying that diverse misfortunes befall one another." [123] On the upper levels, such as the frequent consultations by states and potentates of the Delphian Apollo, the appeals were more often to know the outcome of contemplated actions or to secure approval for the same than for positive blessings. In this sphere the denial by Epicurus of all divine interest in human affairs and consequently of all divine predetermination was applicable. Prophecy could not exist because the gods were exclusively occupied with their own happiness and its continuance.

Of the three divisions commonly recognized in prayer, adoration, confession, and petition, the denial of divine interest almost but not entirely eliminated the last, petition. There was another attitude that severely diminished the sphere of the same, as evidenced by Vatican Saying 65: "It is useless to ask of the gods such blessings as a man is capable of procuring for himself." To this a suitable footnote is furnished by two lines of Horace: "It is enough to pray to Jupiter for what he gives and takes away, that he give length of life, that he give the means of life. As for the quiet mind, I shall provide that for myself." [124] Happiness is self-achieved. It comes of defying Fortune, of building up moral reserves against the exigencies of Necessity, of looking to the past with gratitude and the future with hope while living wisely in the present. The whole life is subject to planning.

The second division of prayer, confession, at no time played a part in the religion of the Greeks. Since they lacked divine commandments, the feeling of disobedience was also lacking and hence the need of confession. Orestes, it is true, offended the gods by slaying his mother, but this offense could not be expiated by confession and petition for pardon. There was no doctrine of grace and forgiveness. Consequently there was no occasion for Epicurus to deal with this aspect of prayer.

In spite of the fact, however, that confession is eliminated and the sphere of petition drastically narrowed, the remaining division of adoration is a large one. It was with this that Epicurus was in complete sympathy. A magnificat was completely to his taste, because in his view a feeling of reverence for the surpassing sanctity and dignity of the gods was especially dependent upon liturgy. It was this feeling of adoration that impelled him to censor the epithets applied to the gods, so that no suggestion of pettiness or meanness should attach to them. It was this also that accounts for his approval of the festivals celebrated in honor of the gods. His personal enjoyment of the rites of a musical character has been already mentioned.

CHAPTER XIV ✝ THE NEW VIRTUES

ASYNOPTIC glance over the topic of virtue is essential for bringing to light the historical sequence and the shift from one matrix of meanings to another. Plato viewed the topic of ethics within a political context. His four cardinal virtues, Wisdom, Temperance, Courage, and Justice, were defined within the political context and they were meshed alike with the division of citizens into men of gold, silver, and iron and with the tripartite division of the soul as rational, appetitive, and passionate. Aristotle honored the political context when he discussed the Best Life under the head of Politics, but he tacitly recognized the social context when he defined virtue as the mean between two extremes in his *Nicomachean Ethics.*

With Epicurus there is no wavering between the political and the social contexts. He favored a minimum of government and chose to look upon men as free individuals in a society transcending local political boundaries. This shift gave rise to a new matrix of meanings and not only called for fresh definitions of recognized virtues but also demanded recognition for new virtues theretofore only conventionally interpreted.

When Epicurus rejected Reason and adopted Nature as the norm, discovering in the behavior of the newly born, "not yet perverted," the basis for identifying pleasure as the end or telos, he created by implication a doctrine of what may be called original honesty. To preserve this natural honesty became the main objective of the new education, and thus the virtue of Honesty was raised to a status of prime importance. The Greek name is *parresia*; it has several facets: frankness, outspokenness, truthfulness. The chief corrupting agencies were rhetoric, dialectic, and mathematics, which were denounced either as useless or as leading to various "false opinions" about the capacity of wealth, glory, and power to render men happy.

Prominent also among the new virtues was Faith, a prerequisite of serenity of soul. It was the shift from skepticism to dogmatism that made

289

a virtue of Faith. Dogmatism meant assertion of the possibility of knowledge and Epicurus believed his teachings to be "true philosophy." His utterances enjoyed the status of divine oracles, and he provided his disciples with forty — unluckily not thirty-nine — Authorized Doctrines, which served as Articles of Faith. Memorization was required.

While Plato's doctrines possessed a dynamic quality only for the talented and privileged few and Aristotle's doctrine of the mean, however intriguing to the intellect, was no more inspiring than the multiplication table, the new creed of Epicurus discovered a powerful stimulus to action in love of mankind, or philanthropy. In local circles of the sect the stress laid upon good companionship or fellowship as a coefficient of the happy life bestowed new and enhanced importance upon friendship. The need of making and keeping friends, in its turn, gained specific importance for Suavity, Courtesy, and Considerateness.

While the good Platonist, like the Christian, lived in contemplation of immortality, the Epicurean was taught to live in contemplation of mortality. The chance of achieving happiness was narrowly confined to the interval between birth and death. This had the effect of bestowing great urgency upon the business of living rightly; procrastination became the greater folly. Only the present is within man's control; the future is unpredictable, and to alter the past is beyond the power of Jupiter himself. This way of looking at the problem of living constitutes a matrix of meanings for Patience, Hope, and Gratitude, corresponding respectively to present, future, and past.

Since Epicurus was initiating the process of shifting the attention from the political to the social context, it was inevitable that the number of virtues should be increased. Only four had been emphasized by Plato; this number was more than doubled by Epicurus. In the New Testament, where the process initiated by him was continued, a legion of minor virtues was brought to the fore.

By way of clearing the ground for the elaboration of this topic the cardinal virtues of Plato, Wisdom, Courage, Temperance, and Justice will be briefly discussed. About these we are informed by Cicero that Epicurus had little to say; the truth of this statement is confirmed by the knowledge that he dismissed the topic in a single roll, *On Justice and the Other Virtues*.[1] This brevity was logically inevitable; the political and psychological contexts within which these virtues had arrived at definition were no longer acceptable.

THE NEW VIRTUES

WISDOM

In Plato's psychology Wisdom was associated with the rational part of the soul; its highest activity was the study of mathematics, and in ethical and political investigations its instrument was dialectic. Since Epicurus dethroned Reason and found in Nature the source of ethical and political truth it followed that dialectic became superfluous. Mathematics was rejected from the course of study as having no bearing upon the conduct of life and as likely to increase the disquietude of those who in the pursuit of it discovered more gods to fear. Moreover, Wisdom in Plato's thought was the prerogative of the men of gold, whose privilege it was to impose regimentation upon the classes of grosser metal. This classification was derided by Epicurus, to whom all men were of one class insofar as they stood in need of emancipation from false opinions and the fears and miseries by these entailed. In derision he dubbed Plato "the Golden." He also rejected Plato's division of the soul into rational, passionate, and appetitive parts; his own ethic had little to do with psychology but depended upon a logic furnished by Nature.

After these subtractions and rejections only a limited scope was left to the first of the cardinal virtues. It was accorded a single mention in the Authorized Doctrines, where the twenty-seventh informs us that the acquisition of friendship was its most precious contribution to the happiness of life. In Vatican Collection 78 it is described as "an understandable good," being ranked below friendship, which is "an immortal good," that is, "passing understanding."

In place of the grandiose notion of Wisdom, identifiable with pure reason and divinity and existing apart from mankind, Epicurus chose to exalt the practical reason, *phronesis*, which was "the greatest good and the beginning of all the other virtues." An alternative title was "sober calculation," of which it was the function "to search out the reasons for every choice and avoidance and to expel the false opinions, which are the chief cause of turmoil in the souls of men."[2] Its method of procedure was to weigh the advantages against the disadvantages in every contemplated action. In Authorized Doctrine 16 it is declared capable of controlling the whole conduct of life, rendering man independent of Fortune.

TEMPERANCE

The virtue of Temperance was also imbedded in philosophic and political contexts. In Plato's philosophy it concerns the appetitive part

291

of the soul, which must be brought into subordination to the rational part. In Greek cities this virtue was the more prized because constantly threatened by homosexual practices. The conduct of citizens in public parks was subject to supervision day and night by officials known as gymnasiarchs. Young boys of well-to-do families were always accompanied, even to school, by guardians known as pedagogues. Access to schools was forbidden by law to all except specified persons. There were also officials called *sophronistae*, whose duty it was to protect the young.[3]

This virtue of Temperance is not even mentioned in the extant writings of Epicurus, although he must have discussed it in the roll above mentioned. Its Platonic context meant nothing to him for two reasons: first, he rejected the threefold partition of the soul and along with this the subjection of the desires to the rational soul; second, he looked not to Reason but to Nature as his norm, which had set definite limits to desires, the so-called "limits of Nature."[4] As for the political setting, Epicurus could not have destroyed it, even had he so wished, but he did diminish its importance by confining his teaching in Athens to private properties.

He also worked out a procedure for developing self-control in his disciples. The working principle, which rather oddly, had its ultimate source in Platonic teaching,[5] was the classification of desires as natural and necessary, natural but not necessary, and neither natural nor necessary. The practical reason was the umpire in every choice and the operation runs as follows, Vatican Saying 71: "To all desires must be applied this question: What will be the result for me if the object of this desire is attained and what if it is not?"

This means the weighing of the pleasure against the consequences, and from Vatican Saying 51 it is possible to reconstruct the procedure precisely in the case of sexual desire: Will I be breaking the laws of the land? Will I be violating the public sense of decency? Will I be wronging any of my neighbors? Will I be ruining my health? Will I be wasting my substance? Epicurus asserts that involvement in at least one of these predicaments is certain, and he adds: "Sexual indulgence never did anyone any good and it is lucky if it does no harm." While this procedure has the merit of confronting the individual squarely with his responsibility, the reasoning is utilitarian and evoked from Cicero a paragraph of scorn and satire in a notorious trial.[6]

THE NEW VIRTUES

It is worth while to note the judgment of Epicurus upon Platonic love. This did not mean an attachment between two people of opposite sex, but the Greek love of man for boy. In his *Symposium* Plato had tried to build up the notion that such a love might be sublimated into a passion for knowledge. Epicurus also wrote a *Symposium* and from it we have this excerpt: "Intercourse never did anyone any good and it is lucky if it does no harm." Knowing the source of this we may substitute "Platonic love" for "intercourse," and in this instance it is heartening to know that Cicero emphatically endorsed the judgment of Epicurus.[7]

COURAGE

The third virtue was Courage, and like the others it had its place in philosophic and political contexts. In Plato's psychology it goes with the passionate part of the soul, which should be ruled by the rational part. To Aristotle it is a mean between feelings of fear and of overconfidence.[8] The factor of knowledge was also joined with it; the courageous man would know what was to be feared and what not. In its political setting it meant specifically the will to fight bravely for one's country against public enemies, and the state assumed the responsibility of imparting the requisite training in the use of arms.

The treatment of the topic by Epicurus is consistent and characteristic. He was no quietist or conscientious objector. He submitted to the usual military training himself, nor is any instance on record where an Epicurean refused to bear arms because of his philosophy. Obedience to the laws was recommended. It was only the deliberate choice of a political or military career that Epicurus discouraged. He esteemed physical courage. He declares that the wise man will not falter under torture and will die for his friend if need be.[9]

In the extant writings of Epicurus not a single mention of Courage is found, but it is clear from Authorized Doctrine 28, which Cicero quotes under the topic of friendship, that Epicurus associated it definitely with enduring torture or dying for a friend. To understand this Doctrine the principle must be carried in mind that "nothing terrible can happen to one while living who has thoroughly grasped the truth that there is nothing terrible in not living." [10] The text, rather curiously worded, runs as follows: "The same argument that assures us of nothing terrible lasting forever or even very long discerns the protection furnished by friendship in this brief life of ours as being the most depend-able of all." [11] If this be kept in mind, it is possible to understand a ying reported of Epicurus at second hand that "Courage comes not by Nature but by a calculation of advantage." [12] The advantage consists in the assurance through friendship of safety from the attacks of men and especially tyrants. This assurance must be reciprocal; if the individual is to enjoy assurance for himself he must also be prepared to furnish assurance to others.

It is apparent from the above that Courage in the view of Epicurus is rather to be called Fortitude. He promises to the disciple who masters his doctrine "an unparalleled robustness as compared with the rest of men." [13] The wise man, because of his philosophy, is scornful of death and patient in pain, which, if acute, is brief, if moderate, is tolerable, and if such as to end in death, he takes his leave of life as if walking out of a theater.[14]

From all this it is plain that Epicurus, while leaving undisturbed the concept of Courage as a virtue of the citizen and the soldier, transfers the responsibility for developing it from the state and the laws to the individual himself and shifts the emphasis from the sphere of politics to that of morals. It may be added also that what we call moral courage will appear in a following section as an aspect of Honesty.

JUSTICE

The innovations of Epicurus with respect to Justice were thorough-going. He sponsored a violent break with both tradition and the prevailing Platonism. In conventional thought the idea of Justice was closely meshed with law and religion. The admiration for lawgivers such as Lycurgus and Solon was a conditioned reflex and under the influence of the Academy enjoyed a renaissance. Laws were regarded not as protective alone but also as creative of the civic virtues; they were educators. The happiness of the citizen was thought of as inseparable from legislation, which regulated also the state religion. This tight context of law, lawgiver, religion, civic virtue, and individual happiness, which as a practical synthesis had run its course, was taken over by Plato for theoretical continuation and extension. First in the *Republic* and afterward in the *Laws,* a significant title in itself, he published his manifesto of a highly regimented polity. Both this theoretical extension and the parent tradition were vigorously rejected by Epicurus.

The importance he attached to the topic is indicated by the relatively ample coverage in the Authorized Doctrines, eight items out of forty, and every one anti-Platonic. In respect of the origin of Justice he holds to the theory of the "social contract," which by no mere coincidence experienced its European revival with Hobbes and Locke during the brief interval that witnessed the only public vogue of Epicurean studies in modern times.[15] Epicurus, however, would have brushed aside the criticism directed against the doctrine in its modern form, that the theory implies a degree of sophistication too advanced for a primitive society. He extended its application to the brute creation. Unlike Plato's Justice, it was not man-made but "of Nature," Authorized Doctrine 31: "The Justice of Nature is a covenant of advantage to the end that men shall not injure one another or be injured." This is one of several instances where Epicurus seized upon a fertile idea in Platonic thought and transferred it to a new matrix of meanings. Plato had written: "It seems advantageous to those who are incapable of escaping the evil of injustice and seizing its rewards to strike a bargain with one another neither to practice injustice nor to suffer it." [16] This is the "political contract"; there is no mention of Nature. By looking to Nature for the sanction of it Epicurus changed it to the "social contract."

Just as the first of the pertinent Doctrines makes clear that the teaching is of Nature and not of man, so the second, 32, makes clear that this teaching of Nature is inferred not only from human behavior but also from that of gregarious animals: "To all animate creatures that have been unable to make the covenants about not injuring one another or being injured nothing is just nor unjust either; this statement holds equally true for all human races that have been unable or unwilling to make the covenant about not injuring or being injured." It is here implied that, so far as the teaching of Nature is concerned, the evidence gathered from the behavior of irrational creatures is superior to that afforded by the behavior of human beings, as was found to be the case in the identification of pleasure as the end or telos.

It is very probable that in speaking of wild animals Epicurus was thinking chiefly of elephants. The data gathered by Alexander's scientific staff were promptly reported, and the later work of Megasthenes on the flora and fauna of India was published in 310 B.C., four years before Epicurus settled down in his Cecropian Garden. The belief that elephants would not harm one another proved so fascinating that, as the elder Pliny informs us, King Bocchus of Numidia decided to make a test of it.[17] It was found that even a herd of specially trained beasts refused to attack another herd. In the same context Pliny credits the elephant with "a divination of Justice." This is the Prolepsis or Anticipation of Justice, to which Epicurus refers twice. It is an innate, an embryonic idea, which exists in advance of experience, anticipates experience and predetermines conduct. In the case of human beings it is capable of development by instruction and reflection but its validity as a criterion comes from Nature. Reason is not necessary to discover it. Dialectic is a superfluity.

The next pronouncement of Epicurus is also distinctly anti-Platonic; it is a denial of the theory of ideas, which presumed the existence of absolute justice, and a declaration of the relativity of justice: "Justice never was anything in and by itself but in the dealings of men with one another from time to time, in regions however large or small, it is a sort of covenant about not injuring or being injured." The companion to this is the declaration that the evil of injustice lies in the consequences, not in the act itself, Doctrine 34: "Injustice is not an evil in and by itself but the evil lies in the fear arising out of the uncertainty that he will not escape detection by those appointed for the punishment of such offenses." By the converse reasoning the good of Justice will not inhere in the act but appertain to the consequences. Justice means serenity, injustice unrest in the soul.

The unity of Justice is not to be found in any heavenly model, preserved among the gods like a standard yardstick in government vaults, but in the omnipresence of advantage. We read in Doctrine 36: "So far as the universal concept is concerned, Justice is the same for all, for it is a kind of advantage in the life they share with one another, but in respect of the particulars of place and all affecting circumstances whatsoever it does not follow that the same thing is just for all." A modern exponent of Epicurus might point out that a law which requires motorists to drive to the right is no more just than one which requires them to drive to the left if both laws alike provide for the safety of all concerned. Safety is the advantage that furnishes sanction to both enactments alike.

Naturally it is Justice as it affects the happiness of the individual that is chiefly pertinent to the present chapter. According to Epicurus the child is not conceived in sin but born in honesty. If not perverted by education or otherwise he lives in harmony with Nature and enjoys serenity of mind. By perversion he means the acquisition of "false opinions," chiefly ascribed to the conventional education, which misled men into thinking that the path to happiness was through wealth, glory, and power. It was the desire for such prizes that tempted men to commit injustice. Such desires were "neither natural nor necessary."

The inherent connection between justice and peace of mind and of injustice with anxiety is stated in Vatican Saying 12: "The just life is marked by the greatest quietude but the unjust overflows with the greatest unrest." The cause of this unrest is ascribed by Epicurus to fear combined with uncertainty. This particular combination seemed to him especially poisonous to happiness. He believed, for instance, that it was worse to feel uncertainty concerning the truth of the myths about Acheron and its punishments than definitely to believe in them.[18] In the case of injustice he believed it the uncertainty of escaping detection that above all else kept the soul in a state of disquietude. Authorized Doctrine 35: "It is impossible for the man who does one of those things which they have covenanted with one another not to do, in order to avoid injuring and being injured, to be confident he will escape, even though for the moment he shall escape numberless times, for till the end it will be uncertain if he will really escape."

This shifting of the good and the evil in conduct from the action to the effect and the emphasis upon the advantage and the disadvantage marks Epicurus as a utilitarian in ethics, and utilitarianism is a vulnerable creed. It laid Epicurus open to the charge of recommending obedience to the laws as a means of avoiding punishment. This charge is specious; the true advantage to be gained was peace of soul and this was a positive objective. Positive also was the obligation to cultivate good will and love toward mankind, which signified a love of justice. The net effect of the teaching of Epicurus was to transfer the idea of Justice from an idealistic to a pragmatic context.

HONESTY

Had Epicurus chosen to name the virtues most necessary for the happy life the list would have included Honesty, Faith, Love, Suavity, Courtesy, Considerateness, Gratitude, Patience, and Hope but the greatest of these, he would have said, was Honesty.

The Greek word around which he chose to build up his cardinal virtues was *parresia*, "freedom of speech." The practice of this was a

297

boast of the Athenians in both public and private life. In the political sphere it signified the right of every citizen to stand up in the public assembly and express his honest opinion. For the contrary vice of shameless assentation the Athenians had developed a special term, sycophancy. It consorted with flattery. During the enforced residence of Epicurus in Lampsacus the Athenian assembly was showering honors upon the Macedonian governor Demetrius Phalereus. After his expulsion it reversed itself and outdid itself in honoring his supplanter.

In the judgment of Epicurus mobs and monarchs fell in the same class, because both demanded servility, the surrender of personal integrity. He observes in Vatican Saying 67: "A life of freedom cannot amass great riches because of success being difficult without servitude to mobs or monarchs." If a difference was to be made, he preferred the monarch, whom he was willing to placate in emergency. From the political life he withdrew absolutely: "Never did I feel the desire to please the multitude, for the tricks that would please them I did not learn and what I did understand was foreign to the outlook of such as they." Belief in the power of a multitude to tempt the speaker to be false to himself was extended even to the audience of a popular lecture. The poet Horace was virtually quoting Epicurus when he wrote: "I do not give readings for anyone unless friends and that under compulsion." The words of Epicurus run: "The wise man will give readings before a crowd but not of his own initiative." [19] The method he preferred for the dissemination of his philosophy may be summed up in the words "Each one teach one."

Outside of the popular assembly *parresia* signified the expression of the speaker's opinion without regard for the feelings of others, and it might mean defiance. Epicurus was exemplifying it when he publicly assailed the Platonists, who in his youth were enjoying a monopoly of favor. He called them "flatterers of Dionysus," and the "deep-voiced." [20] The latter was a term of derision similar to "would-be Hamlets"; it was applied to second-rate actors who pitched their voices absurdly low in the performance of kingly roles. Insofar as they hung around hoping for such parts, they were "flatterers of Dionysus," the god of the theater, comparable to the flatterers of Alexander and his successors. The reference is rendered specific by the derisive language of Metrodorus, who dubbed the young Platonists would-be Lycurguses and Solons. [21] There was a temporary revival of law-giving because of Plato's dream of a philosopher-king, which opened court posts for graduates of the Academy.

On this topic of outspokenness Epicurus issued a veritable manifesto, Vatican Saying 29: "As for myself, I should prefer to practice the outspokenness [*parresia*] demanded by the study of Nature and to issue the kind of oracles that are beneficial for all mankind, even if not a soul shall understand, rather than by falling into step with popular opinions to harvest the lush praise that falls from the favor of the multitude." In this instance, as in many others, it should be borne in mind that by the multitude Epicurus means the people seated in the public assembly. It was his conviction that the democratic political life made dupes of both politicians and people. It was his advice "to avoid publicity."

As for the oracles believed to be beneficial for all mankind, these were exemplified by the Authorized Doctrines. It called for no courage to stand before the assembly and report: "We have sacrificed to Zeus the Savior and to Athena and to Victory, and these sacrifices have been auspicious and salutary for you."[22] It did call for courage to flout popular belief and declare that the gods are immune to anger and gratitude and have no part in human affairs. It called for no courage to exalt virtue; even hypocrites would applaud. It did call for courage to declare that pleasure had been ordained by Nature as the consummation of life; even those who so believed might prefer to be reticent.

The sanction for this outspokenness was discovered by Epicurus in the example of Nature herself. In the passage last quoted above he speaks of "the outspokenness demanded by the study of Nature." Nature demands this virtue because she is incorruptible herself and requires the same virtue in her disciples. In contrast with the effects of this teaching are set those resulting from the popular education in rhetoric, Vatican Saying 45: "The study of Nature turns out men not given to vain display or empty talk or to showing off the education prized by the multitude but rather men who are defiant and self-sufficient and proud of their inalienable blessings instead of the goods of circumstance." Elsewhere he speaks of "an incomparable robustness" as conferred by the study of Nature.[23] The good Epicurean defies Fortune, is self-sufficient under the compulsions of Necessity, and sets these inalienable virtues above wealth, fame, and office, which can be lost.

It was the judgment of Epicurus that human beings are not conceived in sin but born in honesty. The newborn child is "not yet perverted" by the conventional education.[24] To preserve this natural honesty is indispensable for the happy life. "Suffer the little children to come unto me" is in perfect harmony with Epicurean teaching. He did not, as editors would have it, exhort the youthful Pythocles "to flee from every form of culture," but rather "to shun the whole program of education." [25] The dialecticians were called "wholesale corrupters." [26] Socrates, because of his dishonest affectation of ignorance and his concealment of the deadly weapon of dialectic, was judged guilty of cheating.[27]

Epicurus was aiming a sidelong thrust at Socrates when he described the wise man as follows: "The man who has once attained to wisdom never exhibits the opposite diathesis nor does he deliberately simulate it." [28] The honesty of the wise man is absolute; he will have no thoughts that he fears to reveal by talking in his sleep: "He will be the same man in his slumbers." [29] His loyalty to friends will also be absolute: "The wise man alone will know true gratitude and in respect of his friends, whether present or absent, will be the same throughout the journey of life." [30] This absolute loyalty will serve as a rebuke to men who are suspicious of friends and ply them with wine to discover their secret thoughts: "He will put a certain kind of people to confusion and most assuredly will not watch men in their cups." [31] This topic of loyalty, including *in vino veritas,* was handled by Horace in a way acceptable to Epicurus in the fourth satire of the first book.

Another aspect of the necessity imposed upon men by the virtue of absolute honesty was exhibited by Epicurus in respect of his own adventures. The ignominious flight from Mytilene and arrival in Lampsacus as a friendless refugee were things of a sort that many men would have preferred to be forgotten. Not so Epicurus. When the particulars of this incident were published by those who had access to the facts, none other than his friends Idomeneus, Timocrates, and Herodotus, he not only lauded their action but also complimented them for the particular reason that the information published was of a sort that might have been deemed confidential.[32] This approval must have been made known in published letters, since it was known to his enemies. These and other letters, known to Plutarch,[33] must have exhibited a kind of self-revealment that later characterized the *Confessions* of St. Augustine.

Within the sect there were inner and outer circles of friends, but there is no record of esoteric doctrines such as were inherent in Platonism. When in Vatican Saying 29 he speaks of his oracular teachings as "beneficial to all men," there is a probable reference not only to the exclusion of barbarians from Plato's ideal government but also to the necessity of deception of the lower classes by the privileged men of gold. The same universality of appeal is manifest in Vatican Saying 51, where Love is described as "circling in dance around the whole earth veritably shouting to us all to awake to the blessedness of the happy life." The only condition imposed upon barbarians was that of learning Greek, because Epicurus did not restrict his gospel to Greeks but only to those who spoke Greek.

The vogue of philosophy and especially Platonism, which for a time enjoyed the status of orthodoxy, seems to have produced a crop of hypocrisy, just as religion did in later times. On this topic Epicurus expresses himself in Vatican Saying 54: "We should not make a pretense of philosophizing but honestly philosophize, because we need to possess real health and not the mere appearance of it." He set his face against the subtle self-flattery that we know as smugness and in particular against the mummery that went with the cult of the so-called beautiful, *to kalon*: "I spit upon the beautiful and upon those who blindly extol it when it does not give pleasure." [34] In his book *On Kingship* he even advised monarchs to entertain themselves with military anecdotes or coarse buffoonery rather than try to counterfeit a refinement they did not possess. This advice must have been galling to young Platonists who groomed themselves for court appointments. It was galling to Plutarch, who reports it. [35]

Epicurus was resolved to be honest also in treating of the topic of friendship. He was by no means immune to the idealizing tendency. He declared friendship to be the most precious of acquisitions made by wisdom in preparation for the happy life and he esteemed it above wisdom itself as being an "immortal good"; but he stressed the utilitarian aspect in Authorized Doctrine 28 when he praised it as affording the most dependable of all assurances of safety. This sentiment evoked the applause of Cicero but he vigorously rebelled against a balder recognition of utility, extant in Vatican Saying 23: "Every friendship is desirable for its own sake but it takes its beginning from assistance rendered." In his specious essay *On Friendship* Cicero endeavored to base friendship on virtue alone. [36] As an artful pleader he may have deceived even himself for the time being, but his own practice was quite different. Human vanity is a great enemy of honesty; we flatter ourselves by erecting a false façade. Human motives are usually mixed; expediency dons the mask of idealism.

The true gentleman as Epicurus conceived him may be described as combining unfailing courtesy with unfailing sincerity, frankness, and outspokenness. Through the fickleness of tradition this belief can be better documented in Latin than in Greek, a fact which incidentally demonstrates the influence of Epicureanism upon Roman manners and morals. This influence is marked by the new vogue of the word *candor* and the adjective *candid*. Horace was resorting to this new terminology when he declared that Earth had never produced "whiter souls" than Virgil, Plotius, and Varius, a trio still Epicurean at that date.[37] The opposite of ethical whiteness was ethical blackness, associated with treachery and poison.

The Latin for absolute honesty in speech was *severitas*, akin by etymology to English "swear." Cicero complimented a friend for combining it with *humanitas*, "refinement." [38]

The classic definition of the blend, however, was *comitas* with *severitas*. The latter is identical with the *nuda veritas*, "naked truthfulness," which Horace ascribed to the Epicurean Quintilius Varus, the kind but unsparing critic.[39] The combination of this virtue with unfailing courtesy was accorded to the Epicurean Atticus by Cornelius Nepos: "He would neither utter a falsehood nor could he endure to hear one. As a consequence his courtesy was not without sternness nor his reserve without affability, so that it was hard to decide which feeling was uppermost among his friends, respect or affection." [40] Even Marcus Aurelius, by whose time Epicurean virtues were being honored under Stoic labels, expresses his gratitude, itself an Epicurean virtue, to a friend for teaching him to blend graciousness with dignity.[41]

Among Epicureans it was judged an act of infidelity to friends to spare them the truth. Hence comes the *liber amicus*, "the outspoken friend," whom Horace mentions with approval.[42] As a doctrine this *libertas dicendi*, a special sort of freedom of speech, attained such notoriety as to become material for travesty. That epic roisterer, for example, Mark Antony, not only made a fad of it himself but also gave full license to a boon companion to reverse the procedure and mock. the mocker.[43] The generation of Antony had available on the topic the handbook of Philodemus, who seems to have sided with this rival of Augustus Caesar. From this work, extant in extensive fragments, it is clear not only that the practice of mutual criticism was basic in Epicurean friendship but also that the primary objective of elementary education was to habituate the pupil to take correction kindly.[44] St. Paul was cognizant of the doctrine and called it "speaking the truth in love." [45]

Such was honesty as Epicurus conceived it, a total integrity of character. It was enjoined by Nature. To preserve it was the objective of education. It was destroyed by the study of rhetoric and dialectic. It was opposed to sycophancy in politics, obsequiousness in court life, smugness and hypocrisy in private life. It demanded total loyalty to friends combined with absolute frankness in mutual criticism. It called for unreserved self-revelation as practiced by Epicurus himself in his letters, by Horace in his satires and epistles, and by St. Augustine in his *Confessions*.

FAITH

A doctrine of Faith made its appearance for the first time in the philosophy of Epicurus, though it was only in revealed religion that it later attained a full development. It was born of skepticism, a hostile reaction to the teachings of Pyrrho, whose pupil Nausiphanes was the tutor of Epicurus. The latter seems at first to have admired the great skeptic, perhaps for his serenity, but later he revolted violently and resolved that happiness must be based upon the certainty of knowledge rather than upon resignation to the belief that knowledge was impossible. In the heat of this revulsion he declared Pyrrho "incapable either of learning or of being instructed" and became dogmatic on the subject of dogmatism, asserting "that the wise man will dogmatize and not be a doubter." [46]

A brief chain argument will show how the doctrine of Faith fits into the new matrix of meanings. As a dogmatist Epicurus believed that truth was discoverable and also that he had discovered it. He called his teachings "true philosophy." Since this philosophy was presented as ultimate truth it demanded of the disciple the will to believe and in the case of junior pupils subjection to indoctrination.

If this belief had consisted merely in intellectual assent to the doctrine that the universe consists of atoms and void or the like, it would have been on a par with Plato's theory of ideas. It did not, however, stop at this point; it assumed also that the path to true happiness had been discovered, so that over and above mere belief the disciple must feel gratitude and reverence for the discoverer. The new truth attains the status of a revelation and its author the status of a savior. Thus faith in doctrine is conjoined with faith in the leader or guide.

While this conjunction of faith in doctrine with faith in the leader introduces a dynamic emotional element, it still falls short of making a complete picture. The disciple cannot live to himself. Epicurus thought of his oracular teachings as "beneficial for all men," and he planned coherence for all the local brotherhoods in which his disciples were enrolled. All members depended upon one another for what St. Paul referred to as Peace and Safety. This means that the Epicurean must not only feel faith in doctrine and leader but also in friends and friendship. The authority for this is Vatican Saying 34, which exhibits a play upon words that is characteristic of the master's style: "We do not so much have need of help from friends in time of need as faith in help in time of need." This is an excellent commentary upon the words of St. Paul, "faith which worketh by love." [47]

There is a difference, however; Epicurus was more restrained and stopped short of fanatical trust in his creed. Friendship was subject to planning and began with advantage even if developing into affection and faith. Authorized Doctrine 40: "All those who have best succeeded in building up the ability to feel secure from the attacks of those around them have lived the happiest lives with one another, as having the firmest faith." Thus even faith is in part the result of planning.

Epicurus was aware nevertheless of the saving function of faith. He assures his disciples that his account of the soul will result in "the firmest faith," [48] and the sole objective of the study of celestial phenomena is to acquire "tranquillity and a firm faith." [49] His account of the soul would result in emancipating the disciple from the fear of death, and his account of celestial phenomena on a physical basis would spare men the fear of Plato's astral divinities. [50] The supreme function of faith was to banish fears and uncertainties from life.

It is uncertainty rather than outright disbelief that seemed to Epicurus the opposite of faith. Assuredly uncertainty was deemed more destructive of happiness. Two of the Authorized Doctrines, 12 and 13, bear upon this point: "It is impossible for men to dispel the fear concerning things of supreme importance not understanding the nature of the whole universe but suspecting there may be some truth in the stories related in the myths. Consequently it is impossible without the knowledge of Nature to enjoy the pleasures unalloyed." "Nothing is gained by building up the feeling of security in our relations with men if the things above our heads and those beneath the earth and in general those in the unseen are matters of suspicion." The vogue of these teachings among disciples is evidenced by their repetition in the Vatican Collection, 49 and 72.

Another point for which repetition demonstrates importance was the relation of faith to righteousness. Vatican Saying 7 is synoptic: "It is difficult for the wrong-doer to escape and to have faith in escaping is impossible." From Plutarch we possess the unintended favor of a fuller statement: "Even if they are able to escape, to gain faith in escaping is impossible. Because of this, the fear of the future, ever pressing upon them, prevents them from being happy or even being confident for the time being." [51] The same truth was hammered home in Authorized Doctrine 35, with which Vatican Saying 7 is identical.

A warning against error, however, is due for repetition. It was not fear of the law that Epicurus stressed as a deterrent of wrong-doing but the ensuing uncertainty, which was bound to take the joy out of living. It is this refinement of thought that makes applicable the calculus of advantage. The reason that crime does not pay is not the ultimate punishment, which may never arrive, but the misery of fearing it. Adversaries of Epicurus either missed this point or chose to do so.

It may be added that Faith is hardly less a novelty in the New Testament than in the philosophy of Epicurus. There are few objectives of St. Paul so obvious as his desire to integrate the doctrine of Faith with the Old Testament story,[52] and he also unites Justice, Faith, Sin, and the Law in a matrix of meanings not unlike that of Epicurus: "The just shall live by faith" and "The strength of sin is the law." [53] Epicureanism prepared the way for Christianity. Doctrines are not born full-blown; they emerge in outline, gain definiteness by degrees, in pace with slow changes in society, and at last burst from obscurity into full recognition.

LOVE OF MANKIND

The topic of love or friendship is beset by annoying ambiguities. The Greek word *philia*, "love," was applicable to all sorts of attach ments. The Christians gained in precision by adopting the word *agape*. The Latin *amor* tended to denote romantic love, so that *amicitia*, "friendship," was used to translate *philia*; this had the effect of narrowing the meaning unduly. In English the difficulty is renewed because the same word must be used for romantic love, love of mankind, and the love of God. Epicureanism concerned itself with the love of mankind, *philanthropia*, and the love of friends, both denoted by *philia*. It may be added that the vogue of philanthropy as a topic of discussion is attested by its opposite, misanthropy, of which one Timon, famous in literature, made a cult.

The love of mankind is by no necessity consequent upon the love of knowledge, which the Greeks exhibited, or upon the love of liberty, which did not prevent them from enslaving their own countrymen as well as barbarians. Love of mankind was incompatible with the separatism of the Greeks in domestic politics and with the collective feeling of superiority to barbarians, which, to their horror, Alexander the Great ceased to share. It is understandable, therefore, that only within limited circles a certain increase of sympathy with foreign peoples coincided with the increase of precise knowledge concerning Persia, India, and other lands. It is no accident either that a philosophy characterized by love of mankind should have arisen in Ionia rather than in imperialistic Athens, which was self-centered to a degree surpassed only by Sparta.

The first impulse to genuine love of mankind seems to have had its source neither in philosophy nor political theorizing but in Hippocratic medicine. One of its sayings is well known: "Where there is love of mankind there will be love of healing." That the inspiration of Epicurus came to him by this avenue there can hardly be a minimum of doubt. His own mission was conceived to be one of healing: "Vain is the word of that philosopher by which no malady of mankind is healed, for just as there is no benefit in the art of medicine unless it expels the diseases of men's bodies, so there is none in philosophy either unless it expels the malady of the soul." [54] It is on this principle that he denied to Leucippus the right to the name of philosopher and chiefly on the same ground that he broke with Democritus, who seemed in the opinion of his great disciple to impose upon men a paralyzing law of physical necessity.

The love of Epicurus for his native Greece is on record and he preferred to live in Athens even in the days of its tribulations, but his philosophy was valid for all mankind. In his day there was in vogue a weird rite for the cure, as it would seem, of depressive melancholy. The participants were called Corybantes. The patient was seated upon a throne while the celebrants circled round and round with song and dance and a tumult of tambourines and horns. In the normal course of the cure the patient was first overcome with bewilderment, then fell into a coma, and finally awoke in ecstasy, a cured man, to join in the tumult. In the light of this custom we must interpret Vatican Saying 52: "Love goes whirling in dance around the whole earth veritably shouting to us all to awake to the blessedness of the happy life." This tacit allusion to the well-known Corybantic rites should remind us that Epicurus, unlike the Stoics, was not distrustful of emotion; he asserted that the wise man would feel more strongly than the rest of men. His ataraxy, in spite of the dictionaries, cannot be equated with Stoic apathy.

Although Love is said by Epicurus to go whirling in dance around the whole earth, there is no specific command to go into all lands and preach the gospel to every creature. It is true that Epicurus anticipated the apostles in the writing of pastoral epistles, but he did not undertake missionary journeys. Neither did he enjoin this upon others. Each Epicurean household was to become a cell from which the true philosophy should be quietly extended to others. His imperative was "to take advantage of all other intimacies and under no circumstance to slacken in the effort to disseminate the sayings of the true philosophy."

This method will be recognized as the leaven system recommended by Jesus; a little leaven should leaven the whole lump. It won for Epicureanism a vogue of seven centuries but in the meantime was superseded by the organizing genius of Paul, Peter, and other apostles. Epicurus thus occupies, as usual, a middle position between Greek philosophy and Christianity. He was an excellent propagandist but lacked a model for lasting organization. It seems to have been a historical necessity that the foundation of the Roman Empire should precede the establishment of a world religion and reveal to its leaders a pattern for permanence.

FRIENDSHIP

While friendship is a perpetual phenomenon it is capable of assuming special shapes at particular times in particular phases of society. Pythagoras is said to have based his political system upon it, though this included only aristocrats. Epaminondas exploited friendship as a means of gaining robustness for a military organization.

Epicurus was the first to integrate it with an elaborate context of ethical and political doctrine. The first factor in this novel context, as usual, was the attitude or diathesis. Epicurus was extolled for "his humane feeling toward all men." [55] This is the proper attitude toward mankind and was identical with the love of mankind that was enjoined upon physicians by the Hippocratic school. Quite in line with this and yet quite special was the attitude toward friendship, set forth in Authorized Doctrine 27: "Of all the preparations which wisdom makes for the blessedness of the complete life by far the most important is the acquisition of friendship."

The next element in the new context of friendship has elicited adverse criticism because far from flattering to the vanity of mankind. Recognition is given to the utilitarian factor in Vatican Saying 23: "Every friendship is desirable for its own sake but has its beginning in assistance rendered." Cicero, whose pride must have been nettled by the declaration of Epicurus "that he had never been ambitious to please the multitude," as also by his condemnation of the political career, had plenty to say against this utilitarian view of friendship and endeavored to base true friendship upon virtue. In his sly but delightful essay *On Friendship* he won an affirmative verdict from posterity, but his practices in the matter of friendship were different. Human motives are usually mixed.

Cicero was not entirely honest. Neither in Athens nor in Rome were the courts devoted entirely to the administration of justice. They were employed by politicians to destroy one another and the greatest speech of Demosthenes, *On the Crown,* was composed to repel such an attack. So rare was it for a man of wealth or distinction to escape indictment that the orator Cephalus gained a name for himself by this immunity.[56] It is recorded that another was indicted seventy-five times.[57] In Rome after 49 B.C., under Caesar's so-called monarchy, Cicero complained that the courts were silent. This meant only that the political lawsuits had come to an end; the regular criminal and civil courts were functioning regularly.

It was in such conditions of society that Epicurus advised his disciples to seek peace and safety through friendship. He lifted to the status of a creed what other men were already doing by necessity. He made a system out of it and immediately after his discussion of justice, a significant juxtaposition, he laid down his rules. Authorized Doctrine 39: "That man has best forestalled the feeling of insecurity from outside who makes relations friendly where possible, where impossible, at least neutral, and where even this is impossible, avoids contacts, and in all cases where it pays to do so arranges for dynastic support." That the immediate cause for drawing up this article of his creed was the attacks made upon him by the philosophers of Mytilene there can be little doubt, and the mention of dynastic protection as a last resort may be taken as a reference to his own search for sanctuary in the court of Lysimachus. When he speaks of "avoiding contacts," this is precisely what he did later in Athens by confining his teaching to his own private property. The treatment meted out in that city to Anaxagoras, Protagoras, Socrates, and Aristotle was not to be easily forgotten.

In Rome the perfect exemplar of the diplomatic cultivation of friends for the sake of peace and safety was the Epicurean Atticus, famed friend of Cicero, who, though wealthy, succeeded in surviving all the proscriptions and confiscations by rendering his relations friendly with every potentate from the Dictator Sulla to Augustus Caesar.

In drawing up the foregoing rules Epicurus had in mind the threats to safety of person and property through legal proceedings against politicians and philosophers, which might result in exile or excessive fines, as in Athens. When, on the other hand, Epicureans spoke of peace, the reference was to amicable relations with neighbors; the word *neighbor* is almost as frequent in their writings as in the New Testament.

For the sake of enjoying peace the advice is given in a nameless papyrus that a man should make friends with as many as possible.[58] Friendship is not left to chance; it is to be diligently cultivated. In one saying Epicurus stresses the difficulty of the free life arriving at wealth without involvement with mobs or monarchs. He then adds, Vatican Saying 67: "Yet if perchance it shall happen to acquire much wealth, it would readily disburse this to acquire the good will of the neighbor."

A trio of rules has survived for us on the procedure in making friends. While asserting that friendship has its origin in human needs, Epicurus is careful to observe "that the way must be prepared in advance of needs, for we also sow seed in the ground."[59] Upon prospective friends a very discerning eye must be cast. Two sorts will be rejected at the outset, Vatican Saying 39: "Neither is he a true friend who is continually seek-

309

ing help nor he who on no occasion associates friendship with help, because the former is bartering his gratitude for the tangible return and the latter is cutting off good expectations concerning the future." Caution is recommended against hasty judgments, Vatican Saying 28: "We must not be critical either of those who are quick to make friends or those who are slow but be willing to risk the offer of friendship for the sake of winning friendship." In the end it is asserted "that the tie of friendship knits itself through reciprocity of favors among those who have come to enjoy pleasures to the full." [60]

Cicero, with the discerning eye of the trial lawyer, pounced upon the utilitarian aspect of Epicurean friendship as a suitable pretext for throwing discredit upon the whole creed. He chose to exalt virtue as the sole basis of friendship as if Epicurus had ignored it. Yet the latter would tolerate no compromise with evil, Vatican Saying 46: "Evil associations, like wicked men who have long done us great injury, let us banish utterly." He was also capable of expressing himself on the topic of friendship with a depth of feeling that cannot be exceeded, Vatican Saying 78: "The truly noble man concerns himself chiefly with wisdom and friendship, of which the one is an understandable good and the other immortal." This epithet immortal stands for the highest praise in his vocabulary; it denotes a quality of life, the perfection of happiness; by way of contrast with wisdom, the pleasure of friendship is said to pass understanding. Editors ruin a fine sentiment by emendation.

Epicurus virtually established a copyright on the topic of friendship. No sect set more store by good companionship nor cultivated so diligently the virtues that contributed to it. Epicurus himself declared it more necessary to have someone to eat with than something to eat.[61]

SUAVITY

St. Augustine, who, like other churchmen of Africa, possessed a good understanding of Epicureanism and but for its denial of immortality would have awarded it the palm, in one passage selected as its watchwords "pleasure, suavity, and peace." [62] It seems to have been the friendly ethic of Epicurus that won for this virtue of Suavity a manifest vogue among the Romans and for the words *suavis* and *suavitas* a certain currency in a definite context of meaning. They occur so repeatedly in the letters of Cicero and the writings of the Augustan age as to seem characteristic of the Latin vocabulary. However, in the plays of Plautus, who wrote vernacular Latin if any man did, they are found less often and only in the literal sense. Like the words *candid* and *candor*, they took on a fresh color from the Epicurean context; it was the "sweet friendship" of the disdainful Memmius that Lucretius hoped to win for himself by the charm of his verses.[63] In his preface to the fourth book he informs us with clarity what *suavitas* should mean for poetry; he would smear the forbidding teachings of Epicurus "as if with the sweet honey of the muse." Conversion is his objective and suavity is his chief reliance.

It is quite to be expected that in Cicero's sly but genial essay *On Friendship*, a topic for which Epicurus possessed a moral copyright, we should find it briefly defined as "a certain agreeableness of speech and manners." [64] It connoted both a quality of voice and an expression of countenance, as Nepos makes plain in his characterization of the youthful Atticus.[65] Cicero in his letters knew the value of complimenting Epicurean friends upon the possession of it. Even to the lean and hungry Cassius, hardly sweet of disposition though known to have followed Epicurus, is ascribed "an unlimited fund of sweetness." [66] The merry Papirius Paetus deserved better to be told that his letters "overflowed with sweetness." [67] Cicero even claimed the quality for himself, though famed for the acidity of his tongue.[68] It fitted much better the jocular Eutrapelus, whom he addresses as "my sweetest Volumnius." [69] So singular is the usage of the word that it almost ranks as a test for identifying Epicurean correspondents.

Going back to the beginning we discover two necessities for the virtue in the creed of Epicurus. A chain argument, as often elsewhere, will make the logical sequence clear: the objective of life is tranquillity; this cannot be attained without security nor security without friends. Friends, in turn, are not to be won without effort. Friendship is too indispensable as an asset and too precious as a pleasure to be left to the hazards of chance. It is the part of wisdom to make friends systematically. To this end "a certain agreeableness of speech and manners" is essential. "Wear a smile," Epicurus recommended. Moreover, to make friends is not the final objective. These friends, so far as possible, must be made converts, and the creed so attractive they will gladly adhere. Success in this will result in good companionship, which is a final objective.

In addition to this logic of utility there was also a historical reason for cultivating the new virtue of suavity. Epicurus was not born too

late to be a near contemporary to the earlier Cynics, all of whom practiced a kind of "shock treatment" in greeting the public and prospective
students in particular. Antisthenes, when asked why he was so harsh
with his pupils, retorted, "Physicians are so with the sick." Diogenes,
who died when Epicurus was eighteen, interpreted freedom of speech as
freedom to insult. Crates, known as the Gate-Crasher, a contemporary,
was the teacher of Zeno, who adopted and bequeathed to the Stoic school
this practice of asperity. Thus Stoicism by heredity became a scolding,
censorious creed. Epicurus, reacting adversely to the example of the
Cynics, cultivated the opposite virtue. He is on record as having dealt
with this question in the second book of his work *On Lives*, where he
wrote, "The wise man will not adopt the Cynic's way of life." [70]

The suavity of Epicurus was condemned as effusiveness by his enemies,
who rummaged through his letters and assembled a gratifying list of
examples. He addressed his disciple Colotes as Colotarion, as if a Rich-
ard should be called "Dicky dear." The offense was worse when he
addressed the brilliant courtesan Leontion as Leontarion. He was mali-
ciously accused of addressing both her and the barbarian Mithres as
"Lord and Savior," salutations proper to Apollo; the words as he used
them were mere expletives. [71] To friends who had sent him food in a
difficult time he wrote: "You have given heaven-high proofs of your
good will to me." [72] Less fortunate was part of a letter to Pythocles, a
handsome lad: "I shall seat myself and await your lovely and godlike
entrance." [73] It was perhaps such language that prompted the saintly
Epictetus to denounce him as "foul-mouthed." [74] Compliments to pretty
boys aroused suspicions in Greek minds, and the Stoic was censorious.

This cultivation of suavity, while in competitive contrast to Cynic
license and Stoic asperity, serves also in a measure to separate Epicureanism from Platonism, which was the creed of highbrows. Suavity
is more than courtesy. It is active and persuasive. The aristocrat may be
courteous to all but he will be suave only to those whom he admits to
equality. Suavity, as Epicureans practiced it, was a kind of salesmanship.
It was their weapon for making friends and influencing people. It was
partly by means of it that they became the most numerous of all sects.

CONSIDERATENESS

Along with Suavity the virtue of Consideration for the feelings of
others, *epieikeia*, emerged to prominence in Epicureanism. This in-

crease of emphasis was part of a general drift from the study of political to the more purely social virtues. Aristotle had treated of the topic with some fullness, and his onetime colleague Xenocrates made it the subject of a special study.[75]

Aristotle defined it as equity, which mitigates the harshness of strict legality in the administration of law, the latter dealing with general principles while equity is invoked in the particular instance.[76] He wisely observed that it also overlaps the sphere of friendship, though extending beyond it, because consideration is due to the feelings even of those toward whom no affection exists. "The magnanimous man," he writes, "will make it his aim to give pleasure or not to cause pain, referring his actions to the standards of honor and expediency, for, as it seems, he concerns himself with the pleasures and pains that are incidental to social contacts." [77]

The sphere of the virtue is further extended in a papyrus, where it reads that the Epicurean "holds in high regard as many people as possible." [78] This extended attitude is again manifest in the opening lines of the prologue to the *Eunuchus* of Terence, who took over some Epicurean sentiments from Menander: "If there is any man who is eager to give pleasure to as many good men as possible and to cause pain to as few as possible, in that number this poet declares his name." Even Cicero betrays the influence of Epicurus not only by defining the good man, *vir bonus*, as "one who will do a good turn to whom he can and will injure no one unless attacked," but also by arriving at this definition by way of the innate idea, the Prolepsis or Anticipation of Epicurus.[79]

It should be observed, however, that this virtue, although it eventually came to full bloom as the Golden Rule of the New Testament, in its pagan phase stopped short of bidding men to love their enemies. We still possess the pronouncement of Epicurus himself, Vatican Saying 15: "We prize our own characters exactly as we do our private property, whether or not this property be of the best and such as may be coveted by men. In the same way we ought also to respect the characters of our neighbors, if they are considerate." Neighbors who exhibited a lack of consideration were to expect retaliation in kind. The Donatus commentary specifically identifies as an example of *epieikeia* the following sentiment in the prologue of the *Phormio* of Terence: "Let him reflect that the treatment dealt out to him has been the same as was dealt out by him." The commentary attaches the same label to a threat in the prologue of the *Eunuchus*: "I warn that man not to make a mistake and to cease provoking me."

The nature of this virtue is further defined by the virtues with which it is associated. Lucian ascribes it to his Epicurean friend Celsus along with companionability, friendliness, evenness of temper, serenity, and tact, a veritable garland of Epicurean virtues.[80] Epicurus himself is praised for gentleness toward servants, and Cicero allows to the sect in general a freedom from malice.[81] The poet Horace devotes a whole satire to the topic and anticipates more nearly than the others the formulation of the Golden Rule when he exclaims, "Alas, how rashly we enact a harsh law against our very selves," that is, by censoriousness toward the minor faults of others.[82] Even the unfriendly Plutarch grudgingly allows to Epicureans a readiness to forgive.[83]

In the original Epicurean circle of Lampsacus the man especially noted for the virtue was Polyaenus, whom Laertius calls "a considerate and friendly man."[84] It is exemplified in the sympathetic letter to a child, falsely ascribed to Epicurus himself.[85] Because of an excess of the virtue it is said that Epicurus refused to have any part in political life. This may have reference to his declining a court appointment, possibly with the ruler Lysimachus, to whom he was at one time close. The reason for refusal has been interpreted as "modesty" or "deference" or "conscientiousness," but more precision is necessary. The fact that the contemporary Xenocrates had written a book about the virtue is proof that it was under discussion and gaining precision of definition. The meaning must be that Epicurus had too lively a sympathy for the sufferings of the people to consent to benefit by the exactions of the rulers. Even democratic politicians were notorious for self-aggrandizement; their wealth became a scandal in Athens.

For the sake of increasing precision in the understanding of this virtue two points are worthy of mention: the practice of it did not excuse the good Epicurean from candidly reminding the friend of his faults, though this must be done without animus and solely for the good of the advised; "speaking the truth in love" it was called by St. Paul; the second point to be noted is the contrast in which it stood after the time of Epicurus to Stoic censoriousness and specifically to the doctrine that all offenses are equal. Horace makes this opposition abundantly plain;[86] stealing a cabbage is not on a par with robbing a temple; minor faults must be overlooked; the punishment must fit the crime.

THE NEW VIRTUES

To round off this topic it must be mentioned that in the Epicurean design for living this virtue had a specific function. The practice of it was part of the process of building up the feeling of security, of assuring peace and safety. Three motives for injury were recognized by Epicurus, hatred, envy, and contempt. Of these three it is contempt that stands at the opposite extreme to consideration for the feeling of others. People who suffer from the proud man's contumely will be prone to reprisals, and to forestall such persecutions is a chief reason for practicing considerateness. This virtue was discussed by Seneca in one of those letters which disseminated Epicurean teachings under the banner of Stoicism.[87]

For lack of a specific term in Latin the phrase *sensus communis* [88] was sometimes employed to mean considerateness, and enjoyed a permanent vogue, but our English "common sense" has suffered a semantic shift from the original meaning. The original phrase, if strictly interpreted, denoted a feeling that ought to be common to mankind rather than a feeling that is common. It is ideally described in the speech beginning, "The quality of mercy is not strained." It is reciprocal; it is "twice blessed."

HOPE

Among several resemblances between Epicureanism and Christianity is the exaltation of Hope as a factor in happiness. When St. Paul referred to the Epicureans as "others which have no hope," [89] he was in process of constructing a matrix of meanings in which Hope should have a new significance. To him it was to signify the expectation of participating in the grace of God. Epicurus, on the contrary, had denied all divine providence. The matrix of meanings constructed by him had its core in the doctrine that each human life should be thoroughly planned with a view to achieving happiness. To this end a definite attitude or diathesis must be chosen with respect to the past, the present, and the future. Toward the past man should be grateful, in the present patient and cautious, toward the future hopeful.

Gratitude for the past and hope for the future stand in a reciprocal relation, as Cicero makes plain, quoting Epicurus: "He thinks the life of the wise man to overflow with the memories of pleasures past and the hope of pleasures to come." [90] This is an essential part of the new matrix of meanings, though the core of it is total control of experience, including selective memories of the past, patience and caution in the present, and preparedness for the future.

Epicurus drew a clear distinction between the inner life, which Christianity called spiritual, and the outer life as affected by circumstances. So far as the inner life was concerned, man was totally free by a law of Nature, the free play or swerve of the atoms; as for the external life, freedom could be achieved by resolute control of experience. To the lad Menoeceus he wrote: "The life within us knows no master." [91] He was also prepared to go to an extreme in vindicating the feasibility of control over the external life. Speaking of prophecy he wrote: "No art of prophecy exists, and even if it did, external events are to be considered as meaning nothing to the inner life." [92] This does not mean that he utterly denied the play of chance or Fortune; he believed that this play could be practically nullified by rational planning. Neither did he utterly deny Necessity, but "there was no necessity of living with Necessity"; by building up a reserve of self-sufficiency the wise man could forestall the compulsions of poverty, war, or servitude.

The proper attitude toward the future was diligently studied and set forth with disjunctive lucidity: "It must be remembered that the future is neither altogether within our control nor altogether beyond our control, so that we must not await it as going to be altogether within our control nor despair of it as being altogether beyond our control." [93] The new matrix of meanings is here in process of being erected. Along with caution and control goes the active hope of good things to come, as exemplified by the words of Cicero to the merry Epicurean Papirius Paetus: "You, however, as your philosophy teaches, will feel bound to hope for the best, contemplate the worst, and endure whatever shall come." [94]

These same coefficients of the happy life, hope, caution, and control, are exhibited in combination by Horace in his daring admonition to the unstable Licinius, *Odes* 2, 10.13–15:

> sperat infestis, metuit secundis
> alteram sortem bene praeparatum
> pectus.

"The man whose mind is well prepared hopes for a change of fortune in adversity, fears it in prosperity." The allusion to the planned life and controlled experience is made plain by the words "well prepared."

At this point it is timely to be warned against an ambiguity of terms, which may lead to error. In both Greek and Latin hope and expectation are denoted by the same nouns — *elpis* and *spes* respectively. The Hope that chiefly makes for happiness is confident expectation, whether in Epicureanism or Christianity; were this not true, hope would never have been symbolized by an anchor. Only the fool indulges in vain hopes and lives in the future. The wise man lives in the present, facing the future with confident expectation because of preparedness.

The topic was a live one in the time of Epicurus because the contemporary Theophrastus chose to exalt the importance of external influences in human life. "Fortune," he said, "not reason, rules the lives of men." Epicurus, minimizing the role of Fortune, declared "that the inner life knows no master." To Metrodorus, his chief lieutenant, he assigned the task of developing this theme at greater length, and Clement of Alexandria happens to be witness of the fact. He mentions a writing of Metrodorus which aimed to demonstrate "that, viewed as a cause, the inner life is a good of more effect for happiness than are external goods." [95]

"What else," he cites him as demanding, "falls more within the province of the soul than the stable well-being of the flesh and the confident expectation concerning the same?" [96] This doctrine touching the feasibility of counting upon the continuance of health became such a crux of controversy as to be quoted by pagans and churchmen over the space of five centuries. Cicero makes four references to it, ascribing it to Metrodorus, while three others give it to Epicurus.[97] This means that both master and man were hammering home the same teaching. The opposing Platonists and others retorted that the continuance of health was precisely one of those things upon which humanity cannot count, and they gleefully drew up lists of calamities to which flesh is heir, quoting Hippocrates and Aeschylus.[98]

This very vociferousness and its long continuance is sufficient evidence that Epicurus brandished a dialectic which was difficult to combat. The core of this dialectic was the doctrine that experience could be controlled and that man could make himself master of his fate. The controlled experience upon which he pinned his hope was chiefly the simple life, independent of wealth and luxury and far from the madding crowd's ignoble strife, about which no other had more to say. Vatican Saying 33 must have been a favorite: "The cry of the flesh is not to hunger, not to thirst, not to suffer cold, because, possessing these and expecting to possess them, a man may vie with Zeus himself in respect of happiness." That this attitude may attain the rank of a kinetic pleasure is clear from another saying, the one that is mentioned seven times: "The stable condition of well-being in the flesh and the confident hope concerning this means the height of enjoyment and the greatest certainty of it for those who are capable of figuring the problem out." [99] From these quotations it becomes clear that confident hope or expectation is equivalent to faith, and it will be understood why the anchor became a symbol of hope.

This coincidence of confident hope with faith was assumed in the treatment of friendship. Vatican Saying 39 in part: "The man who never associates help with friendship cuts off good expectations concerning the future." In the same connection Epicurus was quoted as viewing faith in help as more important for the untroubled life than was help itself. Here once more it is clear that hope is the aspect of faith that concerns the future.

A minor phase of his attitude toward the future associates itself with his conceit of "condensing pleasures." According to a scholium to Aeschylus Epicurus condemned prophecy on the ground that, if a bit of good fortune should be predicted, the pleasure of it was dissipated by the foreknowledge.[100] The tension of emotion, as he thought, was heightened by surprise and so the pleasure was augmented. Consistently with this view he writes in Vatican Saying 17 of the wise man in his old age "locking in the safe keeping of a grateful memory the recollection of past blessings he had lacked the right to count upon."

It was Epicurean doctrine also that Horace was disseminating when he gave the advice to shun knowledge of the future and "to set down to treasure trove" the gift of the morrow; in the sole passage in which he mentions Epicurus by name he advises Tibullus "to believe that every day that dawns will be your last; welcome will be the surprise of the unexpected hour." [101] This living in the present, it may be added, besides the merit of condensing pleasure through surprise, possessed the advantage of forestalling fear and apprehension, a chief enemy of serenity. The true opposite of hope is not despair but uncertainty.

ATTITUDE TOWARD THE PRESENT

The choice of the proper attitudes toward the past and the future is simple as compared with the choice of attitude toward the present; in the former instances only thought is involved, in the latter both thought and action. Other choices may be made at leisure; the choices and decisions of the present admit of no postponement. They demand previous preparation for good and evil, a degree of self-possession that is proof against all surprises, caution in prosperity, hope in adversity, patience under compulsions.

For Epicurus the chief factor of choice was the denial of immortality, which confined the chance of happiness to the here and now. The effect of this was to endow the present with a tremendous urgency as affording the sole opportunity for action. Conversely, it raised procrastination to the rank of the supreme folly. These reciprocal attitudes, honor for action, scorn for postponement, were displayed by Epicurus, Ecclesiastes, Horace, and Jesus, all of whom belonged in the same tradition of ethical analysis, change, and development.

The urgency of the present is set forth by Epicurus with sweet reasonableness and scriptural simplicity: "He that sayeth the hour for putting philosophy into practice is not yet come or has passed by is like unto him that sayeth the hour for happiness is not yet come or is no more." [102] In contrast to the studied restraint of this admonition stands the forthright vigor of the teacher Ecclesiastes, 9:10, "Whatsoever thy hand findeth to do, do it with thy might," but the motivation is the same, mortality: "for there is no work, nor device, nor knowledge, nor wisdom in the grave, whither thou goest." The imperatives of Horace exhibit a contrast of their own, now gaily admonitory, now peremptory: *carpe diem*, "Gather ye rosebuds while ye may," as it were; *sapere aude, incipe*, "Dare to translate wisdom into action; make a beginning." [103]

In the teachings of Jesus no theme, perhaps, resounds with a greater variety of emphasis than the urgency of the present, but a new motivation has been discovered, the imminence of the kingdom of heaven: "The time is fulfilled and the kingdom of God is at hand; repent ye and believe the gospel."

The folly of procrastination was preached by both Epicurus and Metrodorus. A saying of the former is quoted and expanded by Seneca: "Among other vices this characterizes folly: it is always just beginning to live." [104] Of the same tenor is a second quotation: "It is vexatious to be always just beginning the life of wisdom." A tone of much more distinct melancholy echoes in Vatican Saying 30, ascribed to Metrodorus:

"Some men devote life to accumulating the wherewithal of life, failing to realize that the potion mixed for us all at birth is a draught of death." Diverse tones resound in the sharp words of Epicurus himself, Vatican Saying 14: "We are born once and we cannot be born twice but must to all eternity be no more, and fool that you are, though not master of the morrow, you postpone the hour and life is frittered away in procrastination, and each one of us goes on making excuses till he dies." The last is a familiar theme, Luke 14:18: "And they all with one consent began to make excuse."

There are other aspects of the present, however, besides urgency, self-excusing, and procrastination. All of these are ingredients of the inner life, which is free and knows no master except the individual's own choice. In the same present the individual must face the slings and arrows of outrageous Fortune and the compulsions of Necessity. This topic has already been covered in large part under the heading of the New Freedom and elsewhere, but some minor points deserve mention for the sake of precision.

While the general attitude toward Fortune is one of defiance, it can happen that this false deity seems to bring a shower of blessings. In such a case the proper attitude is caution and distrust. These two attitudes are reciprocal to each other and are so expounded by Epicurus himself: "Nature teaches us when unfortunate not to set great store by good fortune and without being upset to accept the good things from Fortune and to take a defiant stand against the seeming evils from her hand." [105] These reciprocal attitudes served Horace as a conceit for lyrical admonition to the impulsive Dellius in the ode beginning *Aequam memento rebus in arduis*,[106] "Remember to keep the spirit calm when the going is steep, not less restrained from overweening pride when things go well." The good Epicurean was always prepared for either issue, "hoping for the best, contemplating the worst."

The over-all attitude is succinctly expressed in two words by Horace, *nil admirari*,[107] "never to be taken by surprise," which, he adds, "is perhaps the one and only thing that can make and keep one happy." This is not to be confounded with Stoic apathy; the Epicurean did not suppress his emotions but controlled them by preparedness.

Under the head of Necessity fall the compulsions that ensue upon the pranks of Fortune, such as war, famine, and loss of property. Here too the secret of remaining happy is preparedness, which consists mainly in the simple, retired life. Thus Necessity is reduced to impotence. "Necessity is an evil but there is no necessity of living with Necessity" was the principle. The simple life bears fruit by storing up reserves of self-sufficiency against inevitable privations.

The Necessity that could not be overcome was death, and the practical problem was to decide what attitude was proper in bereavement, a question that engendered some heat in the battle of the schools. It overlaps the topic of Gratitude, to be next discussed. Epicurus recommended recognition of the inevitable, but ruled out the wailing that was widely in vogue, Vatican Saying 55: "We must heal our misfortunes by grateful recollection of those who have passed on and by recognizing that what is done cannot be undone." This makes a virtue of patience. As Horace wrote in his memorial ode for Quintilius Varus, addressed to Virgil: "True, it is hard to bear but patience renders easier what fate forbids to rectify." [108]

Patience, like other virtues of the present, is an aspect of preparedness and the latter is the result of sober reflection, so dear to Epicurus. It is sober reflection that recognizes the inevitable and chooses the proper attitude in advance. It is also sober reflection that recognizes, as recorded in Authorized Doctrine 40, the needlessness of bewailing the seemingly premature death of a friend, providing he has reaped already the fullness of pleasure in this life. This was the item of consolation that through Seneca's exposition and enlargement made its way into modern literature.

GRATITUDE

Had Epicurus been called upon to name his cardinal virtues there is little doubt that the foremost place would have been given to honesty or being true to one's self. Neither can there be much doubt that the second place would have been assigned to gratitude. No other virtue, except honesty, possessed for him such breadth of application. While primarily denoting the proper attitude to be assumed toward the past, it applied also to the present and was of ever increasing importance throughout life, reaching a peak in old age. Neither did any other virtue, unless honesty, present so many facets. It was due to teachers, Nature, friends, and patrons. It was extolled as a preserver of youth, as a healing influence in sorrow, as a preventive of vice, and a means of robbing the grave of its victory.

In the conventional ethics of the Greeks there was no lack of emphasis upon gratitude, but in the teachings of Epicurus it gained freshness of definition in proportion as it became integrated with a novel structure of ethics. In relation to happiness, the goal of living, it functioned as a chief coefficient, just as ingratitude was a chief cause of misery. In respect of free will, it represented the proper attitude to be chosen toward the past, though active also in the present. The cultivation of it presumed the feasibility of a total control of experience, including thought itself: "Moreover, it lies in our power to bury, as it were, unhappy memories in everlasting oblivion and to recall happy memories with sweet and agreeable recollection." [109] With fools, on the contrary, to recall the past is to regret it; they torture themselves with the recollection of past mistakes and misfortunes.

As became a moralist, Epicurus was capable of great scorn and was not impressed by tradition, no matter how hallowed by fame and antiquity. He was no more awed by the alleged wisdom of Solon than Solon had been by the riches of Croesus. Solon refused to judge a man happy until death had placed him beyond the reach of misfortune.[110] Epicurus said, Vatican Saying 75: "The adage which says, 'Look to the end of a long life,' bespeaks a lack of gratitude for past blessings." He was equally ready to defy popular belief, above all by denying all gratitude to the gods. Nor did he hesitate to set himself in opposition to the growing cult of Fortune by warning his disciples to look on her favors with distrust.

No less radical was his parting with Plato, whose espousal of the contemplative life along with the belief in immortality was bound to result in construing life as a preparation for death.[111] Epicurus, denying immortality, was equally bound to think of life as narrowly confined to the interval between birth and death and consequently to construe it as a preparation for a happy and triumphant old age. For this victory over death and the grave he found the cause in gratitude for past blessings. The happy life was the grateful life, terminating at last in the fullness of pleasures in old age.

GRATITUDE TO TEACHERS

The duty of gratitude to parents was an assumption of Greek morals and called for no special emphasis. In Hippocratic ethics the obligation of the medical apprentice to the teaching physician was placed on the same basis. This analogy was accepted by Epicurus but underwent a certain enlargement in his thinking, which may be demonstrated by the usual chain argument: the greatest good is life itself and the fulfillment of life is found in tranquillity of mind; this in turn depends upon knowing the true way of life; consequently the greatest gratitude is due to the pathfinder who has discovered the true way and sets the feet of the disciple in the road he must follow.

The thought of a financial nexus between leader and disciple was abhorrent to Epicurus. In his judgment the relationship should be personal and ethical. He scorned the mandatory communism of Pythagoras, "because such a practice was for those who distrusted one another and if men were not to be trusted neither were they friends." [112] He must have scorned also the exactions of the sophists, who were able to collect exorbitant fees so long as Athenian purses were bulging with imperial prosperity. It is a commonplace of handbooks that the Sicilian Gorgias could charge one hundred minas, the price of a house, for a single course of instruction; the garden of Epicurus cost only eighty.[113]

The proper relation between teacher and pupils was regarded as identical with that of father to children. Only in the light of this truth is it possible to arrive at a correct translation of an excerpt from a letter of Epicurus to his chief financial supporter, Idomeneus of Lampsacus: "Send us, therefore, your first-fruits for the sustenance of my sacred person and for that of my children, for so it occurs to me to express it." [114] This attitude was not original with him. A model for it may be recognized in the language of the Hippocratic oath: "I will look upon him who has taught me the art as I do my parents and will share with him my livelihood; if he is in need I will give him money." This is part of the genuinely anthropocentric ethic of Ionian science as opposed to the state-centered philosophy of Athens and Plato.

In the case of Epicurus this gratitude is obscured by the excess of admiration, reverence, and worship on the part of his followers; but the relationship of father and son, which he specifically approved, is also on record in the text of Lucretius: "It is thou, Father, who art the discoverer of truth, it is thou who givest us precepts as a father would." In the course of time, as Greek philosophy drifted closer and closer to religious conceptions, the idea of fatherhood was extended to that of savior. It is this epithet that we find in the Latin inscription of the devoted Plotina,[115] wife of the Emperor Trajan, while the word salvation occurs in the long inscription of the Epicurean Diogenes of Oenoanda.[116]

GRATITUDE TO NATURE

The duty of gratitude to Nature is on record in these words: "Gratitude is due to blessed Nature because she has made life's necessities easy of acquisition and those things that are difficult of acquisition unnecessary."[117] The true basis of the debt to Nature, however, is to be found in her function as a teacher. She is not to Epicurus, as she was to Aristotle, merely the creative force in the universe. She was also the aggregate of animate experience and especially of human experience.

It is Nature that reveals the Canon of truth and bestows upon man the means of contact between his soul and the material world, Sensations, Anticipations, Feelings. The true end of living as she reveals it is "the end of Nature." True justice is "the justice of Nature." The true attitude toward the desires consists in recognizing "the limits of Nature." The true attitude toward riches and poverty demands knowledge of "the wealth of Nature." She is the ethical teacher: "Nature teaches us to think the gifts of Fortune as of minor value and to know that when we are fortunate we are unfortunate."[118] In the language of Lucretius she is so eager for men to know the truth that she "barks" it aloud,[119] like a faithful dog that is keen to give warning. In a magnificent passage toward the end of the third book the poet steps aside and yields the pulpit to her so that in her own person she may lash self-pitying old men for their ingratitude.[120] If we take Nature in this Epicurean sense as a benevolent teacher, then gratitude is an imperative of Nature. It is owed to her by man and she in turn enjoins it upon man.

GRATITUDE TO FRIENDS

It is perhaps worth while to distinguish gratitude for friendship from gratitude to friends. For the former there was the more room and call because no gratitude was due to the gods; even the favors of Fortune were not to be received with gratitude but rather with caution and distrust. The acquisition of friendship was regarded as the most precious of all preparations for the happy life. It was upon friendship that Epicureans depended alike for peace and safety, an essential prerequisite of happiness, and for good companionship, an essential component of happiness.

THE NEW VIRTUES

The topic of friendship suddenly assumed both a new guise and a fresh importance in the life of Epicurus because of the rise of the Macedonian monarchies. Even before the time of Alexander the Platonic dream of a philosopher-king had given a powerful stimulus to the reception of young philosophers in royal courts. After Alexander's death the multiplication of courts served to multiply the opportunities for the graduates of the schools that were partial to monarchy. Even Epicurus himself became a beneficiary of the gifts of Idomeneus of Lampsacus, who, if not a monarch, was a man of power and affluence under a monarchy.

Under these circumstances, therefore, it is not surprising that Epicurus should have published a book to fit the time, entitled *On Gifts and Gratitude*.[121] Not a single specific quotation from this work seems to be on record but with some degree of plausibility a pair of excerpts may be referred to it. The first runs as follows: "Friendship has its origin in human needs. It is necessary, however, to prepare the way for it in advance — for we also sow seed in the ground — but it crystallizes through a reciprocity of benefits among those who have come to enjoy pleasures to the full." [122] The meaning of this is partly clear and partly obscure. Familiar already is the doctrine that friendships must be deliberately cultivated as a matter of expediency in the interests of peace and safety.

The point that may seem obscure is contained in the word reciprocity but this may be cleared up through our good fortune in possessing an epistle of Horace, 1.7, which the title *On Gifts and Gratitude* fits with precision. The poet, addressing Maecenas, who was pressing his rights as patron too rigorously, states his stand as follows: "The good and wise man declares himself willing to assist the deserving and I too shall show myself deserving in proportion to the merit of my benefactor." This is the "reciprocity." The relation must be reciprocal, and the client is no more bound to owe gratitude than is the patron. The relation must be in balance. The pleasure of the one is not to exceed the pleasure of the other.

The second dictum that seems to be an excerpt from the roll of Epicurus above mentioned runs as follows: "The wise man alone will know true gratitude and with respect to friends, whether present or absent, will be of the same mind throughout the whole journey of life." [123] This contains two statements. The meaning of the first is clarified by the negative form of the same truth in the epistle of Horace cited above, lines 20–21: "The open-handed fool makes a gift of that in which he sees no use or value. This is a seed-bed that has produced crops of ingrates in the past and will do so for all years to come." The fool is incapable of giving wisely; he fails to see that true gratitude presumes a reciprocity of benefits.

The second statement, that only the wise man will always be of the same mind toward friends, is clarified by an exposition of the corresponding vice in a satire of Horace.[124] The man who is lacking in true gratitude will speak ill of his friend behind his back, will not defend him when maligned, will betray confidences, and make a sacrifice of friendship to raise a laugh. Such a man is *niger*, "black," the color of poison, which is the opposite of "white," *candidus*; the virtue is candor, a name to which Epicureanism gave vogue in Latin. It denotes a phase of that absolute and incorruptible honesty which to Epicurus was the cardinal virtue. Being unalterably honest, the wise man will be loyal to friends at all times, and being always loyal, he will always be grateful.

FRUITS OF GRATITUDE

Unlike the Stoics who came after him, Epicurus entertained no distrust of the emotions. To the wise man he ascribed an exceptional depth of feeling. At the same time he was mindful of expediency. Emotions under proper control contributed to happiness, and happiness was a form of the advantageous.

One of the foremost recommendations of gratitude was its value as preserver of youthfulness: "Both when young and when old one should devote himself to philosophy in order that while growing old he shall be young in blessings through gratitude for what has been."[125] The converse of this truth is on record in Vatican Saying 19, which refers to an unnamed person: "Forgetting the good that has been, he becomes an old man this very day."

The fruits of gratitude are sometimes emphasized by warnings against the evils of ingratitude, as in Vatican Saying 35: "We must not spoil the enjoyment of the blessings we have by pining for those we have not but rather reflect that these too are among the things desirable." The habit of ingratitude creates an opening for fears: "The life of the fool is marked by ingratitude and apprehension; the drift of his thought is exclusively toward the future."[126] Even gluttony is linked with ingratitude, Vatican Saying 69: "It is the ungratefulness in the soul that renders the creature endlessly lickerish of embellishments in diet." The argument here subsumed is that gratitude is due to Nature for rendering the necessities easy of acquisition, the luxuries difficult.

Gratitude for the blessing of friendship is extolled for its comforting and healing influence, Vatican Saying 55: "One should heal his misfortunes by grateful recollection of friends who have passed on and by reflecting that what has once happened cannot be undone." There is something pathetic about this emphasis among Epicureans upon the irrevocability of the past and the inalienability of past pleasures. When Epicurus, in Vatican Saying 66, wrote, "Let us show our sympathy with our friends, not by wailing but by taking thought," it was almost certainly meant that comfort should be found in the thought, as Horace expressed it,[127] that Jupiter himself was impotent to cancel the recollection of a happy past. This conceit seems to have been built up as part of the counterpoise to the surrender of an afterlife.

It was as a counterpoise that the supreme reward of gratitude was to be reaped. It was not St. Paul but Epicurus who first made an issue of the sting of death. The good Epicurean was to escape this sting through habituating himself to the thought "that death is nothing to us." The wise man takes leave of life as a spectator issuing from the theater or as a satisfied guest taking his departure from a banquet, having enjoyed the fullness of pleasure.[128] The devoted Diogenes of Oenoanda looks forward to taking his leave of life with a paean of victory on his lips.[129] Metrodorus had set a model for him, Vatican Saying 47: "When Necessity does remove us, spitting scornfully upon life and those who foolishly cling to it, we shall depart this life with a beauteous paean of victory, raising the refrain that we have lived a good life."

This thought of victory over death was so captivating to St. Paul as to inspire one of his finest flights of eloquence, 1 Corinthians 15, where he employs the vocabulary of Epicurus while demolishing his doctrine: "O death, where is thy sting? O grave, where is thy victory?" Victory over death was claimed by both creeds, the one by the denial of immortality, the other by the assertion of it.

CHAPTER XV ✛ EXTENSION, SUBMERGENCE, AND REVIVAL

THE time has now come for surveying the fortunes of Epicureanism from the beginning down to the present day. If the synoptic view be first presented as a preparation for the details, it may be said that the creed flourished for the space of seven centuries, three before Christ and four afterward. At the outset it followed the then prevailing migrational trend to the eastward and established itself in the Graeco-Oriental world of Alexander and his successors. After the lapse of a century it followed the reverse trend to the westward and made the conquest of Italy, Rome, and Roman Africa. Thereafter it flourished over the greater part of the Graeco-Roman world for the space of four centuries. During the Middle Ages it survived as an evil name and was overlooked during the first centuries of the Renaissance. At long last it experienced a revival in France in the seventeenth century and enjoyed a brief vogue in England during the period of the Restoration. Its influence for the most part has been exerted anonymously.

To the synoptic view belong also the following items:

During the lifetime of Epicurus and his three colleagues the chief competitors and adversaries were the Platonists and Peripatetics.

During the last two centuries B.C. the chief competitors and adversaries were the Stoics.

With the death of Cicero in 43 B.C. the stage of controversy came to an end, and after the turn of the century the process of syncretism was accelerated. This was the work of Stoics, and the chief names are those of Seneca, Musonius Rufus, Epictetus, and Marcus Aurelius.

Before the year A.D. 200 the Christians had come forward as the chief competitors and adversaries. This rivalry was the last. By the fifth century the Epicureans seem to have been absorbed into the Christian community.

EXTENSION, SUBMERGENCE, AND REVIVAL

GENERAL EVIDENCES OF POPULARITY

Lucretius mentions the philosophy as "disseminated among great races," but Cicero is a more frequent witness. He has no fewer than ten references to the numbers of Epicureans in two of his writings alone. Our biographer Laertius writes of the friends of Epicurus as "so numerous as not to be counted even by whole cities." The best commentary upon this cryptic testimony is the statement of the younger Pliny to the emperor Trajan concerning Christianity: "The contagion of this superstition has permeated not the cities alone but also the villages and country districts." For this reason Cicero could speak of Epicureans as rustics, while Alexander, the false prophet, in a writing of Lucian could complain that "the whole of Pontus was being overrun by them." As for the reference of Laertius to "whole cities," the same Alexander angrily excommunicated from the use of his oracle the whole population of the town of Amastris on the Black Sea because of its Epicurean color, and the name of the Epicurean Roman official whose opposition incensed him is extant in an inscription.[1]

Epicureanism was the only missionary philosophy produced by the Greeks. At its inception it stood to the dominant Platonism as Buddhism to Brahmanism in Asia. Nonconformity, as opposed to orthodoxy, is prone at all times to be militant. Platonism, strange though it may seem, was orthodoxy; its front was to the past and not to the future; it was a theoretical continuation of a political experience that had served its purpose and come to a halt. It kept ethics, religion, and the intellectual life all tied together in a political context. Epicurus socialized the virtues and divorced ethics from religion and politics. While a man could be an active Platonist only in a Greek city-state, a hedonist, as Cicero acutely observed,[2] could go where he chose and still remain a hedonist. A barbarian could hardly be naturalized in a Platonic city but he could readily become an Epicurean. Multitudes of them did so. Cicero informs us, with grudging frankness, that Epicureanism "had a sensational influence not upon Greece and Italy alone but also upon the whole barbarian world."[3]

The popularity of the creed is abundantly attested in Greece itself by tributes of honor and dishonor alike. From the archives of the Academy there is still extant a dialogue called the *Axiochus*, which in defiance of chronology represents none other than Socrates as making sport of Epicurean doctrines. Hostility in the same quarter is also re-

329

vealed by the story that Arcesilaus, sixth successor of Plato, upon being asked "why students deserted from the other schools for that of Epicurus but never from the Epicureans," retorted "that men may become eunuchs but eunuchs cannot become men." [4] Some comedians satirized Epicurus, but the kindly Menander, his classmate, drew upon his teachings for some of his amusing themes.[5] Athens itself honored him with statues of bronze, but the Stoic Chrysippus devoted his life to the demolition of his doctrines.[6] Elsewhere in Greece, as in the Peloponnesus and Crete, two conservative areas, drastic laws were passed against his adherents, and persecutions were not unknown.[7]

Outside of Greece the evidences are also good. In Antioch under Antiochus Epiphanes (d. 164 B.C.) and his successor Epicureanism enjoyed the status of a court philosophy. In Judaea it was so endemic in the same age as to inspire the Book of Ecclesiastes. In Egypt, as already mentioned, it was known from the time of the first Ptolemy. In the first century A.D. the Jewish writer Philo of Alexandria exhibits abundant knowledge of it, as do also Christian scholars of the East in subsequent centuries. In the last century B.C. the East was sending Epicurean teachers to Greece and Italy: Zeno went from Gaza to head the original school in Athens; Philodemus went from Gadara for a career of distinction in Rome.

In the West a curious evidence exists in the form of an anonymous epitaph: *Non fui, fui, non sum, non curo*, "I was not, I was, I am not. I am unconscious of it." With negligible variations this is found in Italy, Gaul, and Africa.[8] It means that death is anesthesia; it means also, according to a conceit of Epicurus, that the unconsciousness of life before birth is a mirror of the unconsciousness of life after death.[9] The anonymity is also Epicurean; it signifies an extension of the precept "Live unknown" to "Die unknown." Horace states the conceit expressly:

Nec vixit male qui natus moriensque fefellit,

"Nor has he missed the good life who in birth and death is unknown to fame." [10]

The ubiquity of the creed is evidenced also by the multitude of books that were written against it. Controversy was so universal as to leap the gap between East and West. The Greek Sotion, for example, who was tutor to the Roman Seneca, wrote twelve books in refutation of Diocles of Magnesia, certainly of Asia Minor, though of which Magnesia it is unknown.[11] Conversely, the churchman Origen of Caesarea composed eight books, which are extant, in refutation of the slashing attack on Christianity by the Epicurean Celsus, who wrote in Rome. In honor of this same Celsus the Syrian Lucian investigated the frauds of the false prophet Alexander, who operated an oracle in a small town in Paphlagonia.

FORTUNES OF THE PARENT SCHOOL

Since the creed of Epicurus was dogmatic, complete, and self-contained and was planned to extend itself from disciple to disciple everywhere, it might seem that the fortunes of the parent school were of minor importance. It is manifest, however, that Epicurus was bent upon ensuring the perpetuity of its existence at least as a shrine. By his will, which is extant, it is learned that he established endowments, which were on record in the public registry, and bequeathed the incomes from the same along with the Garden and the house in Melite to his executors for the use of his disciples forever.[12] The Garden seems to have fared better than the house, because it was in use when Cicero visited Athens in 78 B.C.,[13] while from a letter of 51 B.C. it is learned that the sanctity of the latter was being threatened by a rebuilding for the use of the close-fisted nobleman Memmius, to whose "sweet friendship" Lucretius had vainly aspired. It may have been demolished during the siege of the city by Sulla in 86 B.C. The title, at any rate, had been transferred by the state from the heirs of Epicurus to Memmius.[14]

More important is the succession to the headship. The will designated Hermarchus as the first incumbent with the title "leader among his fellow students in philosophy" and the implication is clear that each leader should select his successor. Of these there were fourteen in the 227 years from the death of Epicurus to the death of Julius Caesar in 44 B.C.[15] Some of these were distinguished men but the names of others have fallen from the record. Laertius deemed worthy of mention after Hermarchus only Polystratus, Dionysius, Basileides, and Apollodorus.[16] It is improbable that Demetrius Laco, a contemporary of Philonides and his "throng of scholars" in Antioch, was ever head of the school but his career marks one of the peaks of Epicurean erudition; both he and Philonides were proficient in mathematics, especially geometry, and both are known chiefly from papyri.[17] It is certain, however, that a younger contemporary, Zeno of Gaza, renewed the distinction of the school in Athens. As a peppery old man he was well known to Cicero and his generation.[18]

After Zeno the school declined again and except for Patro, of whom Cicero had a low opinion, only one head is known by name. This occurs in an inscription of the second century, which yields three mentions in all.[19] In A.D. 121 the then incumbent, Popillius Theotimus, appealed to Plotina, widow of the emperor Trajan and a devoted adherent, to intercede with Hadrian for relief from a requirement that the head should be a Roman citizen, which had resulted in unfortunate choices. This petition was granted and acknowledged with all the gratitude that was proper to the sect. Later in the century it is on record that the school became a beneficiary of the bounty of Marcus Aurelius, who bestowed a stipend of 10,000 drachmas per annum upon the heads of all the recognized schools.

THE BEGINNING OF STOIC HOSTILITY

Before leaving the topic of the parent school it is timely to note the beginning of Stoic hostility to Epicureanism. It is a point of importance to remember that the house and Garden of Epicurus in Athens constituted what was virtually a residential college or private school. The competition with the Academy and the Peripatos was waged with the pen. There is no record of rivalry or animosity between Epicurus and Zeno.[20] There was no need for them to clash. The former was using Athens as a center from which to disseminate his new philosophy among Greeks everywhere. Zeno addressed himself directly to the adult Athenian citizen, as is indicated by the fact that he chose the Painted Stoa adjoining the market place as the stage for his lectures. Even his immediate successors, Cleanthes and Sphaerus, though they wrote against atomism and Democritus,[21] are not on record as having attacked Epicurus.

It was Chrysippus (d. 206 B.C.), the second founder of Stoicism, who first decided that Epicurus and not atomism should be the target. He was bitten by jealousy and set out to outdo his rival even in bulk of publications; his output was upward of 700 rolls, more than double the 300 of Epicurus.[22] Even in death he was determined to have the last word and provided that his tomb in the Cerameicus should be marked by a statue of himself so posed as to demonstrate that pleasure was not the end or telos.[23] It was his great achievement to develop the study of logic, for which he won a permanent place in the curriculum of studies, thus contributing handsomely to the growing sterility of ancient culture. Whatever be the merits of logic it is valueless for the increase of knowledge. A good logician is an intellectual eunuch.

An outstanding effect of the career of Chrysippus was to replace the Platonists and Peripatetics as first-line troops in the campaign against Epicureanism and relegate them to the auxiliaries. While the disciples of Epicurus were uniformly men of good will and desirous of peace, there were different breeds of Stoics, some dignified, others vulgar. Some were unprincipled and among them no weapons were barred; when logic seemed futile they resorted to the poison gas of scandal and imputed to the pen of Epicurus collections of obscene letters.[24] The last stage of this steady but diversified opposition assumed the form of virtual censorship during the regime of Caesar Augustus, who revealed his attitude by welcoming such anti-Epicureans as Dionysius of Halicarnassus and Nicolaus of Damascus.[25]

It may be added, however, that Stoicism enjoyed only a Pyrrhic victory. It is true that the Stoic catchwords of reason, virtue, and duty were welcomed by the Romans as labels, but the Epicurean love of decorum appealed to them more profoundly. When Cicero lavished praise upon Marcus Brutus for his combination of *comitas* with *severitas*, courtesy with unflinching veracity,[26] he was borrowing the language of Epicurus. Stoicism was descended from Cynicism, and the latter signified the philosophy of the dog, the creed and practice of Diogenes, who used an overturned wine cask as a kennel. To this type the vulgar sort of Stoic with his coarse cloak and unkempt hair and beard tended to revert and so become a comic character. Such vulgarity was abhorrent to the dignified sons of Romulus and when Juvenal derided it he was speaking for his countrymen. Epicurean independence of spirit combined with courtesy and decorum was really congenial to Rome. It was the label of hedonism that offended.

THE SCHOOL IN ANTIOCH

The Epicurean school in Antioch is remarkable not only for its strategic importance but also for the fact that its existence is known only from a papyrus. By way of introduction to the story, however, certain warnings are in order, as happens so often in the history of Epicureanism. In spite of the fact that Epicurus seems to have recommended especially the method of extension from disciple to disciple for the

333

propagation of his doctrine, it is quite usual to find his adherents among the teachers of grammar, rhetoric, and even mathematics. The prejudice of the founder against these branches has been greatly exaggerated, especially among modern scholars. Epicurus himself had been a privileged person, enjoying the endowments of generous friends, especially Idomeneus. The sordid necessity of earning a living was more often the lot of his later devotees. They taught their philosophy along with accepted subjects of study.

If this judgment is rendered more credible by examples, the names of Epicureans who essayed to teach grammar or rhetoric in Rome may be found in Suetonius,[27] while it is clear that men like Arnobius, Lactantius, and St. Augustine acquired their knowledge of the creed along with rhetoric.

It is in the light of such knowledge that we should read of the distinguished philosopher Philonides, who set up his headquarters in Antioch and surrounded himself with "a throng of scholars."[28] He made a convert of Antiochus Epiphanes (d. 164 B.C.) and enjoyed not only his patronage but also that of his successor, Demetrius Soter. It was manifestly the ambition of Philonides to make Antioch a capital of Epicureanism. He utilized his privileged position to assemble all the writings of Epicurus for the royal library. Like other leaders of the sect, he was busy with his pen, published 125 books, and rearranged the letters of Epicurus and his three colleagues according to names and subject matter.

That Philonides was also a man of force and persuasion is demonstrated not only by his influence over two monarchs but also by his services as a diplomat. His ability as an administrator was recognized by his appointment in charge of Laodicea on the Sea.

The unique interest that attaches to this school in Antioch is enhanced by other reasons, particularly two: it is probable that it served as a base of operations for the forcible introduction of Epicureanism into Judaea, and it was in this city that, according to Luke, the followers of Jesus were first called Christians. Attention should be drawn to the fact that the word Christian is a Latin and not a Greek formation. Since adherents of the older sect were already known by the name of their founder, it was natural for Roman residents, whether merchants or officials, to designate the adherents of the new sect in a similar way. To these neutral observers, when they heard of Epicureans ridiculing

Christian prophecies and the Christians fighting back, the contenders would have been no more than two warring factions. It was manifestly the resident Romans who coined the word Christian.

As for Antiochus himself, his very name was loathsome to the Jews, because his adopted surname Epiphanes means "the god manifest." He also waged vindictive warfare against them and attempted to force Greek culture upon them and, since Epicureanism was the court philosophy, there can be little doubt that this was part of his program. It is on record that a gymnasium was built in Jerusalem,[29] abhorrent to the orthodox Jew not only as an alien institution but specifically because of nudity in sports and the threat of sodomite practices associated with it. It signified also the virtual licensing of public teachers free of priestly control. That some progress was made in this direction is evidenced by the word Ecclesiastes, which means public teacher. Moreover, the book that goes under this name is abundantly sprinkled with atoms of Epicureanism; it was squeezed into the canon only by drastic and incongruous editing.

It derives its startling literary quality from the combination of luminous Hebraic imagery with the stark materialism of Epicurus. Consider, for example, the following, 9:4–5: "A living dog is better than a dead lion, for the living know that they shall die but the dead know not anything." Here we see transposed into the Hebraic idiom of thought the doctrine of the Garden that the most precious of all things is life itself and "that death is nothing to us"; it is anesthesia. The opinion has been expressed that the author was a Jewish physician of the time of Antiochus Epiphanes.[30]

The hatred of the orthodox Jew for the heretical teaching is on record to this day in the rabbinical term *apikoros*, "unbeliever." Jewish students were exhorted "to study the Law and know how to make answer to an unbeliever [lit. "Epicurean"]." [31]

It may be added that, even apart from attempts at cultural regimentation, an opening had been afforded for the infiltration of Epicurean doctrines among the Jews by the division between Pharisees and Sadducees. The beliefs of the latter, as recorded by Josephus,[32] including the denial of divine providence and the assertion of free will, exhibit an unmistakable coincidence with the teachings of Epicurus. This coincidence is the more noticeable because the reluctance of the Sadducees to hold public office is likewise mentioned. That Epicurus was in the mind of Josephus when penning his account of this sect, even if not mentioned by name, becomes the more probable when it is recalled that his defense of the prophet Daniel concludes with a spirited and extended diatribe against Epicurus and his views on the government of the universe.[33] On this occasion the arch-heretic is specifically named.

In making the transition from the Old to the New Testament it should be remembered that Galilee, in which Nazareth was situated, was a center of conservative Judaism flanked on the east by a network of Greek cities known as the Decapolis and that these were founded or refounded not long before the time of Christ. It was in such urban communities that Epicureanism flourished; from Gadara, for example, a town of the Decapolis, went Philodemus less than a century before Christ to pursue a distinguished career as an Epicurean philosopher in Rome. It would have been in the market places and on the building lots of such towns that the native Jew made his contacts with the immigrant Greeks and learned their way of life and manner of thought. If a local Jew was a fisherman, the Greeks would have been his customers; if he was a carpenter, the Greeks would have been his employers; village labor was probably migratory, as it is today. Moreover, only the homekeeping sort or the less intelligent would have failed to acquire some facility with the Greek tongue; the Greeks themselves were disdainful of all languages other than their own.

It is a reasonable inference that Jesus himself was subjected to these foreign influences. At the age of twelve he was a very orthodox boy, astonishing the doctors in the temple by the precocity of his knowledge. Some twenty odd years later he was scourging the money-lenders from its precincts and hated by the very doctors whose approval and admiration he had previously evoked. In the interval some revolutionary influences must have been at work and it is hard to believe that direct contacts with the gay and intellectual Greeks were not among them. When he speaks of gentiles he means Greeks. It is also difficult to believe that he failed to add some knowledge of their tongue to his own Aramaic and Hebrew.

Before proceeding to enumerate a few points of kinship between Epicureanism and Christianity it may be worth while to show how superficial and illusory are the alleged similarities of Stoicism to Christianity; this is largely a matter of labels only. Belief in one God is common to both but the unity of the Christian God consists in his being a person. The unity of the Stoic God, on the contrary, was qualitative and quantitative: as a quality it was reason; as a quantity it was the divine fire, which was divisible, each human being possessing a portion. Belief in survival after death was common to both, but to the Christian this survival was personal and eternal, while to the Stoic it was temporary, the individual soul being at length united with the great reservoir of divine fire from which it came. Both creeds professed belief in divine providence but for the Stoic this notion signified the maintenance of the astronomical order; to Jesus it meant "Even the very hairs of your head are all numbered."

The Stoic idea of the brotherhood of man was also illusory; it was based upon the possession by all men of a spark of the divine fire. This was not matched by a doctrine of brotherly love; only the few wise men were deemed virtuous and happy; all others were denounced as fools.

Epicureanism, on the contrary, was an integral part of a slow progression in society from Greek philosophy to Christianity. Plato's philosophy was for the talented few, the intellectual aristocrats; the doctrines of Epicurus appealed chiefly to the middle classes, the bourgeoisie; the teachings of Jesus were for the very poor, the lost sheep. Again, the ethics of Plato are tied in with his whole system of knowledge, including politics; the ethics of Epicurus are separated from politics and joined only with physics; the ethics of Jesus are isolated from both physics and politics and fitted into a developing scheme of salvation; this should be recognized as a new matrix of meanings, which we denominate as spiritual.

The vocabulary of the New Testament exhibits numerous similarities to that of Epicurus. An example is the use of the word flesh as opposed to spirit. Since Epicurus believed the soul to be corporeal by nature, the contrast between body and soul all but disappeared, both being of one nature. Yet the opposition from the ethical side still called out for expression and this demand was met by use of the word flesh. Hence we read, "The spirit is willing but the flesh is weak." Even the use of the word *spirit* for *soul* had its analogue on the Greek side. The talented physician Erasistratus of Antioch and Alexandria, an atomist, if not certainly an Epicurean, had proposed the theory that the air breathed

337

into the lungs was transformed by the heart into the vital breath, *pneuma*, Latin *spiritus*, and these words became regular designations for the immortal part of man.[34]

Another catchword of Epicurus is "fullness." It was part of his teaching that a limit to the desires had been set by Nature; thus a normal appetite could easily be satisfied to the full. The consequence was that fullness of pleasure was attainable. In the aggregate it meant that the fullness of all wholesome pleasures was feasible within the limits of mortal life. St. Paul takes over the idea and renders it almost mystical; he holds out the promise of "the fullness of Christ" and "the fullness of the Godhead." [35] In his eagerness to make converts of Epicureans he was adapting their language and ideology to the new creed and also improving upon the promise of their founder.

Both Thessalonica and Corinth must have been strongholds of Epicureanism. We must learn to read between the lines. Paul had been preaching at Thessalonica about the second coming of Christ, and prophecy always aroused the scorn of the Epicureans, who denied all participation of the gods in the affairs of man. The answer of Paul to these scoffers is to condemn them to instant annihilation: "For when they shall say Peace and Safety, then sudden destruction cometh upon them, as travail upon a woman with child, and they shall not escape." [36] The Epicureans were not accorded the honor of mention by name, but Peace and Safety were catchwords of their sect. It was part of their ethics to live a retired life apart from the turmoil of the courts and the market place and so to seek security from the malice and injury of other men. Paul follows up the quarrel and predicts the coming of Antichrist, the model for which was Antiochus Epiphanes, the archenemy of his race and the patron of the hated Epicureans.[37]

Corinth also must have been an Epicurean community. Paul was a fighter and the Epicureans were not mere critics; they were also active competitors. Since they were dogmatists and offered doctrines to be learned by heart, they too realized the need of faith. Like the Christians, they also based their practical ethics upon love of mankind, and it mattered little that they called this love *philia* and the Christians called it *agape*. Since, however, they denied divine providence, they had no hope of being benefited through divine grace or of salvation in the meaning of the Christians. Consequently Paul refers to them as "others which have no hope." [38] That the specific reference is to the Epicureans in this phrase is made evident by the essay of Seneca *De Beneficiis*, where the words "without hope" recur in a revealing context. On this topic there was a spirited controversy, still documented,[39] between Epicureans and their adversaries, especially the Stoics, who championed divine providence, and of this controversy, turning on hope or no hope of benefits from divine goodness, little doubt need exist that Paul was informed.

Add together these three, faith, hope, and charity, and we have the theme of the famous anti-Epicurean document, the thirteenth chapter of 1 Corinthians. It was the zeal of this controversy that inspired Paul to his highest flights of eloquence.

"Corruption" and "incorruption" were also catchwords of Epicureanism. It is true that the classical scholar will use the terms *perishability* and *imperishability*, but the Greek words in the texts of Epicurus and the New Testament are the same. Epicurus taught that the bodies of men are corruptible and the bodies of the gods incorruptible. Consequently, when Paul, preaching to an Epicurean audience, declares the promise "that the dead shall be raised incorruptible," [40] he is telling these Epicureans that the bliss they ascribed to their gods would be their own reward if they came over to his creed. He goes on to speak of "the sting of death," which is an Epicurean catchphrase,[41] because Epicurus before him had essayed to deprive death of its sting, by removing the desire for immortality. Paul tells them "we shall all be changed 'in a moment'," and very curious is the fact that the Greek reads "in an atom," [42] the only occurrence of atom in the New Testament. What better hint could be given that it is people of the Epicurean creed that he strives to win over? No doubt he won many; at long last Epicureanism was absorbed into Christianity.

THE SCHOOL IN ALEXANDRIA

It has been mentioned already that Epicurus established connections with Egypt while still living in Lampsacus, that he was accused of trying "to make recruits among the visitors from Egypt," that the first Ptolemy was not averse to the creed and that Colotes, a Lampsacene colleague of Epicurus, dedicated to him a burlesque of the earlier Greek philosophers. It is probable, therefore, that the impact of Epicureanism upon the Jews of Alexandria was of earlier date than the forced intrusion into Judaea through Antioch. Of the three original wards of the city, founded in 332 B.C., one was Jewish. It is known also that these immigrants succumbed quickly to the allurements of the Hellenistic life and learned the Greek language. It was for their benefit that the translation of the Old Testament known as the Septuagint was undertaken. The motivation of this enterprise has remained obscure, but the known hostility of orthodox Jewry to Epicureanism gives reasonableness to the conjecture that the desire to combat this particular heretical influence was a contributing factor, if not the chief one.

Of Epicurean scholars in the city we have the names of only two, Ptolemaeus the White and Ptolemaeus the Black, which may mean that the former was Greek and the second a native.[43] Their date is unknown but the writings of the famous Jewish writer Philo, of early Christian date, attest to the continued prevalence of the sect. Abundant evidence of the same in the following century is afforded by the writings of Dionysius the Great, Bishop of Alexandria, who is a chief authority for Eusebius on Epicurean doctrine.

EPICUREANISM IN ITALY

As part of the synoptic view, it should be remembered that the Romans received little of their literary culture directly from Greece itself. Their first contacts were with the Greeks of southern Italy and Sicily, and from this region, in the third century B.C., they received the epic and the drama. Philosophy was comprised in the second importation, which took place in the second century and was part of the backwash from the wars in Asia. Panaetius, for example, the Stoic friend of the younger Scipio Africanus (d. 129 B.C.), hailed from Rhodes.

As a detail of the synoptic view, it should also be observed that early Roman Stoicism was restricted to the aristocracy; that its adoption resulted in an exclusive bilingual education; that it depended upon imported Greek tutors and was confined to Rome. Epicureanism, on the contrary, was from its inception a rural and town culture and "took Italy by storm." It was disseminated in Latin translations through reading circles, each convert making new converts, and it required no imported tutors. If Epicurean scholars invaded the capital city of Rome, this was because the soil of patronage was already prepared, not because a virgin field was awaiting missionaries. For the space of a century the new creed spread and flourished openly and unforbidden, but with the transition to the Augustan regime it was forced to become anonymous.

It was already anonymous when the poet Horace penned the candid characterization of his own father, which fits the Epicurean pattern.[44] Thus the genial creed seems to have been known even to humble freedmen far south in Venusia, his birthplace. The cult of the curious *Bona Mens*, part of the Epicurean doublet *bona mens, bona valetudo,* "good health of mind, good health of body," is documented by inscriptions chiefly in Samnite territory south of Rome.[45] The vicinity of Naples became the chief focus of Epicureanism. Under the Republic this region still lay beyond the more congested seaside resorts of Cumae and Baiae;[46] it was there that Cicero retreated for genuine rest to his Pompeian villa, adjacent to his Epicurean friend Marius.[47] It was in Herculaneum that the great find of Epicurean papyri was discovered in the eighteenth century.

Naples itself was not originally on the coast. The port adjacent to it was named Parthenope after one of the Sirens, whose haunt was located by local mythology upon the neighboring peninsula of Sorrento. Thus it seems plausible that the Epicurean philosopher Siro was named for her, being, as it were, the male Siren; the bewitching doctrines of Epicurus himself had been compared to the voices of the Sirens.[48] As for the change of name, parallels are afforded by Plato and Theophrastus, whose given names had been Aristocles and Tyrtamus respectively. Whatever the fact may be, the school of Siro seems to have been located at Parthenope, the burial place of Virgil. Even Naples, however, preserves a memory of Epicurus; the name of the beautiful district called Posilipo is derived from a Greek phrase meaning "surcease from pain," *sans souci.*[49]

That the creed flourished also in the north of Italy is evidenced by the occurrence of the epitaph "I was not, I was, I am not, I am unconscious of it."[50] Inscriptions to the Epicurean *Bona Mens* and *Bona Valetudo* have been found at Aquileia at the head of the Adriatic.[51] From Cremona came Quintilius Varus, a known adherent and friend of Horace and Virgil.[52] Other adherents were of Gallic origin; Cicero's Epicurean friend Marcus Fadius was surnamed Gallus.[53] The best writer of the sect, Catius Insuber, commended by Quintilian, was obviously an Insubrian Gaul by birth or extraction.[54]

From Etruria came the patron of the Augustan poets, Maecenas, who, as Epicurus recommended, took measures to neutralize aristocratic jealousy. He accepted no regular magistracy and affected effeminacy in dress and oddity in speech. Extant from his impish pen are four lines of an outrageous prayer, which baffles the learned: "Cripple me in the arms; make me lame and crippled of foot; raise my back in a hideous hump; if only life is left, it is well with me; preserve this life, even though I sit on a piercing cross."[55] The true explanation is simple. Epicurus had declared life to be the greatest good and that, even though blinded, the wise man will not resort to suicide.[56] Thus it became a crux of discussion at what point of deprivation life ceased to be desirable. As treated by Maecenas this question became fantastic and elicited the desired contempt. The hostility that menaced him was nullified as effectively as posterity has been mystified. No mystery should exist, however, for one who has pondered the advice of Epicurus on the control of environment.

In Rome itself a trickle of information about Epicurus may have arrived as early as 278 B.C., while the master still lived. The horror of Gaius Fabricius at learning of his views on pleasure, the political life and the gods, from Cineas, the envoy of Pyrrhus, was a favorite morsel of historical drama in later days.[57] In the first half of the following century a wave of hostility against foreign teachers was diligently whipped up in senatorial circles and two Epicureans, Alcius and Philiscus, were shown the way to the gates.[58] In spite of this the name of one Nero, a cognomen of the Claudian family, appears in a papyrus as a friend of the ablest Epicurean of the time, Demetrius the Spartan; the latter may have visited Rome.[59] Toward the end of the century the fiery Lucilius was satirizing Titus Albucius, whom Cicero dubbed "a perfected Epicurean."[60]

In the first decade of the ensuing century hostility was whipped up against the teaching of rhetoric in Latin, which was linked with Epicureanism, and by measures taken in 92 B.C. the school of one Aurelius Opilius, freedman of a noble Epicurean, was forced to close along with others.[61] This severity was among the causes that precipitated the Social War. The troublous times that followed for many years, often resulting in exile whether voluntary or involuntary, actually encouraged the life of study and retirement after the rule of Epicurus. Little is known of Velleius, whom Cicero chose to be spokesman for Epicureanism in his book *On the Nature of the Gods*; he may have pursued his studies in Athens. Atticus certainly chose that city as a fit place in which to practice that Epicurean political neutrality by which he won a singular fame. Among Epicureans who pursued a similar course at home were Cicero's friends Marius and Matius.[62]

As for men of action, a special brand of Epicureanism became popular with them, which Cicero described as "pleasure combined with distinction." [63] Calpurnius Piso, prominent senator and provincial governor, father-in-law of Julius Caesar and patron of Philodemus, was an adherent. Titus Manlius Torquatus, scion of a most ancient family, was chosen to speak for the sect in Cicero's books *On the Limits of Good and Evil*. His father was also an adherent.[64] Of distinguished family also was Statilius Taurus, mentioned by Plutarch as excluded from the conspiracy against Caesar, which was headed by Cassius, both of them known to have professed the creed.[65]

Julius Caesar, Rome's greatest man, was very partial to Epicureanism. His boasted clemency happens to be an Epicurean virtue. He opposed the death penalty for the Catilinarian conspirators on the ground that death was no real punishment but rather the end of all human troubles or, as Epicurus held, anesthesia.[66] In his sober middle age he chose to have for his wife the daughter of Calpurnius Piso, patron of Philodemus. Upon leaving the capital for his first absence of five years in Gaul he chose to have his Epicurean father-in-law as his successor in the consulship. Upon planning to depart for his Parthian campaign he chose two Epicureans, Hirtius and Pansa, to succeed him in that office, 43 B.C.[67] The outstanding member of his civil suite in Gaul had been Gaius Matius, a loyal Epicurean friend who defied both the assassins and their sympathizers after the tragic Ides of March.[68] The winter camp in Gaul had exhibited the aspect of an Epicurean colony; the brilliant young lawyer Gaius Trebatius had become a convert there.[69]

It was in the last years of Julius Caesar that the Epicurean school of Siro must have flourished, a solitary example in Italy. A sparkling poem of Virgil is still extant expressing his glee at bidding farewell to the bombast of the rhetoricians and taking leave of Rome for that blessed haven.[70] It was in that "fruitful fellowship," as Tacitus styled it, that "he lived for several years in cultured leisure, enjoying to a singular degree the harmonious and intimate friendship of Quintilius, Tucca and Varius, following the sect of Epicurus." Virgil called Siro a great man; even Cicero wrote of him with respect and the commentators did not forget him.[71] The habit of unsparing mutual criticism practiced by members of his school had much to do with the high quality of the ensuing Augustan literature.

If only the historian were capable of viewing this last century of the Republic with the unbiased gaze of a first explorer, it would seem even more predominantly Epicurean than the previous age had been Stoic. The new philosophy spread more widely, penetrated deeper, and left a permanent stain beneath the Stoic varnish. The career of Panaetius was brief and circumscribed compared with that of the Epicurean Philodemus, who was an outstanding man for thirty years, 70 to 40 B.C., and deeply influenced the poets.[72] Even longer was the prominence of the Epicurean physician Asclepiades, who once stopped a funeral procession and revived the corpse; he flourished from 91 to 40 B.C.[73] In the year 56 B.C. Cicero admitted in a public court that hardly any doctrine was then being taught in Rome except what may be called a Romanized Epicureanism, political distinction joined with pleasure.[74] At the very time that he made this admission some of the finest poetry of all antiquity was being composed by Lucretius under the aegis of Epicurus. In the later years of Cicero the school of Siro was to flourish in Epicurean seclusion, grooming the young poets for the production of a literature surpassing all republican standards of excellence.

THE REACTION AGAINST EPICUREANISM

The turning point in the fortunes of Roman Epicureanism arrived with the publication of the great poem of Lucretius *On the Nature of Things* in 54 B.C. The effect of it upon the intelligentsia of the capital was probably dismay rather than delight. If decent citizens of small towns chose to study Epicurus in bad translations, this was tolerable; it was tolerable also if a section of the nobility chose to adopt such an idle philosophy; but when a new Epicurean literature written in Latin of the highest excellence began to threaten the supremacy of Ennius and the other classics, the limit of endurance was drawing near. The rising anxiety concerning literary standards was aggravated by the emergence of the new poets, the neoterics, "chanters of Euphorion," as Cicero dubbed them,[75] among whom as it happened, were certain of the future Augustans, rebels against prevailing traditions and unabashed partisans of Epicurus. To the old guard it would have seemed incredible that better Latin poetry yet awaited the writing.

Cicero, the spokesman of the intelligentsia, though irked by the complaints of Lucretius about the poverty of the Latin language, confined himself for the time being to grumbling. It was only when the death of his beloved daughter stung him from his complaisance in 45 B.C. that he really took up the challenge. Thereafter by strenuous activity he essayed to mend the damages of delay. During his remaining two years of life he poured forth a stream of anti-Epicurean propaganda, the true nature of which he endeavored to screen by a façade of philosophy, but he skimped his interlocutors for space in expounding the tenets of Epicurus while allowing their respondents more ample room for discharging the ammunition of rebuttal. His true intent was further cloaked by the avowal of a desire to create an indigenous literature of philosophy for the benefit of Roman youth, but this pretense is easily penetrated; [76] he was an elderly man and no such project had previously been announced. Moreover, during the previous four years, from 49 to 45 B.C., his pen had been idle and much of his recent leisure had been spent in the company of merry Epicureans.[77]

His pleas, however, had the desired effect; Epicureanism was discredited both socially and politically. Especially telling was the declaration that the banner of hedonism was one that never could be displayed "in the senate, in the forum, or in the camp." [78] Thus by an ironical and fortuitous timing the way was being prepared by the staunch defender of the Republic for the ensuing imperial regime, which above all things stood in need of unimpeachable banners and labels. If the pretended restoration of the government to the senate and the people was to flourish, not for a moment could a philosophy of political indifference be tolerated. If the old religion was to be revived, not for a moment could a philosophy of divine indifference be tolerated. Thus Epicureanism, too strongly entrenched to be uprooted, was forced to become anonymous. Against Lucretius was inaugurated a tacit conspiracy of silence.

The same circumstantial causes that forced Epicureanism into anonymity were effective in encouraging a revival of Stoicism for the sake of its unimpeachable labels. The essay of Cicero entitled *On Duties* was at the same time a revival of Stoicism and a flank attack upon the menacing Epicureanism. Just as in his direct attacks, he was unwittingly preparing the ground for the Augustan regime. The name of pleasure was quick to acquire a load of disapprobation, but Duty, Virtue, Reason, and Divine Providence, the watchwords of the Stoic, were by their nature immune to calumny. In the first century of the Empire the heroism of suicide among the aristocracy in opposition to the despotism of the Caesars became associated with Stoicism, but the most dramatic of the death scenes described by Tacitus is that of the Epicurean Petronius, who interrupted his enforced departure from life to compose for the benefit of Nero a recital of his imperial crimes.[79] The fact of his affiliation with Epicurus remained unmentioned; to have revealed this would have been a violation of the social and literary convention, the anonymity of the creed. Even to Persius, the satirist of that time, Epicurus was nameless; it was enough to designate him as "the sickly old man." [80]

EPICUREANISM IN THE EARLY EMPIRE

With the end of the Roman republic and the beginning of the Christian era the history of the school entered upon new phases and it is well to select this point of division as an eminence from which to gain a fresh synoptic view. The ensuing two centuries display three trends that are noteworthy: Roman Stoicism found itself for the first time in opposition to government and underwent the last of several transformations; in Greece the original controversy between Platonism and Epicureanism was revived by Plutarch; in the Graeco-Roman world at large a new contention began between the tenacious Epicureanism and the growing Christianity.

To take the first trend first, the transformation of Stoicism invites attention to the changeability of that creed as compared with the tenacity of Epicureanism. The explanation lies partly in the advice of Epicurus, "Avoid publicity." Stoics from the first had sought publicity. While Epicurus founded a private school housed in properties of his own, Zeno chose to discourse in the Painted Porch adjoining the agora in Athens, an even more public place than a gymnasium. In making this choice he was running true to beginnings; Diogenes had frequented the agora and kept his kennel hard by. From him was descended the vulgar breed of Stoics, who by defying the social conventions placed themselves in the same class as naughty boys who to attract attention stick out their tongues at company.

From Zeno was descended the better breed of Stoics, more intellectual and decorous but still characterized by the inverted vanity. They made a great parade of virtue and of fortitude in particular, but this was a quality they sometimes lacked. In prosperity they would maintain a challenging attitude but under compulsion were capable of crumbling. Rome's younger Cato is an example. Lacking the fortitude to become the beneficiary of the victorious Caesar's clemency, he resolved upon suicide but out of vanity dramatized this event for posterity. After banqueting his friends he retired to his quarters, read Plato's *Phaedo* on the immortality of the soul, and then took his leave of life by the most stagy of all ancient techniques of suicide, falling upon the sword.[81] An actor at heart and lustful of attention, he may have given the cue to the greatest actress of ancient times, Cleopatra, who dramatized her own demise with a like sense of the spectacular.

In spite of the bold front usually maintained by Stoicism it was not its way to fight back but to adapt itself. Panaetius, for example, repudiated the cult of Chaldean astrology, which was invading Italy in his day. A century later, after the casting of horoscopes had become standard practice, Posidonius accepted it.[82]

One more feature of the higher Stoicism remains to be mentioned, and the last phase of the creed in Italy can be explained. It depended upon patronage and its code of conduct was set for the aristocratic level. During the Republic this was a felicitous arrangement, but with the swing to the Empire the aristocrats with their Stoicism found themselves in the opposition. Even Seneca experienced the mitigating influence of an enforced absence from Rome; Musonius Rufus went three times into exile and Epictetus accepted this condition as his permanent lot in life.

The outcome of this repression was virtually a new Stoicism, which lowered its sights from the princely and aristocratic level so as to bring the generality of mankind within its purview. The original haughtiness of the sect was mitigated; the emotions were less distrusted than before and the asperity of "the sour and scowling Zeno" was tacitly abandoned in favor of a decent measure of Epicurean courtesy and charitableness. Seneca began to write of clemency, an Epicurean virtue; of tranquillity, which was an accepted synonym for Epicurean ataraxy; and of consolation, which was an Epicurean specialty. In his moral epistles he makes no concealment of his borrowings from Epicurus, quoting him scores of times, and excuses the practice by the sophism that truth is common property, exempt from copyright.[83]

EPICURUS AND HIS PHILOSOPHY

As for Epictetus, he remained a Stoic preacher of the scolding type; he had a keen wit, which he used more like a stiletto than a sword, and he jabbed nastily at Epicurus, but his teachings were as nonpolitical as those of the Garden itself.

Marcus Aurelius passes for a Stoic but is really a hybrid. He stressed the virtue of gratitude, which his school distrusted as a yielding to emotion. He commended courtesy joined with unflinching veracity, which was perhaps the most admirable invention of Epicurean ethics. He exhibits none of the sourness of Zeno and rather resembles Virgil, majestic in his sadness at the doubtful doom of humankind. He betrays no inclination to jab at Epicurus and in general his writings constitute the best amalgam of the doctrines of the once rival schools. His Stoic doctrine of divine providence, however different from that of Jesus, served as a bridge of connection with Christianity for his readers in the days to come. It is this amalgam, typified by the confusion of Epicurean ataraxy with Stoic apathy in modern dictionaries, that survives in English literature.

PLUTARCH, ANTI-EPICUREAN

While Stoicism in Italy was undergoing its final transformation, the learned tradition of interscholastic rivalry was being revived across the Adriatic in Boeotia by the famous Plutarch. His importance for the understanding of Epicureanism equals that of all other external Greek sources combined. His library was enormous and amply stocked with Epicurean rolls. References to Epicurean doctrines are to be found in at least a score of his writings and it is probable that more remain to be identified.

Two of his essays are devoted entirely to the refutation of Epicurean teachings. The first is entitled *Against Colotes* and the work refuted is the burlesque account of Greek philosophers dedicated to the first Ptolemy of Egypt. Epicurus while yet in Lampsacus at the court of Lysimachus was eager to win the ear of Ptolemy through the envoys that were coming and going. With this aim in view he seems to have assigned to Colotes, who had a turn for satire, the task of demonstrating that no philosopher before him had really faced the practical problems of ethics, a charge that was not ill founded. By Colotes himself the thesis was worded to read: "According to the dogmas of other philosophers it is impossible to live at all," to which the reader may add "much less live happily."

348

That this mockery possessed merit cannot be doubted; it survived in the book trade and was deemed worthy of refutation after more than four centuries. Genuine humor has great vitality and is unanswerable by logic. Plutarch did attempt, however, to answer it and parodied the words of Colotes for a title: "It is impossible to live happily after the doctrines of Epicurus." The result is labored but it possesses merits: it preserves much valuable information and it shows how the proud Platonists writhed under the shafts of Epicurean ridicule, a weapon to which pride is especially vulnerable.

Plutarch is an outright Platonist in his attitude toward Epicurus, and his writings should remind us that the original quarrel was between the Academy and the Garden. Recognition of this fact is essential to a correct appraisal of the long contention. The distortion of the modern view must be ascribed chiefly to Cicero. In spite of the fact that, like Plutarch, he was drawing upon the archives of the Academy, he was living in the closing years of the contention between Stoics and Epicureans and he put these contestants in the forefront. After his time there was a lull in the contention, while syncretism of the rival doctrines was going on, until the Christians emerged as fresh antagonists in the second century A.D.

EPICUREANISM IN THE GRAECO-ROMAN WORLD

After the first century A.D. it becomes convenient to scan the evidences of Epicureanism in the Mediterranean countries as a unified cultural area. The development of the new Stoicism of Seneca, Epictetus, and Marcus Aurelius was local and affected only the West. The learned revival instituted by Plutarch, though it must have continued since its memorials still survive, was confined to narrow circles. The collapse of Stoicism as a militant creed, which seems to have been as complete as it was rapid, left the arena to Christianity and the singularly tenacious Epicureanism. This was the last phase of the rivalry of the sects until Christians began to contend with one another in the struggle for orthodoxy.

The evidences from the second century are remarkable. Parallel to the previous refutation of the Epicurean Diocles by the Peripatetic Sotion we find the Christian Origen of Caesarea refuting the Roman Epicurean Celsus in eight books, which are extant. Celsus was the attacker. A man of varied erudition, he composed the most devastating assault upon Christianity ever made in ancient times. Modern scholars have doubted whether a mere Epicurean would have been capable of such a feat, but this judgment is based upon the false assumption of hostility to learning in the sect. Origen himself classified his opponent as Epicurean.[84] The satirist Lucian of the same age mentions an Epicurean friend of this name.[85] Moreover, the very title of the opus, *Alethes Logos*, often rendered *True Account*, though more aptly *True Word*, while satirically suggesting the logos of Jews and Christians, can hardly fail to be recognized as equivalent to the *vera ratio* of Lucretius and the "true philosophy" of Epicurus himself. It was as a tribute to this Celsus that Lucian undertook to expose the frauds of the false prophet Alexander and this study concludes with an exquisite encomium of Epicurus.

Whether Lucian himself was an Epicurean may be doubted, but the very fact that he was a satirist allies him with the sect, which from the beginning employed satire as a chief weapon. The burlesque of Greek philosophers by Colotes may be recalled, as well as the ridicule of young Platonists by Metrodorus as would-be Solons and Lycurguses. To Epicurus young Platonists were "flatterers of Dionysus," that is, candidates for kingly roles. Plato himself was dubbed "the Golden" in derision of his division of citizens into men of gold, silver, and baser metals. Ridicule was the weapon employed by Epicurus to belittle prophecy, as Cicero reminds us. Many passages of Lucretius are pure satire.[86] The Epicurean Horace naturally adopted this literary form in promulgating his ethical creed, and Epicureanism exercised more and more influence over Juvenal, who scorned the Stoics.[87] It is consequently justifiable to infer that the writings of Lucian, which abound in references to Epicurus and his doctrines, depended partly for their appeal upon the ubiquity of the sect and are evidence of this ubiquity.[88]

In the same second century of the Empire, when Lucian was extolling the wisdom of Epicurus, a unique monument of his philosophy was being erected by an obscure old man in an obscure town in Lycia in Asia Minor.[89] The place was Oenoanda and the man bore the name of Diogenes, which so often recurs. "Having arrived," as he informs us, "at the sunset of life, not far from the hour when he should take his leave with a paean of victory upon his lips, having experienced 'the fulness of happiness'," he wished to do something for the happiness of his own townsmen, for visitors, and even for those who were not yet born, because "the whole universe is just one country and the whole earth just one household." To this end it was his choice to have carved on the wall of a portico in the market place his own version of the teachings of Epicurus along with certain doctrines of the master verbatim. After the lapse of seventeen centuries this extraordinary inscription was discovered in 1884 by a pair of French archaeologists, Holleaux and Paris. The stones, even in their battered condition, have yielded sufficient text to make a small volume and their original extension in the portico may have measured as much as three hundred feet. No more eloquent testimony to the popularity of Epicureanism in this age has yet come to light.

In the latter part of this second century fell the career of Galen, the last great medical writer of ancient times. He bears witness to the vitality of Epicureanism by controverting the teachings of Asclepiades,[90] whose name was the foremost among Epicurean physicians. Contemporary with Galen was the physician and writer called Sextus Empiricus, to whose interest in skepticism and dogmatism we owe an imposing number of dependable quotations from Epicurean writings, especially on the topic of sensations.[91]

This century is also characterized by men of miscellaneous learning. Aëtius and Plutarch made collections of the opinions of philosophers, including Epicurus. Diogenes Laertius was compiling his *Lives of the Philosophers*, of uneven merit, but the tenth book, devoted to Epicurus, is the best single account of any ancient philosopher extant. In Athens the capable Alexander of Aphrodisias, commentator on Aristotle, was quoting Epicurus with understanding and respect. In Egypt the indefatigable Athenaeus of Naucratis was compiling an amazing farrago of poetry and philosophy in the form of a symposium of scholars; items from Epicureanism are numerous.

It was in this same century that the false prophet Alexander, an astounding impostor, was complaining of the increasing numbers of Epicureans in the district of Pontus on the Black Sea. All the citizens of the town of Amastris are reported to have been excommunicated from the use of his oracle on account of their adherence to that creed.

In the same age at the opposite end of the Empire in Roman Africa the same creed was flourishing. A hint of this is afforded by the occurrence of the epitaph that declared death to be anesthesia. It there runs: "I was not, I was, I am not, I feel no grief." [92] The sparkling and erudite

Apuleius of the second century classed Epicurus among the great thinkers of Greece and puckishly congratulated himself to have been named
in that same company. No less significant, and perhaps more so, is the
evidence to be gleaned by the activity of African scholars in defense of
Christianity. Among these belongs that Minucius Felix from whose pen
we possess a unique writing in dialogue form, which evinces reasons for
believing that the interlocutors had been Epicureans before becoming
Christians.[93] More outstanding among these apologists was Tertullian,
whose life overlapped the turn of the second and third centuries. It
seemed to him worth while to accord to Epicurus a dozen unfriendly
references.

THIRD AND FOURTH CENTURIES

After Tertullian it becomes convenient to treat of the third and fourth
centuries together. African scholarship, because of its use of the Latin
language, achieves a status of no slight significance. It demonstrates that
Epicureanism penetrated the country through the schools of rhetoric
and in Latin translations. The style of these, it is known, was not in the
learned idiom and closer to the vernacular, like that of the African
Latin itself. As for Greek, it never flourished in Africa, where the second
tongue was Phoenician. Both Tertullian and Cyprian, who knew Greek,
had the benefit of legal training in Rome. Africans of purely provincial
education such as Arnobius, Lactantius, and St. Augustine knew little
Greek and acquired it late; they wrote in Latin.

Arnobius and Lactantius, associated as master and pupil, resemble
each other in displaying a very deficient knowledge of Holy Scripture
and a rather abundant knowledge of Epicureanism. The former seems
to have known his Lucretius by heart. It has been suggested that he was
an Epicurean before his conversion.[94] The same may be suspected of his
pupil Lactantius, who not only shows himself at home in handling the
repudiated doctrines but also exhibits the sort of zeal that is proper to a
deserter. In A.D. 310 he thought it worth while to assemble a long list
of invidious reasons for the wide appeal of Epicureanism.[95] As for St.
Augustine, it is somewhat startling to have him confess "that he would
have awarded the palm to Epicureanism but for the denial of immortality and divine judgment." [96]

Outside of Africa it is evident that Epicureanism still held its own.
Eusebius of Caesarea did not consider it a dead issue; very considerable
references to it have been culled from his writings. St. Basil, his successor

as bishop, seems to have known "Live unknown" as a catchword of the creed.[97] St. Ambrose in Milan was reading Epicurus in an epitome.[98] Julian the Apostate (d. A.D. 363) was seeking certain of his writings, though he was pleased to find them difficult to obtain.[99] At the end of the century St. Augustine seems to have retreated from his earlier partiality; speaking of Epicureans and Stoics, he informs us "that in the rhetorical schools the question is hardly so much as mentioned any more what their doctrines were, while from the babel of Greek gymnasiums their contentions have been rooted out and reduced to silence." [100]

Since a general statement is now in order, the judgment may be ventured that Epicureanism reached its peak of extension in the second century, though failing to penetrate deeply into Spain or Gaul. In the third and fourth centuries it slowly lost ground, chiefly through the absorption of its adherents into the Christian communities. Thereafter the knowledge of it was confined to the learned. The service for which it was adapted as half philosophy and half religion, to function as a bridge between the classical Greek philosophies and Christianity, had long since been performed.

If in retrospect the question be raised by what particular superiority Christianity triumphed over Epicureanism and all other rivals, one answer is easy to find: it was organization. Here, as in some other respects, Epicureanism stands midway between the classical Greek philosophy and the Christian religion. Jesus compared the kingdom of heaven to leaven and Paul said "a little leaven leaveneth the whole lump," but it was not by the leaven method that Christianity conquered the ancient world. The leaven method, though not the metaphor, was that of Epicureanism "taking numberless fresh beginnings from one disciple to another." The really effective device was organization: deacons, elders, bishops, archbishops, and popes. Epicureanism likewise had a ladder of titles, but these were based upon reverence and this was feeble in comparison with a ladder of titles based upon authority. The Church had available a model of organization which Epicurus never knew, the Roman Empire, and the imitation of this was a main reason for its survival.

EPICUREANISM IN THE MIDDLE AGES

It was impossible for a name so long notorious as that of Epicurus to drop from memory in the Middle Ages. The writings of Cicero, the chief source of information in Latin, never passed out of knowledge. In the course of time, as Latin became the sole language of learning, Christian writings in Greek were either lost or confined in their circulation to the East. Yet in the West there were still to be had, besides Cicero, the numerous Latin works of Tertullian, Arnobius, Lactantius, St. Ambrose, and St. Augustine, all of whom preserved the memory of Epicurus. To these should be added the name of Seneca, who, though a pagan, was yet acceptable as a moralist. After the study of Greek was revived the eight books of Origen in defense of Christianity against Epicurean criticism, not to mention other writings, became available. In a list of more than one hundred original sources for Epicureanism no fewer than eighteen are Christian.

Outside of strictly Christian circles the tradition of ancient philosophy shrank to a trickle but never quite perished. Already in the second century A.D. the custom of tabulating the opinions of philosophers in the form of succinct statements had begun; specimens of this activity still survive from that time under the names of Aëtius and Plutarch. In the same class belong the miscellany of Stobaeus of the fifth century and a sort of classical dictionary known by the name of Suidas of the tenth century. Such writings are symptomatic of the senility of learning but they preserved some valuable information about Epicurus. Even after it was thought that the last grain of information had been garnered from such sources a mild surprise was occasioned in 1888 by the discovery of a collection of eighty-one Epicurean apothegms, chiefly of Epicurus himself, in the Vatican Library.[101]

This trickle of the literary tradition was of course confined to the Byzantine region of Europe until the revival of learning in the West. On the other hand, the repudiation of Epicurus as a sensualist did not depend upon knowledge of Greek. It had been taken over by art. On one piece of the Bosco Reale silver treasure, rescued from a villa overwhelmed at the same time as Pompeii in A.D. 79 and now in the Louvre in Paris, he is represented as reaching out his hands for food while Zeno the Stoic rejects it. A similar motive inspired a painting now in the Palazzo Diamanti in Ferrara, Italy, which is entitled "The Triumph of St. Augustine."[102] To the right of the saint in the upper register appear Aristotle, Plato, Socrates, and Seneca. In the middle register the Virtues are represented as punishing the sinners, among whom appear Epicurus and Sardanapalus, an Assyrian monarch whose name had been a synonym for voluptuary throughout antiquity.

This reputation of Epicurus as an out-and-out sensualist has been toned down and survives only in the innocuous "epicure," restricted in application to matters of food and drink. In rabbinical writings, in the form *apikoros*, the name signifies unbeliever. It was this heretical connotation that seems to have been most prevalent in the Middle Ages. Dante paid to Epicureans in general the high honor of devising for them a punishment ingeniously unique. On the day of the resurrection, because they had denied the survival of the soul apart from the body, their souls were to be imprisoned in sealed coffins along with their bodies. In anticipation of the execution of this ironical judgment a cemetery of lidless coffins was exhibited in the sixth circle of the Inferno. To explain their intention could hardly have been a congenial duty for Virgil, his guide, a man who never lost his Epicurean kindliness of heart.

In spite of Christian hostility, however, it need not be inferred that the loss of Epicurean writings was due to deliberate destruction. Apart from the new Stoicism of Epictetus and Marcus Aurelius, the writings of that sect have fared rather worse. The survival of the sixty-nine pages of the texts of Epicurus which we possess has been due to their inclusion in the *Lives of the Philosophers* by Diogenes Laertius. The survival of this, in turn, was assured by the rising interest in the works of Aristotle. The earliest manuscripts date from the twelfth and thirteenth centuries and it was only the part that deals with Theophrastus and Aristotle that found its way into print before the year 1500. The first translation was naturally in Latin, the work of one Ambrosius, and appeared at Venice in 1475, though previously without date at Rome. Five printings of the Greek text were issued between 1533 and 1615 at Basel, Paris, and Geneva.

These facts do not indicate that scholars of the Renaissance were interested in Epicurus. They passed him by or knew him only at second hand, through reading Cicero, Seneca, and Plutarch. The moral essays of Seneca were favorite reading and encouraged the confusion of Epicurean with Stoic ethics.

THE EPICUREAN REVIVAL

The renaissance of Epicurean studies was delayed until the seventeenth century and was at first confined to France. Strange to say, it was

begun by a man in holy orders, Pierre Gassendi, who was attracted
by both the ethical and the physical doctrines of Epicurus. The ethics
presented little difficulty; the difference was not so much in content as
in the absence and presence of divine sanction. The difficulty was greater
in the case of the physics but Gassendi solved it neatly by declaring that
it was God who had created the atoms. This combination of Christian
with Epicurean doctrine was taken over by Sir Isaac Newton and by
means of it he made acceptable to religious people his revolutionary
account of the universe.

In France itself the writings of Gassendi, first printed at Leyden in
1649 and twice again within sixteen years, won a distinguished following. Among his disciples was the dramatist Molière, who wrote comedies
in the style of Menander, the congenial classmate of Epicurus. From
France the doctrines of Gassendi were carried to England in the Restoration period and won a vogue for Epicurean studies which lasted for
about seventy-five years, roughly from 1650 to 1725. Just as in ancient
Rome, however, the threat to morals and religion was eventually recognized and the adverse reaction set in. As a repressing agent the grim
Puritan was extremely efficient, and the suspected creed was once more
driven into anonymity. The atomic theory could be made acceptable
by Sir Isaac Newton only upon condition that God was represented
as the creator of the atoms.

Even in anonymity, however, Epicureanism exhibited its characteristic tenacity. Its secret influence upon the trend of political and philosophical thinking since the late seventeenth century has exceeded that
of all other ancient philosophies. It can be no mere accident that John
Locke, who during his sojourn in France from 1675 to 1679 became a
friend of François Bernier, the most outstanding exponent of Gassendi's
doctrines, should have been the one to write an *Essay concerning Human
Understanding* and fix upon the sensations as the source of all knowledge. The thesis as he develops it is not true to the doctrines of Epicurus.
It is based upon a mistranslation of a sentence, rightly attributed to
Epicurus, which to Gassendi seemed to mean "that there is nothing in
the intellect which has not been in the senses." Thus by a sort of irony
Epicurus seems to have furnished a starting point for modern empiricism; in reality he was something of an intuitionist and his concept
of innate ideas was incompatible with empiricism.

The mistake of Gassendi, to which Locke fell a prey, was in confusing the test of knowledge with the source of knowledge. Epicurus based his Ethics upon his Physics and as a basis of his Physics he laid down the Twelve Elementary Principles, derived chiefly from his predecessors, the truth of which he made no pretence of deriving from sensation. Moreover, the test of the truth of all inferential conclusions was not single but triple, Sensations, Anticipations (innate ideas), and Feelings. The mind of the newborn infant, so far from seeming to him a blank tablet, was thought to have dimly inscribed upon it, as the venous system is outlined in the embryo, the patterns of the thoughts of the mature man. Locke's theory of cognition, compared to that of Epicurus, is naïve.

It is no mere accident either, that it was John Locke, the friend of Bernier, who was to write *Treatises of Government*, in which was set forth the principle that the function of government was to protect the property of the citizen. This was the teaching of Epicurus, who was in rebellion against the teachings of Plato's *Laws*, which proposed a maximum of regimentation. The difference between Locke and Epicurus is only one of names and assumptions. Epicurus taught that the function of government was to protect the safety or security of the citizen, that is, his person, assuming that it was idle to protect his person if his property was not also protected. Locke reversed the terms and in declaring that the function of government was to protect the property of the citizen assumed that it was idle to protect the property unless the person of the citizen was also assured protection.

In respect of this item of political thought a remarkable instance of fortuitous timing should be brought to attention. In the age of Cromwell and the Restoration in England, it was a pressing problem to decide how much authority a government should possess. It was precisely then that Epicureanism arrived with its doctrine that a minimum of government was best. Thereupon began that momentous series of writings of which the chief authors were Hobbes, Locke, Berkeley, Hume, Jeremy Bentham, and John Stuart Mill. A concurrent impulse was, of course, the rapid increase of trade and industry and the beginnings of political science. Among the end results were utilitarianism, universalistic hedonism, and nineteenth-century liberalism. This was all anti-Platonic and behind it was a fertile seed of Epicureanism.

In the new United States of America there was no such chain of reaction. American political thought started with Locke and remained largely with Locke, who was the favored philosopher during the revolu-

357

tionary period. The doctrine of the minimum of government was incorporated in the Constitution. It survived and still survives, though gravely questioned and threatened, as the system of free enterprise. As a matter of interest it may be added that its chief champion, Thomas Jefferson, was an avowed Epicurean and capable of reading the texts in the original.

As for classical scholars, their attitude toward Epicurus has been contemptuous in the main and their treatment perfunctory. In bibliographies his name runs a poor second to that of his alphabetical neighbor Epictetus. Since 1900 a slow increase of interest has become apparent and still persists, but many tedious investigations remain to be made if the misrepresentations of centuries are to be rectified. In particular the New Testament must be diligently studied anew for traces of the language and thought of Epicureanism, which in that day was flourishing both in Judaea and in the Greek cities where the apostles sought their converts. This background was helping to shape the new doctrine.

BIBLIOGRAPHY, ABBREVIATIONS
NOTES, AND INDEX

BIBLIOGRAPHY

TRADITIONAL errors have vitiated expositions and translations alike, but peculiar to England is a progressive amplification of fallacies. This is barely noticeable in W. Wallace's *Epicureanism* (London, 1880), which retains great merit, but is well under way in A. W. Benn's *Greek Philosophers* (London, 1882). John Watson's *Hedonistic Theories* (London, 1895), exhibits vilification rather than an amplification of errors, but the latter tendency reasserts itself in John Masson's *Lucretius, Epicurean and Poet* (London, 1909), and is attended by a certain virulence in A. E. Taylor's *Epicurus* (London, 1911), which is the worst book on the subject by a reputable scholar. Meanwhile a return to moderation becomes observable in R. D. Hicks' *Stoic and Epicurean* (London, 1910), and to this virtue urbanity was added by Cyril Bailey in his *Epicurus* and his *Greek Atomists* (Oxford, 1925 and 1928); but the amplification of fallacy still went on, culminating in the ascription to Epicurus of belief in "the infallibility of sensation."

Exempt from this criticism is a refreshing article, "Epicurus and his Sayings," in the *Quarterly Review*, 185 (1897) 68–93, possibly by A. W. Mair, whose article on Epicurus in the *Encyclopaedia Britannica* is commendable, as also that of K. O. Brink in the *Oxford Classical Dictionary*.

General histories of philosophy in English are perfunctory in their treatment of Epicurus and valueless for integrating him with the succession of ancient thinkers. The reader will profit more, though in a different way, from Benjamin Farrington's *Science and Politics in the Ancient World* (London, 1939), a broad survey spiced with provocativeness.

The fortunes of Epicurus and Lucretius have not followed the same curve in the continuum of western thought but the reader will profit from *Lucretius and His Influence* by G. D. Hadzsits (New York, 1935). This should be supplemented by T. F. Mayo's *Epicurus in England (1650–1725)* (Dallas: Southwest Press, 1934). A disorderly and inaccurate book of this same Restoration period, *Epicurus, Morals: collected and faithfully Englished*, by W. Charleton, was republished by F. Manning in 1926.

Translations of Epicurus have failed to throw much light upon Lucretius but the experiment has been tried by C. Giussani (Turin, 1896) and by A. Ernout (Paris, 1925), as also by Bailey. The relation of the disciple to the master and to other Epicureans still awaits full exploration. A specimen of what can be done is P. H. DeLacy's "Lucretius and the History of Epicureanism," *Transactions of the American Philological Association*, 79 (1948) 12–23.

There is an orthodox translation in German by A. Kochalsky (Leipzig, 1914), but the Germans themselves have done more for the minor Epicureans, especially Philodemus. Noteworthy but indecisive has been the controversy over the gods of Epicurus, where the studies of R. Philippson stand out: *Hermes* 51 (1916) 568–608 and 53 (1918) 359–395. Very illuminating, especially for the astral gods of Plato, is A.-J. Festugière's *Epicure et ses Dieux* (Paris, 1947).

On the continent of Europe Epicurus has commanded more interest with the reading public than in Britain or the United States. Two attractive pocket books have

361

recently appeared in Switzerland: J. von Haringer, *Epikur, Lebenskunst* (Zurich: Werner Classen, 1947) and Olof Gigon, *Epikur, von der Überwindung der Furcht* (Zurich: Artemis-Verlag, 1949).

Other recent books of merit are C. Diano's *Epicuri Ethica* and *Lettere di Epicuro e dei suoi* (Florence: Sansoni, 1946). The latter is for the expert; the former is a collection of texts with scholarly Latin notes and indexes. Additional titles are cited below under Abbreviations.

The best Greek text is that of P. Von der Muehll, *Epistulae Tres at Ratae Sententiae* (Leipzig: Teubner, 1922). It includes the Vatican Collection but lacks the fragments. Of the latter a brief but judicious selection may be found in Bailey's *Epicurus* along with a bibliography, pp. 423–424. Unluckily the indispensable aid, H. Usener's *Epicurea* (Leipzig: Teubner, 1887) is long out of print. The same is true of Ettore Bignone's *Epicurus* (Bari: Laterza, 1920).

As things are, however, the student will benefit more by resolute study of the texts of Epicurus himself than by excursions into the bewildering auxiliary literature, still bedeviled by a hostile tradition. It is the aim of the present study to have pioneered in this direction.

ABBREVIATIONS

AJP: American Journal of Philology
Atomists: Cyril Bailey, *The Greek Atomists and Epicurus,* Oxford, 1928
Bailey: *Epicurus,* Text and Translation, Oxford, 1925
Bignone: Ettore Bignone, *L'Aristotele perduto e la formazione filosofica di Epicuro,*
   Florence, 1936
CIG: Corpus Inscriptionum Graecarum
CIL: Corpus Inscriptionum Latinarum
CP: Classical Philology
CQ: Classical Quarterly
Croenert: W. Croenert, *Kolotes und Menedemos,* Leipzig, 1906
CW: Classical Weekly
D.L.: Diogenes Laertius, *Lives of the Ancient Philosophers,* Translation by R. D.
   Hicks, *Loeb Classical Library,* 1925
HN: Historia Naturalis (Pliny)
Koerte: A. Koerte, *Metrodori Epicurei Fragmenta,* Leipzig, 1890
ND: De Natura Deorum (Cicero)
PW: Pauly-Wissowa-Kroll, *Real Encyclopaedie*
RFIC: Rivista de Filologica e Di Instruzione Classica
RhM: Rheinisches Museum
RS: Ratae Sententiae. See D.L. above, vol. 2, pp. 663–677, or Bailey, pp. 94–105.
SV: Sententiae Vaticanae. See Bailey above, pp. 107–119.
TAPA: Transactions of the American Philological Association
Us.: Usener's *Epicurea*
Vogliano: A. Vogliano, *Epicuri et Epicureorum Scripta in Herculanensibus Papyris*
   Servata, Berlin: Weidmann, 1928

NOTES

Chapter II. Samos and Athens

[1] D.L. 10.3; Suidas *s.v. Epicurus.*
[2] *Non posse* 1100a–b.
[3] D.L. 10.10.
[4] *Ibid.*
[5] Diog. Oen., frag. 64, col. 2.4–9.
[6] Strabo 638; scholium to Aeschin., *c. Timarch.* 12; Philochorus frag. 131; Diod. 18.18.9.
[7] D.L. 10.4.
[8] Demosth., *On the Crown* 258; D.L. 7.18.
[9] D.L. 10.4.
[10] *Ibid.* 10.3.
[11] *Ibid.* 10.8.
[12] *SV* 21.
[13] 51.13, vol. 6, p. 63 (Loeb).
[14] D.L. 10.1.
[15] Frag. 59.5–9.
[16] *Non posse* 1095e.
[17] D.L. 10.4.
[18] *On the Crown* 259.
[19] Diog. Oen., frag. 63, cols. 2.10–3.3.
[20] Frederic Manning, *Epicurus's Morals* (London, 1926), p. xxiii (reprint of Walter Charleton).
[21] *Tusc. Disp.* 1.23.55.
[22] *Ibid.* 1.17.39.
[23] Benjamin Farrington, *Science and Politics in the Ancient World* (London: Allen, 1939), pp. 228–232.
[24] D.L. 10.2; Hesiod, *Theog.* 116.
[25] *Adv. Math.* 10.18–19.
[26] See pp. 73–75.
[27] D.L. 10.14.
[28] *Ibid.* 10.2.
[29] *N.D.* 1.26.72.
[30] D.L. 10.14; Suidas *s.v.* Epicurus. Us., p. 366.10, reads *Antigonus,* a needless change.
[31] D.L. 10.2.
[32] D.L. 10.6; Us. 163.

[33] *Non posse* 1097c; *Inst.* 2.17.15; 12.2.24; cf. Cic., *De Fin.* 1.7.26.
[34] Us. 117, but the reading of Athenaeus 588a, as in footnote, should be retained.
[35] *Non posse* 1094d.
[36] Bignone, followed by Bailey, frag. 24.
[37] Alexis, frag. 25 (Kock); Sen., *Dial.* 7.13.2.
[38] *Confess.* 6.16.
[39] Elias, *Comment. in Arist. Graeca* 18.1–3, p. 118.18.
[40] D.L. 10.13, 31.
[41] *Ibid.*; Us. 55, end; Cic., *De Fin.* 1.9.63; *SV* 29, 45.
[42] D.L. 10.79.
[43] *Ibid.* 56.
[44] Sextus Emp., *adv. Math.* 1.2.
[45] Us. p. xli.
[46] D.L. 10.125.
[47] Us., p. xlii, n. 2, cites 1–7, 9, 10, 16.
[48] Philodemus, *On Frankness,* frag. 6.9–11.
[49] Vol. 2., pp. 51–52, cols. 48.37.12–49.37.16 (Sudhaus).
[50] Cic., *Brutus* 85.292.
[51] D.L. 10.27.
[52] *De Fin.* 1.7.22.
[53] D.L. 10.13; *N.D.* 1.26.72.
[54] D.L. 5.37.
[55] *Ibid.* 10.120.
[56] *Non posse* 1095c.
[57] D.L. 10.14, 18.
[58] Plut., *Phocion* 28; Eurip., *Ion.* 1076.
[59] Strabo 638.
[60] *PW* 15.1, pp. 710–711.
[61] 7.72.
[62] *PW* 15.1, pp. 709–710.
[63] *Ibid.*
[64] Lines 650–665 (Wilamowitz, *Das Schiedsgericht,* Berlin: Weidmann, 1925).
[65] Wilamowitz, *op. cit.,* p. 110.

NOTES

[66] D.L. 76–77.
[67] SV 21.
[68] *Heauton Tim.* 77.
[69] D.L. 10.4.

[70] *Ibid.* 10.1.
[71] *Ibid.* 10.4.
[72] *Ibid.* 10.10.
[73] *Ibid.* 10.9.

Chapter III. Colophon: Development of Doctrine

[1] 655.
[2] Proclus (d. A.D. 485) in one passage calls him pupil and in another friend of Theophrastus: K. O. Brink, *CQ* 40 (1940) 21, frags. 5(6) and 6(5). This supersedes Croenert, p. 74.
[3] *Ibid.* p. 20, T3, T5(b), T8.
[4] *Ibid.* T8.
[5] *Ibid.* pp. 19–26.
[6] *Ibid.* p. 20, T9 a, b.
[7] *Ibid.* p. 21, F3.
[8] *Ibid.* p. 20, T5.
[9] Croenert, pp. 69–74.
[10] *Ibid.* 71, col. 16, lines 6–14.
[11] See n. 2.
[12] D.L. 10.13.
[13] *Ibid.*
[14] *Ibid.* 3.8.
[15] *Ibid.* 10.10.
[16] Diog. Oen., frag. 64, pp. 59–60.
[17] D.L. 10.4–5.
[18] Diog. Oen., frag. 65, p. 60.
[19] D.L. 10.10.
[20] A. Gellius 13.3.
[21] *N.D.* 1.26.73.
[22] Aristotle, Xenocrates, Erastus, Coriscus, and Hermias, all of Plato's school, lived at Assos or Atarneus; Neleus of Scepsis inherited Aristotle's library: Strabo 608, 610.
[23] Herod. 1.168; Strabo 644.
[24] Sextus Emp., *adv. Math.* 1.2.
[25] Philodemus, *Rhet.*, vol. 2, pp. 51–52, cols. 48.37.12–49.37.16 (Sudhaus).
[26] D.L. 9.64.
[27] *Ibid.*
[28] *N.D.* 1.26.73.

[29] D.L. 10.8; Sextus Emp., *adv. Math.* 1.4.
[30] *H.N.* 9.154; Sextus Emp., *adv. Math.* 1.4. *Cf.* Plato, *Philebus* 21c; Plautus, *Epid.* 5.1.21 (dubious).
[31] D.L. 10.14.
[32] *Tusc. Disp.* 4.33.70–34.72.
[33] D.L. 10.118; Us. 62, which shows it to be often quoted.
[34] Us. 114.
[35] *Ibid.*
[36] D.L. 10.7; Us. 93, but I read ἴτω σαλάκων instead of ἴτωσαν as being more consistent with the context and the MSS.
[37] D.L. 10.2.
[38] *Ibid.* 10.138.
[39] *Ibid.* 10.9.
[40] Cic., *De Fin.* 1.21.71.
[41] Us. 116.
[42] See pp.186–187.
[43] See pp. 116–117.
[44] *N.D.* 1.26.73; *De Fin.* 1.6.17.
[45] Diels, *Vorsokratiker*[5] 49, vol. 2, p. 97.
[46] Lucr. 2.216–293; p. 120.
[47] D.L. 10.23.
[48] *Ibid.* 2.11.
[49] Lucr. 4.822–876.
[50] *RS* 32.
[51] Demosth. 51.38, vol. 7, p. 69 (Loeb).
[52] D.L. 10.13, usually mistranslated to mean he "denied his existence."
[53] Us. 221.
[54] *Ibid.*
[55] Us. 423; Plut., *Non posse* 1091b.
[56] D.L. 10.85.
[57] Bignone, I, 121–149.
[58] D.L. 10.8.

Chapter IV. Mytilene and Lampsacus

[1] Vogliano, frag. 6, col. 2, lines 9–12, p. 59.
[2] *Non posse* 1090e.
[3] D.L. 10.15.
[4] Bignone, II, 43.
[5] A. Momigliano, *Su alcuni dati della vita di Epicuro, RFIC* 13 (1935) 302–316.
[6] D.L. 6.90; *cf.* Val. Max. 9.10.2, *Ext.* 2; 9.12.8, *Ext.* 7.
[7] 35.48 (940).
[8] *Ath. Const.* 57.

[9] *Tusc. Disp.* 3.18.42.
[10] D.L. 10.8; Us. 114; "flatterers of Dionysus," the "deep-voiced", pretentious actors, "would-be law-givers."
[11] *Tusc. Disp.* 3.18.41; Athenaeus 280a–b.
[12] Scholium to *Odyssey* 9.28; Athenaeus 513a; Lucan, *Parasite* 10–11; Ps. Plut., *Vita Homeri* II, 150; Eustatius *Com. on Odyssey,* p. 1612.10; Heracleitus, *Homeric Allegories* 75; Sen., *Ep.* 88.5; Bignone, II, 291–292.

[13] *Odyssey* 9.5–10.

[14] D.L. 10.136, end; Plato, *Timaeus* 80b; Bignone would discern a polemic against Aristotle: I, 321–324, 358; II, 37–39, 170–171.

[15] *Pol.* (VIII) 3.1338a. 27ff.

[16] *Odyssey* 4.805; *Iliad* 6.138.

[17] D.L. 10.137.

[18] D.L. 10.24.

[19] Pytho and Heracleides assassinated King Cotys of Thrace: Plut., *adv. Colot.* 1126c; Evaeon and Timolaus attempted revolution in Lampsacus and Cyzicus respectively: Athenaeus, 508f–509a.

[20] Athenaeus 509b.

[21] Plut., *Non posse* 1090e.

[22] D.L. 10.2. Corrupt text but surviving letters point to ἀπέστη; Usener's reading is sheer invention.

[23] See n. 19.

[24] See n. 19.

[25] Plut., *adv. Colot.* 1126c.

[26] In 309 B.C.: Diod. 20.29.

[27] Us. 389.

[28] D.L. 10.4.

[29] Plut., *adv. Colot.* 1126e–f.

[30] D.L. 10.28.

[31] *Ibid.* 2.102.

[32] *Ibid.* 2.97.

[33] *Ibid.* 2.140; 6.97.

[34] *Ibid.* 2.102.

[35] *Ibid.* 10.5. The MSS. read *Theodotus* (unknown).

[36] Us. 107.

[37] *Non posse* 1095d–e; *adv. Colot.* 1107d–e, 1111f. Croenert differs, p. 13.

[38] *Tusc. Disp.* 5.34.97.

[39] *SV* 41.

[40] D.L. 2.102, beginning, and 103; he had been expelled from Cyrene and prosecuted in Athens.

[41] 13.589.

[42] Sen., *Ep.* 21.3–4. The king is not named, but he must be Lysimachus.

[43] D.L. 2.20; 6.8; Bignone II, 81, n. 2.

[44] *Non posse* 1098b.

[45] D.L. 10.24.

[46] Vogliano, pp. 114–117, esp. 116–117.

[47] D.L. 10.23.

[48] *Ibid.* 2.11.

[49] *In Pisonem* 26.63.

[50] D.L. 10.5.

[51] Vogliano, frag. 6, col. 3, p. 60.

[52] Plato, *Epin.* 981d; *cf.* 985d.

[53] D.L. 10.8.

[54] Croenert, pp. 4–8.

[55] Us. 176; Vogliano, frag. 5, col. 23, p. 49.

[56] Us. 135.

[57] *Odes* 3.16.39–44; Sen., *Ep.* 21.7; Us. 135.

[58] D.L. 10.4, 6–7; one of the papyri throws light on this: Chr. Iensen, *Ein neuer Brief Epikurs* (Berlin: Weidmann, 1933).

[59] *Ibid.* 10.4.

[60] *Ibid.* 10.5.

[61] 589.

[62] Us. 107.

[63] *Ibid.* 101, 107–110.

[64] *Anab.* 1.9.11.

[65] 3.1,8.

[66] *SV* 79.

[67] 9.4.

[68] It may denote *akedia*, freedom from a feeling of responsibility; *aponia*, exemption from responsibility; or ataraxy, freedom from turmoil of soul. See Latin lexicon.

[69] I Thess. 5:3.

[70] 6, 7, 13, 14, 28, 31, 32, 39, 40.

[71] D.L. 10.121.

[72] *Epodes* 8.15–16.

[73] *Ep.* 1.7. Epicurus wrote *On Gifts and Gratitude*: D.L. 10.28.

[74] Plut., *adv. Colot.* 1125c.

[75] *Ibid.* 1120b–c.

[76] *Tusc. Disp.* 2.3.7–8.

Chapter V. The New School in Athens

[1] D.L. 5.38.

[2] Athenaeus 508–509.

[3] Bignone, II, 134–143.

[4] D.L. 10.5.

[5] Wilamowitz, *Antigonos von Carystos* (Berlin: Weidmann, 1881), pp. 263–291.

[6] *De Fin.* 1.20.65.

[7] D.L. 4.3.

[8] Elias, *Com. in Arist. Graeca: Categ.* 118.18.

[9] Plato, *Lysis*, chap. 1.

[10] D.L. 5.51–57.

[11] *Ibid.* 7.185.

[12] *Ibid.* 10.16–21.

[13] N. W. DeWitt, "The Three-Wheeled Chair of Epicurus," *CP* 35(1940) 183–185.

[14] D.L. 10.17.
[15] *De Fin.* 5.
[16] Diod. 12.53.2.
[17] Plut., *Non posse* 1098b.
[18] D.L. 10.20.
[19] *Tusc. Disp.* 3.17.37.
[20] Sen., *Ep.* 52.3.
[21] 6.26–28.
[22] See n. 19.
[23] Philod., *On Frankness*, frag. 45.9–11.
[24] Philod., *On Anger*, frag. 45.1; *On Management*, col. 12.20; *Rhet.*, vol. 1, col. 23.22, p. 49 (Sudhaus).
[25] See n. 20.
[26] Sen., *Ep.* 52.4.
[27] Vogliano, frag. 5, cols. 22–28, pp. 48–54.
[28] N. W. DeWitt, "Organization and Procedure in Epicurean Groups," *CP* 31(1936) 208.
[29] Cic., *Tusc. Disp.* 5.26.73; Plut., *adv. Colot.* 1117c.
[30] DeWitt, *op. cit.* (see n. 28), p. 206.
[31] Vogliano, frag. 5, col. 26, lines 4–10, p. 52.
[32] D.L. 10.3, 21.
[33] *Ibid.* 10.19, 23.
[34] *Orator* 151; *N.D.* 1.33.93; Pliny, *H.N.*, Praefat. 29.
[35] Pliny, *H.N.* 35.99, 144.
[36] Athenaeus 593b–d.
[37] Plut., *Non posse* 1097e; D.L. 10.7.
[38] D.L. 10.21.
[39] *Ibid.* 10.17, 21.
[40] Plut., *adv. Colot.* 1117b–c.
[41] See n. 31.
[42] DeWitt, *op. cit.* (see n. 28), pp. 207–209.
[43] *Ibid.*, p. 207.
[44] D.L. 4.63.
[45] *Adv. Colot.* 1117a.
[46] D.L. 4.22; Bignone, I, 53, n. 2.
[47] D.L. 10.19, 26.
[48] Plut., *adv. Colot.* 1117b–c.
[49] *Tusc. Disp.* 5.26.73.

[50] Plut., *adv. Colot.* 1117d–e; Athenaeus 279f.
[51] Us. 49, p. 111.3–7.
[52] *Ibid.* 185.
[53] DeWitt, *op. cit.* (see n. 28), p. 206. For the value of reverence see Sen., *Ep.* 11.8–10.
[54] *Ep.* 1.1.48.
[55] *Brutus* 35.131.
[56] *In Pisonem* 25.59.
[57] *De Fin.* 5.1.3.
[58] *H.N.* 35.5.
[59] Us. 390.
[60] *Ibid.* 390–391.
[61] *SV* 52.
[62] D.L. 10.9.
[63] *Ibid.*
[64] *Ibid.*; the scholarchs were not innumerable, as translators misconstrue it.
[65] Us. 181.
[66] D.L. 10.120, end.
[67] Eph. 3:19; 4:13.
[68] N. W. DeWitt, "Epicurean Contubernium," *TAPA* 67(1936) 55–63.
[69] *Dialogus* 13.
[70] *Ep.* 6.6.
[71] D.L. 10.20.
[72] *Ibid.* 10.27–28; five rolls on Metrodorus; one each on his three brothers and Hegesianax; large rolls on Themista: Cic., *De Fin.* 2.21.68.
[73] Plut., *Non posse* 1089c.
[74] D.L. 10.130–131.
[75] *Ibid.* 10.6.
[76] *SV* 10. Eurip., *Ion* 1076.
[77] Plut., *Phocion* 28.
[78] *SV* 29; Lucr. 5.111–112.
[79] D.L. 6.101.
[80] If Bignone (II, 239–241) correctly interprets D.L. 10.4.
[81] Menippus D.L. 6.101; Cic., *De Fin.* 2.31.103; Pliny, *H.N.* 35.5; Plut., *Non posse* 1089c; Athenaeus 298d.
[82] *Anth. Pal.* 9.44.

Chapter VI. The New Education

[1] Plut., *Non posse* 1095e.
[2] *De Musica* 4, cols. 3, 18, 24, pp. 64–66, 84–85, 92–93 (Kemke).
[3] D.L. 10.77.
[4] *Ibid.* 120.
[5] Plut., *Non posse* 1086f–1087a.
[6] N. W. DeWitt, *CP*(1936) 207–208; Philonides at the court of Antiochus Epiphanes was surrounded by a throng of them: *RhM* 56(1901) 145.
[7] D.L. 10.120.
[8] Us. 8, p. 95.5–8.
[9] D.L. 10.79; H. J. Leon, *Astronomy in Lucretius* (Rand Studies, 1938), pp. 163–176.
[10] 246–247.
[11] 3.16–18.

[12] *Ibid.* 25.
[13] Plut., *adv. Colot.* 1117b.
[14] D.L. 10.36.
[15] *Tusc. Disp.* 5.39.114.
[16] 3.74.
[17] D.L. 10.36.
[18] *Ibid.* 35.
[19] *Eth. Nic.* 1094a.
[20] D.L. 10.36.
[21] *Ibid.* 10.79.
[22] *De Fin.* 2.7.20.
[23] Probably A. W. Mair: *Quarterly Review* 185(1897) 75.
[24] D.L. 10.84.
[25] *Ibid.* 83, end; 85.
[26] 1.407–408; *cf.* 1115–1117.
[27] D.L. 10.36. Both Hicks and Bailey mistranslate. Usener's text is best.
[28] *Ibid.* 10.39–40.
[29] *Ibid.* 10.36. Usener's text is best.
[30] *Eth. Nic.* 1095a, end.
[31] D.L. 10.45.
[32] One Philistas praised by Carneiscus: Croenert, pp. 69–72; the unknown author of No. 176 was writing of the friends of Epicurus, beginning with Hermarchus: Vogliano, frag. 5, col. 24, p. 50; No. 1044 was in praise of Philonides: brief account by Usener, *RhM* 56(1901) 145–148 with refs. to earlier literature.
[33] D.L. 10.25.
[34] *Ep.* 33.4.
[35] Lists in D.L. 10.24–28.
[36] *Ibid.*: list in 10.24.
[37] *In Pisonem* 26.63; Us., p. 101.
[38] *Lover of Lies*, end.
[39] Cic., *N.D.* 1.33.93; Pliny *H.N.*, Praefat. 29.

[40] Plut., *adv. Colot.* 1127c.
[41] Us. 114; Platonists were not named, but they were the usual target of scorn. Plutarch relates how the Macedonians lowered their voices "like tragic actors" after assuming the title of king: *Demetrius* 18; *cf.* Demosth., *On the Crown* 262.
[42] D.L. 10.8.
[43] *Ibid.* 2.60; 3.36.
[44] *Timaeus* 81c–d.
[45] Us. 174.
[46] D.L. 2.14; 10.12.
[47] Lucr. 3.371, 1039–1041; 5.622.
[48] D.L. 10.27.
[49] *Ibid.* 10.25.
[50] *Ibid.* 10.24.
[51] Plut., *De Occulte Vivendo* 1129a.
[52] I Cor. 12:20.
[53] Sen., *Ep.* 79.16.
[54] Lucr. 3.874, 1019.
[55] Croenert, pp. 69–72.
[56] D.L. 10.27–28.
[57] *Ibid.* 10.27.
[58] *De Fin.* 2.21.67–68.
[59] D.L. 10.28.
[60] Usener, *RhM* 56(1901) 145–148.
[61] II Thess. 2:3–4.
[62] Usener, *RhM* 56 (1901) 146.
[63] R. T. Ohl, "Ironic Reserve in Horace," *CW* 43(1949) 35–40. An unintended tribute to Epicurean ethics.
[64] Us. 176; Bailey, frag. 35; Vogliano, frag. 5, col. 23, p. 49.
[65] Vogliano, pp. 116–118.
[66] Usener, *RhM* 56 (1901) 148.
[67] *Non posse* 1101b.
[68] 7.5, 9; 10.11, 13, 22, 30.

Chapter VII. The Canon, Reason and Nature

[1] Us. 242.
[2] 4.513–521.
[3] D.L. 10.39.
[4] *Ibid.* 44.
[5] *Ibid.* 32.
[6] Cic., *De Fin.* 9.30.
[7] D.L. 10.31.
[8] *Ibid.*
[9] *Ibid.*
[10] *Ibid.*
[11] *De Sensu* 442b.
[12] D.L. 10.32. Modern empiricism has arisen from the mistranslation of this sentence.
[13] *Ibid.* 10.59, end. Mistranslated by both Hicks and Bailey.
[14] *Ibid.* 10.42.
[15] *N.D.* 1.16.43; *De Fin.* 1.19.63.
[16] *Adv. Colot.* 1118a.
[17] *Ep.* 2.2.2. (Loeb 4.17, p. 309).
[18] 5.1362.
[19] *SV* 21.
[20] D.L. 10.75.
[21] Us. 469.

²² *De Fin.* 1.9.30.
²³ D.L. 10.33.
²⁴ *Eth. Nic.* 1173a.4–5 (Oxford).
²⁵ This is citable only in Latin: Hor., *Sat.* 1.1.49–50; but see *RS* 3, 18, 20.
²⁶ D.L. 10.75.
²⁷ 5.953–987, 1011–1027, 1281–1296.
²⁸ Us. 335.
²⁹ D.L. 10.76.
³⁰ 5.1046–1049.

³¹ 5.181–186.
³² *De Fin.* 1.19.63.
³³ D.L. 10.37–38.
³⁴ *Ibid.* 10.120.
³⁵ *Ibid.* 10.13.
³⁶ *Ibid.*
³⁷ *Ibid.*
³⁸ *Ibid.* 10.120.
³⁹ *Ibid.* 10.31.
⁴⁰ *Ibid.* 10.34.
⁴¹ *Ibid.* 10.37.

Chapter VIII. Sensations, Anticipations, and Feelings

¹ 10.31–32; Lucr. 4.379–468.
² Us. 250, esp. p. 184.27–31.
³ Cic., *De Fin.* 1.9.30.
⁴ Bailey, p. 163; Hicks 10.32.
⁵ D.L. 10.45. Editors misunderstand and emend.
⁶ *Ibid.* 10.63; Lucr. 3.161–167.
⁷ *De Anima* 427b–428b (four times); *De Sensu* 442b (Oxford).
⁸ *Adv. Colot.* 1121d; Us. 247, p. 180.5, 9–10; 248, 250, p. 184.1–3.
⁹ 4.387–396, 420–425, 443–446.
¹⁰ *De Anima* 428a.
¹¹ D.L. 10.32, 51, 88, 102, 110.
¹² *Ibid.* 10.80.
¹³ *Ibid.* 10.32.
¹⁴ Us. 247, pp. 180.16–181.6.
¹⁵ Lucr. 4.438–442.
¹⁶ D.L. 10.32.
¹⁷ N. W. DeWitt, "Epicurus: All Sensations are True," *TAPA* 74(1943) 32.
¹⁸ D.L. 10.38.
¹⁹ *Ibid.* 10.32.
²⁰ *Ibid.* 10.31.
²¹ *Ibid.* 10.82.
²² *Ibid.* 10.80. Cf. Us. 247.20–21, where *phantasia* is equated with clear vision.
²³ *Ibid.* 10.91; Lucr. 5.564–591; Cleomedes, *Cyclic. Theor.* 2.1.87; *De Fin.* 1.6.20; *Acad.* 82.123.
²⁴ D.L. 10.87.
²⁵ *Ibid.* 10.34.
²⁶ The language of the law-court is regular: "confirm by evidence," "contradict by evidence," "decision." See *RS* 147, end; D.L. 10.34, 50, 51.
²⁷ D.L. 10.38.
²⁸ *Ibid.* 10.82.
²⁹ J. S. Reid, Cicero's *Academica* (London: MacMillan, 1885), p. 55.
³⁰ See n. 8.

³¹ *H.N.* 8.5.
³² *Ibid.* 1.
³³ *N.D.* 1.17.44.
³⁴ 10.34.
³⁵ Otto Jespersen, *Language, Its Nature, Development and Origin* (London: Allen and Unwin, 1922), 388–390.
³⁶ D.L. 10.124.
³⁷ *RS* 10.37, 38.
³⁸ *N.D.* 1.17.44.
³⁹ *Ibid.*
⁴⁰ *Atomists* 557.1.
⁴¹ 5.1028–1040.
⁴² Cic., *De Fin.* 1.9.30.
⁴³ *Meno* 81d; *Phaedrus* 249b; *Phaedo* 72e.
⁴⁴ D.L. 10.124.
⁴⁵ 2.6.29 (753b).
⁴⁶ D.L. 10.72–73; Us. 294.
⁴⁷ *Ibid.* 7.54.
⁴⁸ *De Fin.* 1.9.31.
⁴⁹ Eleven examples cited by C. J. Vooys, *Index Philodemius* (Purmerend: J. Muusses, 1934 and 1941).
⁵⁰ Cols. 21.35–22.3.
⁵¹ A poem with this title is found in the *Appendix Vergiliana* (R. Ellis, Oxford, 1907).
⁵² *De Off.* 3.20.81, end; cf. *Tusc. Disp.* 4.24.53; *Top.* 31.
⁵³ *Ibid.* 19.76.
⁵⁴ *Rep.* 462a; Cic., *N.D.* 1.14.37.
⁵⁵ *Orator* 5.18; 38.133.
⁵⁶ *Rhet.*, vol. 1, p. 255, col. 21.10–20 (Sudhaus).
⁵⁷ 5.1046–1049.
⁵⁸ *Ibid.* 181–186.
⁵⁹ D.L. 10.34.
⁶⁰ *De Anima* 13b, 14b, 34a; *Eth. Nic.* 1174b.20–23 (Oxford).
⁶¹ D.L. 10.66 scholium; Lucr. 3.140–144; 273–275.

[62] *SV* 48.
[63] *Ibid.* 81.
[64] Us. 68.
[65] See Chap. XII.
[66] See n. 61.
[67] 10.128.
[68] *SV* 17.
[69] D.L. 10.79.
[70] *Ibid.* 85.

[71] Theophrastus, *Characters* 28 (Jebb-Sandys).
[72] Cf. *RS* 35; *SV* 6, 7, 12, 70.
[73] Plut., *Non posse* 1104b.
[74] Frag. 57, p. 54.
[75] *RS* 14, 15; *SV* 25, 45, 63, 67, 68, 69, 81.
[76] *SV* 71.
[77] Plut., *Non posse* 1091b.

Chapter IX. The New Physics

[1] D.L. 10.85.
[2] *Lover of Lies*, end.
[3] D.L. 10.44 scholium.
[4] *Ibid.* 10.38, end; Lucr. 1.159–207.
[5] D.L. 10.39; Lucr. 1.215–264.
[6] D.L. 10.39–40; Lucr. 1.265–328, 339–397, esp. 357–369.
[7] 1.418–448, esp. 433–439.
[8] D.L. 10.40–41.
[9] *Ibid.* 10.67–68. Volition and sensation are not named, but the soul is viewed as capable "of acting and of being acted upon."
[10] *Atomists* 324–325; Gilbert Murray, *Five Stages of Greek Religion* (Oxford, 1925), p. 133.
[11] D.L. 10.69, end.
[12] 1.453.
[13] *Ibid.* 449–458.
[14] *Ibid.* 70–71.
[15] Plut., *adv. Colot.* 1110c.
[16] 2.730–841, 1004–1012.
[17] D.L. 10.55–56.
[18] *Ibid.* 10.56, beginning.
[19] *Ibid.* 10.42; Lucr. 2.478–521.
[20] D.L. 10.42–43; Lucr. 2.522–568.
[21] Lucr. 5.783–820.
[22] D.L. 10.58–59.
[23] *Ibid.* 10.59, second sentence.
[24] *Ibid.*, end. Sections 58 and 59 are simple; Hicks and Bailey make them abstruse.
[25] *Ibid.* 10.46–47.
[26] *Ibid.* 10.62.
[27] *Ibid.* 10.60.
[28] *Ibid.* 10.46.

[29] *Ibid.* 10.61, end.
[30] *Ibid.* 10.62, *bis*.
[31] *Ibid.* 10.77, end.
[32] *Physics* 216a.15; *De Caelo* 277b.4–5; 308b.20–21.
[33] D.L. 10.62.
[34] Lucr. 2.446.
[35] D.L. 10.48.
[36] *Ibid.* 10.43.
[37] *Ibid.*, end.
[38] *Ibid.* 10.44.
[39] Lucr. 2.214–224.
[40] *Ibid.* 251–293.
[41] D.L. 10.47.
[42] *Ibid.* 10.61.
[43] *Ibid.* 10.46, end; 10.61.
[44] *Ibid.* 10.46, end; novel discussion by Israel E. Drabkin, "Notes on Epicurean Kinetics," *TAPA* 69(1938) 364–374.
[45] *Ibid.* 10.62.
[46] *Ibid.* 10.60.
[47] *Timaeus* 62c–63a. Hicks in *CR* 37 (1923) 108, though elucidating the meaning, fails to see that the argument is directed against Plato.
[48] Even in an infinite universe motions can be opposed to one another.
[49] D.L. 10.60.
[50] Bailey, p. 215.7.
[51] D.L. 10.79, middle.
[52] 2.284–293.
[53] *Ibid.* 216–224.
[54] *Ibid.* 251–293, esp. 255.
[55] 2.930, 975–990; the whole passage, 865–990.

Chapter X. The New Freedom

[1] D.L. 10.133; Us. 375.
[2] D.L. 10.77, end.
[3] Us. 376.
[4] D.L. 10.27.
[5] See διώκω and φεύγω in lexicon.

[6] I Cor. 14:1; I Thess. 5.15.
[7] W. C. Greene, *Moira: Fate, Good and Evil, in Greek Thought* (Cambridge, Harvard University Press, 1944).
[8] For example, the advice of Athena to

NOTES

Telemachus, *Odyssey* 1.279–305 and thereafter.
[9] D.L. 10.134.
[10] *Ibid.* 10.13. He did not deny his existence, as editors claim.
[11] Lucr. 2.257.
[12] *Ibid.* 251–262, esp. 259–260.
[13] Cic., *Div.* 2.47.97; August., *Civ. Dei* 5.2; Suidas 3055A (Gaisford).
[14] D.L. 10.134; Aristotle, *Phys.* 2.5; *De Caelo* 311a 1–6.
[15] Plut., *Demetrius* 34.
[16] *SV* 40.
[17] *Ep.* 1.1.68–69.
[18] *SV* 45.
[19] *Ibid.* 47.
[20] *SV* 17.
[21] D.L. 10.134–135.
[22] Us. 489.
[23] D.L. 10.118.
[24] *Tusc. Disp.* 2.7.17.
[25] *Ep.* 66.18.
[26] Lactantius, *Div. Mot.* 2.8.50 (Brandt).
[27] Chrysippus wrote at length on the topic: D.L. 7.138.
[28] D.L. 10.123.
[29] 7.10, middle.
[30] *Rep.* 379c; *Timaeus* 42d.
[31] *Timaeus* 41c–d, 42d–e.
[32] The case for Plato is stated by Rupert C. Lodge, *Proceedings of the Royal Society of Canada* 43(1949) 87–101.
[33] Bailey errs in the translation.
[34] *Aen.* 10.467–469.
[35] Us. 530.
[36] Us. 387.
[37] Lucr. 5.199.
[38] D.L. 9.63.

[39] D.L. 9.64.
[40] *Ibid.* 5.42, end; Cic., *Ad Att.* 2.16.3.
[41] Frag. 57.1–3.
[42] *Ep.* 22.5.
[43] Us. 8, p. 95.5–8.
[44] *Ad Att.* 14.20.5.
[45] D.L. 10.117.
[46] See the complaint of Demosthenes, *Ep.* 3.31–32, vol. 7, pp. 245–247 (Loeb).
[47] *De Occulte Vivendo* 1128f.
[48] Sen., *Ep.* 21.3; by his will he provided for the preservation of his fame.
[49] *Ibid.* 79.15–16.
[50] D.L. 10.120.
[51] *Odes* 2.10.5–8.
[52] *SV* 81.
[53] *Ibid.* 67.
[54] *De Fin.* 1.20.68.
[55] *Ep.* 1.16.79.
[56] *Tusc. Disp.* 5.32.89.
[57] *Odes* 2.16.13–16; *Sat.* 2.2.70–136.
[58] *SV* 77.
[59] *Ibid.* 44.
[60] Sen., *Ep.* 19.10.
[61] D.L. 10.130–131.
[62] Plut., *Non posse* 1089c.
[63] D.L. 10.130.
[64] *Ibid.* 131.
[65] *Odes* 4.12.28; *cf.* 2.7.27–28.
[66] *Ep.* 1.2.62.
[67] Sen., *Ep.* 18.14.
[68] *Tusc. Disp.* 3.21.50.
[69] *Adv. Colot.* 1118e.
[70] D.L. 10.10.
[71] *Alexander*, end.
[72] Cic., *Brutus* 35.131; *In Pisonem* 25.59.
[73] 3.319–322.

Chapter XI. Soul, Sensation, and Mind

[1] D.L. 10.67.
[2] *Ibid.* 10.63.
[3] *Ibid.*
[4] Lucr. 3.302–306.
[5] D.L. 10.63.
[6] *Ibid.*
[7] 3.316–318.
[8] 3.555, 604, 614, 793, 936, 1009; 5.137; 6.17–18.
[9] 3.425–444.
[10] 12.6.
[11] Acts 9:15; I Thess. 4:4; I Pet. 3:7. But there was also the Hebrew notion of God as the potter, man the vessel: Jer. 18:6; Rom. 9:21.

[12] D.L. 10.64.
[13] *Ibid.* 10.66.
[14] *Non posse* 1089d.
[15] D.L. 10.64.
[16] Lucr. 3.152–160.
[17] *Ibid.* 3.345.
[18] D.L. 10.63; 10.64, end.
[19] *Ibid.* 10.65.
[20] Lucr. 3.370–373.
[21] *Ibid.* 381–390. For weight see 211–215.
[22] D.L. 10.66.
[23] Lucr. 3.266–268.
[24] D.L. 10.66.
[25] Lucr. 3.273–275.

[26] *Aen.* 10.601.
[27] 3.476–505.
[28] 3.421–424.
[29] D.L. 10.28.
[30] *Ibid.* 10.32.
[31] *Eth. Nic.* 1154b.7–9 (Oxford).
[32] *Timaeus* 45b–d.
[33] Theophrastus, *De Sensu* 50.
[34] D.L. 10.49.
[35] *Ibid.* 10.50.
[36] *Ibid.* 10.50, 51.
[37] *Ibid.* 10.32, 52, 53.
[38] *Ibid.* 10.50.
[39] *Ibid.* 10.49–50.
[40] *Ibid.* 10.50: *symmetron.*
[41] *Timaeus* 45c.
[42] D.L. 10.50.
[43] *Ibid.* 10.75; hearing, 52–53.
[44] Lucr. 4.526–546.
[45] *Ibid.* 2.410–413.

[46] D.L. 10.53.
[47] *Ibid.* 52; Lucr. 4.563–567.
[48] D.L. 10.53.
[49] 4.677–686.
[50] D.L. 10.53.
[51] 4.677–686.
[52] 6.76–78.
[53] *Ibid.* 3.246–251.
[54] *Ibid.* 3.152–160, 256–257.
[55] *Ibid.* 4.883.
[56] *Ibid.* 5.534–563.
[57] 3.140–142.
[58] D.L. 10.31. Hicks goes totally astray in his note.
[59] *Ibid.*, end.
[60] *Ibid.* 10.51.
[61] *Ibid.* 10.32, 82.
[62] *RS* 11–13.
[63] D.L. 10.85, end.
[64] *Ibid.* 10.132.

Chapter XII. The New Hedonism

[1] Editors follow Usener in changing ἀπολύσεως to ἀπολαύσεως, "termination" to "enjoyment."
[2] Us. 423.
[3] Cic., *De Fin.* 1.9.31.
[4] Arist., *Eth. Nic.* 1172b.9–10 (Oxford).
[5] Lovejoy and Boas, *A Documentary History of Primitivism* (Baltimore, Johns Hopkins Press, 1935), pp. 103–116.
[6] Arist., *Eth. Nic.* 1173a.4–5.
[7] *De Fin.* 1.9.30.
[8] D.L. 10.132, middle.
[9] See n. 6.
[10] *Odes* 1.31.17–19.
[11] *Cena* 61; *cf.* Lucian, *On the Blunder in Salutation*, 728, 732.
[12] Koerte, col. 6, lines 3–8, p. 581.
[13] *Ep.* 1.18, end.
[14] Us. 68.
[15] D.L. 10.117.
[16] *Ibid.* 10.37.
[17] Us. 413.21–25.
[18] *Tusc. Disp.* 5.34.97.
[19] Plut., *adv. Colot.* 1107e, 1111f; *Non posse* 1095d–e. Croenert differs, p. 13.
[20] *Tusc. Disp.* 3.18.41, 43.
[21] He employed the hedonist Theodorus as envoy: D.L. 2.102.
[22] D.L. 10.130–131.
[23] *Rep.* 588c; for insatiability see 562c, 586b.
[24] *Ep.* 66.46.

[25] *De Fin.* 1.11.38; 2.3.10.
[26] 5.1427–1429.
[27] Us. 181.
[28] *Ibid.* 207.
[29] D.L. 10.128.
[30] 4.18–20.
[31] 3.945, 1081.
[32] 3.938, 960.
[33] Frag. 2.2.7–3.1.
[34] D.L. 10.124.
[35] *Ep.* 93.
[36] Us. 68.
[37] D.L. 10.124, middle.
[38] *De Fin.* 2.4.12–13.
[39] *Ibid.* 2.5.17.
[40] Frag. 2, pp. 349–350 (Kock).
[41] Us. 432.
[42] Us. 181.
[43] See Chapter IV.
[44] *Eth. Nic.* 1175b.36—1176a.1–3 (Oxford).
[45] Pytho and Heracleides murdered Cotys, king of Thrace; Chion and Leonides murdered Clearchus, tyrant of Pontic Heraclea; Dion of Syracuse was done in by a fellow-Platonist, Callippus, who met a like fate. Consult *PW*.
[46] Us. 409.
[47] D.L. 10.129, beginning.
[48] D.L. 10.128, end.
[49] *SV* 29.
[50] 5.110–113.

[51] Us. 221.
[52] D.L. 10.128, end.
[53] De Fin. 2.3.9–5.17.
[54] P. E. More, Hellenistic Philosophies (Princeton University Press, 1923) 20.
[55] D.L. 10.131, middle.
[56] Atomists 526.
[57] RS 4; D.L. 10.130.
[58] Tusc. Disp. 5.10.30, 31.87; 2.7.17–10.25.
[59] D.L. 10.118.
[60] Ibid. 10.22.
[61] Ibid. 10.136.

[62] Tusc. Disp. 5.9.24–25.
[63] Us. 447.
[64] D.L. 10.130.
[65] Us. 116.
[66] See n. 58.
[67] Eth. Nic. 1175a.29–37 (Oxford).
[68] Ibid. 1172b.31–32.
[69] 1.450–454; 3.327–330.
[70] Us. 512.
[71] Ep. 1.6.31–32.
[72] Dio Cass. 47.49.
[73] Us. 116.

Chapter XIII. The True Piety

[1] D.L. 10.123.
[2] Ibid. 77.
[3] Ibid. 115–116.
[4] Frag. 57.1–3.
[5] D.L. 10.123.
[6] Origen, c. Celsum 4.71–72.
[7] Ibid.
[8] Us. 366.
[9] N.D. 1.56.
[10] Us. 358, end.
[11] D.L. 10.77; Cic., N.D. 2.17.46.
[12] Timaeus 41a; Epin. 984d.
[13] D.L. 10.8, end. Editors wrongly emend to read "Cynics."
[14] Ibid. 123.
[15] N.D. 1.16.43.
[16] Ibid., middle: impressisset. D.L. 10.49.
[17] N.D. 1.17.45.
[18] 4.881–884.
[19] Us. 353.
[20] 5.1161–1193.
[21] Us. 353.
[22] N.D. 1.18.46. Admonet, "gives a hint." Imperfective prefix.
[23] 5.148–149.
[24] N.D. 1.19.49, middle; Us. 355.
[25] N.D. 1.18.46.
[26] 6.77.
[27] Us. 358, end.
[28] Ibid. 352, end.
[29] D.L. 10.123.
[30] Ibid. 67.
[31] I Cor. 15:44.
[32] See Oxford Classical Dictionary, p. 40.8.
[33] H.N. 9.17.
[34] Cic., N.D. 1.18.48.
[35] Lucr. 3.784–793.
[36] Ibid. 3.615–623, 273–275.
[37] Ibid. 5.138–143.
[38] Cic., N.D. 1.18.46–48.

[39] Ibid. 1.10.24.
[40] Ibid.
[41] Ibid. 1.18.47.
[42] Ibid. 1.18–19.49.
[43] Iliad 5.339–340.
[44] Bailey, p. 348.
[45] Us. 394, end; cf. 393.
[46] Us. 355.11–13.
[47] On the Gods 3, col. 10.2–6 (Diels).
[48] N.D. 1.19.49.
[49] Ibid. 1.39.109.
[50] Us. 40.
[51] Aristot., Metaph. 999b, 1016b.
[52] See n. 48; Lucr. 5.1176.
[53] On Anger, col. 30.19–21 (Wilke); Philip Merlan, Zwei Fragen der Epikureischen Theologie, Hermes 68(1933) 196–217.
[54] See n. 48.
[55] Ibid.
[56] N.D. 1.41.114. Both afflux and efflux mentioned.
[57] De Defectu Orac. 420d.
[58] Us. 361.
[59] D.L. 10.124.
[60] 5.82; Sat. 1.5.101.
[61] 959–961.
[62] D.L. 10.135; SV 78.
[63] De Defectu Orac. 420d.
[64] Us. 364, p. 243, top.
[65] 3.18–24.
[66] D.L. 10.117.
[67] Timaeus 41a.
[68] D.L. 10.166.
[69] N.D. 1.19.50.
[70] Bailey would dissent: Atomists, pp. 461–467.
[71] Us. 368, pp. 247–248, bottom and top.
[72] N.D. 2.46.
[73] Ibid. 1.19.50.
[74] Koerte, p. 570, bottom; P. H. and E. A.

EPICURUS AND HIS PHILOSOPHY

DeLacy, *Philodemus: On Methods of Inference* (Lancaster, Pa.: Lancaster Press, 1941), col. 14, lines 26–27, p. 55.
75 *N.D.* 1.19.50.
76 Bailey would dissent: *Atomists*, p. 464.
77 Lucr. 5.91–109.
78 D.L. 10.39.
79 *N.D.* 1.19.50.
80 *Iliad* 6.138; *Odyssey* 4.805.
81 D.L. 10.121.
82 *Ibid.* 10.8; editors wrongly emend to read "Cynics."
83 D.L. 10.76–77.
84 *Acad.* 2.38.121; very commendable is A.-J. Festugière, *Epicure et ses Dieux* (Paris: Presses Universitaires de France, 1946), esp. chap. 5.
85 D.L. 10.124.
86 Us. 374.
87 *De Beneficiis* 4.19.2.
88 Col. 22.1–3; 33.11–18, 23–32; 26.7–14, 24–28.
89 Us. 356.
90 *Ibid.*
91 *Ibid.*
92 D.L. 10.117; Us. 226.
93 *De Fin.* 1.3.10; 3.2–5; *N.D.* 1.4.8; *Tusc. Disp.* 3.5.10, 8.16.
94 Sext. Emp., *adv. Math.* 9.177–178.
95 Us. 387.
96 *Ibid.* 169.

97 *Ibid.* 386.
98 D.L. 10.77.
99 *Adv. Colot.* 1119d–e.
100 D.L. 10.120.
101 *Non posse* 1095e.
102 Us. 386. 8–10.
103 *Ibid.* 386.11–14.
104 *Ibid.* 386.15–18.
105 Plut., *Non posse* 1102b–d; Cic., *N.D.* 1.44.23.
106 Us. 389.
107 Us. 390.
108 Sen., *Ep.* 25.5; 11.8.
109 *Aen.* 10.468–469.
110 3.319–322.
111 D.L. 10.135.
112 *SV* 24.
113 D.L. 10.135.
114 *N.D.* 2.65.162.
115 *Alexander* 25.
116 D.L. 10.115–116.
117 *Alexander* 25, 44–46.
118 I Thess. 5:3.
119 *Antiq. Iud.* 10.11.7.
120 *Alexander* 5, 8.
121 *Prometh.* 624; Us. 395.16–20.
122 Cic., *Ad Fam.* 9.17.3, end.
123 Us. 388.
124 *Ep.* 1.18.111–112; G. D. Hadzsits, "Significance of Worship and Prayer among the Epicureans," *TAPA* 39(1908) 73–88.

Chapter XIV. The New Virtues

1 *De Fin.* 2.16.51; D.L. 10.28.
2 D.L. 10.132.
3 Aeschines, *c. Timarch.* 9–11; Aristotle, *Ath. Const.* 42.18, 25, 27.
4 *RS* 3, 8; Hor., *Sat.* 1.1.49–51, 2.111–113.
5 *Rep.* 558d–559d; cf. Arist., *Eth. Nic.* 1118b 8–9; 1147b 23–31; 1149b 4–7; 1150a 16–17 (Oxford).
6 *Pro Caelio* 18.42.
7 *Tusc. Disp.* 4.33.70, 34.71.
8 *Eth. Nic.* 1115a–1117a (Oxford).
9 D.L. 10.118, 120.
10 *Ibid.* 10.125.
11 *RS* 28; Cic., *De Fin.* 1.20.68.
12 D.L. 10.120.
13 *Ibid.* 10.83; Cic., *De Fin.* 1.15.49.
14 Us. 446–448; Cic., *De Fin.* 1.15.49.
15 T. F. Mayo, *Epicurus in England* (Dallas: Southwest Press, 1934), p. xi.
16 *Rep.* 359a.
17 *H.N.* 8.15.
18 D.L. 10.81; *SV* 49, 72.

19 *Sat.* 1.4.73–74; D.L. 10.120.
20 D.L. 10.8; Us. 114.
21 Plut., *adv. Colot.* 1127b–c.
22 Demosth., *Exordium* 54 (Loeb, vol. 7, p. 187).
23 D.L. 10.83.
24 Cic., *De Fin.* 1.9.30.
25 Us. 163.
26 D.L. 10.8.
27 Plut., *adv. Colot.* 1118a, d. His irony was condemned: Cic., *Brutus* 85.292.
28 D.L. 10.117.
29 *Ibid.* 10.120.
30 *Ibid.* 10.118. Various emendations: read διὰ ὁδοῦ; for life as a journey see *SV* 48.
31 D.L. 10.119. Hicks and Bailey both misinterpret.
32 *Ibid.* 10.5.
33 *Non posse* 1101b.
34 Us. 512.
35 *Non posse* 1095c.
36 5.18; 6.20; 8.28.

374

[37] *Sat.* 5.39–42.
[38] *Ad Fam.* 12.27.
[39] *Odes* 1.24.7.
[40] *Vita* 15; R. J. Leslie, *The Epicureanism of Titus Pomponius Atticus* (Columbia dissertation, 1950), pp. 66–73, differs.
[41] *Meditations* 1.15.
[42] *Sat.* 1.4.132.
[43] Plut., *Antony* 24, end; Cic., *Phil.* 2.17.42.
[44] N. W. DeWitt, "Organization and Procedure in Epicurean Groups," *CP* 31(1936) 207–209.
[45] *Eph.* 4:15.
[46] D.L. 10.8, 120.
[47] *Gal.* 5:6.
[48] D.L. 10.63.
[49] *Ibid.* 10.85.
[50] *Ibid.* 10.78–79. Plato, as usual, is not named.
[51] *Us.* 532.
[52] *Heb.* 11.
[53] *Gal.* 3:11; I *Cor.* 15:56.
[54] *Us.* 221.
[55] D.L. 10.9.
[56] Demosth., *On the Crown* 251.
[57] *Aeschines* 3.194.
[58] W. Schmid, *Studia Herculanensia*, Fasc. I, *Ethica Epikurea*, Pap. Herc. 1251 (Leipzig; Harrassowitz, 1939), col. 22, lines 15–21.
[59] D.L. 10.120.
[60] *Ibid.*, end.
[61] Sen., *Ep.* 19.10.
[62] *Confess.* 6.16; *Us.* 397, end.
[63] 1.141.
[64] 18.66.
[65] Chap. 1.
[66] *Ad Fam.* 15.14.6.
[67] *Ibid.* 9.18.1.
[68] *Ibid.* 9.11.1.
[69] *Ibid.* 7.33.1.
[70] D.L. 10.119.
[71] Plut., *adv. Colot.* 1107d. D.L. 10.4–5.
[72] *Us.* 183.
[73] D.L. 10.5.
[74] *Ibid.* 10.6.
[75] *Ibid.* 4.12.
[76] *Eth. Nic.* 1137b.24–27 (Oxford).
[77] *Ibid.* 1126b.22–31.
[78] See n. 58.
[79] *De Off.* 3.19.76, 20.81.
[80] *Alexander* 61.
[81] D.L. 10.10; *Tusc. Disp.* 3.21.50.
[82] *Sat.* 1.3.66–67.
[83] *Adv. Colot.* 1118d.

[84] D.L. 10.24.
[85] *Us.* 176. The context in the papyrus requires ascription to Polyaenus: Vogliano, pp. 114–119.
[86] *Sat.* 1.3.115–119.
[87] *Ep.* 105.
[88] Hor., *Sat.* 1.3.66; Sen., *Ep.* 105.4; *Harper's Latin Dictionary s.v. sensus* II.3.
[89] I *Thess.* 4:13.
[90] *Tusc. Disp.* 3.15.33.
[91] D.L. 10.133.
[92] *Ibid.* 10.135.
[93] *Ibid.* 10.127.
[94] *Ad Fam.* 9.17.3.
[95] *Stromata* 2.21.131, p. 498; Koerte, col. 6, p. 540.
[96] *Ibid.*
[97] *De Fin.* 2.28.92; *Tusc. Disp.* 2.6.17; 5.9.27; *De Off.* 3.33.117; A. Gellius 9.5.2; for Cleomedes see Us., p. 89.18–29; Plut., *Non posse* 1090; Origen *c. Celsum* 3.80, end.
[98] *Non posse* 1090a–c.
[99] *Ibid.* 1089d. See n. 97.
[100] *Us.* 395.
[101] *Odes* 1.9.13–15; *Ep.* 1.4.14–15.
[102] D.L. 10.122. *Cf.* Hor., *Ep.* 1.2.41–42.
[103] *Odes* 1.11.8; *Ep.* 1.2.40–41.
[104] *Ep.* 13.16; 23.9.
[105] *Us.* 489 in part.
[106] *Odes* 2.3.
[107] *Ep.* 1.6.
[108] 1.24.19–20.
[109] Cic., *De Fin.* 1.17.57; 2.32.104–105.
[110] Herod. 1.32; Plut., *Solon* 27.
[111] *Phaedo* 67c–68; Cic., *Tusc. Disp.* 1.30.74.
[112] D.L. 10.11.
[113] *Ibid.* 10.10; Diod. 12.53.2.
[114] *Us.* 130.
[115] Dittenberger, *Sylloge* 834.21.
[116] Frag. 2.5.14.
[117] *Us.* 469.
[118] *Ibid.* 489, in part.
[119] 2.17.
[120] *Ibid.* 3.931–962.
[121] D.L. 10.28.
[122] *Ibid.* 10.120, end.
[123] *Ibid.* 10.118.
[124] 1.4.81–85.
[125] D.L. 10.122.
[126] Sen., *Ep.* 15.9.
[127] *Odes* 3.29.43–48.
[128] Cic., *De Fin.* 1.15.49; Lucr. 3.960; Hor., *Sat.*, 1.1.117–118.
[129] Frag. 2.2.7–13.

Chapter XV. Extension, Submergence, and Revival

[1] Evidences assembled: Lactantius *Div. Inst.* 3.17; Lucr. 5.19–21; Cic., *De Fin.* 1.7.25; 2.9.28, 14.44, 15.49, 25.81, 34.115; *Tusc. Disp.* 2.3.7; 3.21.50; 4.3.6; 5.10.28; *De Off.* 3.33.116; whole cities: D.L. 10.9; Pliny, *Ep.* 10.96; Lucian, *Alexander* 25; *CIG* 4149.

[2] *Tusc. Disp.* 5.37.108.

[3] *De Fin.* 2.15.49.

[4] D.L. 4.43.

[5] The contrast between the new and the old education in the *Adelphi*; the scene where Syrus makes game of Demea in the same, 405–432; comparison of lovers with gods, *Andria* 959–961.

[6] D.L. 10.26–27.

[7] Plut., *Non posse* 1100d; Athenaeus 547a.

[8] *CIL* 5.1813, 1939, 2893; 13.350; 8.3463.

[9] Lucr. 3.972–975.

[10] *Ep.* 1.17.10.

[11] D.L. 10.4.

[12] *Ibid.* 10.16–18.

[13] *De Fin.* 5.1.3.

[14] *Ad Fam.* 13.1.3–5.

[15] Suidas, *s.v. Epicurus*; Us. p. 373n.

[16] D.L. 10.25.

[17] Croenert, pp. 100–125; Usener, *RhM* 56 (1901) 146–147; De Falco, *L'Epicureo Dimitrio Lacone* (1923).

[18] *Tusc. Disp.* 3.17.38.

[19] Dessau, *Inscriptiones Selectae* 7784; Dittenberger, *Sylloge* 834; J. H. Oliver, "An Inscription Concerning the Epicurean School at Athens," *TAPA* 69 (1938) 494–499; Lucian, *Eunuchus* 3; Philostratus, *Vitae Soph.* 2.3; Dio Cass. 72.31 (Boissevain).

[20] Two refs. of Epicurus to Zeno are extant, neither unfriendly: D.L. 7.5, 9.

[21] *Ibid.* 7.174, 178.

[22] *Ibid.* 7.180.

[23] Cic., *De Fin.* 1.11.39.

[24] D.L. 10.31.

[25] *Ibid.* 10.4. The time is certain, the welcome inferred.

[26] *Orator* 10.34.

[27] Suetonius, *De Grammaticis* (Roth) 6, 8.

[28] H. Usener, *RhM* 56 (1901) 145.

[29] I Macc. 1:13–14.

[30] Paul Haupt, *AJP* 26 (1905), 125.

[31] H. Danby, *The Mishnah* (Oxford, 1933), p. 449.

[32] *Antiq.* 18.1.4; *Bell. Iud.* 2.8.14.

[33] *Antiq.* 10.11.7.

[34] According to I Thess. 5:23, man is composed of "spirit, soul, and body."

[35] Eph. 4:13; Col. 2:9.

[36] I Thess. 5:3.

[37] II Thess. 2:3–4.

[38] I Thess. 4:13.

[39] Bignone, vol. 2, chap. 11, esp. pp. 561–563.

[40] I Cor. 15:52.

[41] *Ibid.* 55–56: Lucr. 3.874, 1019; *stimulus* as in Vulgate; D.L. 10.124.

[42] I Cor. 15:52. For the association of Epicureans with Christians in popular opinion see Adelaide D. Simpson, "Epicureans, Christians, Atheists in the Second Century," *TAPA* 72 (1941) 372–381.

[43] D.L. 10.25.

[44] *Sat.* 1.6.65–88.

[45] *PW* 15.1, pp. 936–937.

[46] N. W. DeWitt, *Virgil's Biographia Litteraria* (Oxford, 1923), pp. 41–44.

[47] *Ad Fam.* 7.3.1.

[48] D.L. 10.9.

[49] παυσίλυπον.

[50] *CIL* 5.1813.

[51] *PW* 15.1, p. 937.

[52] Eusebius: Quintilius Cremonensis Vergili et Horati familiaris.

[53] *Ad Fam.* 7.26.

[54] *Inst.* 10.1.124.

[55] P. Lunderstedt, *De C. Maecenatis Fragmentis* (Leipzig: Teubner, 1911), 35–36, 46–51; Sen., *Ep.* 101.10–13.

[56] D.L. 10.119, 125–127; *SV* 38.

[57] Valerius Maximus 4.3.6; Plut., *Pyrrhus* 20.395.

[58] Athenaeus 547a; A. Gellius 15.11 assigns the decree authorizing expulsion to 161 B.C.

[59] Croenert, pp. 100, 124; R. Philippson, "Papyrus Herculanensis 831," *AJP* 64 (1943) 161–162.

[60] *De Fin.* 1.3.9; *Brutus* 35.131.

[61] Suet., *De Gram.* 6 (Roth); A. Gellius 5.11.

[62] *Ad Fam.* 7.1.5; 11.28.2.

[63] *Pro Caelio* 17.41.

[64] *De Fin.* 1.11.39.

[65] Plut., *Brutus* 12, 37; Cic., *Ad Fam.* 15.16.

[66] Sall., *Catiline* 51.20.

[67] Pansa's adherence is certain: Cic., *Ad Fam.* 15.19.3. Hirtius moved in Epicurean

circles and was given to good companionship: *Ibid.* 6.12.2; 7.33.1; 9.16.7, 20.2; 16.27.2; *Ad Att.* 12.2.2.

[68] *Ibid.* 11.28.

[69] *Ibid.* 7.12.

[70] *Catalepton* 5.

[71] *Ibid.* 5.9; *Ad Fam.* 6.11.3; *Eclogue* 6.13; *Aen.* 6.264.

[72] J. I. M. Tait, *Philodemus' Influence on the Latin Poets* (Bryn Mawr dissertation, 1941), pp. 1–4.

[73] Pliny *H.N.* 29.15.

[74] *Pro Caelio* 17.41.

[75] *Tusc. Disp.* 3.19.45.

[76] *De Fin.* 4.10; *Tusc. Disp.* 4.7; *De Div.* 2.1–2.

[77] *Ad Fam.* 9.18, 26.

[78] *Tusc. Disp.* 1.23.25; for a study sympathetic toward both Cicero and Epicureanism see Mary N. Porter Packer, *Cicero's Presentation of Epicurean Ethics* (Columbia dissertation, 1938).

[79] Tac., *Ann.* 16.19; G. Highet, "Petronius the Moralist," *TAPA* 72(1941) 176–194.

[80] J. W. Spaeth, Jr., "Persius on Epicurus: A Note on *Satires* 3.83–84," *TAPA* 73(1942) 119–122.

[81] Plut., *Cato* 67–70.

[82] Cic., *Div.* 2.47.97; August., *Civ. Dei* 5.2; Suidas 3055A (Gaisford).

[83] *Ep.* 12.11; 21.9; 33.2.

[84] He accuses him a dozen times of concealing his identity as an Epicurean: see Koetschau's Index *s.v. Epicureus.*

[85] *Alexander* 1, 61.

[86] C. Murley, "Lucretius and the History of Satire," *TAPA* 70 (1939) 380–395.

[87] G. Highet, "The Philosophy of Juvenal," *TAPA* 80(1949) 254–270.

[88] See Teubner edition, Index *s.v. Epicurus*; anonymous refs. frequent, as in the *Parasite*

[89] J. Williams, *Diogenis Oenoandensis Fragmenta* (Leipzig: Teubner, 1907).

[90] Us., *Index Fontium,* p. 427.

[91] *Ibid.*, pp. 438–439.

[92] *Alexander* 25.

[93] Adelaide D. Simpson, *TAPA* 72(1941) 379–381.

[94] George E. McCracken, Arnobius of Sicca ("Ancient Christian Writings," Westminster, Md.: Newman Press, 1949), pp. 29–30, 37–38.

[95] *Div. Inst.* 3.17–18.

[96] *Confess.* 6.16.

[97] *Ep.* 9, p. 99 (Loeb).

[98] Us. 385a, p. 356.

[99] Letter to a priest, 301c.

[100] *Ep.* 118.21.

[101] C. Wotke, *Wiener Studien* 10(1888) 191ff; Von der Muehll, pp. 60–69; Bailey, pp. 107–119.

[102] Raymond van Marle, *The Development of the Italian Schools of Painting* (The Hague, 1923), VII, 240.

INDEX

Academy, as property, 91–93
Acceleration and retardation, 166
Acts of the Apostles, 119
Addition of opinion, 212
Adulation, 97
Advanced studies, 271
aequabilis tributio, 271, 274
aequam memento, 320
Aeschines, s. of sausage-maker, 117
Aëtius, on the gods, 263
Afflux and efflux of images, 264, 266
agapai, 105
agape, 338
Air and serenity, 198
aisthesis, 137, 139–140, 142
akrisia, indecision, 213
Albucius, Titus, 100, 342
Alciphron, ridicules the Canon, 127
Alcius and Philiscus, 342
alethes logos, 155, 350
Alexander, false prophet, 285, 286, 351
Alexander of Aphrodisias, 351
Ambrose, Saint, read Epicurus, 353
amicitia, inadequate, 306
Analogy: tricky, 246; and form of the gods, 251; and seat of reason, 260, 261; and number of the gods, 272–273; and transition, 277
anamnesis, 146
Anaxagoras, 37, 77, 81
Anaxarchus: in India, 21; rebuked, 185–186
Anger, and slaves, 194; physical explanation of, 195–196; reciprocal to gratitude, 253
anima = psyche, 211
Animal behavior, 19, 67, 133–134, 143, 145, 207, 216, 220, 295–296
animus, mind, 203; *dianoia,* 211
Antichrist, 338
anticipatio, 143, 150

Anticipations, 13, 142–149; as witnesses, 213
Antigonus, the One-Eyed, 71, 76, 77
antikope, 166
Antioch, school in, 333–334
Antiochus Epiphanes, 119, 120, 335
Antisthenes, harsh, 312
Apathy, not ataraxy, 225
apikoros, unbeliever, 335
apistia, 213
Apocalypse, Epicurean, 108
Apollo, as prophet, 286; Clarius, 284, 286
Apollodorus, historian, 58
Apollodorus, tyrant of the Garden, 114
Apuleius, 352
Arcesilaus, witticism of, 330
arche, 238
Archytas, 109
Aristippus, criticized, 232
Aristobulus, writer, 143
Ariston, on Epicurus, 43
Aristotle: influence of, 10, 13, 65, 220; on sensation, 124; criticized, 167–168, 203; quoted, 204, 236; on *epieikeia,* 313
Arnobius and Lucretius, 45, 352
Articles of Faith, 111
Ascending scale in nature, 161, 260
Ascent and descent, 109, 110
Asclepiades: influence of, 22, 344; attacked, 351
Astrology, 176
Ataraxy: an objective, 5; origin of, 61; not apathy, 225; defined, 226; static pleasure, 240
Athenaeus, 351
Atom: defined, 159; varieties of atoms innumerable, 160; *plektikai,* 165; occurrence of word in New Testament, 339
Atticus: on images, 100; on political activity, 187; praised, 302, 309; lived in Athens, 343

378

INDEX

Attitudes, the right, 173. *See also* Diathesis

Attributes and accidents, 148, 159–160

Augustine, Saint: on size of images, 258–259; partial to Epicurus, 352, 353

Aurelius Opilius, 342

Authorized Doctrines: anti-Platonic, 11, 48; memorized, 38; excerpted, 47; and Homer, 75; on safety, 79, 85–86; meaning of name, 111; and skepticism, 140–141; and prolepsis, 147

Axiochus, 329

Bailey, Cyril, 361, 362, 368, 369, 370, 371, 373

Banquets of Epicureans, 104–105, 192

Basil, Saint, 353

beatus, 242

Beginning and end, 238–239

bene vixi, 230

Benn, A. W., 361

Bereavement, attitude toward, 321

Bernier, François, 356

Big Epitome, 5

Bignone, Ettore, 362, 364, 365, 366, 367

Biology, influence of, 13, 22–23, 133–134, 263

Blushing, *etc.*, 200, 210

Bocchus, King, 296

Body: envelope or vessel, 199–200; not a prison, 224

bona mens, 224, 341

Bosco Reale treasure, 354

Breast, seat of soul, 202

Brilliant letter, 47, 117

Brink, K. O., 361, 364

Brothers of Epicurus, 95

Brutus, Marcus: last words, 247; praised, 333

Cadetship, 49–51

Calculus of Advantage, 192, 194, 244

Calpurnius Piso, 343

Candor, 302, 311, 326

Canon, 21, 24, 62, 64–65; meaning of word, 121; ridicule of, 126–127

Carneiscus, 57, 119

carpe diem, 319

Cassius, 343

Catechumens, 96

Catius, 30, 341

Cato, 347

Cause, problem of, 168–170, 171–172

Ceilings of pleasure, 226–229

Celsus: against Christianity, 155, 349–350; on god of wrath, 253; and Lucian, 331

Centaur, 138, 208–209, 284

Chaerestrate, m. of Epicurus, 39, 41–42; letter to, 58–59

Chain arguments, examples of, 253–254, 260, 270, 303–304, 311, 323

Chance, 172. *See also* Fortune

Chaos, 42, 43

chara, peak of pleasure, 151

Choosing and Avoiding, 173

Christ, images of, 101

Christian, the name, 334

Christians: competitors of Epicureans, 328; superior in organization, 328

Chrysippus: hostile, 11, 332–333; introduced logic, 219–220

Cicero: mentions pamphlet, 30; prefers Plato, 42; scornful, 64, 292; quoted, 73; quotes Ptolemy, 80; *Dream of Scipio*, 110; his knowledge, 144; on prolepsis, 145; *On Duties*, 149; unfair, 178–179, 234, 240, 242; on gods, 254, 256, 258, 266, 272; criticized, 256, 308; on human form, 261; on afflux and efflux, 264; his purpose, 267; on infinity, 271; on forces, 273–274; on Latin language, 278; *On Friendship*, 301, 310; on considerateness, 313; on hope, 316; and Epicureanism, 329, 345–346; and Zeno of Gaza, 332; distorts tradition, 349

Civilization, origin of, 129–130

Cleanthes, 332

Clement of Alexandria, 317

Cleruch, 40, 41

Colophon, 56

Color, not corporeal, 160

Colotes, satirist, 80, 83, 87, 96, 97, 227, 348

comitas, 302, 333

Communion: of saints, 282; according to Stoics, 279

Comte, Auguste, 7, 18–20

Condensation of image, 206, 235, 241, 267, 318

consensus, new meaning of, 201

Considerateness, 312–315

Control: of environment, 342; of experience, 171, 182, 186, 217, 233, 317–318; of thought, 233, 322

contubernium, 103

Corinth, Epicurean city, 338

Cornelius Nepos, 302
Corruption and incorruption, in New Testament, 339
Corybantes, 307
Cosensitivity, 198, 200–201
Counterpoise to immortality, 327
Courage, 293–294
Courtesans, names of, 96
Crates, 79
Crime, why it does not pay, 305
Croenert, W., 363, 364, 366, 368, 376
Cultural context, 8–11
Cynics, 9. See also Diogenes
Cyzicus, 77; seat of school of Eudoxus, 82–83

Daemons, nonexistent, 262–263
Damoxenos, 235
Danaë, d. of Leontion, 95
Danby, H., 376
Daniel, Book of, 286, 336
Dante, 200, 355
Dareius, on thirst, 227
Death, necessity of, 182–183
Declaration of Independence, 35
declinatio, 165
Deductive reasoning, examples, 9, 156, 157–158, 197–198, 260
De Falco, V., 376
DeLacy, P. H., 361, 374
Demetrius Laco, 331, 342
Demetrius of Magnesia, 50
Demetrius Phalereus, 53, 77: ousted, 84; honored, 298
Demetrius Poliorcetes, 89
Democritus: his cheerfulness, 61, 65; determinism, 66; criticized, 202, 204–205
Democracy, favored by Epicurus, 86–87
Demosthenes, 10, 41, 72
Desires, control of, 193–196
Determinism, 65, 175. See also Necessity
Dialectic: superfluous, 12, 23, 131; dramatized logic, 17; evils of, 47–49; function of, 146
Dialecticians, wholesale destroyers, 300
Diano, C., 362
dianoeseis, 198
dianoia, 125, 203, 205
Diathesis: importance of, 4, 251–252; toward careers, 153; choice of, 173; toward gods, 252–255
Dicaearchus, on Lives, 186
Diocles of Magnesia and Sotion, 330
Diogenes the Cynic, 51, 192, 312, 333, 346

Diogenes Laertius, 6, 38, 43, 76, 351: editions of, 355; on Sensations, 135–137; on Anticipations, 144–145
Diogenes of Oenoanda, 41, 58, 153, 350–351: on death, 186, 252; on victory over death, 230, 327; on salvation, 324
Dionysius, Bishop: on oaths, 281; and Eusebius, 340
Dionysius of Halicarnassus, 333
Disjunctive syllogism: examples of, 140–141, 172, 278; of Lactantius, 276
Divination, evils of, 286
Divine Providence, 179–182
Dogmatic writings, 113–115
Donatus, 269; on epieikeia, 313–314
Double choice, the, 173
Double reactions, 207, 209–210, 212
Drabkin, Israel E., 370
Dreams: explained, 208–209; value as evidence, 209, 257; valueless for prophecy, 284
Dualistic good, 223–226
Dynastic protection, 189–190

Ecclesiastes, 50, 81, 85, 199, 330, 335: on urgency, 182, 319; on fullness of pleasure, 230
Egypt, recruits from, 79–80
eikadistai, 105
Elephants, 23, 143, 295–296
Embryo, 256
Emotional level, 134
Empiricism, 7, 26, 356. See also Epicurus
ennoemata, 136
ennoiai, 135, 136
Envelope, important, 164
Environment, control of, 187–191. See also Control
epaisthema, 205
epaisthesis, 140, 205
epereismos, 205
Epictetus, 328; censorious, 312, 348
Epicureanism: influence of, 8; its two fronts, 8, 32–33; literature, 5; schools, 26; missionary philosophy, 26–29, 329; relation to pragmatism, 30; nonpolitical, 31; and Christianity, 31–32; survival, 33–35; perfection possible, 100; romantic, 270; popularity, 328–332; in Italy, 340–346; in Rome, 342–346; anonymity, 345, 356; in Middle Ages, 353–355; modern revival, 355–358
Epicureans: pamphleteers, 30; bourgeois, 86, 337

INDEX

Epicurus: parentage, 36, 41, 42; appearance, 32; effusiveness, 59, 312; lovable, 194; revered and reviled, 3; as a father, 323; dominance, 88, 114; dogmatist, 7, 20–22; not an egoistic hedonist, 8, 30; erudite, 12–14; self-taught, 64–67; moral reformer, 14–15; as propagandist, 18; as philosopher, 18–20; Antiplatonist, 7, 10; a teaser, 236; educator, 7, 25–26, 63–64; pragmatist, 65, 67–68, 69, 171, 233, 239; intuitionist, 215; his teleology, 221–222; inconsistent, 125–126; polytheist, 258, 262, 273; traditionalist, 262; not an empiricist, 7, 25–26, 112–113, 125, 135; not a martyr, 279; not a prolific writer, 120; accused of disloyalty, 53–54; of hypocrisy, 281, 282; attitude toward fame, 188; toward liturgies, 280–281; toward music, 106–107; on human life, 224–225; on prayer, 224–225, 287; on style, 131; last words, 242; will, 96; in art, 354–355

epieikeia, 48, 312–313

epinoiai, 113, 125, 135, 136–137, 203: of gods, 258; for adults, 252

Epistle, origin of, 87

Epitaph, Epicurean, 330, 341; in Africa, 351

Epithets of gods, 280

Epitomes, use of, 111–113

Erasistratus, 259, 337

Ernout, A., 361

Euclid, influence of, 9, 25, 45

Eudoxans, enemies of Hellas, 255, 275

Eudoxus, 45, 81–82: on the telos, 220; criticized, 255

eukinesia, 198

eunomia, 272

Euphranta, 104

euphrosyne, 74, 104, 107, 151

eusebeia, 254

Eusebius: on Epicureanism, 352–353; on providence, 268; quoted, 281

Evaeon, Platonist, 77, 90

Extramural students, 96

Faculty psychology, 197

Fadius, M., 341

Faith, 5, 213–214, 289–290, 303–305

False opinions, 6–8, 113–114, 153, 189, 297

familiares, 282

Fantastic, defined, 138, 140, 212

Farrington, Benjamin, 361, 364

Fate, fatalism, 174–176

fatis avolsa potestas, 175

Feelings, 150–154; as witnesses, 213

Fellowship, 102–103, 278–283, 343

Festivals, 279, 280–281

Festugière, A.-J., 361, 374

finita potestas, 169

Flesh, opposed to soul or spirit, 216, 225, 337

Flight of the soul, 109

foedera naturae, 175

Forces, pairs of, 273

Fortune, chance, 172: not a fickle cause, 176; and Necessity, 176; and Freedom, 177–179; attitude toward, 320

Four, not canonical, 199

Fourth ingredient of soul, 198

Frankness, exemplified, 84. *See also* Honesty

Freedom: and Necessity, 174–176; and Fortune, 177–178; and the gods, 179–182; and government, 183–185; an option of man, 185; and public careers, 185–187; not a right, 193; of gods, 286

Free will, 62: and the swerve, 169–170; not an ancient concept, 179

Friendship, 101–102, 190–191, 307–310

Fullness, of pleasure, 102–103, 230–232; in New Testament, 338

Galen, 351

galenismos, 226

Gandhi, Mahatma, 98

Garden of Epicurus: as property, 93; cost, 323; visited, 331

Gargettus, deme of Epicurus, 41

Gassendi, Pierre, mistake of, 121–122, 124, 215, 356–357

General concepts, 144, 148

Generation of Animals, 147

Genetic approach, 133–134, 152, 237; process, 256

Geometry: rejected, 12, 25, 108; inspired romanticism, 16; as used by Eudoxus and Plato, 45–46

Gestalt psychology anticipated, 210, 257

Gigon, Olof, 362

Giussani, C., 361

gnorimoi, 102

Gods: nature of, 5; theology reserved for advance study, 26; some of limited substance, 130; in need of freedom, 179; and free will, 179–182; anthropomorphic, 209, 257–261; happiness of, 231; summary, 249–250; knowledge of, 250–252;

not transcendent, 254; existence of, 255–257; not deathless, 267–268; virtue of, 268; must be vigilant, 269, 276; number of, 273; life of, 274–278; immune from labor, 275–276; indifferent to wickedness, 275–276; language of, 277; images of, 279. *See also* Fellowship
Good companionship, 277. *See also* Fellowship
Good will, catchword, 190
Gorgias, his fees, 323
Government, attitude toward, 87
Gradations: in the atoms, 160–161, 202; in godhead, 261–267
Graded texts, 26
Gratitude, 321–327
Greatest good, not pleasure but life, 154, 218; how identified, 219
Greene, W. C., 370
Gymnasiarch, 69, 70, 72, 76, 96–97
Gymnosophists, 98

Habituation, necessary, 233
Hadzsits, G. D., 361, 374
halitus vitalis, 259
Happiness, of two kinds, 275
Haringer, Jakob von, 362
Haupt, Paul, 376
Heap of atoms, impossible, 162
Hearing, 206–207
Hedone, of the body, 104, 151. *See also euphrosyne*
Hedonism: altruistic, egoistic, or universalistic, 8, 31; repellent to many, 33; not learned by Epicurus from teachers, 66; revamped by Epicurus, 216–218
hegemon, 93
Heracleides Ponticus, 77
Heraclitus, on flux, 265
Herculanean papyri, 114, 341
Hermarchus, rhetorician, 47, 76: characterized, 94; as writer, 117–118
Herodotus, deserter, 53–54, 84
Heroes, nonexistent, 262
Hicks, R. D., 361, 368, 369, 370, 372
Highet, Gilbert, 377
Hippocratic medicine, influence of, 27–29, 99, 183, 306, 323
Hirtius and Pansa, 343
Hodgepodge, moral teachings of poets a, 107
Homer: as hedonist, 42–43, 73; textbook on morals, 74; on the gods, 261, 264
homo sum, 30
Homosexuality, 62–63, 292

Honesty, 289, 297–303
Hope, 315–318; and Faith, 318
Horace: partial to Epicurus, 10, 45; on lessening desires, 83; on safety, 85; independent, 86, 120; on Fortune, 177, 320; on ostentation, 188–189; on death, 191, 219; on condensing pleasure, 193, 318; on the dualistic good, 224; on virtue, 247; on prayer, 287–288; on recitations, 298; on loyalty, 300; on candor, 302; on considerateness, 314; on hope, 316; on urgency, 319; on bereavement, 321; on reciprocity of benefits, 325–326; on the past, 327; on the good life, 330; his father Epicurean, 341
Human nature, diversity explained, 195
hupographo, 147
Hylozoism, imputed to Epicurus, 159
ichor, 261
Idols, images, 266
Idomeneus: wrote on Socratics, 81, 116–117; patron, 88, 325; warned, 186–187; letter to, 323
Iliad, 74–75
Images of Epicurus, 100–101, 282
Imagination, associated with reason, 197
Immortal, denotes a quality, 97–98, 226, 269
Immortality, a quality, 270–271
immunitas, of gods, 275
Impiety, as a charge, 69, 72
Impulses: volitional and emotional, 203, 209–210; motor, 210–211
Inconceivable, meaning of, 166
Incorruptible, why retained, 252–253
Incorruptibility and virtue, 267–270
Indecision, evil of, 213
Infallibility of sensation, absurd, 121, 138, 142
infinita species, 265
Infinity: importance of, 271–272; of time, 273
Innate ideas, 145. *See also* Anticipations
Inner life, free, 284, 316, 317
Interference, 166
intermundia, 274
Intuitionism, incompatible with empiricism, 122, 136
Irony condemned, 47, 48, 114, 300
Isocrates, 9, 10, 46, 58
Isonomy, 113, 251, 271–274
Jefferson, Thomas, an Epicurean, 8, 35, 358
Jensen, Chr., 366

INDEX

Jesperson, Otto, 369
Jesus: on urgency, 319; and Epicureanism, 336
Jews, in Alexandria, 339–340
Jonson, Ben, 231–232
Josephus: on Epicurus, 285–286; on Sadducees, 335–336
Julian the apostate, 353
Julius Caesar, 343
Justice, 294–297. See also Social Contract
Juvenal: partial to Epicurus, 10; and Themista, 81; on dualistic good, 224; critical of Stoics, 333

kata homoeideian, 265
kat' arithmon, 265
kataskeuazomenoi, 96
katastematikos, 243
kat' eidos, 265
kathegemon, 94
kathegetes, 94
kedemonia, 47
kinesis, stimulus or reaction, 204, 205, 208, 212, 235
kinetic. See Pleasure
Kochalsky, A., 361
Koerte, A., 363, 372, 373, 375
kuriai doxai, III. See also Authorized Doctrines

Lactantius, 45: on divine wrath, 253–254; on existence of the divine, 272; cites disjunctive syllogism, 276; familiar with Epicureanism, 352
Laertius. See Diogenes Laertius
Lampsacus, 77–84; windy city, 210–211
Language: origin of, 27, 130; nature of, 206
lathe biosas, 188, 299, 330
Laws: and freedom, 183–185; not educators, 294
Leaven, system of, 307, 353
Leon, H. J., 367
Leonteus, patron, 80, 81, 88
Leontion, courtesan, 90; distinguished, 95
Leslie, R. J., 375
Letters of Epicurus, 38, 120, 243. See also Menoeceus
Leucippus, criticized by Epicurus, 67, 175, 306
Levels of experience, 134
liber amicus, 302
Life: the greatest good, 218; a preparation for old age, 322

Linear and vibratory motion, 163–165
Liturgies, esteemed by Epicurus, 288
Lives, as a topic, 186
Locke, John, 8, 35, 122, 215; friend of Bernier, 356–358
Lodge, Rupert C., 371
Logos, as imagination, 163
Love of mankind, 290, 305–307
Lovejoy and Boas, 372
Loyalty to friends, 300
Lucian: on Epicureanism, 116; kinship with Epicureans as satirist, 187, 350; On Salaried Posts, 187; on Epicurus, 194, 285; on Alexander the false prophet, 331; on Epicurean virtues, 314; friend of Celsus, 350
Lucretius: on process of learning, 4–5; on life, 33–34; on flight of the soul, 109; on civilization, 129; on proleptic behavior, 145; deficient on prolepsis, 150; on diversity of character, 195; misleading, 198–199, 270; on conception, 201; on soul, 202; on mortality of mind, 203; inaccurate, 209, 267; on oracles, 239; on dreams, 257; on form of the gods, 258; romantic, 270; on poverty of the Latin language, 278; on life of the gods, 283; hails Epicurus as father, 323; on ingratitude, 324; personifies Nature, 324; his poem a turning point, 344
Luke, Saint: on procrastination, 183, 220; on the name Christian, 334
Lunderstedt, P., 376
Lung-fish, 62
Lyceum, as property, 92
Lycurguses and Solons, would-be, 116
Lysimachus, court of, 78, 80

McCracken, George E., 377
Maecenas, 341–342
Mair, A. W., 361–368
Manlius Torquatus, 343
Manning, Frederic, 361, 364
Marcus Aurelius: influenced by Epicurus, 302, 328, 348; endowed schools, 332
Mark Antony, 302
Marle, Raymond van, 377
Masson, John, 361
Matius, Gaius, 343
Mayo, T. F., 361, 374
Megasthenes, 10, 143, 295
Memmius, 331
Memorial writings, 114, 118–120
Memorization, 25, 112

Menander, 52–53, 180, 269, 313, 330
Menippus, satirist, 105
Menoeceus, letter to: written artfully, 9, 12, 46–47; protreptic, 68; on nature of the gods, 146; on Fortune, 178; on hunger, 227; on tetrapharmacon, 229; on counterpoise for immortality 231; on the gods, 255–256; on the future, 316
mens, meaning of, 211
mens sana in corpore sano, 106
Merlan, Philip, 373
Metrodorus: his assignments, 14; *On Nobility of Birth*, 41; second Epicurus, 81; characterized, 94; on orgies, 109–110; writings, 115, 118; on death, 182, 307; on procrastination, 183, 319–320; on mortality, 218; on pleasure, 238, 243; satirical, 298; on the inner life, 317
Micrometry of atom, 161–162
Mind: automatic or volitional, 141, 208; a mechanism, 208; automatic, 211–212; errs, 212–213; volitional superior, 213; as judge, 213, 214; and soul, how related, 203; summary, 211–215
Minucius Felix, 352
Miserliness and contempt, 188
Mithres, 78–79, 80, 84
Mobs and monarchs, 298
Molière, friend of Gassendi, 356
Momigliano, A., 365
Monarchy, attitude toward, 86
Moral invalidism, refuted, 383
More, P. E., 373
Mortality, calls for counterpoise, 230–231
motio, kinesis, 235
Motion, 162–167
Mourning for dead, 102–103
Murley, C., 377
Murray, Gilbert, 370
Museum, inscription on Plato's, 91
Musonius Rufus, 328, 347
Mys, 95
Mytilene, 71

Naples, Epicureanism at, 341
natura creatrix, 26–27, 128
Nature: furnishes the norm, 10, 127–128; new order of, 22–23; living according to, 23; as teacher, 25, 130–131, 324; meanings of word, 122, 128; priority of, 128–131, 146; before Epicurus, 220; honest, 221, 229; nonpurposive, 223; personified, 222, 230
Nausiphanes, 40, 46, 60–64

Nearchus, writer, 143
Necessity: of the physicists, 165–166; kinds of, 172; and Fortune, 176–177; and freedom, 174–176; of death, 182–183; attitude toward, 320–321. *See also* Determinism
Neighbor, frequent, 309
Neocles, b. of Epicurus, 39
Neocles, f. of Epicurus, 36, 40; rites in honor of, 103
New Testament, 259, 309, 336–339, 358; vocabulary of, 337
Newton, Sir Isaac, and the atom, 356
Nexus between gods and men, 250, 262, 266, 283
nil admirari, 320
Nocturnal sessions, 96
noesis koine, 147
notities, 150
nous, 124
nuda veritas, 302
numerum, ad, 266

Oaths, 281
Odyssey, 73
Oenoanda, 350. *See also* Diogenes of Oenoanda
Ohl, R. T., 368
oikeiotes, 103
Oliver, J. H., 376
Omens from birds, 285
Onesicritus, writer, 143
Origen: accuses Epicurus, 78, and Epicureans, 282; on images, 100–101; on wrath of God, 253; against Celsus, 331; wrote 6,000 books, 120
ousia, 159

Packer, Mary N., Porter, 377
paideia fallacy, 44
Pain: and disease, 216, 223; subtractable, 241–242; not continuous, 244–245
Pamphilus, 43
Panaetius: condemned astrology, 176, 347; in Rome, 340, 344
Papirius Paetus, 316
paregklisis, 165
parresia: and irony, 47; facets of, 289; defined, 297–299. *See also* Honesty
pathe: and criteria, 133; Feelings and Sensations, 151
Patience, 321
Paucity of atoms in soul, 210
Paul, Saint: not taught by man, 14–15;

INDEX

and Peace and Safety, 85, 189, 338; on sin and the law, 153; on fullness, 217; angered by Epicureans, 285; speaking the truth in love, 303, 314; on faith and love, 304; on hope, 315, 338; on death, 327; in 1 Cor. 13

Peace: among neighbors, 189; and Safety, 85, 189, 338

peregrinatio, 110

perfectus Epicureus, 195

periodeia, periodos, 110

Perpendicular universe, 168

Persius, 346

Perversion by education, 221

Petronius: partial to Epicureanism, 10; on dualistic good, 224

Phaedrium, 96

Phanias, Aristotelian, 81

phantasia, defined, 137–138, 140, 141, 205

Phantasm, defined, 137

Philanthropy, 290, 306

philia, amicitia, 101, 305–306, 338

Philippson, R., 361, 376

Philo and Epicureanism, 330, 340

Philodemus: on honesty, 26, 30, 99, 302–303; his life of Epicurus, 81; his epigram, 105; *On the Management of an Estate*, 149; on gods, 264, 277; on units, 264–265; on anger, 265; *On Evidences*, 273; on festivals, 281; on fellowship, 282; in Rome, 344

philologus, 107

Philonides: memoir of, 119; his activities, 120; mathematician, 331

phronesis, prized, 195–196, 214, 291. *See also* Practical reason

Physicists, criticized, 175

Plato: criticized, 16–18, 123–124, 141, 167–168, 170, 180–181, 185, 203, 204, 227, 232, 234, 241, 245–246, 247, 255, 261, 275, 300–301, 322; a romantic, 22; the Golden, 97; viewed as a skeptic, 122

Platonic love, scorned, 293

Platonism, 9: orthodox creed, 43; lapse from popularity, 90; criticized, 300–301

Platonists: violent men, 76, 77; satirized, 116; tyrannicides, 237; criticized, 141, 152, 187, 260, 328

Pleasure: pleasures classified, 66; genetic approach to, 216; and health, 216, 223; and pain, 217; ceilings of, 217; its true nature, 223; basic or decorative, 228–229, 239–240; not increased by immortality, 229–230; its unity, 232–236; ki-

netic or static, 233, 235, 242–243; root of all good, 236; continuous, 239, 244; and virtue, 245–248; priority over virtue, 246

Pledge to Epicurus, 94, 282–283

Pliny: on images of Epicurus, 100; on elephants, 143, 296; on the vital breath, 259

Plotina, Empress: viewed Epicurus as savior, 323–324; interceded for school in Athens, 332

Plutarch: on island birth, 41; against Colotes, 80; on rhetoric, 108; on epithets, 280; on gods of Epicurus, 268, 269; his importance, 348–349

Poetry, Epicurus' attitude toward, 107

poikilmata, 228

Political careers, 185: two kinds, 186; discouraged, 186–187

Political contract, 295

Polyaenus, mathematician, 81: characterized, 94; his letter to a child, 120; considerateness, 314

Popillius Theotimus, 332, 347

Porphyry, commentator, 269

Posidonius, condoned astrology, 176

Posilipo, 341   ,

Practical reason, 193, 214, 222, 292. *See also phronesis*

praenotio, 143, 150

Pragmatism, 194. *See also* Epicurus

Praxiphanes, 13, 36, 46, 51, 56–58

Precision, an objective, 112

Predestination, 181

Preparedness, 320

Prèsent, urgency of, 18, 290, 319

Procedure, logical: from general to particular, 4; deductive, 25–26, 45

Proclus, 57–59

Procrastination, 183, 319–320. *See also* Luke, Saint

Progress toward wisdom, 99, 237, 238

Prolepsis, 143, 144; an innovation, 145. *See also* Anticipations

pronoia, 179, 180

Prophecy and prayer, 283–288

Prudence, personified, 222

Psychical, meaning corporeal, 259

Psychology of Epicurus: psychosomatic, 200; summarized, 211–215

Ptolemaeus, name of two Epicureans, 340

Ptolemy I: and Colotes,79–80; on hunger, 80, 227

puknoma, 110

Pyrrho, skeptic, 21: in India, 61; imperturbable, 62; attracted Epicurus, 143; criticized, 303
Pythagoras: and friendship, 27, 28; criticized, 323
Pythocles, disciple of Epicurus, 83: advice concerning, 300; handsome boy, 312

Quick as thought, 163, 165
Quintilius Varus, 302, 341

Rabbinical literature, 31
ramosus, 165
Rational and irrational soul, 203–210
Reactions, psychosomatic, 133, 203
Reason: and sensation, 128–129, 136; a contingent capacity, 203
Recognition, 205, 206–207
Refutative writings, 113, 115–118
Reid, J. S., 169
Residue of image, 206
Restoration, vogue of Epicureanism under, 357
Revelation, 239
Reverence: due to gods, 82, 107, 254, 285, 279–280; due to Epicurus, 97–100; its guiding power, 254–255, 280
Rhetoric: studied by Epicurus, 46–47; taught by Epicurus, 63; remunerative branch, 75–76; rejected, 108
Rhodes, 59–60

Sadducees, 335
Safety, 147. *See also* Peace
Sardanapalus, 355
Satire: affinity of Epicureanism with, 10; on irony of Socrates, 114; as a weapon, 116; of Colotes, 349; examples of, 350
Savior sentiment, 323
scala naturae, 259, 260
Schmid, W., 375
Scholarchs, list of, 375
Scholium: on causation, 171–172; on parts of the soul, 202; on the gods, 258, 264; to Aeschylus, 287, 318
School, of Epicurus: elementary, 68; as property, 90–93; graded, 99–100; later history, 331–332; in Antioch, 333–336; in Alexandria, 339–340
Schoolteacher, word banned, 93
Seal, simile of, 205
Security, 184. *See also* Peace
Self-sufficiency, 176–177; and freedom, 191

semnoma, 254
Seneca: unfair, 179; on consolation, 231; on gods of Epicurus, 270, 277; on contempt, 315; syncretizer, 328; on hope, 339; on Epicurean themes, 347; in Middle Ages, 354
Sensation: word ambiguous, 135; an accident, 159; workings of, 203–206; irrational, 208
Sensations: discussed, 134–142; as witnesses, 141, 213; not all true, 142
Sensitivity, how shared, 200
sensus: ambiguous, 135; and *phantasia*, 137; *communis*, 315
Septuagint, 340
severitas, 302, 333
Sextus, Empiricus: on life of Epicurus, 42, 64; on *phantasia*, 137; on dreams, 257; on size of images, 258; his disjunctive syllogism, 278
Sibyls, 283–284
Similars, argument from, 272–273, 277. *See also* Analogy
Simple life, and freedom, 191–193
Simpson, Adelaide D., 376, 377
Siro, 341, 343–344
Skepticism, attacked, 140–141. *See also* Pyrrho
Slander, against Epicurus, 6, 28
Smell, 207
Social contract, 29, 34–35, 295
Social level of experience, 134, 152
Socrates, in *Axiochus*, 329. *See also* Irony
Solon, and happiness, 322
soma, 225
Somatic level of experience, 134, 152
Sophists, criticized, 323
Sophocles, law of, 89–90
Sophocles, quoted, 75
sophronistae, 292
Sorites syllogism, 72–73
Sotion, 105, 330
Soul: composition, 197–200; nature, 197–198; unity, 202–203
Spaeth, J. W., 377
speciem, ad, 265; *infinita species*, 265
Spencer, Herbert, 7
Speusippus, invalid, 91
Sphaerus, 332
Sphericity, and the gods, 261
Spiritual beings, a new category, 249, 259–260

INDEX

Static. *See* Pleasure
Statilius Taurus, 343
Sting of death, 119, 327, 339
Stobaeus, 354
stocheion, 159
Stoicism: later than Epicureanism, 6–7, 10; mitigated by Epicureanism, 248; and Christianity, 336; Roman, 340; under the Empire, 345–348
Stoics: as chaplains, 187; censorious, 312, 314; as competitors, 328; differences in kind, 333
Style, learned from Nature, 130–131
suavis, suavitas, 242, 310–312
sub specie mortalitatis, 183
Suetonius, 334
summum bonum fallacy, 218–219
Sun, size of, 141
sunetheis, 282
Supersense, mind a, 207–209
Swerve, 165–166: a cause, 169; active or permissive, 170; and free will, 175
sympatheia, given new meaning, 201, 205
Symposium of Epicurus, 293
Syncretism of philosophies, 328
Synoptic view, 4

Tacitus: on fellowship, 103, 343; on Petronius, 346
Tait, J. I. M., 373
Talented few, 130
Taylor, A. E., 361
Teleology: of Epicurus, 66–67; of Aristotle, 128
Telos: a criterion, 134, 238–239; not *summum bonum*, 218; identified, 219–220; aspects of, 232
Temperance, 291–293
Teos, 60–61
Terence, 53, 269, 313
Tertullian, 352
Tetrapharmacon, 38
Textbook: origin of, 9, 25, 26; textbooks, Epicurean and Christian, 32
Themista, influence of, 79, 80, 81; honored, 119
Theodorus, hedonist, 79, 80
Theology, reserved for advanced study, 251. *See also* Gods
Theophrastus: popular, 50–51; and Praxiphanes, 57–58; friend of Demetrius Phalereus, 77; exiled, 90; on Lives, 186; on Fortune, 243–244, 317

Thessalonica, Epicurean city, 338
Timaeus, parodied, 234
Time, accident of accidents, 147–148
Timocrates, deserter: maligns Epicurus, 54; attacked by Epicurus, 78; brother of Metrodorus, 83; on banquets, 104
Timolaus, Platonic conspirator, 40, 77
Timon, misanthrope, 188
Timon, satirist, 40
Touch, all sensations reduced to, 204
Tour of the universe, 110
Tower at a distance, 135, 139
tranquillitas, 226
Trebatius, Gaius, convert, 343
Tripod of Nausiphanes, 62, 65
True, ambiguous, 135
Truth and value confused, 135, 138–139
Tusculan Disputations, 244–245
Twelve Elementary Principles, 113, 123: listed, 156–157; a code, 214
Twentieth, 51–52
Twentyers, 105

Uncertainty, misery of, 297; and crime, 305
Universal idea of gods, 256
"Up" and "down," 167–168
Urgency of the present, 18, 290, 319
Usener, H., 362 *et saepe*
Utilitarianism, 297, 301–302

Vatican Collection discovered, 354
Velleius, 342
vera ratio, 155
Vessel, body a, 164–165: in New Testament, 199; ridiculed, 200
Victory over death, 327
vir bonus, 149
Virgil: partial to Epicurus, 45; on urgency, 182–183; on soul, 202; on immortality, 283; short poem of, 343
Virtue: a mere name, 247; and pleasure, 245–248
Vision, 204–206
Vogliano, A., 363, 366, 367, 368, 375
Volition, an accident, 159. *See also* **Mind**
Von der Muehll, P., 362

Wallace, W., 361
Watson, John, 361
Wilamowitz, U. von, 364, 366
Will, will power, 173
Wind and heat, 198

Wisdom, 291
Words, corporeal, 206
Wotke, C., 377

Xenocrates, 50
Xenophanes, skeptic, 82

Zeno, founder of Stoicism, 332; sought
   publicity, 346
Zeno of Gaza, head of the Garden, 330,
   331–332
zoa, the gods are, 259, 263, 267
Zoroaster, 272

EPICURUS AND HIS PHILOSOPHY

by NORMAN W. DeWITT

Traditional theories and interpretations of Epicurean philosophy are challenged by this book, in which a distinguished scholar demonstrates the fallacies and shortcomings of most of the previous works on the subject.

Professor DeWitt provides, for the first time, a biographical account which relates existing data on the life of Epicurus to the development of his doctrine. The philosopher is shown to have been an innovator throughout his whole career, the founder of a new kind of school, and a pioneer in deducing ethics from physical theories.

A major finding of Professor DeWitt's study centers on the importance of Epicureanism as a source of numerous Christian beliefs. The author shows that Epicurus brought forth a new group of